MW01105684

to Léo, a fellow
admirer of Russian
literature.

Best wishes
Ron

*Slavic Sins of the Flesh*

BECOMING MODERN: *New Nineteenth-Century Studies*
*Series Editors*
Sarah Way Sherman, Department of English, University of New Hampshire
Janet Aikins Yount, Department of English, University of New Hampshire
Rohan McWilliam, Anglia Ruskin University, Cambridge, England
Janet Polasky, Department of History, University of New Hampshire

This book series maps the complexity of historical change and assesses the formation of ideas, movements, and institutions crucial to our own time by publishing books that examine the emergence of modernity in North America and Europe. Set primarily but not exclusively in the nineteenth century, the series shifts attention from modernity's twentieth-century forms to its earlier moments of uncertain and often disputed construction. Seeking books of interest to scholars on both sides of the Atlantic, it thereby encourages the expansion of nineteenth-century studies and the exploration of more global patterns of development.

For a complete list of books that are available in this series, see www.upne.com

# Slavic Sins of the Flesh

FOOD, SEX, AND CARNAL APPETITE

IN NINETEENTH-CENTURY RUSSIAN

FICTION *Ronald D. LeBlanc*

UNIVERSITY OF NEW HAMPSHIRE PRESS

*Durham, New Hampshire*

Published by University Press of New England

*Hanover and London*

University of New Hampshire Press
Published by University Press of New England,
One Court Street, Lebanon, NH 03766
www.upne.com

© 2009 by University of New Hampshire Press

Printed in the United States of America
5   4   3   2   1

All rights reserved. No part of this book may be reproduced in any
form or by any electronic or mechanical means, including storage
and retrieval systems, without permission in writing from the
publisher, except by a reviewer, who may quote brief passages in a
review. Members of educational institutions and organizations
wishing to photocopy any of the work for classroom use, or authors
and publishers who would like to obtain permission for any of the
material in the work, should contact Permissions, University Press
of New England, One Court Street, Lebanon, NH 03766.

Library of Congress Cataloging-in-Publication Data
LeBlanc, Ronald Denis.
Slavic sins of the flesh : food, sex, and carnal appetite in nineteenth-
century Russian fiction / Ronald D. LeBlanc.
    p. cm. — (Becoming modern: new nineteenth-century studies)
Includes bibliographical references and index.
ISBN 978-1-58465-767-5 (cloth : alk. paper)
1. Tolstoy, Leo, graf, 1828–1910—Criticism and interpretation.
2. Dostoyevsky, Fyodor, 1821–1881—Criticism and interpretation.
3. Pleasure in literature.  4. Desire in literature.  5. Food in
literature. 6. Sex in literature.  7. Russian fiction—19th century—
History and criticism.  I. Title.
PG3415.P55L43 2009
891.73'309353—dc22        2009006594

University Press of New England is a member of the Green Press
Initiative. The paper used in this book meets their minimum
requirement for recycled paper.

# Contents

## Acknowledgments

This book project grew out of a stimulating conference sponsored by the Russian Research Center (now the Davis Center for Russian and Eurasian Studies) at Harvard University held back in 1993. The event was co-organized by Musya Glants and Joyce Toomre, who subsequently coedited the collection of essays that resulted from the conference, *Food in Russian History and Culture* (1997). The two essays of mine that appeared in that volume—one on Dostoevsky, the other on Tolstoy—provided the foundation for this current study, which builds upon the contrasting gastrosexual poetics of these two Russian literary giants that I had outlined there.

My initial interest in examining food imagery and eating metaphors in Russian literature was generated several years earlier by a lecture I attended, "Thought for Food: Comedy and Gastronomy in Molière's Theatre," delivered at Washington State University in 1986 by Ronald Tobin, a specialist in seventeenth-century French literature. Professor Tobin's memorable lecture, his wise counsel, and his generous mentorship over the years have sustained my work on gastronomic and alimentary issues in literature ever since. I also acknowledge the contributions of those pioneers of "gastrocriticism" in the Slavic field—especially Darra Goldstein and Joyce Toomre—who have generously shared their considerable knowledge with me and who have consistently encouraged my work in this field. Two of my colleagues at the University of New Hampshire, historian Cathy Frierson and animal scientist Sam Smith, have likewise been valuable and generous sources of intellectual support.

My research has been facilitated by the helpful staffs at a number of libraries, primary among them, the former Lenin Library in Moscow, Widener Library at Harvard University, the Library of Congress, the Russian and East European Library at the University of Illinois at Urbana–Champaign, the Suzzallo Library at the University of Washington, and the interlibrary loan division of the Dimond Library at the University of New Hampshire. Financial support for research visits has been provided by the National Endowment for the Humanities; the Kennan Institute for Advanced Russian Studies; the American Council of Learned Societies; and the Office of Academic Affairs, the Center for the Humanities, the Center for International Education, and the College of Liberal Arts at the University of New Hampshire.

At various stages in its long gestation, this book manuscript has benefited from being read and critiqued by generous colleagues whose feedback is both highly valued and deeply appreciated. They include, among others, Richard Borden, Greg Carleton, Caryl Emerson, Donald Fanger, Michael Katz, Deborah Martinsen, Gary Saul Morson, Robin Miller, Eric Naiman, Donna Orwin, Daniel Rancour-Laferriere, James Roney, Nancy Ruttenburg, and Andrei Zorin.

I gratefully acknowledge permission from the editors and publishers listed below to reprint, in modified form, some of the following material I have previously published:

"Alimentary Violence: Eating as a Trope in Russian Literature." In *Times of Trouble: Violence in Russian Literature and Culture*, edited by Marcus Levitt and Tatyana Novikov, pp. 154–77. Madison: University of Wisconsin Press, 2007. Reprinted by permission from the University of Wisconsin Press. All rights reserved.

"An Appetite for Power: Predators, Carnivores, and Cannibals in Dostoevsky's Novels." In *Food in Russian History and Culture*, edited by Joyce Toomre and Musya Glants, 124–45. Bloomington: Indiana University Press, 1997. Reprinted by permission from Indiana University Press. All rights reserved.

"Food, Orality, and Nostalgia for Childhood: Gastronomic Slavophilism in Midnineteenth-Century Russian Fiction." *Russian Review* 58, no. 2 (1999): 244–67. Reprinted by permission from Blackwell Publishing. All rights reserved.

"Gluttony and Power in Iurii Olesha's *Envy*." *Russian Review* 60, no. 2 (2001): 220–37. Reprinted by permission from Blackwell Publishing. All rights reserved.

"Oblomov's Consuming Passion: Food, Eating, and the Search for Communion." In *Goncharov's Oblomov: A Critical Companion*, edited by Galya Diment, pp. 110–135. Evanston, Ill.: Northwestern University Press, 1997. © Ronald LeBlanc. Reprinted by permission from Northwestern University Press. All rights reserved.

"Saninism Versus Tolstoyism: The Anti-Tolstoyan Subtext in Mikhail Artsybashev's *Sanin*." *Tolstoy Studies Journal* 18 (2006): 16–32. Reprinted by permission from the *Tolstoy Studies Journal*. All rights reserved.

"The Sweet Seduction of Sin: Food, Sexual Desire, and Ideological Purity in Alexander Tarasov Rodionov's *Shokolad*." *Gastronomica: The Journal of Food and Culture* 3, no. 4 (2003): 31–41. Copyright © 2003 by the Regents of the University of California. Reprinted by permission from the University of California Press. All rights reserved.

"Tolstoy's Body: Diet, Desire, and Denial." In *Cultures of the Abdomen: Diet, Digestion and Fat in the Modern World*, edited by Christopher E. Forth and Ana Carden-Coyne, pp. 147–66. London: Palgrave Macmillan, 2004. Reprinted by permission from Palgrave Macmillan. All rights reserved.

"Tolstoy's Way of No Flesh: Abstinence, Vegetarianism, and Christian Physiology." In *Food in Russian History and Culture*, edited by Joyce Toomre and Musya Glants, pp. 81–102. Bloomington: Indiana University Press, 1997. Reprinted by permission from Indiana University Press. All rights reserved.

"Trapped in a Spider's Web of Animal Lust: Human Bestiality in Lev Gumilevsky's *Dog Alley*." *Russian Review* 65, no. 2 (2006): 171–93. Reprinted by permission from Blackwell Publishing. All rights reserved.

"Unpalatable Pleasures: Tolstoy, Food, and Sex." *Tolstoy Studies Journal* 6 (1993): 1–32. Reprinted by permission from the *Tolstoy Studies Journal*. All rights reserved.

I dedicate this book to my wife, Lynda, whose unflagging love, patience, forbearance, and support throughout the long years of this project have enabled me to complete this book.

## Note on Transliteration, Citation, and Translation

For ease of reading, I have used J. Thomas Shaw's transliteration System I in the text, where personal and place names are rendered in a more recognizable (and pronounceable) form for readers unfamiliar with Russian: for example, Dostoevskii becomes Dostoevsky, Tolstoi becomes Tolstoy, Gumilevskii becomes Gumilyovsky. In the notes and bibliography, meanwhile, I have adhered more strictly to the Library of Congress system with the diacritical marks omitted (Shaw's System II) because of its greater accuracy. The many references in this book to the works of Dostoevsky and Tolstoy, which are cited parenthetically in the text by volume and page number, come from the Soviet editions of their complete works: F. M. Dostoevskii, *Polnoe sobranie sochinenii v tridtsati tomakh*, edited by V. G. Bazanov (Leningrad: Nauka, 1972–90) and L. N. Tolstoi, *Polnoe sobranie sochinenii v devianosta tomakh*, edited by V. G. Chertkov (Moscow: Khudozhestvennaia literatura, 1928–58). Except where otherwise noted, all translations from the Russian are my own.

*Slavic Sins of the Flesh*

# Introduction

## Food and Sex in Russian Literature

1

THOMASINA: Septimus, what is carnal embrace?

SEPTIMUS: Carnal embrace is the practice of throwing one's
arms around a side of beef.

THOMASINA: Is that all?

SEPTIMUS: No . . . a shoulder of mutton, a haunch of venison
well hugged, an embrace of grouse . . . *caro, carnis*; feminine;
flesh.

THOMASINA: Is it a sin?

SEPTIMUS: Not necessarily, my lady, but when carnal embrace is
sinful, it is a sin of the flesh, QED. We had *caro* in our Gallic
Wars—'The Britons live on milk and meat'—'*lacte et carne
vivunt*.' I am sorry that the seed fell on stony ground.[1]

## Dostoevsky, Tolstoy, and the Carnal

The humorous exchange above between the precocious thirteen-year-old pupil, Thomasina Coverly, and her twenty-
two-year-old tutor, Septimus Hodge, at the opening of Tom
Stoppard's play *Arcadia* (1993) illustrates nicely the double
meaning of the word "carnal." Septimus's comic explanation
of what "carnal embrace" means ("the practice of throwing
one's arms around a side of beef") reminds us that "carnal"
(literally, "of the flesh") possesses, in addition to its more
common sexual referent, an alimentary one as well: that is,
it can just as easily refer to the meat consumed in one's diet
as to the bodily pleasure enjoyed in sexual intercourse. As
Septimus later elucidates for his young charge, "Carnal embrace is sexual congress, which is the insertion of the male
genital organ into the female genital organ for purposes of

procreation and pleasure."[2] In this book we shall be concerned with the "carnal" in both of its meanings—the alimentary and the sexual—as we examine how food and sex are represented in a number of works of nineteenth- and early-twentieth-century Russian literature. More specifically, we shall be concerned with how certain Russian writers used the language of food and the imagery of eating to express male heterosexual desire.

Although this study examines works written by various Russian writers, it focuses primarily on the two giants of nineteenth-century Russian prose fiction: Fyodor Mikhailovich Dostoevsky and Lev Nikolaevich Tolstoy. As Slavic scholars are only too well aware, a customary way to approach the poetics of either Dostoevsky or Tolstoy has been to contrast the literary style or artistic method of the one with that of the other.[3] This procedure has been so well rehearsed, in fact, that D. S. Mirsky once quipped that Tolstoy "seems to have been given to the world for the special purpose of being contrasted with Dostoevsky."[4] Nikolay Berdyaev was among the first to help create this polarization when he asserted that readers may feel an affinity for one or the other of these two Russian literary giants, but not for both, as these writers appeal to two such distinctly different types of human soul, "those who are drawn to Tolstoy's mind and those drawn to Dostoievsky's."[5] There is an "unbridgeable gap," Berdyaev claims, that separates the holders of these two radically differing "fundamental conceptions of existence."[6] Whether or not we accept Berdyaev's sweeping claim, we must admit that the differences between these two great Russian writers are indeed profound and substantial. Where Dostoevsky, who possessed the plebeian nature of a democrat, tends to write mainly about lower-class types and petit-bourgeois life in the city, the aristocratic Tolstoy writes largely about upper-class life upon gentry estates in the countryside. Where Dostoevsky probes the deep subconscious layers of the human psyche and dramatizes the ideological conflicts of his age, Tolstoy instead paints a broad epic canvas of nineteenth-century Russian life.[7] Where Dostoevsky is a "seer of the spirit," Tolstoy is a "seer of the flesh."[8] Where Dostoevsky is the Russian Shakespeare, Tolstoy is the Russian Homer.[9] Where Dostoevsky's novelistic discourse is quintessentially dialogic, Tolstoy's is essentially monologic.[10] Joseph Brodsky once argued that this "Dostoevsky versus Tolstoy" dichotomy can even be applied to the direction Russian literature chose to take during the greater part of the twentieth century. Seeking to spare itself the need to climb to what he calls "the heights of Dostoevsky's spiritual pitch," twentieth-century Russian prose, in Brodsky's opinion, shunned Dostoevsky and the path of modernism mapped out by this visionary artist. It instead followed Tolstoy's road of mimetic writing—the one that led eventually to the ponderous Soviet production novel of Socialist Realism.[11]

To the already lengthy list of dichotomies that purportedly separate these two influential Russian writers, this book will seek to add yet another defining distinction: their "gastropoetics"; that is to say, the contrasting treatment of food motifs and eating metaphors that we find in their works. Ronald Tobin provides a conceptual model that proves especially useful for comprehending the nature of the gastronomic discourse—as well as the structure of the male sexual appetite—that operates within the respective fictional worlds of Dostoevsky and Tolstoy. In his study of *L'Ecole des femmes* (1662), Tobin interprets the central romantic plot in Molière's comic play as a clash between two quite different semiotic codes: he sees the rivalry between the violently aggressive Arnolphe and the gentle, hedonistic Horace for the love of young Agnes as a semiotic collision between the code of power, communicated by the French verb *manger* (to devour), and the code of pleasure, with its concomitant notion of *goûter* (to taste).[12] Whereas the carnivoristic and predatory Arnolphe seeks to "devour" Agnes, hoping to dominate and control her as soon as she becomes his property as a wife, Horace wishes instead to enjoy a "taste" of Agnes's sexuality and tender affection as a love partner. Molière, in short, contrasts Arnolphe's sexual aggressiveness, his desire to dominate, to Horace's affection and desire to pleasure and to be pleasured. If we apply Tobin's distinction between *manger* and *goûter* to nineteenth-century Russian literature, we could say that whereas the characters in Tolstoy's fiction tend to "taste," those in Dostoevsky's works tend to "devour."[13] We find, in other words, a polar opposition, as far as food and sex are concerned, between Dostoevskian "carnivorousness," where eating and sexual intercourse are both portrayed as acts of violence, aggression, and domination, and Tolstoyan "voluptuousness," where eating and sex are instead understood as acts of libidinal enjoyment, delight, and indulgence. In Russian lexical terms, this gastropoetic opposition may be said to be one between Dostoevskian *plotoiadnost'* (literally, an appetite for eating "flesh") and Tolstoyan *sladostrastie* (literally, a passion for things that taste "sweet"). Where Stiva Oblonsky in Tolstoy's *Anna Karenina* (1877) personifies the passion for enjoying sweet-tasting pleasures of the flesh, Pyotr Verkhovensky in Dostoevsky's *The Devils* (1872) represents the carnivoristic appetite for eating and devouring the flesh. With Stiva, who seems motivated mainly by the epicurean desire for libidinal pleasure, eating constitutes "tasting"; thus the narrative emphasis is placed upon the tongue and the palate as organs of gustation. With Pyotr, on the other hand, the psychological desire for autonomy, domination, and control turns eating into an act of carnal violence; for him, to eat means to "devour," and Dostoevsky focuses the reader's attention accordingly upon organs of mastication, such as the teeth and the throat, as flesh is violently attacked and consumed.

Dostoevsky's poetics, it could reasonably be argued, would hardly appear to contain a well-developed "gastrological" dimension. Unlike most Russian writers, Dostoevsky as a rule seems to show little narrative interest in depicting food and scenes of eating in his novels. While some readers might claim that the dearth of culinary imagery in Dostoevsky's fiction stems from the author's putative lack of concern for depicting the physical details of everyday life, I would suggest that in his novels the act of eating simply operates according to a different semiotic code and serves a different narrative function than it does with most of his Russian compatriots. Where the fictional characters who populate the works of other Russian writers are apt to enjoy food primarily for the sensual delight it brings them, for Dostoevsky's highly volitional creatures (who are generally obsessed with a desire to dominate and control one another) the ingestion of food—whether as a mimetic or metaphoric act—tends to indicate not taste, enjoyment, and nourishment, but rather violence, aggression, and domination. What one critic calls a "devouring aggressiveness"—a desire to negate and destroy the Other—seems to permeate the act of eating in Dostoevsky's fiction.[14] His characters, as a result, do not merely eat; they seek to devour, digest, and destroy. As we shall see in the next chapter, the will to power—the desire for absolute possession of, and mastery over, other people—that seems to motivate many of the egoistic human beings portrayed in Dostoevsky's novels finds its physiological as well as psychological expression in predatoriness, carnivorousness, and ultimately cannibalism. Sociologically and psychologically considered, Dostoevsky depicts a Darwinian world of intense capitalistic competition, where men, as merciless socioeconomic animals, seek ruthlessly to devour one another. Human relations have here become mercenary, rather than empathetic; predatory, rather than symbiotic. In Dostoevsky's fictional world, intercourse between the self and the other tends in most cases to be reduced to the cynical dictum: eat or be eaten. This novelist, in other words, portrays egoistic human beings as predominantly cruel and aggressive creatures who hunger insatiably to assume power and thus consume one another. In Dostoevsky's novels, accordingly, we frequently witness the rich devouring the poor, the strong devouring the weak, the proud devouring the meek. The physical act of copulation is here conceived more as an act of violence than as an erotic experience: as rape or sexual assault rather than consensual sex or mutual lovemaking.

With Tolstoy, on the other hand, people tend to "taste" rather than "devour." The predominant semiotic code in his fictional world is that of pleasure rather than power: of hedonism and epicureanism rather than carnivorousness and cannibalism. Tolstoy's male characters, in other words, enjoy food primarily for the sensual delight it brings them. Given what we know of Tolstoy's own powerful instinctual urges, as well as the equally obsessive striving for moral self-perfection that he undertook in his personal life, it should not surprise us too greatly to find in his works the development of a growing strain of anti-hedonistic and anti-epicurean philosophy, a puritanical ethic that comes increasingly to condemn categorically both gastronomical and sexual pleasure. Like women, food and drink come to serve for Tolstoy as recurrent emblems for the erotic objects that tempt adult males in this life, offering them instant physical gratification of the senses as a substitute for the more difficult (and temporally deferred) satisfaction of the soul that comes only with true spiritual fulfillment. In Tolstoy's later fictional works, especially *The Kreutzer Sonata* (1889), this direct connection between eating and fornicating becomes especially explicit and prominent. In essayistic writings, such as *The First Step* (1892) and "Why Do People Stupefy Themselves?" (1888), meanwhile, Tolstoy comes to espouse a rigorous brand of Christian asceticism that advocates both sexual continence and gastronomical abstinence: a renunciation of the pleasures of the palate as well as the flesh, of the delights of the stomach as well as the loins. Tolstoy, in other words, comes to renounce the "carnal" in both of its basic meanings.

## Gastrocriticism: The Study of Food and Eating in Literature

Given that we tend to identify both Dostoevsky and Tolstoy with literary masterpieces that explore compelling philosophical, moral, religious, and social issues, we might initially find odd the suggestion that gastronomic concerns figure prominently and significantly in the poetics of either of these two great writers and thinkers, both of whom seem eminently more concerned with the minds and spirits of human beings than with their mouths or stomachs. Anthropological and sociological studies during the past fifty years have amply demonstrated, however, that the act of eating represents much more than merely the satisfaction of a basic biological need for human beings. The ingestion of food constitutes an act that is in important ways culturally shaped and socially determined. It is in this sense that Claude Lévi-Strauss is to be understood when he observes that food not only nourishes, it also signifies; food is not only good to eat, but good to think. Using "gustemes" as a culinary analogue to the "phonemes" of language, Lévi-Strauss theorized how the constituent elements of a society's cuisine are organized according to certain structures of opposition and correlation (he was seeking to distinguish English cooking from French cooking).[15] In such groundbreaking studies as *The Raw and the Cooked* (1964) and "The Culinary Triangle" (1965), meanwhile, Lévi-Strauss examined the broad ramifications of the essentially transformational nature of cookery. Noting how distinctions between raw food and cooked food are linked in human thought with a fundamental distinction between "nature" and "culture" (between what is found in a natural state and what is transformed or elaborated by human effort), this pioneer sought to discover the basic structures that underlie our thinking about food, structures that he saw as symptomatic of human thinking in general. Another pioneering food anthropologist, Mary Douglas, who adopts a cultural rather than a structural approach, has studied the way that food functions as a symbol of social relationships. Her main concern has been with the task of "deciphering" a meal in its social context: by unearthing the chain that links meals together and thus explaining how food categories help to encode social events.[16] Jack Goody and Pierre Bourdieu, meanwhile, have examined mainly the social stratification that characterizes human eating behaviors, showing how tastes and food preferences, long considered highly individualized traits, are, in fact, closely tied to socioeconomic class.[17]

The meaning of food in human culture has begun to be elaborated for us, however, not only by these and other anthropologists and sociologists, but also by semioticians and cultural theorists. Roland Barthes, for instance, proposed that we search for the code—or "grammar"—that underlies the selection, preparation, service, and consumption of the foods that people eat. In his *Eléments de Sémiologie* (1964), Barthes appropriated for semiotics Ferdinand de Saussure's distinction between *langue* (the linguistic system one appropriates when one learns a language) and *parole* (the actual speech utterances one makes in that language). Much like Saussurean linguistics, Barthes's semiology attempts to describe the underlying system of rules and distinctions that make signification possible in a semiotic system such as food: for example, rules of exclusion (food taboos), rules of association, signifying oppositions, rituals of use (what Barthes calls "alimentary rhetoric").[18] "For a semiologist studying the food system of a culture," Jonathan Culler explains,

> parole consists of all the events of eating and langue is the system of rules underlying these events, rules that define what is edible, what dishes go with or contrast with one another, how they are combined to form meals, in short, all the rules and prescriptions that enable meals to be culturally orthodox or unorthodox. A restaurant menu represents a sample of a society's "food grammar." There are "syntactic" slots (soups, appetizers, entrées, salads, desserts) and paradigm classes of contrasting items that can fill each slot (the soups among which one chooses). There are conventions governing the syntactic ordering of items within a meal (soup, entrée, dessert is orthodox, while dessert, entrée, soup is ungrammatical). And the contrasts between dishes within classes (main course, dessert, etc.) bear meaning: hamburger and roast pheasant have different second-order meanings. Approaching such material with the linguistic model, the semiologist has a clear task: to reconstruct the system of distinctions and conventions that enable a group of phenomena to have the meaning they do for members of a culture.[19]

In an essay titled "Toward a Psychosociology of Contemporary Food Consumption" (1961), Barthes even went so far as to suggest that it might be possible, by drawing up exhaustive lists of contrasts in national food habits, to compare the gastronomic grammars of different countries, just as the structures of their national languages can be compared.[20]

The gastrological legacy left by thinkers such as Lévi-Strauss, Douglas, Goody, Bourdieu, Barthes, and others has made itself felt in the efforts made by some literary critics during the past few decades to explore the various codes—whether anthropological, psychological, semiotic, linguistic, aesthetic, or structural in nature—that underlie the use of food motifs and the depictions of fictional meals in works of literature. These so-called gastrocritics have examined the various roles played by food and fictional meals in the works of such diverse authors as, among others, François Rabelais, Molière, Alain René Lesage, Jean-Jacques Rousseau, the Marquis de Sade, Jacques-Henri Bernardin de Saint-Pierre, Lord Byron, Gustave Flaubert, Anton Chekhov, Nikolay Gogol, and Lev Tolstoy.[21] In some cases, unfortunately, the connection between gastronomy and literature has not extended much farther than popular anthologies—such as Linda Wolfe's *Literary Gourmet* (1962) or Joan and John Digby's *Food for Thought* (1987)—which merely collect various references to food and drink found in the works of authors ranging from Fielding and Dickens to Whitman and Proust. As a rule, however, the authors of studies in literary gastronomy have been more apt to posit a series of basic binary oppositions underlying artistic texts and then to examine how these contrastive pairs—wealth versus poverty, urban versus rural, simplicity versus sophistication, foreign versus native, carnivorous versus vegetarian, ingestion versus elimination, abstinence versus gluttony, need versus desire, feasting versus fasting, public versus private dining, and so forth—help to illuminate a text's meaning. Gastrocritical studies of this sort have increasingly demonstrated that the food items literary characters choose to eat, as well as the manner in which they eat them, tell us much not only about the personality and psychology of this particular individual but also about the sociology and cultural values of the world he or she inhabits.[22] Because eating is a human activity that by its very nature encompasses a social, psychological, as well as biological dimension, the depiction of fictional meals in literature allows this everyday event to be transformed into a narrative sign with vast semiotic possibilities, not only within the world of the literary work itself but also within a broader cultural context.

James W. Brown, for instance, who has studied fictional meals and their function in the nineteenth-century French novel, shows how Balzac regularly juxtaposes wealth and poverty in gastronomical terms, contrasting the elegant haute cuisine and fashionable dining rooms of Parisian bon vivants with the more modest repasts served in the countryside by impoverished provincial landowners. By identifying physical hunger with poverty and culinary extravagance with wealth, Balzac, as a literary realist, uses scenes of dining in a highly mimetic way to criticize the social and economic inequities of bourgeois life in early-nineteenth-century France.[23] Ronald Tobin, writing about the connection between comedy and gastronomy in the theater of Molière, notes how the playwright is able, through the comic confusion of spiritual with corporeal appetites (of intellectual with physical ingestion), to deflate the mistaken notion that humans are by nature essentially noble and spiritual rather than base material beings.[24] And, of course, Mikhail Bakhtin has explored how images of eating and drinking can function as the most significant manifestation of what he calls the medieval "grotesque body," whose open-ended, unfinished carnivalesque nature is celebrated so memorably in François Rabelais's seriocomic masterpiece, *Gargantua et Pantagruel* (1532–42).[25] In his study of Rabelais and the medieval popular-festive tradition, Bakhtin outlines how in carnivalized literature—with its atmosphere of license, gaiety, and liberating laughter—eating and drinking reflect the sense of freedom, collectivity, and abundance that was experienced in the inverted world of popular folk culture. As symbols of life and sensuality, food and drink help to sustain the comic mode in Rabelais's fiction and its carnivalesque spirit of life affirmation, regeneration, and renewal.

Among the most notable monographs of gastrocriticism is Gian-Paolo Biasin's *I sapori della modernità: Cibo e romanzo* (1991), which the author characterizes as "a re-reading of the Italian novel *sub specie culinaria.*" Biasin's study, which does not pretend to be a systematic historiographic inquiry into the fate of the culinary sign in the modern Italian novel, analyzes a sampling of literary texts where food imagery and scenes of dining are especially privileged by their authors. In his gastrocritical readings of novels by Alessandro Mazoni, Giovanni Verga, Gabriele D'Annunzio, Giuseppi Tomasi di Lampedusa, Carlo Emilio Gadda, Italo Calvino, and Primo Levi, Biasin illustrates several of the varied functions that the representation of food can fulfill in a literary text: from the mimetic and narrative to the cognitive and tropological, from the referential to the figurative. As Biasin notes (in a statement that has particular resonance for our current study), "The discourse on food inevitably becomes a discourse on pleasure and on power."[26] Louis Marin's *La parole mangée et autres essais théologico-politiques* (1986) concerns itself mainly with various representations of the body—the human body, the divine body, the Eucharistic body, the royal body, the pathetic body, the utopic Rabelaisian body. It also deals with the relationship between the two different spheres of orality: between linguistic utterance (the mouth as site of verbal expression) and eating (the mouth as site of the mastication and ingestion of food).[27] Michel Jeanneret's *Des mets et des mots: banquets et propos de table à la Renaissance* (1987) examines the banquet (symposium) as a paradigm of art, morality, and intellectual life during the High Renaissance. "The combination of words and food in a convivial scene gives rise to a special moment when thought and the senses enhance rather than just tolerate each other," Jeanneret writes. "The symposium ideal reconciles the angel and the beast in the human, and it renews the interdependence between the mouth that eats and the mouth that speaks."[28]

### Food and Eating in Nineteenth-Century Russian Fiction

French and Italian texts are not the only works of world literature that should attract the interest of a gastrocritic, of course. As readers of nineteenth- and twentieth-century Russian literature will readily attest, food and eating figure prominently in Russian prose fiction of the past two hundred years. From the sumptuous old-world repasts conjured up in his reveries by the somnolent hero of Ivan Goncharov's *Oblomov* (1859) to the cheap but nutritious salami with which the food commissar, Andrey Babichev, hopes to feed the Soviet people in Yury Olesha's *Envy* (1927), many of the characters who populate Russian fiction seem intent upon reminding us of Lévi-Strauss's dictum that in literature as in culture food not only nourishes, it also signifies. The thick descriptions of what Tatyana Tolstaya calls "oblivious gorging" (found in literary works by Nikolay Gogol, Anton Chekhov, Ivan Bunin, and numerous other Russian authors) reveal more than just a casual relationship between Russian literature and gastronomy, however. They come to constitute, in her words, "a process that literally becomes orgiastic, virtually a sexual activity."[29] Indeed, Tolstaya asserts that

"Russian literature's reserve in regard to eroticism and carnal love is compensated for many times over by the lengthy unbridled epic poems devoted to the joys of the stomach."[30] As Lev Losev puts it, Russian literature has always been "nurtured by Russian cuisine."[31] One of the aims of this study is to explore why certain Russian authors, who generally seem so reticent concerning sexual matters, have written so effusively about food and dining and have waxed so lyrically about the joys of the palate and the stomach.

Initially, a primary function that food imagery fulfilled within artistic literature in Russia was to break some of the lingering aesthetic taboos against corporeality that had been established during the neoclassical period. Those taboos had for a long time regulated the choice of appropriate subject matter and proper artistic methodology to be used for literary representations of the human body in what was considered serious literature.[32] In the early part of the nineteenth century, for instance, Vasily Narezhny and Aleksandr Izmaylov were each dubbed the "Russian Teniers," a sobriquet that was intended mainly to censure these two fledgling realists for the robust and decidedly inelegant manner in which they depicted native life in Russia. Like David Teniers the Younger (1610–90), the seventeenth-century Flemish genre painter to whom they were often compared, these two Russian prose writers enjoyed depicting everyday scenes of common life (*byt*) in which peasants indulged in pleasures of the flesh. Both Izmaylov and Narezhny were repeatedly chastised in particular for depicting so many scenes of eating and drinking in their works and for seating their characters so often at table, whether in pubs, taverns, or public houses. In the case of Izmaylov, he was frequently compared, in an unflattering way, to Russia's more decorous fabulist Ivan Krylov. "The fable writer Izmaylov is a Krylov who has had a drop too much to drink," complained Prince Vyazemsky.[33] Izmaylov, observed another contemporary, "is a Krylov who has wandered into a pub, a barracks, or a public house."[34] Where Krylov had brought the genre of the fable out onto the public square, as one epigram of the day explained it, Izmaylov now brought it into the tavern.[35] Here is how P. N. Polevoy later characterized the fictional world Izmaylov creates and the characters who inhabit it:

A public house, a tavern, low-ranking policemen (right down to noncoms) in the midst of fulfilling their duties by maintaining order in the streets, drunken rowdies and intoxicated deacons, poverty and dirt and banal folk with their drunken revelry and cheap binges—that's the world which Izmaylov's modest Muse frequents and in which she rummages, that's where she gets her images and her moralizing, both the humorous elements and the serious ones![36]

Izmaylov's fictional world, Belinsky observed, is inhabited by "retired police sergeants, drunken peasant men and women, herb-flavored vodka, raw vodka, beer, pressed caviar, onions, and salt sturgeon; the locales of his action are peasant huts, taverns, and eating houses."[37]

Narezhny fared little better with contemporary critics. "All his pictures belong to the Flemish School," complained Faddey Bulgarin, "and they give him the right to the title of the Russian Teniers."[38] Commenting upon what he called the "gastronomic profusion" in Narezhny's novels, Jean Chopin, an early-nineteenth-century French critic who wrote about Russian literature, notes that "we could reproach the author for seating his characters too often at table."[39] Elsewhere in his review of Narezhny's works, Chopin speaks of the prevalence there of domestic merrymaking, traced in the manner of Teniers, in which inebriating liquors play a primary role.[40] "Narezhny was a Teniers of the novel, and what is more, a Russian Teniers," Baron Anton Delvig wrote shortly after the author's death in 1825. "Just as Chinese novels give off to us the smell of tea so that while reading them you feel as if you are sitting up to your ears in a tea chest, so do Narezhny's novels give off the aroma of Ukrainian hot spiced vodka [*varenukha*], and no matter where the author leads us, you feel as if you never leave a tavern."[41] Even a modern-day critic like John Mersereau, Jr., feels it necessary to note that, even in the most trying circumstances, Narezhny's characters "hardly ever miss a meal, and they never lack for some intoxicating beverage to wash it down."[42] Pavel Mikhed, who has noted that "prandial images" (*pirshestvennye obrazy*) occupy a central place in the narrative structure of Narezhny's novels, argues that the hyperbolic depictions of banquets in many of his works bear a striking resemblance to the images of jolly festivity often found in Rabelais.[43] Such is especially the case in the novel *The Black Year* (1829), where Narezhny uses the enjoyment of food and drink as a way to maintain the comic spirit, to celebrate the sheer physical joy of life, and to highlight the primitive sensual gratifications of the human body. Indeed, *The Black Year* can be considered

"Rabelaisian" largely for the way Narezhny foregrounds broad physical humor and robust coarseness, both of which, as Bakhtin points out, he derives directly from the popular folk culture (*smekhovaia kul'tura*) of his native Ukraine.[44] The robust coarseness that characterizes the works of a Rabelaisian writer like Narezhny manifests itself largely in an emphasis upon the material and corporeal aspects of human life and especially in the predominant role played by what Bakhtin calls the "material bodily principle": "images of the human body with its food, drink, defecation and sexual life."[45] Scenes of eating and drinking are thus rife in Rabelaisian works of fiction; these two alimentary acts, Bakhtin observes, "are one of the most significant manifestations of the grotesque body."[46] By portraying men and women in the act of satisfying the most basic and primitive of human instinctual urges, such earthy scenes help both to create a comic atmosphere and to debunk idealistic pretensions.

A generation after Izmaylov and Narezhny had passed from the literary scene, Gogol and several members of the so-called Natural School would likewise be accused of cultivating a coarse brand of word painting, a literary "Flemishness" that manifested itself largely through culinary, gastronomical, and alimentary imagery. As Bakhtin points out in his essay "Rabelais and Gogol," Russia's greatest comic writer inherited much of his earthy, humorous style from his fellow Ukrainian, Narezhny, whose works are "thoroughly saturated" with elements of grotesque realism.[47] The colorful way Gogol and other members of the Natural School depicted lower-class types continued to be dismissed by conservative critics as merely dirty pictures of life in urban and rural Russia, distasteful tableaux vivants depicting the crude, vulgar side of humanity and expressing mainly the base animal urges of human beings.[48] When he surveyed the sources of artistic inspiration that motivated this new generation of realist writers in Russia, one conservative critic during the 1840s noted sadly that "the classical Olympus and the romantic Valhalla have been replaced by the eating house."[49] During the 1850s, however, by which time Realism, as a literary aesthetic, had risen to a position of ascendancy within Russian literature, this coarse Flemishness was no longer categorically disdained in critical circles. Throughout the second half of the nineteenth century, especially during the heyday of the novel, the artistic representation of food imagery and fictional meals in works of Russian prose fiction was implicitly authorized by the aesthetic principles of literary realism. In the classic nineteenth-century Russian novel, the enjoyment of food and drink is often used by realist writers as a way to condemn the banality of those philistines who care more for stuffing their bellies than for developing their minds or elevating their souls. In Gogol's *Dead Souls* (1842), for example, Sobakevich's gluttonous gorging at the dinner table implicitly suggests his mental, moral, and emotional malnourishment. The essentially bovine existence led by Sobakevich and several other provincial characters in the novel invites the reader to infer that low, mundane interests—such as feeding the body with food—hinder the development of higher concerns such as nourishing the intellect with knowledge or nurturing the heart with love and affection. In Anton Chekhov's works as well, we witness how the enjoyment of food and drink is frequently a sign of *poshlost'*; that is to say, it is usually coded as a marker for a character's crass materialism, spiritual vacuity, and bourgeois philistinism.[50]

In addition to satirically juxtaposing the concerns of the stomach to those of the head or heart, Russian writers during the nineteenth century also used food and eating in their novels to reflect the debate over the national identity. What Lynn Visson calls a "gastronomic dialectic" between Slavophilism and Westernism is at work throughout nineteenth-century Russian literature and culture, where the simple, hearty, native cooking of the Russian peasantry is often pitted against the more elegant and sophisticated cuisine that the Europeanized gentry imported from abroad.[51] This gastronomic rivalry between East and West, Visson argues, plays itself out in a number of memorable scenes from the pages of Russian fiction. In Aleksandr Pushkin's *Eugene Onegin* (1825–32), for instance, the highly "westernized" meal that the dandified Onegin enjoys at Pierre Talon's fancy restaurant on Nevsky Prospekt in cosmopolitan St. Petersburg—a meal described in considerable detail in the novel's opening chapter—provides a sharp contrast to the more traditional "Russian" feast held in the provinces to celebrate Tatyana Larina's nameday party in chapter 5. Pushkin's thoroughly Europeanized hero displays a fondness for such exotic culinary treats as English roast beef, French wine, *pâté de foie gras en croûte* (from Strasbourg), Limburger cheese, and pineapple. The rustic Larins, meanwhile, feast on such traditional native dishes as meat pie, mushrooms, *kvas,* and *bliny*. These references to food and drink in Pushkin's famous "novel in verse," Visson notes, highlight the differences between "the elegant, urbane, westernized hero and the provincial Russian heroine."[52] Likewise, in part 1 of Tolstoy's *Anna Karenina* (1879) the urbane Stiva Oblonsky's ordering of Cachet Blanc, oysters, turbot, roast beef, capon, and Chablis for a meal at the Hotel Angliia restaurant contrasts sharply with Konstantin Levin's rustic preference for such plain peasant fare as bread, kasha, and cabbage soup.[53] Such vivid illustrations within nineteenth-century Russian literature of this gastronomic dialectic between East and West seem to validate Stepan Shevyryov's 1840s contention that life in nineteenth-century Russia continued to be polarized around two cultural extremes: "kvass and champagne, Asiatism and Frenchism."[54]

## Gastronomic Slavophilism: Nostalgia for the Eden of Childhood Russia

One way the gastronomic dialectic between Westernizers and Slavophiles reflects the debate over national identity in nineteenth-century Russia is through the rhetoric of nostalgia. Works such as Gogol's "Old-World Landowners" (1835), Goncharov's *Oblomov*, and Kvitka-Osnovyanenko's *Pan Khalyavsky* (1840) reveal the direct connection established between the nostalgia for childhood experienced by some male characters in mid-nineteenth-century Russian fiction and the regret over Russia's own lost innocence expressed by the Slavophile authors who created these fictional characters. Nostalgia for childhood innocence, as Richard Coe reminds us in *When the Grass Was Taller* (1984), his aptly named study of childhood autobiography, is generated in large part by the disillusionment and disdain that the adult now feels about the world that currently surrounds him:

> it is not so much that the child itself, now an adult, has forever outgrown the splendors of the past, but rather that civilization and "progress" have annihilated, perhaps totally and irretrievably, an ancient way of life and replaced it with something crude, rootless, and modern. This is more than nostalgia; it is nostalgia shot through with bitterness, resentment, and disgust.[55]

Coe refers to this bitter feeling as "black" nostalgia, explaining that "far from being sentimental, it is an outburst of despair or protest against the wanton murder of countryside, village, and even town, a lament for the deliberate destruction of beauty.[56] The sense of loss that some Slavophile writers felt over the gradual disappearance of a pastoral and patriarchal Russia during the nineteenth century, when a rural agrarian society was to their mind being systematically destroyed by modernizing "Western" forces such as commercialization, industrialization, secularization, and urbanization, was not nearly so "black" as the bitter nostalgia that Coe describes above. Nonetheless, the sense of regret and loss that these writers felt was likewise generated in large part by the passing of an ancient way of life, what Benedict Anderson would characterize as an "imagined community," as Russia at midcentury headed toward the reform of its traditional feudal ways.[57]

In the case of Gogol, Goncharov, and Kvitka-Osnovyanenko, this sense of loss and regret over the demise of "old" Russia expresses itself in terms that are at once pastoral and gastronomical: the "good old days" are portrayed in their works, largely through the use of food imagery, as an idealized time of innocence, authenticity, and abundance—both in their own childhoods and in the childhood of Russia as a country. Not only was the grass taller in this mythologized "old" Russia; the crops were also larger and the meals tastier. These three writers tend to use gastronomic motifs in their fiction not simply to comment satirically on the spiritual vacuity of their fictional heroes (characters whose interests in life seem to extend no further than stuffing their bellies with food and drink) but also to voice the serious concerns of literary patriots, lamenting the demise of native values and traditions in their homeland. It is in their virulent attacks upon Gallomania, when they castigate their countrymen who indiscriminately adopt all manner of foreign habits and tastes, that these nativist writers reveal decidedly anti-Western (and anti-modernizing) sensibilities.[58] In gastronomic terms, their staunch defense of native values and old-fashioned customs often takes the form of detailed descriptions of fictional meals, especially ceremonial repasts at estates, characterized by both an abundance of wholesome foodstuffs and a festive spirit of brotherhood and goodwill. Although often laden with ironic overtones (especially in those cases where the paean to the gastronomic glories of the past is voiced by a *skaz* narrator), these literary representations of gentry meals nonetheless paint an idyllic picture of rural life in agrarian, precapitalist, "old" Russia, a nostalgic picture imbued with large doses of pastoral simplicity and homespun authenticity. They constitute what, for lack of a better term, we might call "gastronomic Slavophilism."[59]

The idealization of Russian—and especially "Little Russian" (Ukrainian)—childhood life that we encounter in the works of Gogol, Goncharov, and Kvitka-Osnovyanenko neutralizes much of the satire in these literary texts. This idealization is conveyed largely by the feelings of well-being, comfort, security, and joy that food and eating can provide. Literary idealizations of childhood, as Raymond Williams has argued, tend to reflect the adult male fantasy of retrieving an imagined lost reality, a golden age characterized by a state of total identity and harmony between subject and object.[60] "Such Golden Ages," another critic explains, "typically appear as worlds of plenitude, in which all appetites are satisfied by a generous nature that involuntarily offers itself to man, and in which there is no private property or sense of divisions at all."[61] The golden age, as a paradigm of original happiness, is closely associated with the festive banquet table. As Jeanneret, writing about the Renaissance banquet, puts it: "The fecundity and abundance, the participation of the one in the whole and the universal well-being, can be read as relics of the Garden of Eden, of Arcadia or of the Land of Cockaigne; signs of some paradise regained through the gift of inexhaustible food."[62] In their fond reminiscences of their childhood pasts, in their idealized description of the bucolic idyll enjoyed by old-world landowners, the male characters in the fictional works by Gogol, Goncharov, and Kvitka-Osnovyanenko create just such a paradisaical world of plenitude.

This idealization of feudal relations in the nation's past as a time of true human community was prompted, in part, by actual historical developments. Throughout the first half of the nineteenth century, Russia experienced the early stages of modernization. By the time of the emancipation of the serfs in 1861, the socioeconomic conditions that had long before given rise to agrarian capitalism in Europe were only beginning to take root on Russian soil and the country found itself increasingly immersed in the painful process of embourgeoisement. In public discourse as well as in literary representations, an incipient capitalism imported from the West was implicitly being blamed for a pernicious economic environment within Russian society that severely exacerbated the bestial inclinations of human beings—a "dog-eat-dog" world. By the late 1840s, Gogol (in response to Belinsky's claim that

Russia's salvation lay in adopting European civilization) warned that in Europe one finds "all sorts of people who are ready to devour one another."[63] In the immediate wake of the emancipation of the serfs, widespread discussion about—and reevaluation of—the nature of human beings and their social relations began to take place. As we shall see in the next chapter, this debate was fueled by the publication in 1864 of a Russian translation of Darwin's *On the Origin of Species* (1859); its themes of "the struggle for existence" and "the survival of the fittest" suggested that the biological laws of nature were not fundamentally different from the human laws of society. During the period of sudden and rapid capitalist development that took place on Russian soil following the reforms of 1861, native writers began to make extensive use of imagery from the animal kingdom and to portray the dynamics of human relationships in Darwinian terms. In works such as Nikolay Ostrovsky's *Wolves and Sheep* (1875), Aleksey Pisemsky's *The Predators* (1873), and Fyodor Dostoevsky's *A Raw Youth* (1875), for example, powerful "predatory" characters are repeatedly shown to feed upon weaker and more defenseless human prey. In gastronomic and alimentary terms, a paradigm shift was beginning to take place by midcentury as Russia moved closer and closer toward full-scale capitalist modernization: the act of eating was becoming associated not with the idea of pleasure but rather with the idea of power. Life in post-emancipation Russia was seen as pervaded more by the spirit of carnivorism and cannibalism than by commensalism and communion.[64]

It is within this historical, psychoanalytical, and gastronomical context that we ought to read and interpret Gogol's "Old-World Landowners," Goncharov's *Oblomov*, and Kvitka-Osnovyanenko's *Pan Khalyavsky*, recognizing them as instantiations of the "pastoral of childhood," a literary genre that responds to the onset of Western-style capitalist modernization by creating an Eden out of an idealized, precapitalist, feudal Russia.[65] Melancholy is expressed in these three works of gastronomic Slavophilism largely through the language and imagery of food and eating. A longing for the culinary pleasures of the past (personal as well as national) leads Gogol, Goncharov, and Kvitka-Osnovyanenko at midcentury to mythologize the setting of gentry childhood and thus to create out of the eighteenth-century estate a gastronomic paradise that perhaps never really existed. Within the trajectory traced by the development of nineteenth-century Russian prose, the movement away from the idyllic spirit of eating as an act of sharing and communion toward the modern bourgeois spirit of eating as an act of violence and power (encountered especially in Dostoevsky's fiction) may be said to have reached its apotheosis in Mikhail Saltykov-Shchedrin's *The Golovlyov Family* (1875–80), a dark and somber work that inverts and thus negates the idyllic tradition of pastoral prose generally and the family novel in particular.[66] Besides debunking what Andrew Wachtel has characterized as the myth of the "happy gentry childhood" in Russia, Saltykov-Shchedrin's novel explodes the myth of nourishment by portraying the Golovlyov family as a "death-oriented, self-devouring matriarchy" rather than as the nurturing body posited by the Great Mother archetype.[67] The bleak and gloomy picture of dysfunctional family life that Saltykov-Shchedrin paints in this late-nineteenth-century Russian novel is not designed to portray (in the person of Arina Petrovna) a nurturing and nourishing mother figure or to arouse a gustatory nostalgia—a *nostalgie du goût*—for the "good old days" spent in a gastronomic paradise. Rather, it produces a disturbing and upsetting *dégoût* in the reader, an almost dyspeptic disgust at an oppressive way of life whose literary representation conjures up a masticatory image more in keeping with the predatory spirit of the times: the terrifying jaws of an all-devouring demon, sitting in hell, who threatens to eat human beings alive.[68]

## The Childhood Idyll as Oral Regression

As modern readers, we seem inclined to view the significance of the childhood idylls created by Gogol, Goncharov, and Kvitka-Osnovyanenko within a psychoanalytic context. Hugh McLean, for instance, has demonstrated how Gogol's narrator in "Old-World Landowners" may be seen as "retreating" from the sexual demands typically associated with romantic love: in psychoanalytic terms, he is renouncing sexual maturity and regressing from adult genitality by reviving and glorifying infantile (pregenital) modes of libidinal expression. Like the author himself, who seems to have associated sexual activity very closely with death, he is one of Gogol's many male characters who escape or overcome their paralyzing fear of sexual intimacy with a great love of food and drink.[69] For Gogol's male heroes, McLean notes, "The forbidden genital gratifications are compensated for by the delights of the table."[70]

In the words of the Freudian critic Ivan Yermakov, "Old-World Land-owners" describes "a typically regressive pregenital erotism: the relationship between husband and wife depending exclusively on the consumption of food."[71] The relationship between Afanasy Ivanovich and Pulkheria Ivanovna, which the narrator depicts as being devoid of any sexual passion, can be understood not as a conjugal relationship between husband and wife, nor even as a platonic one between brother and sister (note their shared patronymic), but rather as a symbiotic relationship between a mother and her pre-Oedipal child.[72] Afanasy Ivanovich, after all, is portrayed in the story as a helpless, dependent child whose only libidinal outlet is pregenital (oral) rather than genital (sexual) in nature; Pulkheria Ivanovna, for her part, expresses her love for Afanasy Ivanovich in a maternal way, providing him with constant oral satisfaction through the delights of her table.[73] When she dies, there is no one left to care for her helpless child of a spouse. "The death of his wife," Renato Poggioli writes of the infantile Afanasy Ivanovich, "has left him not so much a widower as an orphan, crying because his mother-wife is no longer there to nurse and to feed him."[74]

Like Gogol's narrator in "Old-World Landowners," Oblomov displays an intense longing to recapture a bucolic "paradise lost" of his mythologized childhood in the Russian countryside. Considered as a psychological condition rather than as a social or moral ailment, the purported "Oblomovitis" of Goncharov's lethargic hero can be seen as a case of arrested personal development, whereby Ilya Ilyich displays an inability or unwillingness to adapt himself to the normal exigencies of mature adult life.[75] According to François de LaBriolle, Oblomov suffers from a weaning complex and separation anxiety: his over-protected, coddled childhood experience in Oblomovka has rendered him ill-equipped to form normal human relationships or to display mature adult behavior.[76] As a result of his chronic infantilism and the severe "mother complex" he seems to suffer from, Ilya Ilyich not only dreams nostalgically about his childhood days in Oblomovka; he also seeks in his present-day life in St. Petersburg to return to that joyous presexual and prelapsarian state, when his every need—whether physiological, alimentary, or emotional—was attentively taken care of. With his imagination enflamed by his nanny's fairy tales about some wonderful country "where rivers flowed with milk and honey, where no one did a stroke of work all year round," the adult Oblomov seeks to find a real-life version of Militrissa Kirbitievna, the legendary maiden of indescribable beauty who inhabits this magical kingdom and who personifies the plenitude and solicitude that reign there. And he seems eventually to find her—not, however, in the beautiful music and delicate flowers of the vivacious Olga Ilinskaya, but rather in the delicious soups and homemade pies of the hospitable Agafya Matveevna Pshenitsyna, who embodies both sustenance and fecundity. What the hero searches for throughout his adult life, in other words, is not actually a wife but a mother: not a young and vital life partner who will make it necessary for him to exhibit adult responsibility as well as mature (genital) sexuality, but a matronly cook who, in addition to nurturing and protecting this overgrown child, will satisfy his oral needs by providing him with good-tasting meals. In keeping with his infantile orality, the only eroticism that Oblomov seems interested in, one commentator notes, is a "gustatory" one.[77] Understood as a movement from "paradise lost" to "paradise regained," Oblomov's quest to return to the idyllic condition of his Oblomovkan childhood involves a psychological regression to a carefree, presexual existence where libidinal pleasure is derived primarily, if not exclusively, from the ingestion of food and drink.[78] Agafya Matveevna's well-stocked larder and well-provisioned kitchen, as twin embodiments of gastronomic plenty, thus promise Oblomov the appeasement of his physical and emotional hunger through the kind of unbounded motherly love he had once enjoyed as a well-fed, pampered child in Oblomovka.[79]

Psychoanalytical readings of Oblomov's regression wish usually emphasize the hero's desire to return to the womb; that is, to the peace, calm, and repose of the prenatal state as emblematized in the novel by his dressing gown (*khalat*).[80] Oblomov's desire to return to the womb, John Givens observes in a Freudian reading, is "the most oft-cited psychoanalytical interpretation" of *Oblomov* and has become "a commonplace in Western critiques of the novel."[81] The food imagery in *Oblomov*, however, suggests that the hero's regression wish is not so much a death wish as a longing to recapture what Natalie Baratoff, in a Jungian analysis, calls "the original maternal symbiosis"; that is, the perfect symbiotic union of the pre-Oedipal child feeding at the mother's breast.[82] In Goncharov's novel, food is made to serve, among other things, as an emblem of all the comfort, security, and warmth that characterize the hero's idealized infantile past. It represents a lost state of total unity and undifferentiated oneness with the mother that exists in very early childhood, during the oral stage, before the infant is weaned away from the maternal breast. Hence the magnetic appeal that Oblomov finds in the high, firm bosom of Agafya Matveevna, who becomes at once his mother-surrogate and nanny-substitute.[83] As Givens notes, the narrator's frequent reference to Agafya Matveevna's bare neck, shoulders, and arms, her busily moving elbows, and her ample bosom results in her becoming metonymically identified by "that part of the mother's anatomy from which nourishment and sensual pleasure is first derived, the place between the crook of the elbows cradling the child and holding it to the exposed breast that feeds it and the bare arms and shoulders that form the borders of the baby's world during feeding."[84] Oblomov's regressive wish to return to the idyllic condition of his Oblomovkan childhood is thus granted through the caretaking and cooking of Agafya Matveevna, his surrogate nanny, nursemaid, and mother all rolled into one. In the person of Agafya Matveevna, Oblomov finds the fulfillment of his wish to regress to an infantile state, not only that of a baby at repose in the mother's womb, but also that of an infant suckling at the nurse's breast.[85]

In his fond reminiscences about the "good old days" in rustic Ukraine, the elderly Pan Khalyavsky may be seen as expressing a similar sentimental longing to regain a lost pastoral ideal, seeking to revisit a childhood world that he idealizes into a veritable "land of milk and honey," a Land of Cockaigne where happiness consists almost entirely in oral gratification.[86] Kvitka-Osnovyanenko's narrator mentions on several occasions how he was spoiled as a child by being constantly given extra portions of food, an emblem of her love and affection, by his overprotective mother: "Since I was mommy's little pet, that is, her favorite, I was allowed to eat whatever was served at any time of day and I could eat it all up without leaving any food leftovers."[87] Indeed, Mrs. Khalyavsky, who, like Oblomov's mother and nanny, seems to know of no other way to express her maternal love and affection for her favorite child than by showering him with kisses, hugs, and food treats, seeks to shield little Trushko from the emotional bumps and bruises that life has in store for him by repeatedly sneaking comfort foods to him at trying moments: for example, when he leaves home for the first time to attend school, when his father reprimands him for his poor academic performance there, and when he is forced to undergo basic military training. Although it is never made absolutely clear whether Pan Khalyavsky, as an adult, suffers from the type of severely arrested personal development that afflicts Oblomov, there is little doubt that deeply felt separation anxieties characterize this mother-son relationship as well. Pan Khalyavsky's "mother complex" reveals itself in the narrator's inability—or unwillingness—to cut the emotional umbilical cord that attaches him to his dearest "mommy" (mamen'ka) and thus to achieve sexual maturity on his own.[88] Indeed, sexual maturity continues to elude Kvitka-Osnovyanenko's hero throughout his adult life; he is tricked into marrying a woman who, he tells us, ceases to be affectionate with him from the day of their wedding. As Roman Koropeckyj explains, "erotic desires are effectively foreclosed" for the male characters in Pan Khalyavsky and in Kvitka-Osnovyanenko's other works of prose fiction. This Ukrainian writer's oeuvre, he argues, is marked, as is Gogol's, by the author's own sexual anxiety, reflected in the need his characters feel to repress or sublimate their sexual desire.[89]

In Freudian terms, it appears that the sexually immature and orally regressive Pan Khalyavsky is also attempting during his twilight years to recapture the perfect symbiotic union of the pre-Oedipal child feeding at the mother's breast, characteristic of the oral stage of psychosexual development, when sexual appetite has not yet been differentiated in the child's psyche from gastronomic appetite.[90] As he avoids the responsibilities of mature genital sexuality and opts instead for the oral gratification that comes from eating and drinking, Kvitka-Osnovyanenko's narrator experiences the same nostalgia for the "original maternal symbiosis" we have already discussed. In Jungian terms, meanwhile, Pan Khalyavsky could be said to suffer, again like Oblomov, from a severe mother complex: his nostalgia for childhood signals his compensatory need as an adult to be held, sheltered, warmed, nourished, and loved. Like the coddled and pampered Ilya Ilyich, whose gaze is fixated upon the plump elbows and high breasts of Agafya Matveevna, Pan Khalyavsky is seduced by an unconscious attraction to the soothing caresses offered by the archetypal Great Mother.

## Paradise Lost: Hospitality and Commensality in Prelapsarian Russia

As was noted earlier, a psychoanalytical reading of the nostalgia for childhood portrayed in Gogol's "Old-World Landowners," Goncharov's

*Oblomov*, and Kvitka-Osnovyanenko's *Pan Khalyavsky* suggests at the same time a historical, national, and cultural analogue. The psychosexual regression experienced by the adult male characters may also be understood as the expression of their secret longing to return to an earlier, prelapsarian stage in tsarist Russia's historical development. These male characters seek to return, that is, to an idyllic golden age of patriarchal relations imagined as having existed before the advent of modernization in Russia, a recent development that was disrupting the country's autochthonous culture and its primitive natural economy through Western-style industrialization, secularization, and urbanization. "Westernization of the upper classes, which proceeded through the eighteenth century and resulted in a forcible divorce from their traditional culture, was repeated with each generation through the customs of child-rearing," Joanna Hubbs points out.

> The higher ranks of the nobility continued to place their infant offspring at the breasts of peasant nurses, while the gentry mothers remained a shadowy presence. The peasant woman came to represent, for her charges, the bountiful and ever-nurturing avatar of Mother Earth. It is perhaps for this reason that the idyllic memory of childhood floats over the writings of a number of nineteenth-century intellectuals.[91]

Hubbs proceeds to note the lost "sense of communion" these Russian intellectuals sought to rediscover in their adult years. Understood in the Russian historical context, each of the fictional characters we have been examining may be said to be experiencing nostalgia for a more primitive but happier way of life that is believed to have existed in his nation's past; he is longing to return to a mythic Slavic Ausonia, where communalism and commensalism—rather than individualism and differentiation—shaped human relationships. The literary genre of neo-pastoral that arose in Europe in the wake of the industrial revolution, Raymond Williams has observed, invariably portrayed an idyllic life characterized by what he calls the "happy ethic of consuming," where the dining table—the site of hospitable and abundant eating and drinking—is central in conveying a spirit of community.[92] As Michel Jeanneret puts it in his study of Renaissance banqueting, "at table we rediscover, in the imagination, elements of original happiness and unity."[93]

Such elements are evident in the idyllic domestic household of Gogol's Afanasy Ivanovich and Pulkheria Ivanovna. The narrator of "Old-World Landowners," a disillusioned denizen of modern-day Saint Petersburg, greatly admires the quiet country life led by the elderly couple and their household's bucolic setting, not just for the world of munificence represented here, but also for the hospitality the old-world landowners provide. The faces of Afanasy Ivanovich and Pulkheria Ivanovna, he informs us, "always betray such kindness, such hospitality and sincerity."[94]

> But the old couple seemed interesting to me most of all on those occasions when they had guests. Then everything in their house assumed a different aspect. These good-natured people, one may say, lived for visitors. The best of everything they had was all brought out. They vied with each other in trying to regale you with everything their husbandry produced. But what pleased me most of all was that in all their solicitude there was not a trace of unctuousness. This cordiality and readiness to please were so gently expressed in their faces and so well suited them that one could not help but capitulate to their entreaties. (2:17)

It is not merely the abundant meals and delicious foods served by Pulkheria Ivanovna, therefore, that inspire the narrator's nostalgia for this rapidly disappearing, old-fashioned way of life; it is equally the solicitude shown to the guests who join the elderly couple at table for one of their festive repasts. In Gogol's Ukrainian version of the agrarian, pastoral dream, Poggioli observes, the narrator is presented with "a way of life free from the taint of the acquisitive spirit, as well as from the curse of money."[95] In short, the charm these old-world landowners hold for Gogol's urban, modern narrator consists largely in the old-fashioned spirit of commensality and communion that emanates from their idyllic way of life.

Pan Khalyavsky, likewise, is nostalgic for the old-world hospitality of his family's ancestral estate. Indeed, the resplendent banquet his parents held in honor of a powerful Cossack commander, described at great length and in considerable detail early in part 1 of the novel, is recalled mainly to illustrate the narrator's contention that hospitality (obkhozhdenie) has declined precipitously since the days of his childhood, when a host used to show great generosity in his treatment of the guests at his table. Although formal decorum is rigidly observed throughout this scene of epic feasting, where everything from seating assignments around the table to the order in which the guests are served is done strictly according to a patriarchal hierarchy of rank and gender, the banquet meal itself is characterized not only by the impressive abundance of food and drink provided by Pan Khalyavsky's parents, but also by the genuine hospitality displayed by the host and hostess as they tend to the alimentary and gustatory well-being of their many invited guests.[96] While the mother, "in keeping with her solicitude," prepares an enormous "light meal" (*poldnik*) following the main banquet meal, the father makes the rounds of their guests at table, "asking whether they cared for any of the fruit liqueurs of various sorts, colors, tastes, and kinds that were being passed around in abundance" (58). "In the Homeric banquet feasts his father used to host," writes one commentator, "Trushko Khalyavsky sees a sort of ideal model of existence, where mead and beer, flowing not down one's mustache but directly into the mouth, create an atmosphere of idyllic, universal well-being."[97] "Is there nowadays even just the vestige of a similar kind of sincere, joyous, decorous, and profuse banquet feasting?" Pan Khalyavsky asks rhetorically (62). Hospitality of this kind, the narrator sadly observes, has all but disappeared from present-day Ukraine. He complains, for instance, about an old friend who recently hosted a dinner at his home in one of the principal towns of their province: "During the entire meal he got up from his seat and made the rounds of his guests but once, asking whether they wished to have more to eat and drink. And, if the truth be told, he did not even ask those seated right next to him whether they themselves were eating in exceedingly good order. Formerly, when he would have guests dining at his table, he would not sit down at all; all the time he would be walking around to his guests and entreating them: please try this, add some of that, drink some of this" (29–30). Whereas in the past, at least as far as Pan Khalyavsky remembers it, festive repasts used to be warm, kind, convivial, and generous, meals among the present generation of Ukrainians seem cold, inhospitable, niggardly, and tasteless.

Of the three works of gastronomic Slavophilism we have been examining, it is Goncharov's novel, set in present-day St. Petersburg, that provides the most compelling artistic portrayal of the putative decline of hospitality and commensalism. The meals at Oblomovka, about which the hero reminisces in dream visions of his childhood past, convey a precapitalist kinship model (and a connection with folk mythology) that has at its center a sense of nurturing, harmony, and communion woefully lacking in the bustling St. Petersburg life that surrounds Oblomov as an adult. Whereas in Oblomovka a ritualistic attitude toward the renewal of life that comes each year at springtime had been marked by the traditional baking of "larks," now it is "the importing of oysters and lobsters which defines Spring for the inhabitants of St. Petersburg."[98] Likewise, in Oblomovka the ritual preparation of dinner was seen largely as a communal activity. "The whole household was consulted about the dinner: the aged aunt, too, was invited to the council," we are told. "Each person suggested his or her own dish: one person giblet soup, another noodle soup or brawn, another tripe, another red or white sauce. Every advice was taken into consideration, thoroughly discussed, and then accepted or rejected in accordance with the final decision of the mistress of the house."[99] In cosmopolitan St. Petersburg, on the other hand, meals are prepared and served more privately and individually, without any of this communitarian spirit.

Not only were the plans and preparations for a meal completed in a collective fashion in Oblomovka; so too was the consumption of the meal a community event: remnants of the large stuffed pie, baked for the master on Sundays and holidays, would be eaten throughout the rest of the week by members of the family as well as by the maids and house-serfs. Yury Loshchits, who refers to Goncharov's style in the novel as a kind of "mythological realism,"[100] notes that the communal eating of this enormous pie, a food item that is meant to symbolize prosperity and well-being, apotheosizes not only the feeling of satiety enjoyed by the inhabitants of Oblomovka, but also their folkloric sense of belonging to a greater and more meaningful whole:

What, after all, is Oblomov's existence, if not the fragment of a life that at one time was full-valued and all-embracing? And what is Oblomovka, if not a "blessed corner" forgotten by everyone and remaining intact due to a miracle—a fragment of Eden? The local inhabitants eat up an archeological fragment, a piece of what was once an enormous pie. We recall that in the folk *Weltanschauung* the pie is one of the most graphic symbols of a happy, abundant, prosperous life. The pie is a "lavish feast," a cornucopia, the acme of universal merriment and contentment. Around the pie gathers the feasting, festive folk. From the pie emanates warmth and fragrance; the pie is the central and most archaic symbol of the folk utopia. It is not for nothing that a very real cult of the pie reigns in Oblomovka. The preparation of an enormous pastry and its consumption recall a kind of sacramental ceremony that is strictly fulfilled according to the calendar, from week to week, and month to month. The "dream kingdom" of Oblomovka revolves around its pie, as if around a hot, luminous sphere.[101]

As another commentator observes, in Goncharov's text, the food shared by the inhabitants of Oblomovka (*sovmestnaia eda*) is not just a mere detail of everyday life. More important, it serves as a literary motif, conveying the spirit of communion (*uedinenie*) that unites these people.[102]

The holistic nature of this imagined community at Oblomovka, a community that seems free of any sense of disharmony, exclusion, or class conflict, is especially visible at the family dinner table. "Food and drink in the idyll partake of a nature that is social or, more often, family," Bakhtin reminds us, "all *generations* and *age-groups* come together around the table."[103] Thus young Oblomov's typical day, at age seven, would begin, appropriately enough, with his being caressed lovingly by family and friends gathered around the breakfast table, adults who offer him their affection and acceptance by way of kisses, hugs, and food. "All these members of the Oblomov retinue and establishment picked up Ilya Ilyich and began showering him with caresses and praises," the narator relates, "he had hardly time to wipe away the traces of the unbidden kisses. After that they began stuffing him with rolls, biscuits, and cream. Then his mother hugged and kissed him again" (4:110–11). "Little Oblomov," notes Milton Mays, "enjoys a regime much like that of the Oblomovka geese, marinated in affection as in goodies."[104] This warm, loving atmosphere of Oblomovkan commensality is markedly absent, of course, from the rather lonely bachelor life that Oblomov leads as an adult in the capital, where—as a "spiritual exile"[105]—he is usually shown to be dining alone at home. "Waking up, he saw before him the table set for dinner: cold fish soup with beet greens and kvass, and a tenderized cutlet," we read in part 2. "He had his dinner and then sat down by the window. It was so boring, so absurd—always alone!" (4:236). Even when he does dine out with others, Oblomov continues to pine for the absent spirit of communion and commensality that he idealizes from his childhood. What Oblomov particularly dislikes about the bustling St. Petersburg lifestyle (into which Stolz is seeking to reintroduce him during part 2 of the novel) is precisely this lack of love, fellowship, and goodwill at table. The members of the urbane bourgeois society in the capital, he complains, young and old alike,

> gather, entertain each other at meals, but there is no real good-fellowship, no real hospitality, no mutual attraction! If they gather at a dinner or a party, it is just the same as at their office—coldly, without a spark of gaiety, to boast of their chef or their drawing room, and then to jeer at each other in a discreet aside, to trip one another up. The other day at dinner I honestly did not know where to look and wished I could hide under the table, when they began tearing to shreds the reputations of those who did not happen to be there: "This one is a fool, that one is a mean scoundrel; another one is a thief; and another one is ridiculous"—a regular massacre! . . . Why, then, do they come together if they are like that? Why do they press each other's hands so warmly? No genuine laughter, not a glimmer of sympathy! (4:180–81)

It is worth noting in this regard that Oblomov, whose early retirement from government service stemmed largely from the disenchantment and disappointment he felt when he realized that the civil servants employed in one department were not "one big happy family, unremittingly concerned about one another's peace and pleasures" (4:57), experiences terrible embarrassment and discomfort when he dines for the first time with Olga Ilinskaya. "The footman brought him a cup of tea and a tray with cakes," the narrator relates. "He wanted to suppress his feeling of embarrassment and to be free and easy—and in this mood of undue familiarity he picked up such a pile of rusks, biscuits and cakes that a little girl who sat next to him started to giggle. Others eyed the pile curiously" (4:198). The hero suffers "the same agonies at dinner" (4:201) on the following day, when once again he finds himself struggling to remain calm and relaxed under Olga's watchful gaze at the dinner table. "It's sheer agony!" he laments. "Have I come here then to be laughed at by her?" (4:201).

Later in part 2, Oblomov's earlier embarrassment, when Olga had noticed his gaucherie with the biscuits, returns in the form of the severe self-consciousness he suffers at her aunt's dinner table, where, at the mere mention of a love story, he "would suddenly seize, in his confusion, such a fistful of rusks that someone was quite sure to laugh" (4:278). By part 3 of the novel, Oblomov's embarrassment and discomfort at the dinner table turn to panic as he imagines how his health will be toasted at the official dinner held to celebrate his engagement to Olga. Being betrothed to Olga, in Oblomov's view, would mean that "you must never eat and drink properly and adequately, but live on air and bouquets!" (4:335).[106] In his attempt to flee from the harsh psychological and emotional realities he encounters in St. Petersburg, Oblomov pictures in his imagination what his ideal future life in the country will be like: an idyll replete with abundant meals, the companionship of a kind helpmate, and warm goodwill among family and friends:

> Now he became absorbed in his favorite idea: he was thinking of a small group of friends settling in villages and farms within ten or fifteen miles of his estate, who would visit each other daily in turn, and would dine, sup, and dance together; he saw nothing but bright days and bright, laughing people, without a care or a wrinkle, with round faces and rosy cheeks, double chins and insatiable appetites; it was going to be a perpetual summer, everlasting gaiety, lovely food, and sweet leisure. (4:79)

"You will not hear someone delivering a violent philippic against an absent friend," Oblomov tells Stolz when he describes how a meal will be enjoyed in this utopian future life. "You will not catch a glance thrown your way that promises the same to you the moment you go out the door. You will not break bread with anyone you do not like or with anyone who is not nice. You will see sympathy in the eyes of your companions, sincere and good-natured laughter in their jokes. . . . Everything is to one's liking! Everybody looks and says what is in his heart!" (4:185–86). Happiness for Oblomov thus consists not merely in having copious amounts of food and beverages, but also in sharing the dining experience with people he loves and who love him. His ideal meal is characterized by a loving goodwill that envelops everyone at table.

Oblomov seems eventually to regain the commensal spirit that he remembers from childhood. He recaptures it around the family dinner table at Agafya Matveevna's home, where his meals are now taken in the pleasant company of the landlady herself, her young children, and, on occasion, his friend Alekseev. One of the hero's favorite activities during the final, Vyborg period of his life consists in loading his family into a carriage and driving out of the city to the Gunpowder Works for a picnic on his name day. Indeed, Oblomov wishes to share the happiness of these family excursions with his old friend Stolz and his wife Olga, suggesting that they purchase a summer cottage nearby so that the couple could join him and his new family in such pleasant activities. "You'd love it!" he gushes to Stolz. "We'd have tea in the grove, go to the Gunpowder Works on St. Elijah's Day, with a cart laden with provisions and samovar following us. We'd lie down on the grass there—on a rug! Agafya Matveevna would teach Olga Sergeevna how to run a house. Truly she would!" (4:454). Picnicking with family and friends on the grass and sharing food as well as fellowship evoke the Oblomovkan spirit of commensality that he desperately seeks to recapture.

Oblomov comes closest to attaining this spirit at Agafya Matveevna's home, where "everything of a hostile nature had disappeared from Ilya Ilyich's life. He was now surrounded by simple, kind, and loving people who all consented to do their best to make his life as comfortable as possible" (4:491). One evening following his stroke, the convalescent Oblomov, reclining on the sofa, drowsily recalls a peaceful domestic scene from his childhood years in Oblomovka. It seems—at least in his imagination—that he has indeed managed to recapture that lost spirit of commensality he so yearns for:

> Lazily, mechanically, almost unconsciously he looked into Agafya Matveevna's eyes, and out of the depths of his memory there arose a familiar image he had seen somewhere before. He tried to think hard where and when he had heard it all. . . . And he saw before him the large, dark drawing-room in his parents' house, lighted by a tallow candle, and his deceased mother and her visitors sitting at a round table; they were sewing in silence; his father was walking up and down the room in silence. The present and the past had merged and intermingled. He dreamt that he had reached the promised land, flowing with milk and honey, where people ate bread they had not earned and wore gold and silver garments. He heard the stories of dreams and signs, the clatter of knives, and the rattle of crockery.

He clung to his nurse and listened to her old shaky voice: "Militrissa Kirbitievna!" she said, pointing to Agafya Matveevna. (4:500)

Where the child Oblomov used to daydream constantly of "that magic country where there were no evils, troubles, or sorrows, where Militrissa Kirbitievna lived, where they fed you such excellent food and such fine clothes could be had for nothing" (4:123), the adult Oblomov now entertains the wish-fulfillment fantasy that he has at last arrived at that magic country, the Slavic Ausonia, where human relationships are nurtured in a convivial atmosphere of love, fellowship, and goodwill.

## Sex and Sexuality in Russian Literature

Although food and eating came eventually to occupy a rather prominent (or at least legitimate) position in works of modern Russian fiction, the same cannot be said for sex and sexuality. "We have no sex here" (*U nas seksa net*), claimed one female participant from the USSR during a Soviet-American television bridge hosted in 1986 by Vladimir Pozner. This now famous line has generally been taken to mean not that there was no sexual activity going on in the former Soviet Union, but rather that there was not any open public discourse about sex and sexuality. Of course, the repressive silence on sexual matters (if not outright sexophobia) experienced during most of the Soviet era is now very much a thing of the past. Indeed, the post-Soviet period has been providing us with what Eliot Borenstein calls "a veritable orgy of sexual discourse in and about Russia." As a result, he notes, "Russian culture in all its manifestations would appear to have become thoroughly and overtly sexualized."[107] In addition to the explicit and widespread sexual expression (often pornographic) that has appeared in the Russian mass media, film, and fiction since the collapse of Communist rule in 1991, cultural historians have examined the social construction of sexuality in Russia's long history: from the religiosity of the Middle Ages through the libertinism of the fin de siècle to the sexual repression of the Soviet period. What emerges from these recent histories of sexuality in Russia is the marked absence of an established erotic tradition in its literature and painting. Russian chauvinists usually interpret the absence of eroticism in Russian cultural history as a positive development, of course. The early-twentieth-century metaphysical philosopher Nikolay Berdyaev, for instance, attributed the nonerotic legacy in literature and art to the innate spirituality of the heroic Russian people, who grant little value to the physical body and are thus better equipped than those who live in the decadent West to forgo the sensual pleasures of the material world. In terms of human sexuality, Berdyaev's so-called Russian idea in large part celebrates in his homeland "the triumph of morality and sublimation over the temptations of the flesh."[108]

The roots of sexual puritanism in Russian culture, most critics agree, extend back to the adoption of Orthodox Christianity late in the tenth century, when a lively prosexual culture, which was believed to have thrived for a long time among the pagan Slavs, was suddenly driven underground. For many centuries to follow, Russia would be forced to lead a double life, as far as sexuality was concerned: official high culture, which was dominated by the teachings of the Russian Orthodox Church, would remain antisexual in its orientation, while the low everyday culture of the common people would be guiltlessly prosexual. "The contradiction between the 'high' culture's supreme spirituality and utter disregard for the life of the body and the 'low' culture's insistence on the inescapable reality of natural life runs like a thread through the entire history of Russian culture," writes Igor Kon, who has examined how the intense spirituality and rigorous asceticism found in Russian Orthodox doctrine contributed mightily to the antisexual ethos that dominated official high culture throughout the medieval period.[109] Eve Levin, in *Sex and Society in the World of the Orthodox Slavs, 900–1700* (1989), has shown how the Russian Orthodox Church viewed sexual desire as something extraneous to (rather than innate in) human nature, regarding concupiscence as an evil inclination, originating with Satan, something alien to spiritual love or moral virtue that thus needs to be strictly regulated, if not eliminated altogether, in earthly life.[110] "In the official view of the medieval Russian Orthodox Church, sex was always suspect, even in marriage for procreation," she explains:

> The ideal life was marked by total abstinence. The desire for sex originated with the devil, who used this greatest of all temptations to lead humankind astray, beginning in Eden. Childbearing resulted from God's blessing, not from sexual intercourse. Any form of sexual expression was essentially unnatural, unhealthy, and indecent. Sex was also, as Russian churchmen granted, inevitable. Human

weakness and propensity to sin led men and women into sexual desire and sexual activity. Thus God, in His infinite mercy, had granted dispensation to human beings to marry, in order to channel the sexual impulses to which they were all too susceptible.[111]

Russian Orthodox teachings were not only antisexual and puritanical in nature, but also highly misogynistic, conceptualizing Eve as the creature who introduced sin into the world and thus categorizing woman as a dangerous source of sexual temptation. Woman was viewed as "the cosmic carrier of all that is elemental, natural, and bestial in human sexuality."[112]

Such a repressive religious morality actively discouraged Russian artists from developing an openly erotic tradition in literature and art. Granted, as a secular culture gradually began to develop in Russia during the eighteenth century, when texts about love and romance from Western Europe (especially from France) began to find their way into the country, the situation did start to change somewhat. But erotic poetry—whether it be the bawdy poems of Ivan Barkov or Pushkin's ribald *Gavriliada*—existed only at the very periphery of serious literature in post-Petrine Russia, where the myth of the Madonna and the idealization of motherhood helped to perpetuate the anxieties about the human body and sexuality that had been nurtured by Russian Orthodoxy.[113] A heightened poetic attitude toward women, which eschewed coarse sensuality, came to dominate mainstream nineteenth-century Russian literature, where "carnal 'love for sex' usually stands in opposition to a purely spiritual 'love for the person' or a serene 'love for wedlock,' founded on marital fidelity."[114] As Igor Kon puts it, "the ideal woman in Russian literature was either the innocent maiden or the overweening mother, but never the lover."[115] Where Eve, the archetypal sexual creature, was seen as having introduced sin into the world, Mary—at once the virgin maiden and the Mother of God (*bogoroditsa*)—was seen as having brought spiritual salvation to a fallen humankind. Eroticism in Russian culture found an especially assiduous foe in the Social Democrats (*raznochintsy*), writers and critics such as Nikolay Chernyshevsky, Nikolay Dobrolyubov, and Dmitry Pisarev, whose zealous devotion to the revolutionary cause led them to renounce sensuality in general and sexual desire in particular. Carnal pleasures were deemed base and vulgar personal indulgences unworthy of such committed political activists as these; carnality only distracted them from pursuing their noble ideological mission.

The sole historical exception to the pattern of dominance enjoyed by antisexuality and antieroticism within Russian culture is provided by the brief interlude—what James Billington calls the "new sensualism"—that occurs at the end of the nineteenth century, when a reaction against traditional religious moralism and ascetic puritanism ushered in a period when writers, artists, and critics became preoccupied with issues of sex and sexuality.[116] The so-called sexual question that arose in Russian cultural discourse during the last decade of the nineteenth century and first decade of the twentieth century, as we shall see in chapter 4, was launched largely with the publication in 1891 of Tolstoy's controversial novella *The Kreutzer Sonata*, a work that prompted many people at the time to question the nature of sex, the meaning of love, and the viability of the institution of marriage. The fin de siècle debate over human sexuality not only involved important philosophers such as Vladimir Solovyov, Nikolay Berdyaev, Dmitry Merezhkovsky, and Vasily Rozanov; it also witnessed the veritable cult of eros proclaimed by Symbolist poets such as Konstantin Balmont, Vyacheslav Ivanov, and Valery Bryussov and Silver Age painters such as Mikhail Vrubel, Valentin Serov, and Leon Bakst. Russian works of erotic prose fiction— such as Mikhail Artsybashev's *Sanin* (1907), Fyodor Sologub's *Petty Demon* (1907), Evdokia Nagrodskaya's *The Wrath of Dionysus* (1910), and Anastasia Verbitskaya's *The Keys to Happiness* (1913)—also appeared for the first time during this short-lived era of unprecedented openness in the artistic representation of sexuality. The turn-of-the-century explosion of interest in eroticism and sensuality in Russian literature and art soon ran its course, however. By the late 1920s and early 1930s the repressive antisexual ethos that had dominated official high culture in tsarist Russia for so many centuries was restored by the Soviet leadership under Stalin and remained in place until the collapse of Communist rule in 1991.[117]

## Food, Sex, and Carnal Appetite

The aim of this study, however, is not to produce a comprehensive historical survey that traces the use of food imagery and/or sexual representation in Russian literature during the past two centuries. Instead the focus will be placed specifically on the nexus of the alimentary and the sexual in the works of the two most famous writers of prose fiction in nineteenth-century Russia. Of course, this gastronomical/ sexual nexus is not unique to the works of Dostoevsky and Tolstoy. "Writers throughout history have always linked food with sexuality," writes James W. Brown, "food because of the pleasures one obtains from oral gratification, eating because of the intimacy growing out of close and immediate contact with the world."[118] Indeed, the gastronomical and the sexual, as contemporary anthropologists remind us, are appetites that are closely associated biologically as well as socially and culturally.[119] Where eating is a basic biological drive that is necessary for the perpetuation of life for the individual (self-preservation), the sex drive is necessary for the perpetuation of life for the species (procreation, reproduction). And just as human sexuality has evolved to undergo a functional bifurcation, whereby the act of sexual intercourse can serve both pleasure and procreation, so too has the act of eating become split between pleasure and necessity—between eating to live (food as a source of nourishment) and living to eat (food as a source of pleasure).[120] Because food and sex are needed to satisfy the two most basic drives of our animal nature, several ancient Greek philosophers, including Plato and Aristotle, advocated temperance and moderation in our indulgence in the pleasures of touch (sex) and of taste (food), alert to the danger of human beings becoming enslaved by such bestial enjoyments of the body.[121] Plato, for instance, warned of the inevitable diminution of our humanity when human beings do not "master" themselves: that is, when they fail to allow the higher, "rational" part of their soul to control the lower, "desiring" part (when they fail to tame and temper the wild, unruly, bestial part that lusts after food, drink, and sex) and thus to keep it from gorging itself in the animal pleasures of the body.[122] "Like cattle," Socrates laments, "they always look down, stooped to the earth and their tables, grazing, feeding, and copulating, kicking and butting each other out of greed for these delights."[123] And, as Cephalus learns from the elderly Sophocles in *The Republic*, one of the great happinesses found in old age is that men are at last freed from bondage to the cruel and raging tyranny of sexual desire.[124]

Christian moralists throughout the Middle Ages shared this basic distrust of the animal nature of human beings and their carnal appetites. Like the ancient Greek philosophers, Catholic churchmen in the

West—such as St. Augustine and St. Thomas Aquinas—believed that carnal pleasures rendered man incapable of pursuing and attaining higher spiritual aspirations. They also believed that the desire for tasty foods and drink is closely linked to the desire for sex—that our lust for oral pleasure is linked to our lust for sexual pleasure. Iconic representations of a naked Eve standing seductively with an apple in her hand conjoined the gastronomical with the sexual in the minds of many. As Tobin notes, "the symbolic history of the Judaeo-Christian tradition opens with the episode of the tasting of the fruit in the Garden of Eden: eating precedes sexual shame, food comes, therefore, before eroticism."[125] In his *Summa Theologica* (1265–74), St. Thomas Aquinas thus conceives of "temperance" in very broad terms with an emphasis on moderation in matters of food and drink as well as sexual relations.[126] The same linkage is made between food and sex in Eastern Christendom, especially in Russian Orthodox teachings, where abstaining from eating meat (fasting) and from drinking alcoholic beverages was advocated as a method for avoiding sexual temptation. "Overindulgence in food, too much sleep, or a sense of superiority," Eve Levin points out, were to be avoided as they were believed to arouse sexual desire in men.[127]

Even modern secular thinkers persist in making this connection between oral and sexual appetites, albeit for vastly different reasons than did Christian moralists. Freudian psychoanalysis, for instance, considers the "oral" and the "genital" to be stages in the development of sexual maturity in human beings. We have already seen how Gogol, Goncharov, and Kvitka-Osnovyanenko portray male characters whose paralyzing fear of sexual intimacy is compensated by their great love of food and drink. In psychoanalytic terms, these male characters may be said to be regressing from adult genitality to infantile (pregenital) modes of libidinal enjoyment. Food and sex, however, are just as frequently conceptualized as operating in tandem rather than by way of contrast—as "both/and" rather than "either/or." Indeed, they are more likely to be portrayed as accompanying each other, not compensating for or replacing each other. From a psychoanalytical point of view, the table and the bed are never very far apart: in dreams, Freud has noted, "a table is very often found to represent a bed."[128] If we understand eating to be an act of incorporation—an act whereby an external object is taken inside another—then it is the most basic model of what

Bakhtin calls man's joyful, exultant, and triumphant "encounter with the world."[129] Sexual intercourse likewise serves as a bodily image for incorporation, whereby two bodies are made one. The desire to become one with another sexually, not surprisingly, is often represented as a kind of eating. As objects of sexual attraction, beautiful women are frequently referred to as "tasty morsels," while handsome men are regarded as "hunks" or "beefcakes." Carnal appetite, in short, is traditionally equated with gastronomical appetite.

In this book, we shall be examining how carnal appetite and gastronomical appetite are represented in works by Dostoevsky and Tolstoy. Although several other Russian writers of the late nineteenth and early twentieth century will be discussed, the main objective is to explore the contrasting treatments of food and sex by those two giants of the nineteenth-century Russian novel. As noted earlier, I shall extend the useful distinction that Ronald Tobin posits (and that Michel Foucault seems much too eager to collapse) between *manger* and *goûter*: that is, between conceptualizations of the acts of eating and sexual intercourse according to the paradigms of "power" or "pleasure." A polar opposition emerges between Dostoevskian "carnivorousness" (*plotoiadnost'*), where eating and sexual intercourse are both portrayed as acts of psychological violence, aggression, and domination, and Tolstoyan "voluptuousness" (*sladostrastie*), where they are instead understood as acts of libidinal enjoyment, delight, and indulgence.

As we shall see in chapter 2 ("Eating as Power: Dostoevsky and Carnivorousness"), an alimentary dynamic of "eat or be eaten" is operative in Dostoevsky's postlapsarian fictional world, where characters with strong personalities and cruel sensual impulses are portrayed as being ruled by a seemingly insatiable power-lust. Both eating and fornicating signify acts of violence and cruelty rather than of pleasure in Dostoevsky's novels, and carnal desire manifests itself primarily as a rapacious appetite for power: the desire to consume and devour others. In contrast to the male characters of Gogol, Goncharov, and Kvitka-Osnovyanenko, who pine for an idealized childhood world of communion, commensality, and compassion, Dostoevsky's male characters are shown to inhabit a fallen world of capitalism, materialism, and egoism—predatory, carnivoristic, and cannibalistic. In chapter 3 ("Eating as Pleasure: Tolstoy and Voluptuousness"), I trace how the trajectory of Tolstoy's evolving attitude toward human sexuality—his movement from hedonism to asceticism, from self-enjoyment to self-denial—is mirrored by his treatment of gastronomic indulgence. As the carnal pleasures of the flesh come increasingly to be seen as sinful temptations that lure people away from the straight and narrow path of moral righteousness and spiritual self-perfection, Tolstoy tends more and more to regard the gastronomic pleasures of the table with revulsion and disgust: bodily pleasures only, no longer morally or spiritually palatable. Tolstoy's advocacy of such radical ideals in sexual matters as celibacy, chastity, and conjugal continence is thus mirrored by his support of extreme dietary measures as well, such as vegetarianism, abstinence, and fasting. In chapter 4 ("Carnality and Morality in Fin de Siècle and Revolutionary Russia"), I discuss the influence that Dostoevsky's and Tolstoy's contrasting conceptualizations of sexual and gastronomical desire exerted upon Russian writers and thinkers during the late nineteenth and early twentieth century, a period when the reception in Russia of Darwin's theories, Nietzsche's philosophy, and Zola's novels brought to the fore in public discourse the allegedly "zoological" nature of human beings: that is, the unleashing of the "beast within man." For Dostoevsky the "beast" that lies hidden within each human being is a ferocious, rapacious, and brutalizing appetite for power. For Tolstoy that inner "beast" is the pleasure-seeking part of our animal nature that instinctively pursues corporeal gratification and sensual satisfaction.

# Eating as Power
## Dostoevsky and Carnivorousness

2

In *The Abortion* (1970), a rather fanciful American novel set in the late 1960s, Richard Brautigan describes a public library located somewhere in California that accepts books from its patrons rather than lends them out. One of the titles brought to this mythical library is *The Culinary Dostoevski*, written by a man named James Fallon, who refers to his literary creation as "a cookbook of recipes" culled from Dostoevsky's novels and who claims to have eaten everything the Russian author ever cooked.[1] "Brautigan's fancy is delightful," Simon Karlinsky observes in regard to this fictitious Dostoevsky cookbook,

> but in actual fact his character would end up very poorly nourished. Gogol, Tolstoy, and Chekhov, among Russian writers, have written lovingly and at length about various foods eaten by their characters. But Dostoevsky, who can be so magnificent in his own realm of irrational passions and spiritual insights, had very little interest in the physical basis of human life or in man's natural surroundings. The only kinds of food that it would occur to him to use for literary purposes are a crust of dry bread someone denies to a starving little boy or a pineapple compote that a neurotic young girl dreams she would eat if she were witnessing the crucifixion of a child.[2]

Few readers, I think, would dispute the accuracy or validity of this analysis, nor would they seriously challenge Karlinsky's additional claim that "for the flavor and the feel of actual life as it was lived in Russia, reproduced with all the fidelity and subtlety that literary art is capable of," we have to turn to other Russian authors than Dostoevsky.[3] The "culinary Dostoevsky," therefore, turns out to be a rather ironic (if not oxymoronic) choice of title for a cookbook; the novels by this Russian author appear to be the last place one would choose to explore in search of tasty recipes, kitchen expertise, or cooking tips.[4]

It seems to me, however, that we can account for the rarity (not to mention the morbid perversity) of descriptions of food and scenes of eating we observe in Dostoevsky's fiction by more than merely what Karlinsky calls the Russian author's putative lack of interest in "the physical basis of human life" or in "man's natural surroundings."[5] Dostoevsky, I would argue, simply utilizes food motifs and eating metaphors for quite different narrative purposes than do most nineteenth-century Russian writers. Moreover, the "poet of the underground" proceeds to encode these gastronomic images with a peculiar symbolic significance. Visits to inns, taverns, and restaurants in a Dostoevsky novel serve not as a means for the author to paint a picture—rich in physical detail and pictorial expressiveness—of contemporary culinary practice in Russia; they instead provide him with an opportunity to orchestrate shocking scandal scenes and impassioned dialogic confrontations involving some of his characters. The memorable encounters between Prince Valkovsky and Ivan Petrovich in *The Insulted and Injured*, Svidrigaylov and Raskolnikov in *Crime and Punishment*, Arkady Dolgoruky and Versilov in *A Raw Youth*, and Ivan and Alyosha Karamazov in *The Brothers Karamazov* well illustrate how this orchestration is true of the author's poetics with respect to scenes that are set inside public eateries. As a verbal artist, Dostoevsky seems eminently more interested in appropriating the discourse of gastronomy as a trope for describing the emotional state or psychological motivation of his characters than in providing readers with the artistic representation of actual meals. In short, Dostoevsky tends to exploit food and the act of eating less as mimetic devices for realistically representing the details of everyday life in nineteenth-century Russia than as metaphors for illustrating human conflicts in modern life between the sexes, between the generations, and between the social classes.

Moreover, in Dostoevsky's postlapsarian fictional world, where many of the characters are highly volitional, egoistic creatures almost obsessed with a desire to dominate and control one another, the act of eating—like the sex act—serves not as a paradigm of pleasure, but as a paradigm of power. This alimentary dynamic is especially evident in those works written upon the author's return from Siberian exile, where fictional characters with strong personalities and sensual impulses are often portrayed as being ruled by a seemingly insatiable appetite for power, an unappeasable power-lust that one critic has termed a *libido dominandi*.[6] For these egoistic Dostoevskian characters, the ingestion of food—whether as a mimetic or metaphoric act—tends to indicate not taste, enjoyment, and nourishment, but violence, aggression, and domination. Where food and women are concerned, bloodthirsty and power-hungry people such as these do not merely eat; they seek to devour, digest, and destroy. In this sense, they share the same pathology of desire that Pechorin claims to experience in *A Hero of Our Time* (1841), where Lermontov's jaded hero confesses to satisfying a strange inner need that compels him, vampire-like, to "feed" upon the feelings and emotions of other people. "I have an insatiable craving inside me that consumes everything," Pechorin explains, "and that makes me regard the joys and sufferings of others only in their relationship to me, as food to sustain my spiritual powers."[7] As a function of the violent and often cruel "masculinist" psychology that Dostoevsky seems to feel compelled to depict (and expose) in his fiction, food—like women—comes to serve as an object of male heterosexual desire that is coveted not for the libidinal satisfaction it can bring, but for the sense of autonomy, domination, and control it can bestow.[8] Both eating and fornicating thus signify acts of violence and cruelty rather than pleasure in Dostoevsky's fictional universe, where carnal desire manifests itself primarily as a rapacious appetite for power.

What I shall be exploring in this chapter is how Dostoevsky conveys this insatiable will to power within human beings in large part through the language and imagery of eating. I shall not be concerned, therefore, with retrieving the few recipes one might manage to cull from the pages of his novels in search of the mythical "culinary" Dostoevsky. Rather I shall be examining the way that an evil and destructive egoistic appetite for power is often expressed in his fiction by means of masticatory and predatory images. Like Dickens in England, this nineteenth-century

Russian writer repeatedly uses different kinds of animal imagery (birds of prey, spiders, reptiles, and so on) to convey how the dynamics of various relationships of power—political, sociological, sexual, psychological—operate between and among human beings.[9] To help reinforce this animal imagery, he selects certain masticatory terms—such as "to swallow" (*proglotit'*), "to eat up" (*s"est'*), and "to devour" (*zhrat'*)—whose literal meanings and etymological origins are designed to compete semantically with what would seem to be their more neutral figurative value of "to destroy" or "to annihilate." We shall see, in addition, how the carnivoristic appetite that develops within some people—a metaphorical hunger for "flesh" that Dostoevsky identifies closely with the psychological desire to dominate and control others—can ultimately devolve into anthropophagy (or man-eating), especially when that rapacious will to power is fueled by a highly competitive social and economic environment, such as the one taking shape in post-emancipation Russia, a country that at the time was undergoing a process of rapid industrialization and capitalist development. Filtered through his unique artistic imagination, his abiding Christian faith, and his profoundly apocalyptic vision of mankind's future, the bestial carnivorousness that Dostoevsky saw at the basis of human relations in the modern secular world threatens to make people degenerate eventually into bloodthirsty cannibals.

## The Belly Versus the Soul: Hunger, Fasting, and Suffering

If one were foolhardy enough to venture forth in search of the mythical "culinary Dostoevsky," one would quickly discover that in his fictional works this Russian author describes a world where food is generally stripped of much of its traditionally strong positive value as the source of life—as the main provider of physical nourishment, vitality, and health for the human body. As Karlinsky strongly insinuated in his example of the neurotic Lise Khokhlakova, who can derive a sadistic sense of pleasure from contemplating herself eating a sweet and exotic culinary delight like pineapple compote while she watches the painful suffering of a young child as he is being crucified (15:24), the act of eating in Dostoevsky's fictional universe is more likely to be negatively rather than positively valorized, because it is so often associated with the prurient, the perverse, and the pathological. With very few exceptions (such as, for instance, in the case of the hearty appetite for food manifested by the robust Yepanchin daughters in *The Idiot*), it is not physical vitality or gastronomic satiety that tends to predominate among the fictional characters—considered as eaters—who populate a Dostoevsky novel.[10] On the contrary, we are more apt to encounter people who, if they are not afflicted with some debilitating form of bodily illness, suffer from chronic hunger due to a shortage of food. Indeed, physical hunger is made to serve in Dostoevsky's fiction as an important sociological indicator of the type of oppressive urban environment these unfortunate individuals are forced to inhabit and is, as a result, closely associated with conditions of economic poverty, material deprivation, and physical suffering.[11] As an impoverished writer who himself was for many years pressured to produce literary works to keep himself and his family from starvation, Dostoevsky knew firsthand just how difficult procuring one's daily bread could prove to be.[12]

Such poverty-stricken families as the Marmeladovs in *Crime and Punishment* and the Snegiryovs in *The Brothers Karamazov* are thus shown to suffer terribly from hunger, to the extent that many of the family members are forced to survive on seriously inadequate and substandard diets. Nina Snegiryov, for instance, is reduced to eating other people's leavings ("What you would scarcely give to a dog," Captain Snegiryov comments sadly [14:191]), while in Ivan Karamazov's anecdote about the French murderer Richard, that poor creature is glad just to be able to eat the slops that are served to pigs (14:218). In many cases, a dire shortage of edible food prompts characters to take rather drastic measures. Sonya Marmeladova, for example, is forced into prostitution to help feed her younger brother and sisters (6:21), while her widowed stepmother, after being cruelly repulsed in her entreaties for financial assistance from her late husband's well-fed but indifferent superior, decides to take her own children out onto the streets to perform like circus animals, forcing them to sing and dance like beggars for a meal. "Now I shall feed the children myself, I won't be beholden to anybody!" she exclaims in anguish (6:329–30). The "irritations of hunger" (as Svidrigaylov phrases it) even figure among those several reasons that are advanced in that novel as possible motivations for the terrible crime committed by the chronically undernourished and seriously malnutritioned Raskolnikov (6:378).[13] The vulnerable young heroine in "A Gentle Creature," a sixteen-year-old girl who was regularly beaten at the home of her two aunts, where the poor orphan was begrudged "every bite of bread she ate" (24:10), agrees to a loveless marriage to a much older man strictly, it seems, as a matter of her own physical survival. "I told her directly that she would have enough to eat," explains the pawnbroker, whose petty tyranny (as a dominating husband intent upon subjugating his new wife) eventually drives the emotionally brutalized young bride to suicide (24:11). In *The Brothers Karamazov*, Captain Snegiryov is driven by the demands of hunger to swallow his fierce "pride of the poor"; rather than fight a duel to defend his honor, he accepts the money offered him as compensation for the public humiliation he suffered earlier at the hands of the brutish Dmitry Karamazov. "And if I challenge him and he kills me on the spot, what then? What will become of them?" Captain Snegiryov asks with respect to his children. "Who would feed them all?" (14:186). For hungry and impoverished families such as the Marmeladovs and Snegiryovs, who must struggle to survive at a basic level of material subsistence (what gastrocritics would call the *degré zéro alimentaire*) and who are forced to live in a realm of dire physical necessity that Roland Barthes has labeled *l'ordre de besoin*, food thus indicates acute material deprivation, need, and want.[14] It is not surprising, therefore, that one way Dostoevsky marks the brutal victimization of many of his gentle and humble fictional characters—as we witness, for example, in the case of the simpleminded Swiss girl Marie in *The Idiot* (8:59), Marya Lebyadkina in *The Devils* (10:114), and Stinking Lizaveta in *The Brothers Karamazov* (14:91)—is to mention how they have been deprived of adequate food by those people who are directly responsible for providing for their material welfare. Indeed, those characters in Dostoevsky's fiction who are guilty of cruelly tormenting other human beings often manifest their petty tyranny and domestic despotism by refusing to allow those under their dominion to enjoy an adequate diet.

Dostoevsky also exploits in his works the traditional symbolism associated with "bread" as the staff of life, using it to indicate the basic physical sustenance without which human beings cannot continue to live. When a person approaches extreme material deprivation in one of Dostoevsky's narratives, such as in the case of the little boy who starves to death at Christ's Christmas tree in *Diary of a Writer* (22:15), that person is often said to have been reduced to his or her proverbial last "piece of bread" (*kusok khleba*) or "crust of bread" (*korochka*). Indeed, "bread" in Dostoevsky's writings comes to serve as a basic metonym for food in general. In "A Gentle Creature," for instance, the young heroine reaches a point of such desperation in her miserable home life that she takes out an advertisement in a local newspaper offering to work without salary—simply "for food" (*iz khleba*) (24:8). In both *The Idiot* (8:312) and *The Devils* (10:172), we encounter—as symbols for the philanthropic intentions of liberal secular humanism and socialism—the motif of rumbling carts bringing "bread" (that is, food) to a starving mankind.[15] In *The Brothers Karamazov*, meanwhile, the Grand Inquisitor chastises Christ for having refused to turn the stones in the wilderness to "bread" and in this way having forfeited the opportunity to satisfy not only the human need for physical self-preservation but also the desire (or "appetite") for epistemological certainty and community of worship. "Feed men and then ask of them virtue," Christ is advised by the Grand Inquisitor, who maintains that humankind is only too eager to believe that "there is no crime, no sin . . . there is only hunger" (14:230).

The danger in so easily satisfying men's physical appetite by feeding them "bread," as Dostoevsky makes clear in a letter written to Vasily Alekseev in June 1876, is that this socioeconomic solution to the problem of human hunger will take away our essential moral freedom, depriving us of our "labor, personality, the sacrifice of one's own good for the sake of another" (29.2:85). The motif of "turning stones into bread," the author explains, was designed to challenge and counter the Socialists' fundamental belief that "man's most important vices and troubles have come from hunger, cold, poverty, and every kind of struggle for existence" (29.2:85). Christ's response to this demonic temptation (his famous rejoinder that "man does not live by bread alone") states an important axiom about man's spiritual—and not just animal—nature. Rather than seek to renew humankind with earthly bread, Christ instead provides more nourishing sustenance in the form of heavenly bread, instilling in our souls the ideal of beauty and the law of love. By striving toward these difficult spiritual ideals, human beings can eventually attain the goal of becoming brothers to one another. "While if you give them bread," Dostoevsky observes, "out of boredom they will perhaps become enemies to each other" (29.2:85). Once humankind is fed and each person has eaten his fill, Dostoevsky feared, people will immediately become bored. "A man will eat his fill and then forget about it," Prince Versilov predicts. "Right away he'll start saying: 'Well, I've had enough to eat, so what am I to do now?'"(13:173).

In a religious and spiritual context, as a result, some of Dostoevsky's characters actually cherish the hunger that results from gastronomic self-denial, from a self-imposed deprivation of "bread" (food) as physical nourishment. Whereas others are suffering from hunger, these people seem masochistically to hunger for suffering.[16] Father Ferapont, we recall, is renowned far and wide for the great rigor and devotion he displays in observing the ecclesiastical fasts: all year round, even at Easter, the holy monk takes nothing but bread and water, restricting himself to two pounds of bread in three days and consuming in seven days what usually lasts the fasting monks at the Obdorsk monastery only two days (14:153). Indeed, food becomes closely associated with the devil and evil temptation for this religious fanatic, who accuses his former spiritual rival, the recently deceased Father Zosima (who did not believe in fasting), of having been "seduced by sweets" and of having "worshipped the belly by filling it up with sweets" (14:303).[17] In a similar vein, when Alyosha's faith in God is severely put to the test by the putrid odor of corruption that emanates prematurely and profusely from the corpse of his beloved spiritual mentor, the "elder" Zosima, this near fall from grace—"from the saints to the sinners" (14:310)—involves not only the attraction of sex (visiting the voluptuous Grushenka, who has long been waiting to get the young monk "in her clutches" so that she might pull his cassock off) but also the lure of food and drink: that is, he plans to break the Lenten fast by eating sausage and drinking vodka with Rakitin (14:309). The Grand Inquisitor speaks to Christ of the suffering that he himself experienced (as one of those elite few who are strong rather than the masses who are weak) by living on "roots and locusts" in the wilderness (14:237), while later Ivan's devil will mockingly assert that Ivan too—as one of the strong—is prepared to "dine on locusts" (15:80). In *The Idiot*, Lebedev boasts that he is ready to live on a meager diet of bread and water (8:163), and Rogozhin actually undertakes a hunger strike in an effort to show Nastasya Filippovna that he is prepared to accept great physical suffering—risking death itself—in order to prove his passionate love for her (8:175–76). In *Crime and Punishment*, meanwhile, Raskolnikov insists that his sister Dunya would eat only black bread and water rather than sell her soul by marrying for money (6:37). Likewise in *The Village of Stepanchikovo*, marriageable young women such as Sashenka and Nastenka voice their willingness to live on black bread and water in defiance of the petty tyranny exerted in the fiefdom of Foma Opiskin (3:58).

## The Belly-as-God: Sensual Indulgence and Sybaritism

Although Dostoevsky's narratives tend to privilege physical suffering (and thus its gastronomic correlatives of hunger and fasting) over the pleasures of feasting and satiation, there are nevertheless occasional representations in his novels of the joy and delight that are to be derived from gastronomic indulgence. Mention is sometimes made of notorious epicures, gourmets, or bon vivants, most notably, Radomsky's uncle in *The Idiot* (8:262, 297), who inhabit not *l'ordre de besoin* but *l'ordre de désir*, where food indicates self-indulgence and extravagance rather than self-denial and deprivation. The gastronomic activities of these Dostoevskian pleasure-seekers, however, are seldom graphically depicted for us in the text. One such sybarite, Fyodor Pavlovich, the rapacious head of the Karamazov tribe of voluptuaries, castigates the monks at the local monastery who seek to bribe God and hope to reap blessings in the afterlife by every day eating only an unappetizing type of fish called gudgeon. "Father monks, why do you fast? Why do you expect reward in heaven for that?" he asks. "Come and see me now in the town. It is fun there. . . . Instead of lenten oil, I will give you sucking pig and kasha. We will have dinner with some brandy and liqueur to it" (14:84). Dmitry, the son who appears most fully to have inherited the sensual lust—or "Karamazovism"—that is his father's legacy, orders a lengthy grocery list of culinary delights as he prepares to set off to meet Grushenka at Mokroe on the night of his father's murder (14:360). Not unlike Gogol's Pyotr Petrovich Petukh, who delivers a veritable "ode to an epicure" in part 2 of *Dead Souls* as he instructs his chef about the preparations required for the next day's dinner meal,[18] Dmitry's appetite for pleasure seems acutely whetted, in anticipation of the orgiastic feast he has planned for that night, as he enumerates the various comestibles (most of them rich and exotic food items) to be delivered to Mokroe:

> Stay, listen; tell them to put in cheese, Strasbourg pâté, smoked fish, ham, caviar, and everything, everything they've got, up to a hundred

rubles, or a hundred and twenty as before. . . . But wait: don't let them forget dessert, sweets, pears, watermelons, two or three or four—no, one melon's enough, and chocolate, candy, toffee, fondants; in fact, everything I took to Mokroe before, three hundred rubles' worth with the champagne . . . let it be just the same again. (14:360)[19]

In *The Idiot*, meanwhile, life itself is seen—in terms at once gastronomic as well as metaphysical—as a joyful and festive "banquet" (*pir*) to which Ippolit, with his fatal illness of consumption (8:343), and Myshkin, with his chronic epilepsy (8:351), both feel uninvited to attend.

Whereas Gogol, Goncharov, and Kvitka-Osnovyanenko, as we saw in the previous chapter, are at times inclined to portray gluttonous over-indulgence in eating and drinking in a satiric light (as a way to condemn a character's banal philistinism and to imply his intellectual and spiritual bankruptcy), Dostoevsky's motivations for such negative gastronomic valorizations seem to derive less from the literary poetics of "Enlightenment realism" and more from the ascetic traditions of Eastern Christianity and particularly the Russian Orthodox religious belief that man's physical nature interferes with his attainment of spiritual salvation.[20] Whether on religious and spiritual grounds or even for moral and philosophical reasons, sensual indulgence of a gastronomic nature tends to be categorically condemned in Dostoevsky's fictional world; the belly—as the emblem for man's lowly animal inclinations—is invariably counterposed to the soul, which represents instead man's lofty spiritual aspirations and his transcendent quest for the sublime. The legend of the Grand Inquisitor, as we noted above, quite memorably contrasts man's hunger for earthly bread (physical sustenance) with his desire for heavenly bread (spiritual nourishment) (14:231),[21] while Father Zosima in his series of exhortations warns against the "cruel pleasures" to be found in the tyranny of material things generally and in particular from the sin of gluttony (14:288). It is interesting that the spiritual metamorphosis of Grushenka we witness during the course of the novel, whereby she is transformed from a sinful voluptuary of the flesh to a true soul "sister" to two of the Karamazov brothers (Dmitry and Alyosha), is depicted in imagery that is primarily corporeal and culinary. Initially she is described to the reader as having "a full figure, with soft, as it were, noiseless movements, softened to a peculiar over-sweetness, like her voice" (14:136). Following her encounter with Alyosha, however, (when, out of compassion, she gives him an "onion") and after the events at Mokroe on the night of Mitya's arrest (when she declares her genuinely spiritual love for him), Grushenka is now said to look considerably thinner and firmer than before, without any traces of her former sweetness, softness, or voluptuousness (15:5). The strong implication here is that Grushenka, who has at last been awakened to the benign and charitable impulses of her Christian soul, has ceased to live exclusively for her "belly" (and/or her loins): that is, for the carnal pleasures of the flesh.

This opposition between the belly and the soul in Dostoevsky's fiction is often made for moral or philosophical reasons as well. In *The Devils*, for instance, Stepan Trofimovich, the liberal Westernizer who himself suffers from chronic attacks of gastric catarrh, thunders forth against the utilitarian aesthetics of the young radicals, who, "in the name of equality, envy and—and digestion" (*pishchevarenie*), would reject the ideal beauty embodied in Raphael's Madonna (10:266). Mankind, according to Stepan, "can get on without bread, but without beauty it cannot carry on, for there will be nothing more to do in the world!" (10:373). Expressing the apparently mistaken belief that there was "something higher than food" in his personal relationship with Varvara Petrovna (10:266), Stepan castigates his longtime female friend and close companion for having sold out her values so cheaply and so readily to the younger generation of Nihilists, whose aesthetic and ethical views she now parrots quite unconscionably. "For what a mess of pottage have you sold them your freedom!" exclaims Stepan in disgust (10:263), echoing the author's opinion that there are more exalted aims in human life than merely satisfying physical hunger (material need). The dichotomy between physical and spiritual ingestion—between feeding the belly and feeding the soul—is likewise maintained in the narrator's depiction of the ill-starred fete in the opening chapters of part 3 of *The Devils*, where local philistines (who are referred to in the text, appropriately enough, as "our incontinent public") seem much more interested in the gastronomic pleasure they will derive from the refreshments to be served at the free luncheon than in the aesthetic pleasure of observing the "literary quadrilles" that will be presented on stage (10:356–57).[22] "The attainment of objects which are of universal human interest is of incomparably greater importance than any transient bodily enjoyments," Mrs. Von Lembke reminds her colleagues during the preparations for the fete (10:356). The rabble that shows up at this event, fully expecting to be treated to a "Belshazzar's feast," gets upset, however, and begins acting rowdily, once it is learned that the "literary quadrille" has been substituted for these bodily delights and thus there will be no free buffet. When the "great writer" Karmazinov, near the end of his reading of *Merci*, makes the mistake of noting ironically that "laurels are in this age more appropriate in the hands of a skillful cook than in mine," one member of the audience (who obviously shares the utilitarian ethos of the young radicals) responds, "Yes, a cook is more useful." "I'd give an extra three rubles for a cook this instant," volunteers another voice in the audience (10:370).

It is worth remembering in this regard that Dostoevsky was prone to castigate the advocates of those social and political ideologies imported from the West that he particularly abhorred (such as nihilism, socialism, and liberalism) by imputing to them a concern with merely filling the human "belly." As Joseph Frank reminds us, Dostoevsky strongly believed that "there are more exalted aims in human life than satisfying hunger, and he too wished that mankind, when faced with the alternative, would choose suffering over satiation."[23] Dostoevsky, according to Frank, insisted that "mankind would always display an irresistible inclination to choose suffering in preference to the satisfaction of material need."[24] He was greatly aggrieved, therefore, to observe around him how the Socialists, in their efforts to attract recruits to their cause, pandered to the material needs and corporeal desires of the Russian people. In his essay, "Mr. Shchedrin, or a Schism Among the Nihilists" (1864), he bitterly parodies the Socialist belief, promulgated by radical democrats such as Pisarev and Zaytsev, that man's physiological needs are more important that any moral truths or scientific discoveries. In Dostoevsky's parody, the editors of a Nihilist journal are shown briefing a new coeditor about the leading tenets of their philosophy. "You need to be penetrated by the most essential idea of our movement," they tell him, "namely, that for the happiness of all mankind, just as for the happiness of each individual separately, first and most important of all ought to be the belly—in other words, the stomach" (20:109). They explain further,

You need to understand that the belly is everything, that all other things, almost without exception, are merely a luxury, and a worthless luxury at that! What good are politics, nationality, senseless foundations, the arts, and even science, if the belly is not filled? Stuff the belly, and all the rest will be found by itself. . . . The belly, the belly, and only the belly—that, my dear sir, is our great conviction! (20:110–11)

In another (unfinished) essay, "Socialism and Christianity," Dostoevsky complains that "the Socialists go no farther than the belly" and that "Socialism posits the goal of a full belly as the whole future basis and standard of the social anthill" (20:192). Christ, on the other hand, teaches that "there is something much higher, more sublime, than the belly-as-god" (*bog-chrevo*) (20:193). Like St. Augustine, Dostoevsky thus directly opposes Christ, who symbolizes our spiritual appetite, to the belly, which symbolizes our bodily appetite.[25]

### Carnal Love in Dostoevsky: Male Aggression, Violence, and Cruelty

Another way Dostoevsky supports the dichotomy between the corporeal and the spiritual is to link food imagery with sexuality, which in Eastern Orthodox religious terms constitutes, besides food, the other major sinful temptation of the flesh. Indeed, the Russian term for "sensualists" (*sladostrastniki*), which is applied directly to the Karamazov clan in the title to book 3 of his final novel, is itself a lexical compound that combines etymologically both the culinary (*slado* or "sweet") and the sexual (*strastie* or "passion"). In Russian, "sensuality" thus means, in a literal sense, a passion or strong libidinal desire for what is sweet and pleasurable. It is only fitting, therefore, that when Fyodor Pavlovich assures Alyosha, the most spiritual and religious of his sons, that he has no intention whatsoever of reforming his debauched way of life, this aged voluptuary should proclaim that for him "sin is sweet" (14: 157). In the testing of Alyosha's religious faith by Rakitin, who offers his troubled friend sausage and vodka as well as Grushenka's body, the sinful temptation that visits upon him in the wake of Zosima's death seeks to stimulate, during a Lenten period of obligatory abstinence (from food and drink) and continence (from sexual activity), both of man's basic physical appetites. A similar conflation of these two desires of the flesh occurs at the orgiastic feast at Mokroe, where Maksimov is shown to be interested in both the local peasant girls and the chocolate sweets that Dmitry has brought to please them (14:393). Katerina Ivanovna, it should be noted, likewise has recourse to chocolates earlier in the novel as a way to entice Grushenka into renouncing her romantic claims upon Dmitry (14:316). Indeed, the latter's sexual appetite for Grushenka is indicated for us by the way his mouth is said to "water" at the very thought of her (14:75). In a similar vein, during the crowd scene following the final arguments at Mitya's trial a male spectator is heard to observe that one of the women present is a "tasty little morsel" (*pikantnen'kaia*) (15:152). Food and sex are linked in Dostoevsky's fiction not only in these lexical and thematic ways, but also in a structural sense through the pattern whereby a group of men gathers to dine, to drink, and then to go off whoring together. We witness this pattern both in part 2 of *Notes from Underground*, where the farewell dinner arranged for Zverkov at the Hôtel de Paris is immediately followed by a trip to the brothel where Olympia and Liza work (5:148), and in *The Brothers Karamazov* in the account of the gang rape of Stinking Lizaveta by a band of five or six drunken revelers (Fyodor Karamazov among them), all of whom are primed for an escapade of sexual violence after an evening of dining and drinking at the local club (14:91).

Both of these episodes of feasting followed by whoring and/or raping ought to remind us once again that in Dostoevsky's fictional world the desire for sex—like the appetite for food—acts according to the paradigm of power rather than pleasure. Sexual union for many of his male characters usually means the violence of rape and masculinist conquest over the female victim rather than the mutual gratification of the body's senses.[26] "Dostoevsky's view of sexual relationships is distorted by intensity and operates along an axis of violence and pain," observes one commentator. "In Dostoevsky's world the object of one's desire tends to become a victim, to be tortured without mercy. The torturer derives his pleasure from the victim's suffering."[27]

A Pechorinesque "vampirism" of this kind is evident, for instance, in the reprehensible sexual behavior exhibited by Dostoevsky's Underground Man at the brothel: his loveless act of sex with Liza is revealed to be nothing other than a violent and cruel outburst of passion whose sinister aim is to wreak vengeance upon her for the pain and humiliation he had himself suffered earlier that evening. "I had been humiliated, so I too wanted to humiliate someone," he explains to her, "they wiped the floor with me, so I too wanted to show my power. . . . I wanted power. Power was what I wanted then" (5:173). The narrator, who admits that he cannot imagine living without the feeling that he has someone completely in his power ("that I am free to tyrannize over some human being" [5:175]), proceeds to spell out a perverted ethos of "love" that echoes Pechorin's cynical view of human relationships, whereby the sufferings of others are seen as food to sustain one's powers. It also anticipates the sexual philosophy of power, domination, and humiliation to which many other Dostoevskian male characters from the 1860s and 1870s will subscribe: "to me love meant to tyrannize and to be morally superior. . . . I cannot help thinking even now that love only consists in the right to tyrannize over the woman you love, who grants you this right of her own free will. Even in my most secret dreams I could not imagine love except as a struggle, and always embarked on it with hatred and ended it with moral subjugation" (5:176).

Equally cynical, mean-spirited, and carnivoristic is the view on love propounded in *The Gambler* (1866) by Aleksey Petrovich, whose love-hate relationship with Polina is patterned in large measure upon Dostoevsky's own turbulent affair with Apollinaria Suslova. "But enjoyment is always useful, and a savage, unbounded power—even if only over a fly—is also a pleasure in its own way," confesses the young male hero. "Man is a despot by nature, and he loves to be a tormentor" (5:231). The narrator openly admits that he is tempted to kill the woman he claims to love so passionately. "I shall kill you not because I shall cease to love you or be jealous," he explains to Polina. "I shall kill you simply because I have an impulse to devour [s"est'] you" (5:231).

Some commentators have linked the cynical views on love and sexuality shared by many of Dostoevsky's fictional characters with the personality of the author himself. According to A. Kashina-Evreynova, a Freudian critic from the 1920s, all of Dostoevsky's sexually perverse characters—from Netochka Nezvanova to Fyodor Pavlovich Karamazov—are spiritual progeny of the same artistic father, whose own disturbing "psychic baggage" is expressed through their thoughts, desires, and actions.[28] One of Dostoevsky's contemporaries, his close friend and colleague, Nikolay Strakhov, considered the writer's psychic baggage to be not only extremely heavy, but also disturbingly evil, pathological, and perverse. According to Strakhov, Dostoevsky was an "evil," "nasty," and "debauched" man who "was drawn to debaucheries and boasted about them."[29] As an example, Strakhov, in a letter written to

Tolstoy shortly after he had completed writing Dostoevsky's biography, mentions the unsubstantiated claim, circulated by P. A. Viskovatov, that Dostoevsky had once bragged about raping a young girl in a bath-house. Strakhov goes on to say that all of Dostoevsky's novels, which to his mind constitute exercises in self-justification, only serve to prove that, together with nobility of spirit, all sorts of vile moral abominations can coexist within the soul of one and the same person. The Dostoevskian characters who most closely resemble their creator, Strakhov asserts, are such supreme moral degenerates and sexual abusers as the Underground Man, Svidrigaylov, and Stavrogin.[30] It seems highly unlikely, however, that Dostoevsky ever was, in fact, guilty of committing "Stavrogin's sin" (the rape of a child), and Strakhov's damning profile of the author hardly appears to be either fair or accurate.[31] Nonetheless, there are still those who persist in identifying Dostoevsky himself with the sexual perversities of some of his male characters. One of Dostoevsky's recent biographers, for instance, notes that the author's conception of love is "inseparable from suffering and pain. It was difficult for him to love without also suffering. For him, love was hurting and being hurt."[32] T. Yenko's post-Soviet study of Dostoevsky's "intimate sex life," meanwhile, traces the author's relationships with the various women in his life, including the tempestuous Apollinaria Suslova, whose seductive figure—she is draped in a diaphanous gown while reclining on a couch, holding a rose in one hand and having Dostoevsky kiss her upraised foot—adorns the book's lurid cover. Yenko characterizes Dostoevsky as someone who by temperament was "a person of large passions, deep sensuality, and insatiable sexual appetite," someone for whom "to love meant to torture oneself, to cause another to suffer, to painfully wound the creature one loves."[33]

What is of primary importance for our purposes, however, is not Dostoevsky's psychic profile or his personal sex life, but rather how the author represented sexual desire as a brutalizing passion in his works of fiction. "Cruelty, a desire to torment others, is a leitmotif of Dostoevsky's oeuvre," observes one commentator, "the disclosure of the evil and the impulse to torment that lurk in the souls of his characters is the secret behind the powerful impression one gets from reading his works."[34] Another commentator writes, "Pain and suffering, as an inseparable part of love, the desire to torment another physically, in connection with the sex act, and the desire to torment another mentally, in connection with the entire sensual sphere of intimacy between a man and a woman, this is Dostoevsky's eroticism in his mature years."[35]

An episode in Dostoevsky's writings that illustrates quite graphically the cruelty and the impulse to torment others that so often characterize the relations between the sexes in his fictional world occurs in his *Diary of a Writer* for 1873. In the third chapter, "Environment," Dostoevsky relates an account that had appeared in the newspapers not long before about a peasant woman who was cursed, beaten, and maimed over many years by her abusive husband, whose physical and psychological torments eventually drove her to hang herself. Witnesses testified that the husband was a person with a "cruel character" (21:20) who would catch a domestic chicken and hang it upside down by its legs simply for his own pleasure. Like the impecunious and mean-spirited caretakers mentioned earlier in this chapter, this surly peasant would starve his poor wife for days at a time, refusing to allow her to eat any food (literally, any "bread"). Then he would suddenly place some bread on the shelf, call her over, and tell her not to dare to touch the bread. "This is *my* bread!" he would warn her (21:21). Dostoevsky proceeds to describe how a peasant husband such as this one goes about whipping his wife with a branch or a strap; he would do so, we are told,

> methodically, cold-bloodedly, drowsily even, with measured blows, not listening to her cries and entreaties; to be precise, he actually does listen to them, he listens to them with pleasure, otherwise what enjoyment would there be for him in whipping her? . . . the blows rain down upon her with greater and greater frequency, more sharply, more innumerably; he begins to get flushed, to develop a taste for it. He has already turned completely into a wild beast [*ozverel*] and is himself pleased to know this. The animal cries of his suffering wife intoxicate him like wine. (21:21)

The following day the sadistic peasant reiterates to his chastised wife: "Don't you dare eat this bread: this is *my* bread!" (21:21). In the days leading up to her suicide, Dostoevsky adds, the peasant started to enjoy hanging his wife upside down by her feet, just as he would do with the chicken: "He would hang her, no doubt, but would himself move away a little and sit down to start eating his porridge. He would finish his meal and then suddenly pick up the strap again and begin to lash his wife as she was hanging there" (21:21).

This brutal scene from Russian peasant life reveals more than the sadistic cruelty of which Dostoevsky believed human beings are capable and the extreme possessiveness that selfish egoism can engender. It also reflects the violent aggression that often characterizes the relations between the sexes in the author's oeuvre, especially the masculinist psychology that seems to endorse male aggression and violence toward women. "Dostoevsky's eroticism is constructed upon the fact that for the characters in his works sensuality—in their imagination, feelings, and dreams—is inseparable from the desire to torment others," explains one critic. "What appears in the forefront for all of his characters, as the fundamental motif of their sexuality, is either a thirst for power over the other sex or a thirst to become a sexual victim."[36] For many of Dostoevsky's male heroes, accordingly, "love opens out upon a dark abyss of cruelty, hatred, pride, and the urge to dominate."[37] In Dostoevsky's novelistic universe, love-egoism of this sort, as Konstantin Mochulsky once observed, can quite easily—even quite naturally—drive a man to murder his beloved (such as the passionate and rapacious Rogozhin does to Nastasya Filippovna in *The Idiot*). Passion here generally "borders on madness": it is "irrational, demonic, and destructive"; it is "the yearning for power over another."[38] Sexual passion, as a voluptuous and nearly obsessive love of power, permeates romantic relationships throughout Dostoevsky's works, from the tyrannical love Murin possesses for Katerina in "The Landlady" to the despotic dominion over his inexperienced young bride the pawnbroker-husband seeks so diligently to establish in "A Gentle Creature."[39] In alimentary terms, male sexual appetite in Dostoevsky's fictional world is predominantly an egoistic desire that drives men to seek ultimately to "devour" their female victim by tyrannically possessing, dominating, and controlling her will.[40] The true essence of Dostoevsky's power-hungry male characters is, as one commentator puts it, their "insatiable carnivorousness" (*plotoiadnost'*).[41]

### After the Fall: From Commensalism to Carnivorousness

If, as we asserted in the opening chapter of this book, the main difference between the treatment of food and sex in Tolstoy and Dostoevsky can be understood as an opposition between the semiotic codes of pleasure (*goûter*) and power (*manger*), then the oral preoccupations we find in the texts of Gogol, Goncharov, and Kvitka-Osnovyanenko present a contrast to Dostoevsky's gastropoetics that calls for a somewhat different interpretive scheme. Maggie Kilgour provides us with a conceptual model that helps us to understand the nature of the paradigm shift, in terms of food and sex, that occurs as we move from the idyllic spirit of eating (as an act of sharing and communion) that characterizes the three pre-reform works of gastronomic Slavophilism we examined in the preceding chapter to the modern bourgeois spirit of eating (as an act of violence and power) that informs the novels of a postreform writer such as Dostoevsky. In her study, *From Communion to Cannibalism: An Anatomy of Metaphors of Incorporation* (1990), Kilgour posits a whole spectrum of tropes for the process of ingestion, ranging from "communion," which indicates a relationship that encompasses unity, identity, and harmony, to the opposite extreme of "cannibalism," an act that represents, in her words, "the most demonic image for the impulse to incorporate external reality."[42] If we adopt for the moment Kilgour's terminology, we might say that the male protagonists we encounter in the works by Gogol, Goncharov, and Kvitka-Osnovyanenko reveal a similar nostalgia for "total unity and oneness," for "a state of total incorporation" that suggests Freud's oral stage seen as a golden age in the infantile past—a presexual idyll that is at once national as well as personal, ideological as well as psychological.[43] Observing the modernizing changes that were already beginning to take place in their homeland and anticipating the institutional reforms that threatened to sound the death knell for Russia's old-fashioned feudal ways, these three authors—through their male fictional characters—looked back longingly and lovingly at their own old-world childhoods and at childhood Russia, both of which at midcentury seemed destined for imminent extinction.

When we move from the prereform fictions of Gogol, Goncharov, and Kvitka-Osnovyanenko to the postreform works of Dostoevsky, however, we encounter a writer whose artistic gaze is fixed critically and harshly upon the present rather than nostalgically and dreamily upon the past. In historical and national terms, we leave the pastoral idyll of childhood in feudal Russia to experience all the poverty, misery, and alienation associated with adult life in a Russian society that has become much more modern, urban, and European. In gastronomical and psychological terms, we leave the oral stage of psychosexual development for the genital stage and find ourselves at the opposite end of Kilgour's spectrum. In Dostoevsky's literary representation of the decidedly "fallen" world of post-emancipation Russia, the act of eating loses the benign features that had been assigned to it by Gogol, Goncharov, and Kvitka-Osnovyanenko through their pastoral vision of social harmony, peace, and abundance in an earlier, more innocent time. Instead of pre-Oedipal children, such as the orally regressive Afanasy Ivanovich, Oblomov and Pan Khalyavsky, who seek as adult males to nurse at their mother's breast once again, we encounter angry adolescent sons, such as the rebellious Raskolnikov, who murders two women (and entertains Napoleonic fantasies about masculinist supremacy that involve destroying "symbolic maternity"),[44] and the murderous Karamazov brothers, who seek Oedipally to consume their tyrannical father and usurp his power. Oral regression, in short, has given way to sexual and alimentary aggression.

Eating in Dostoevsky's novels serves as a barometer for the fundamental changes in social and economic relations that were taking place in Russia during his lifetime, reflecting all the cruelty, brutality, and horror involved in the ruthless struggle for survival occurring within an increasingly capitalistic, mercantile, and consumeristic society. Dostoevsky, accordingly, provides his readers with a vision of human relationships that bears close affinities to the worldview of Dickens in England, Balzac in France, and other so-called romantic realists in mid-nineteenth-century Europe who likewise sought to depict the angst of modern bourgeois life within an urban, industrial society.[45] Historically considered, this cynical vision of human relations, Mervyn Nicholson observes, follows immediately upon "the triumph of market forces in Western Europe, the supplanting of earlier social relations by the cash nexus."[46] Human relations have here become mercenary, rather than empathetic; predatory, rather than symbiotic.[47] Exchanges between the self and the other within this modern "consuming" society, a postlapsarian world ruled by the merciless law of the jungle, tend more and more to be reduced to the rather cynical alimentary dictum: "eat or be eaten."[48] In their efforts to capture accurately and to condemn categorically this new bourgeois ethos, writers such as Balzac, Dickens, and Dostoevsky portray those human beings who epitomize the dehumanized values of market culture during the modern age as predominantly cruel and aggressive creatures who hunger insatiably to acquire power and, metaphorically, to consume one another. "Not only is eating itself of huge importance in the Dickens world," John Bayley points out about the British novelist, "but in a broad sense all his characters are engaged in eating each other, or being eaten."[49] Gail Turly Houston, in her study of "consumption" in Dickens's fiction, demonstrates quite convincingly how his novels reveal what she calls "the cannibalistic nature of capitalist economy," exposing "an economic and social system that devoured some of its members."[50]

In the nineteenth-century model of social reality as a fiercely competitive struggle that was posited by social thinkers such as Hobbes, Malthus, and Darwin, human exchanges have become primarily struggles between rivals—be those struggles psychological, social, sexual, generational, or economic in nature. Dostoevsky, who often reveals in his correspondence his own deep-seated fear that he will be "eaten alive"—whether by his creditors (29.1:213, 227), by the peasant convicts in the Omsk prison camp (28.2:169), or by the leading literary critics in Russia (30.1:121)—creates fictional characters whose human relationships are frequently portrayed as rapacious and predatory. The petty tyrant Foma Opiskin, in *The Village of Stepanchikovo*, for instance, is feared precisely because he implicitly threatens to "eat alive" those who might be foolish enough to seek to challenge the position of dominance and control he has come to enjoy over the household at Colonel Rostanev's estate. "Or am I a crocodile that would rather devour you than give you worthy counsel?" this Russian Tartuffe asks rhetorically and disingenuously. "Or am I some kind of vile insect that would sting you rather than be conducive to your happiness?" (3:148). Foma's essentially predatory nature is conspicuously obvious to the denizens of Stepanchikovo, however. "We sat down to eat dinner," reports his neighbor, Mr. Bakhcheev, "and I tell you he nearly ate me alive at that dinner! Right from the start I could see that he was sitting there fuming, such that his entire soul was squeaking. He would have been glad to drown me in a spoonful of water, the viper!" (3:28). Colonel Rostanev's daughter Sasha likewise comments upon the voracious and carnivorous nature of Foma's appetite: "he gobbles up everything put before him and keeps coming back for more. Just you wait, he'll eat us all up. . . . Horrible, horrible Foma Fomich!" (3:57–58). Even Colonel Rostanev himself, the impotent estate owner who has unwittingly allowed

Opiskin's tyranny to prevail, bemoans the fact that he has been "eaten alive and whole" by that despot (3:102). For his part, Foma insidiously projects onto others his own carnivoristic appetite for power, accusing even such a mild sheep as Colonel Rostanev of being a "crocodile" and a "sea monster in human form" who "wants to devour me, to gobble me up alive in one gulp!" (3:74).

## *Human Bestiality:* Notes from the House of the Dead

Considered not in the socioeconomic and historical context of the rise of capitalism in modern Europe and Russia, however, but rather in the biographical context of his own life and career as a writer, Dostoevsky's rather cynical view of human relations in the contemporary world may be said to have taken definite shape during the 1850s as a direct result of his years spent in prison in Omsk and then in exile in Siberia. As Joseph Frank observes, "the juxtaposition of refined aestheticism and lustful depravity emerges in Dostoevsky's works sharply only after his return from Siberia in the 1860s."[51] In terms of the development of his philosophical views (especially his political and social ideology), the Siberian prison experience is widely considered to have "cured" Dostoevsky irrevocably of his youthful infatuation with the liberal European ideas of Saint-Simon, Fourier, and other utopian socialists, ideas that had circulated freely among the idealistic members of the Petrashevsky circle. In prison, having come face-to-face at last with the "real" Russian people (*narod*) and having witnessed firsthand their deep-seated hostility toward both the gentry and the intelligentsia, Dostoevsky, so this conversion narrative runs, abandoned his earlier, misguided Russian Westernism, rediscovered Russian Orthodox Christianity, and enthusiastically embraced a neo-Slavophile ideology of "native soil enthusiasm" (*pochvennichestvo*) that would leave its indelible imprint upon his work and thought for the remainder of his life.[52] Edward Wasiolek reminds us, however, that Dostoevsky's Siberian penal experience not only introduced him to the good, positive qualities of a somewhat idealized Russian *narod*; it also exposed him to all the human cruelty, amorality, and bestiality of the hardened criminals with whom he came into daily contact. "Almost without exception," Wasiolek writes concerning these fellow prisoners, "Dostoevsky saw them as pitiless, cruel, and emptied of any suggestion of moral feeling."[53] This intimate contact with ruthless murderers and hardened criminals, Wasiolek argues, had a profound effect upon Dostoevsky's thinking and his art:

> All the evidence of *The House of the Dead* suggests that Dostoevsky's abstract and simplified conception of human nature gives way to an astonished insight into the complexity of man and his tragically evil nature. *The House of the Dead* profoundly changed Dostoevsky, but not from atheism to faith in the golden heart of the masses, as many critics have led us to believe. Rather, he is brought to the terrifying perception of the moral abyss of human nature. . . . once having seen man in the "house of the dead," he knew that evil was part of man's nature.[54]

Wasiolek's sweeping claim about the sobering effect the Siberian prison camp experience had upon Dostoevsky's view of human nature may seem a bit exaggerated; the narrator of *Notes from the House of the Dead* does, after all, speak of having encountered people in Siberia whose Christian goodness and kindness were boundless.[55] Nonetheless, Wasiolek's reading does draw our attention to the indisputable fact that bestial images of human behavior begin to make their appearance in Dostoevsky's writings immediately upon the author's return from Siberian exile.

Indeed, Dostoevsky's fictionalized account of his penal servitude is the first of his writings that contains in considerable quantity the kind of language and imagery that emphasizes how people can derive a cruel and sadistic pleasure from satisfying base animalistic desires. In *Notes from the House of the Dead*, we read about how some of the prisoners possess "bestial inclinations" (4:14), a "bestial insensitivity" (4:16), and a "bestial character" (4:189). We also read about how a man in prison can grow morally depraved, lose his basic humanity, and "turn into a beast" (4:16). The narrator speaks, for instance, about the monstrous Gazin, who, when drunk, would reveal "all the bestiality of his nature" (4:41), a man who would slowly and voluptuously slit the throats of young children solely for the pleasure, deriving great enjoyment from the terror and anguish felt by his wretched little victims (4:40–41). The prisoner Korenyov, meanwhile, is characterized as a totally "wild beast" (4:47) whose spiritual torpor is so great that there is nothing left inside him except "a ferocious appetite for bodily pleasure, sensuality, and carnal satisfaction" (4:47). No doubt the most loathsome and disgusting example of moral degradation in a human being, however, is provided by Aristov, an inveterate sensualist who has become addicted to the coarsest, vilest pleasures. Dostoevsky, appropriately enough, describes this convict's spiritual degradation and moral corruption in predominantly anatomical and animalistic terms:

> Aristov was simply a lump of meat, with teeth and a stomach, and with an insatiable appetite for the grossest and most bestial [*samykh zverskikh*] physical pleasures, for the satisfaction of the least and most capricious of which he was capable of the most cold-blooded violence, murder, or, in short, anything at all, provided he could hide his traces. I am not exaggerating anything; I knew Aristov well. He was an example of the lengths to which the purely physical side of a man could go, unrestrained by any internal standard or discipline. . . . He was a monster, a moral Quasimodo. (4:63)

Inside the stockade at the Omsk prison, Dostoevsky thus came to meet a large number of cruel and violent murderers—the real-life prototypes for Gazin, Korenyov, Aristov, and the other fictionalized inmates later portrayed in *Notes from the House of the Dead*—whose lack of remorse over committing even the most atrocious crimes certainly did much to shape the author's view of human desire in the modern world as being rapacious and bestial.

The worst excesses of cruelty and brutality, however, that Dostoevsky witnessed at the Omsk prison were not exhibited solely—or even primarily—by his fellow convicts. Even more "bestial" than the behavior of these fearless convicted murderers, some of whom had killed simply for pleasure, was the perverse tyranny displayed by the camp "executioners," such as Lieutenant Zherebyatnikov, whose pleasure in administering floggings and birch-rod beatings to the prisoners amounted to a sick passion. This mean-spirited lieutenant, the narrator tells us (with a highly revealing metaphor), was something of a "highly refined gastronome" (4:148) when it came to matters of inflicting corporal punishment. "He loved, passionately loved, the art of the executioner, loved it purely as an art," the narrator writes. "He relished it highly and, like some jaded patrician of Imperial Rome, sated with pleasures, invented various refinements and unnatural variations in order to provide some small stimulation and pleasurable titillation for his soul, already lapped in layers of fat" (4:148). Indeed, the narrator openly

compares the cruel feeling of pleasure enjoyed by Siberian executioners such as Lieutenant Zherebyatnikov to the perversities of the marquis de Sade and Madame de Brinvilliers, speculating that there must
have been "something in those sensations, at once sweet and painful,
that made these gentlemen's hearts swoon with pleasure" (4:154).[56] In
his attempt to explain the perverse psychology of these bestial sadists,
the narrator directly links their intoxicating will-to-power with the
behavior of wild predatory animals:

> There are people who, like tigers, thirst for blood. Any man who has
> once tasted this power, this unlimited dominion over the body,
> blood, and spirit of a human creature like himself . . . this boundless
> opportunity to humiliate with the deepest degradation another being
> made in the image of God, loses control over his own sensations.
> Tyranny is a habit; it has the capacity to develop and it does develop,
> in the end, into a disease. I maintain that the best of men may be-
> come coarsened and degraded, by force of habit, to the level of a
> beast. Blood and power are intoxicating; insensitivity and perversity
> develop and grow; the greatest perversions become acceptable and
> finally sweet to the mind and heart. (4:154)

As we clearly see, Dostoevsky's narrator is here describing the psychology (or, more accurately, the psychopathology) rather than the sociology of this bestial and intoxicating lust for power. But the cultural and
ideological implications of the executioner's sadistic behavior are unmistakable when the narrator notes that "both the man and the citizen
perish eternally in the tyrant" (4:154). The narrator then proceeds
to discuss how society looks upon this despotic lust for power among
both professional and "gentlemen" executioners, observing that "every
manufacturer and entrepreneur must inevitably find some stimulating
pleasure in the fact that his workmen and their families are sometimes
wholly and solely dependent upon him" (4:155). Dostoevsky seems to
have had the socioeconomic environment of modern capitalism specifically in mind when he writes that "the executioner's nature is found
in embryonic form in almost every contemporary man, but the bestial
traits of a human being do not develop equally in all men" (4:155).

In the major novels about life in post-emancipation Russia that were
to follow *Notes from the House of the Dead* during the 1860s and 1870s,
Dostoevsky reveals quite graphically the extent to which human nature

was being perverted by the new secular ethos of dog-eat-dog capitalism that was rapidly replacing the traditional Christian ethos of compassion, brotherly love, and self-sacrifice. In gastronomic terms, Dostoevsky's post-Siberian fiction shows us how commensalism (the fraternal sharing of bread) has now given way to carnivorousness (the rapacious devouring of flesh) and how the pyramidal "food chain" from zoology has permeated an increasingly secularized Russian society and the national psyche. In this regard, Dostoevsky's use of eating imagery anticipates in many ways the gastropoetics of Joris-Karl Huysmans, in whose works eating is made to serve as "an outlet for cruel, sadistic impulses whose expression reduces a human being to a primitive and savage level. Eating here is an act of neurotic frenzy rather than the normal pursuit of pleasure."[57] In Dostoevsky's novels, we watch, accordingly, as the rich proceed to devour the poor, the strong to devour the weak, and the proud to devour the meek. The pawnbroker Alyona in *Crime and Punishment*, for example, is considered to be, by the very nature of her profession, a human louse who "grows fat" by "sucking" the lifeblood out of the urban poor in St. Petersburg (6:54). According to Razumikhin, members of the new entrepreneurial class in Russia—greedy businessmen such as Luzhin, for instance—listen to the sensitive and honest person as he pours out his heart and take it all in, the better to "swallow up" the honest fellow (6:98). The monks in *The Brothers Karamazov* likewise are accused of constituting an entire class of socioeconomic parasites. "The Russian peasant, the laborer," Fyodor Karamazov asserts at the monastery, "brings here the half-kopeck earned by his calloused hand, wringing it from his family and the tax collector! Holy fathers, you are sucking the blood of the common people, you know" (14:83). Father Zosima, for his part, bemoans the fact that an entirely new class of "blood-sucking" kulaks (he refers to them as *miroedy*: literally, "eaters" of the peasant commune) has been devouring the livelihood of the Russian common people ever since the emancipation of the serfs (14:285).[58]

In many cases, psychological exploitation and/or socioeconomic parasitism merge with gender domination in Dostoevsky's fiction; thus we encounter numerous instances where rich and powerful males take advantage of poor, meek, defenseless females. Indeed, Dostoevsky's fictional world, as contemporary feminist critics point out, is filled with men—such as Prince Valkovsky, Svidrigaylov, Stavrogin, Fyodor

Karamazov—who ruthlessly exploit the privileges granted them by their male gender and/or their socioeconomic class by committing acts of sexual violence against women.[59] As one might well expect, Dostoevsky often expresses the dynamics of this sexual domination, violence, and brutality through the language of eating. In part 1 of *Crime and Punishment*, for example, in the scene where Raskolnikov witnesses a "fat" dandy trying to proposition a young woman who is sitting drunk on a park bench, Dostoevsky's hero changes his mind about intervening on the poor girl's behalf and we hear him exclaim instead, "Let one devour the other alive" (6:42).[60] Even the emotional tyranny that underlies personal relationships is often communicated in Dostoevsky's novels through masticatory and alimentary terms. The hard-drinking, garrulous, and decidedly impecunious General Ivolgin in *The Idiot*, for instance, is accused of "sucking dry" (8:111) his widowed friend Mrs. Terentiev, not only financially but also emotionally, much as Mrs. Ivolgin's fear that her son's dying (yet still very talkative) friend Ippolit will "devour her alive" (8:488) is to be understood mainly in a psychological and emotional sense.[61] In *The Devils*, meanwhile, where several of the women who cross Stavrogin's path end up sexually violated and/or murdered, such "devouring" is, in one feminist critic's opinion, "never ungendered."[62] If post-emancipation Russia was seen by many to be a world where man was a wolf to man (*homo homini lupus est*), man was especially a wolf to woman, upon whom he seemed to feed for purposes of his own sexual gratification and sense of psychological domination.

## Darwinism, Native Soil Enthusiasm, and the Discourse of Predation

The carnivoristic nature of human appetite in general and of the egoistic will-to-power in particular that Dostoevsky represents in his fictional works during the 1860s and 1870s coincides with the critical reaction within Russian intellectual circles to the appearance of Darwin's theory of evolution. Thanks in large part to the deep strain of religious fundamentalism that underlies mainstream American culture, as well as to the memorable courtroom performances delivered by William Jennings Bryan and Clarence Darrow at the celebrated Scopes "monkey trial," we tend in our country to identify Charles Darwin mainly with the "descent" of man: that is, with an evolutionary theory based on natural science rather than biblical creationism. In Russia, on the other hand, Darwin's name is more likely to be associated with the notion of the "struggle for existence," a phrase that is used as the title of chapter 3 in his groundbreaking work, *On the Origin of Species* (1859), which appeared in Russia in a French translation in 1862 and in a Russian translation in 1864.[63] Although Darwin as a scientist was generally accorded a sympathetic welcome in mid-nineteenth-century Russia, especially by the radical socialists (who regarded science as the keystone to their materialistic philosophy of rational egoism), many intellectuals there did take issue with what they saw as the pernicious social implications of Darwin's evolutionary theory. They were particularly upset when such notions as the "struggle for existence" and the "survival of the fittest" were transferred from the realm of the animal or vegetable kingdom and applied to human society.

These two concepts were, of course, closely associated with Darwin's theory of natural selection, but they did not in fact originate with him. Herbert Spencer had used the phrase "survival of the fittest" as early as 1852, while Thomas Malthus made the "struggle for existence" a central idea in the *Essay on the Principle of Population* he published in 1798. The ideology that was supposedly based on Darwin's theory and that would later come to be known as "Social Darwinism" turns out, upon closer inspection, to be what we might more accurately call "Social Spencerianism" or "Social Malthusianism." Darwin himself, of course, made no secret of the fact that his famous metaphor, the "struggle for existence," is merely the social doctrine of Malthus applied to the animal and vegetable kingdoms. As a result, Russian intellectuals generally revered Darwin as a scientist, but they were almost equally unanimous in their condemnation of Darwinism as a detestable ideological movement that they associated primarily with the pessimistic social theories of Malthus and Spencer.[64]

As in the United States, the public reaction in Russia to Darwin's theory of evolution was grounded more in social, political, and even religious ideology than in natural science. Indeed, the controversy in Russia over Darwinism, one critic notes, "acquired the character not of a scientific, but of a philosophical dispute."[65] But whereas American society, with its ethos of rugged individualism and its tradition of laissez-faire economics, merely saw its own image faithfully reflected in the "tooth-and-claw version" of Darwin's theory of natural selection, the sensibilities of many educated Russians of the nineteenth century were highly offended by the application of Darwin's Spencerian and Malthusian metaphors to their social order. The drive to obtain food that Darwin posited as underlying the struggle for existence among animals in the natural world seemed a not entirely appropriate analogue for human behavior within a civilized society, even a society such as the one in post-emancipation Russia, which found itself increasingly affected by the free economic competition that characterized the incipient era of capitalist development.

Most Russian thinkers, therefore, objected strongly to the contention made by Darwinists that the laws of nature are not fundamentally different from the laws of society—that biology, in other words, can join hands with political economy and social theory to help explain the human condition. For them, such metaphors as the "struggle for existence" and the "survival of the fittest" tarnished the self-image of a collectivist and spiritual Russia. As a number of reception studies amply demonstrate, intellectuals from across the political spectrum in nineteenth-century Russia condemned as morally repugnant and ontologically inaccurate Malthus's belief that intense struggle among individuals for a limited supply of food and shelter is the inevitable result of our basic human situation. Such a soulless, divisive, and atomistic ideology, Russian social thinkers argued, merely reflected the British enthusiasm for competition and the European respect for individualism, materialism, and bourgeois egoism. Indeed, the standard argument for discrediting Malthusianism in Russia, invoked by radical socialists and conservative Slavophiles alike, seems to have consisted in identifying the "struggle for existence" with social conditions that were peculiar to bourgeois Europe (and particularly to industrialized Britain) during the capitalist era, when free and ruthless competition dominated economic life there. As Daniel Todes has observed, the Russians' sense of communitarianism, their cooperative social ethos, and their vision of a cohesive society emblematized by the traditional peasant commune (*mir*) were seriously threatened by Darwin's Malthusianism, which in their eyes exalted individual conflict, competition, and disharmony at the expense of cooperation, brotherhood, and mutual aid.[66] As an alternative to Malthus's bourgeois proposition about the selfish mainsprings of human behavior, Russian intellectuals advanced a view of human nature that better reflected what they

considered to be the Slavic spirit of instinctive communalism, cooperation, and solidarity. This native opposition to Social Darwinism in
Russia culminated in the "theory of mutual aid" propogated by Pyotr
Kropotkin, the anarchist turned amateur naturalist, who asserted that
among individuals of the same species cooperation rather than competition is the primary impulse and dominant behavioral pattern.[67]

Although the debate in nineteenth-century Russia over Darwin's
notion of the "struggle for existence" involved many contemporary
writers, journalists, and thinkers, few were affected more profoundly
than Dostoevsky. For one thing, two of his closest ideological allies, the
patriotic native soil enthusiasts (*pochvenniki*) Nikolay Strakhov and
Nikolay Danilevsky, wrote strongly anti-Darwinian tracts on this theme.
Strakhov published an article entitled "Bad Signs" ("Durnye priznaki")
in the November 1862 issue of Dostoevsky's journal *Time*, in which he
lashed out at the views promulgated earlier that same year by Clémens
Royer in her preface to the French translation of Darwin's *Origin of Species*. Royer, who was one of the first people on the Continent to formu-
late the ideas of Social Darwinism, had rather clumsily and mechani-
cally applied Darwin's concept of the "struggle for existence" to the
area of social life, constructing in the process a highly conservative and
reactionary sociological theory that sought, among other things, to
defend racial superiority and social inequality as natural conditions
within human society. Strakhov begins by praising Darwin's book as
having carried out "a great revolution in the study of organisms" and of
constituting "a mighty step forward in the evolution of natural science"; he then proceeds, however, to take strong exception to Royer's
prefatory remarks: he considers them symptomatic of the current decline in European thought, which now champions philosophical materialism rather than idealism.[68] Darwin's French translator, he notes,
errs by invoking the authority of scientific discourse to justify (out of
self-interest) the "right of might" in social, political, and economic
matters and by questioning the importance that has been placed upon
Christian compassion, charity, self-sacrifice, and brotherhood in human
affairs.[69] Challenging Royer's claim that Darwinian theory is especially
rich in terms of its humanistic and moral implications, Strakhov concludes that one thing is evident about the applicability of Darwin's scientific findings to human beings: "We cease to understand human life,
we lose its meaning, as soon as we fail to separate man from nature, as

soon as we place him on a level with nature's works and begin to make judgments about him from the very same perspective that we do about animals and plants."[70]

Danilevsky, meanwhile, attacked the notion of the "struggle for existence" in the sixth chapter of his controversial book, *Russia and Europe* (1869), where he dismisses the social theory of Darwin—along with the political theory of Hobbes and the economic theory of Adam Smith—as a manifestation of the dominant trait in the English national character: namely, their innate love of personal independence and individual competition.[71] Years later, in a two-volume work titled *Darwinism* (1885–87), Danilevsky elaborates at greater length upon his basic contention that Darwin's "struggle for existence" is merely a product of the highly individualistic mentality of Europeans in general and of Britons in particular.[72]

Besides Strakhov and Danilevsky, another *pochvennik* implicitly encouraged Dostoevsky to address the challenge of Social Darwinism in Russia, especially in light of the novelist's abiding concern about the carnivorous nature of the human appetite for power. Apollon Grigoriev, who, like Strakhov, was a regular contributor to the ill-fated journals *The Epoch* and *Time* published by the Dostoevsky brothers during the early 1860s, wrote an article about Pushkin (it appeared in *The Russian Word* in 1859) that attributed the poet's artistic greatness—and his essential Russianness—to his uncanny ability to represent so memorably the constant struggle waged within nineteenth-century Russian literature and culture against foreign literary ideals and historical types.[73] Indeed, Grigoriev credited Pushkin with being the first writer to have created—in the character Ivan Petrovich Belkin—a genuinely Russian "humble" or "peaceable" (*smirnyi*) type to counter the "predatory" (*khishchnyi*) Western type, characterized by passion and strength, made famous by the heroes of Byron and other European romantics.[74] Strakhov revives these two terms—*smirnyi* and *khishchnyi*—in an article on Tolstoy's *War and Peace* that appeared in *The Dawn* in 1868. According to Strakhov, Grigoriev demonstrated that

> to the alien types, who predominated in our literature, belong almost everything that bears upon itself the mark of the *heroic*—types that may be either brilliant or gloomy, but that are in any event powerful, passionate, or, as our critic expressed it, *predatory*. The Rus-

sian nature, meanwhile, our sincere, cordial type, made its appearance in art mainly in the *simple* and *humble* types, apparently devoid of anything heroic, types such as Pushkin's Ivan Petrovich Belkin, Lermontov's Maksim Maksimych, and others.[75]

In Strakhov's view, Tolstoy's patriotic epic, *War and Peace*, with its memorable portrayal of such quintessentially national characters as Platon Karataev and General Kutuzov (as well as such unsung heroes as Timokhin and Tushin), presents us with the very apotheosis of the "humble" Russian type. The "predatory" types, meanwhile, who are made to represent "evil" and "depravity," include not just the French military and civilian leaders (especially Napoleon) but also those Europeanized Russian aristocrats—such as the Kuragins—who mimic their Gallic ways.[76] The significance of Tolstoy's national epic, for Strakhov, lies mainly in the way it depicts the victory of the "humble" Russian type over the "predatory" French type: "A voice on behalf of the simple and the good against the false and the predatory—this is the essential, principal meaning of *War and Peace*. This is the original and distinctive element of our literature that Apollon Grigoriev discovered in it and traced with great perspicacity."[77] Like Darwinism itself, the "predatory" Western type was considered by Grigoriev and Strakhov alike to be a foreign cultural import of European origin, alien to the Russian national character and to native Russian values.[78]

Not unlike his fellow "native soil enthusiasts," Dostoevsky fervently championed the Russian idea, believing that the tendency in the West to seek scientific and materialistic solutions to fundamental problems of human life posed a grave threat to the moral and spiritual values that traditionally had nurtured the Russian soul.[79] In his *Diary of a Writer* (and in his notebooks for it), Dostoevsky on a number of occasions refers quite openly and negatively to Darwinism, the "struggle for existence," and the instinct for self-preservation.[80] In some of his letters, meanwhile, Dostoevsky repeatedly links the Darwinian notion of the "struggle for existence" with the Socialists' belief that the socioeconomic "environment" is to blame for human vices and that a revamping of the political system and class structure in Russia—"turning stones into bread"—would rectify its most pressing social problems. "Present-day *socialism* in Europe, and with us in Russia too," he writes to Vasily Alekseev on June 7, 1876, "eliminates Christ everywhere and worries above all else about *bread*, calls on science, and asserts that there is but a single reason for all human problems—poverty, the struggle for existence, and 'people prey to the environment'" (29.2:85). Unlike "the current theories of Darwin and others about man's descent from the ape," Dostoevsky adds, Christ's message insists that "in addition to the animal world there is a spiritual world as well" (29.2:85). In a letter to Pavel Polotsky, written just three days later, in which he discusses the recent Pisaryova suicide, Dostoevsky complains that young people in Russia today are being assured that there is no spiritual life and no generosity, that "there is only the struggle for existence" (29.2: 86). If you tell a person "that there is no generosity, that there is only the elemental struggle for existence (egoism)," Dostoevsky explains to his correspondent, "you effectively deprive that person of both personality and freedom (29.2:87).[81]

Dostoevsky repeatedly takes issue with the teachings of both Darwin and Malthus in his novels as well. In *Crime and Punishment*, for instance, Darwin's theories are implicit in Raskolnikov's ambition to prove to himself that he is an "extraordinary" man who belongs to a superior race of Napoleons.[82] "Darwin's theory of evolution replaces the biblical view of creation and disproves the existence of God in the immature mind," writes B. E. Lewis of *Crime and Punishment*. "In the absence of moral sanctions provided by religion, life becomes a mere battle for survival and man an animal who must trample on others, even kill, or be exploited and destroyed himself by others."[83] In *The Idiot*, meanwhile, Ganya Ivolgin insists that "the instinct for self-preservation is the normal law of humanity" (8:311), while Radomsky observes that it is but a short step from the "right of might" to the "right of tigers and crocodiles" (8:245). As this last remark illustrates, Dostoevsky not only resorted to Darwinian slogans and naturalistic metaphors in the prose fiction he wrote during the 1860s and 1870s; he also came increasingly to use predatory animal imagery as a way to characterize—with marked disapproval—the carnivorous relations between human beings in this new world of capitalism and consumption.

Nor was Dostoevsky alone in this regard. The debate over Darwinism in post-emancipation Russia prompted many other Russian writers and journalists at the time, in their discussion of changing social relations, to make mention of the open warfare that is perpetually being waged between predators and their prey in the animal kingdom.

As a result, it was not uncommon in Russia during the 1860s and 1870s to encounter naturalistic metaphors about people behaving like "wolves" and "sheep" (or "pikes" and "carps") as well as animal idioms such as "*homo homini lupus est.*" Indeed, the public discourse (both journalistic and artistic) during this period of sudden and rapid capitalist development on Russian soil fairly resonates with predatory imagery and idiomatic language of this sort.[84] Aleksandr Ostrovsky, for instance, explicitly foregrounds predatory metaphors in his play, *Wolves and Sheep* (1875), where the dynamics of human relations are shown to be dominated almost exclusively by socioeconomic coercion and sexual duress. In the opening act of Ostrovsky's rather bleak comedy about marriages arranged through economic blackmail and extortion, the landowner Lynyaev observes that it is not human beings who live all around them, but rather wolves and sheep. "The wolves devour the sheep," Lynyaev notes, "and the sheep peacefully let themselves be devoured."[85]

Likewise, Aleksey Pisemsky's drama, *The Predators* (1873), makes it clear that the new wave of capitalist entrepreneurs, corrupt bureaucrats, and ambitious social climbers living in Russia during the 1860s and 1870s constitute little more than predatory beasts possessed of an almost insatiable appetite for material comfort, economic power, and worldly success.[86] Meanwhile, in Nikolay Leskov's anti-nihilist novel, *At Daggers Drawn* (1870–71), the opportunistic swindler Gordanov (who at one point in the narrative is characterized as "a wolf in sheep's clothing") openly admits that he is merely seeking to put into practice in his own life Darwin's famous theory about the struggle for existence, which to his mind is accurately encapsulated in the predatory adage: "Swallow up the others or they will swallow you up."[87] Even in Tolstoy's *Anna Karenina* (1877) we find that one of the dark thoughts that enters the troubled mind of the heroine just prior to her suicide is Yashvin's cynical view that "the struggle for existence and mutual enmity are the only things that bind people together" (19:342).

## Dostoevsky's Cruel Talent: Human Predators and Their Prey

Because Dostoevsky was acutely attuned to what Gary Cox has called the "dominance hierarchies" that operated in his society, he saw clearly in the life around him a world dominated by the ruthless struggle for survival.[88] It is not surprising, therefore, to find that in his writings he too makes extensive use of imagery derived from the animal kingdom, frequently portraying the dynamics of human relationships in terms of animal predation. Indeed, Dostoevsky once noted sardonically that in Russia Darwin's theory about the fierce nature of the "struggle for existence" had gone beyond ingenious hypothesis; it had long ago become an axiom (23:8).[89] As we know from some of his letters and notebook entries, Dostoevsky firmly believed that in a godless secular world that believes in Darwin and science rather than in Christ and religion, there can be neither love nor compassion. "There is only egoism," he writes, "that is, the struggle for existence" (24:164).[90]

As a verbal artist, Dostoevsky adds a compelling psychological and religious dimension to this public discourse in Russia during the 1860s and 1870s, a dimension that centered upon the socioeconomic nature of predation. In his famous essay where he attacks Dostoevsky's so-called cruel talent, the populist critic Nikolay Mikhaylovsky observes that "as in the economy of nature there exist wolves and sheep, so in the economy of mutual human relations there exist and must exist the tormentors and the tormented."[91] Mikhaylovsky acknowledges Dosto-evky's keen insight into human psychology, asserting that "no one in Russian literature has analyzed the sensations of a wolf devouring a sheep with such thoroughness, such depth, one might say with such love, as Dostoevsky."[92] This Russian writer's artistic specialty, Mikhay-lovsky notes, is precisely his ability to dig "into the very heart of the wolf's soul, seeking there subtle, complex things—not the simple satisfaction of appetite, but precisely the sensuality of spite and cruelty."[93] Indeed, Dostoevsky's works, he writes, provide readers with "a complete nursery of wolves of different breeds."[94]

As a humanist and a populist, Mikhaylovsky was deeply offended, of course, by the unflattering portrait of human beings painted by Dostoevsky, and especially by what he took to be the gratuitous "cruelty" of his literary talent: he considered him a sadistic writer who actually enjoyed the exaltation of suffering, pain, and humiliation.[95] Years later, Maksim Gorky, another fervent humanist and democrat, would likewise express anger that Dostoevsky portrayed "the bestial, animal element in man" not in order to refute it, but to justify it.[96] Mikhaylovsky and Gorky are not the only commentators who have complained about Dostoevsky's purportedly "cruel talent." As we have seen, several critics of a psychoanalytical bent have accused Dostoevsky of being a sadist. According to these critics, not only did Dostoevsky in his fiction represent cruelty and a desire to inflict torment upon others as an essential truth about human nature; he himself, they claim, derived a perverse pleasure as a verbal artist from depicting sadistic behavior. This is perhaps what Turgenev had in mind when he referred to Dostoevsky as "our" (Russian) marquis de Sade.[97] For our purposes, what is significant about Mikhaylovsky's and Gorky's negative evaluation of Dostoevsky as a "cruel talent" is that both of them couch their assessment of his poetics in alimentary terms and through imagery that is at once bestial and predatory: namely, of wolves "devouring" sheep. Robert Louis Jackson, however, characterizes the motivation behind Dostoevsky's keen interest in human bestiality much more accurately when he writes, "Dostoevsky finds in the human propensity for violence and cruelty only a partial truth—a truth that is counteracted by fundamental moral and spiritual strivings of man."[98] As we shall see later in this chapter, the larger and more important truth for Dostoevsky is that human predatoriness and carnivorousness—both manifestations of a godless egoism—must be transcended by returning to Christ and his law of active love and self-sacrifice.

Dostoevsky's notebooks for *A Raw Youth* bear witness to this novelist's abiding concern with what he repeatedly refers to as the "predatory" (*khishchnyi*) type of person, by which he seems to mean strong, charismatic, but deeply troubled personalities, people in whom tempestuous passion and an attraction to cruelty and evil combine with tremendous strength of will to produce a demonic and debauched moral monster (16:6–7).[99] Dostoevsky's fascination with such "predatory" human types is evident in a number of his other novels as well.[100] In *The Devils*, for instance, the strong-willed, wealthy, and tyrannical Countess Stavrogina is described as pouncing upon Shatov's sister Darya "like a hawk" (10:58); later she seizes by the hand the Bible-selling Sophie Ulitkina (another of Stepan Trofimovich's female friends) much "as a kite seizes a chick" (10:501). "Well, here she is, I haven't eaten her up," Varvara Petrovna reassures Stepan afterward. "You thought I had eaten her, didn't you?" (10:501). Likewise, Marya Lebyadkina, who when speaking of her husband Stavrogin insists that it is impossible for her "falcon" to have become an "owl" (10:218), notes that her mother-in-law "would have been glad to devour me" (10:217). Even before his actual appearance in the novel, of course, the enigmatic "Prince Harry" has himself been characterized as a "wild beast," who, in suddenly biting the governor's ears, finally showed his true "claws" (10:37). Pyotr Verkhovensky, meanwhile, is portrayed as a scavenger whose carnivorousness is made especially prominent by the inclination he reveals to sink his teeth into beefsteaks, cutlets, or chicken at times when less ruthless people would have absolutely no stomach for such distinctively "carnal" culinary fare (for example, just prior to Shatov's murder and Kirillov's suicide). Stepan's son, moreover, the "cunning serpent" Pyotr, is presented to us throughout the novel as a parasitic "louse" who lives quite comfortably off the generous hospitality of those unwitting gulls, the Governor and Mrs. Von Lembke. In *The Brothers Karamazov*, meanwhile, the voluptuous Grushenka is characterized by some of the town's inhabitants as being a "tigress" (14:141), a fearsome predator who claims that she will "devour" (14:101) and "swallow up" (14:318) the docile Alyosha by taking away his monkish virginity and sexual innocence. Lise Khokhlakova, another rapacious female type who has sexual designs upon Alyosha, cannot understand how it is that she has scared off the youngest of the Karamazov brothers, wondering aloud at one point, "Surely I will not eat him up?" (14:55).

Much has already been written about the "insectology" at work in Dostoevsky's fiction and about how he—in order to foreground the bestial nature of human beings—consistently links his characters with lower forms of animal life, and especially with those from the insect and arachnid realms: spiders, ants, flies, cockroaches, lice, and so on.[101] Readers of Dostoevsky's *Crime and Punishment*, for example, are long apt to remember Svidrigaylov's memorable vision of hell as a bathhouse filled with spiders in the corners (6:221) as well as the tiny red spider that haunts Stavrogin and invalidates his dream of a golden age, reminding him of his despicable abuse of the young girl Matryosha (11:22).[102] The convict Gazin in *Notes from the House of the Dead* is visualized by the narrator as "a huge, gigantic spider, the size of a man" (4:40), while the major in charge of the prisoners at the camp is said to resemble "a vicious spider, hurrying to pounce on the poor fly that had fallen into his web" (4:214). Prince Valkovsky in *The Insulted and Injured*, when he offers the narrator money to marry Natasha, the penniless woman in love with his son, reminds Ivan Petrovich of "some huge spider, which I felt an intense desire to crush" (3:358).[103] Ralph Matlaw correctly notes how Dostoevsky associates the image of the spider with evil: in particular, with the morally dissolute behavior on the part of two of his more demonic characters, Svidrigaylov and Stavrogin, both of whom are rumored to have committed such heinous acts as the sexual violation of children. "The spider," Matlaw writes, "is inevitably connected with evil, not only in a sensual but also in a broader, ethical and moral sense."[104] What has perhaps not been emphasized sufficiently about Dostoevsky's use of insect and arachnid imagery, however, is the highly predatory nature of many of the crawly creatures he mentions, especially spiders and tarantulas, that trap and then devour the other (invariably weaker) insects that have been caught in their sticky web. Such predatory imagery reinforces the dynamics of power relationships between and among human beings in Dostoevsky's fictional universe, which, according to Gary Cox, can be seen as polarized between "tyrants" and "victims," or "masters" and "slaves."[105]

In *The Devils*, for example, the political conspirators who make up Pyotr Verkhovensky's local group of five are correct to feel trapped—in a legal as well as a moral and psychological sense—"like flies caught in the web of a huge spider" (10:421).[106] In *Crime and Punishment*, when Raskolnikov speculates as to what he might have done with the pawnbroker's money after murdering her, the alternatives he poses are either to have become a generous benefactor to mankind or to have spent the rest of his life "like a spider catching everybody in my web and sucking the lifeblood out of them" (6:322). Predatoriness of a socioeconomic nature is likewise the target of the mad speaker's harangue at the fete in *The Devils*. He accuses Western-style modern capitalism of preying upon his homeland; the new railways, he asserts, have "eaten up" all of his country's economic resources and they now cover Russia "like a spider's web" (10:375).[107] In *The Idiot*, Ippolit feels that, in a broader metaphysical sense, we as human beings are all trapped in the clutches of a dark and evil nature, which he envisions as a powerful but deaf-and-dumb and implacably rapacious beast, an enormous "tarantula" that devours Christ—"a great and priceless Being" (8:339)—and thus destroys all that is good in life. Ippolit protests plaintively, "Can't I simply be devoured without being expected to praise what has devoured me?" (8:343).

Quite frequently, however, images of predatory arachnids (as with birds of prey) are used in Dostoevsky's novels to characterize the dynamics of personal relations between individual human beings, especially their sexual relationships. In *A Raw Youth*, Arkady Dolgoruky, who describes his passion for Katerina Nikolaevna as an "animalistic" and "carnivorous" feeling (13:333), admits that there is the soul of a "spider" lurking deep inside him (13:306), an apt characterization in view of the decidedly predatory nature of his attraction:

> "I don't know," I wondered, "whether the spider hates the fly which it has targeted and caught? Poor, dear little fly! I think people love their victims; at least I think it's possible to love them. You see, I am in love with my enemy—for instance, I'm terribly pleased, my dear lady, that you're so haughty and grand, because if you'd been less grand it wouldn't have been anything like the pleasure." (13:35)

Similarly, Dmitry Karamazov, that self-proclaimed "noxious bug" who admits that he loves vice and cruelty, and who senses that his own heart has been "bitten" by a phalange spider (14:105), plans to take advantage of the fact that he has Katerina Ivanovna completely at his mercy when she comes to him for the money she needs to cover her father's alleged embezzlement of government funds. Stung by a cruel and "venomous" thought whose voluptuous appeal he can hardly resist ("My first thought was a Karamazov one," he confesses [14:105]), Dmitry feels strongly tempted to exploit the young lady's position of acute economic and sexual vulnerability, to act toward her, in his words, "like a bug, like a venomous tarantula, without a spark of pity" (14:105). In Dostoevsky's portrayal of sexual relationships, however, it can quite often be the female partner who functions as the predatory spider and the male who serves as her unwitting prey. When discussing Pushkin's *Egyptian Nights* in his "Response to *The Russian Herald*," Dostoevsky characterizes Cleopatra as a black widow spider "who devours her male after mating" (19:136). In his famous Pushkin Speech, meanwhile, he notes how the author of *Egyptian Nights* portrays the ancient gods as desperately seeking diversion "in fantastic bestialities, in the voluptuousness of creeping things, of a female spider devouring its male" (19:146).[108] Although in *The Brothers Karamazov* the voluptuous Grushenka is never explicitly characterized as a black widow spider (she is referred to by other characters in the story variously as a "creature," a "monster," a "hyena," and a "tigress"), she does fit the part of the algolagnic female when she promises that she will "eat up" the docile Alyosha (14:101). The same is true of Lise Khokhlakova, another predatory female who has sexual designs upon Alyosha. It should be noted that poor Alyosha, who is forced to contend with carnivorous males and predatory females alike, is himself identified with defenseless creatures from the animal realm—sacrificial victims who are likely to be "eaten"—such as a dove (15:85) and a chick (14:317).

## From Zoological Carnivorism to Human Cannibalism

In addition to spiders, tarantulas, and birds of prey, reptiles constitute another species of predator Dostoevsky invokes to convey to readers the highly rapacious nature of some of his fictional characters. *The Crocodile*, written in 1865 as a satirical and allegorical lampoon against Chernyshevsky and contemporary Russian Nihilism (as well as against the process of European-style industrialization then taking place), tells the story of how a certain gentleman, Ivan Matveich, is swallowed alive by an enormous reptile. "What is the fundamental characteristic of a crocodile?" the narrator asks philosophically. "The answer is clear: to swallow up people. . . . it can ceaselessly swallow and fill itself up with everything that comes to hand. And that is the sole logical reason why all crocodiles swallow up our brethren" (5:196). Etymologically, he points out, "the name *crocodillo* apparently comes from the verb *croquer*, meaning 'to devour,' 'to eat up,' 'to use as food'" (5:196). Although Ivan Matveich is pleased to find that he and the crocodile are actually managing to nourish each other in a reciprocal fashion ("as I nourish the crocodile with myself, I, in turn, receive sustenance from it," [5:197]), he resists with all his might being digested by the reptile; as he puts it, "I do not want to be turned into what all food is turned into" (5:198).[109] In *The Insulted and Injured*, the power-hungry and debauched Prince Valkovsky produces upon the narrator the impression of "some kind of reptile" (3:358) when he attempts to manipulate him into marrying Natasha. Pyotr Verkhovensky, in *The Devils*, foresees the day when man will be transformed into "a loathsome, cruel, egoistic reptile" (10:325). The notebooks for *A Raw Youth*, meanwhile, reveal the thoughts of a female character who looks upon her male lover "like a crocodile wanting to swallow its prey alive" (106:112). Raskolnikov, we recall, had exclaimed, "Let one reptile devour the other alive," when he observed a sexual predator taking advantage of a drunken girl in *Crime and Punishment* (6:42). And at the scandal scene with which the opening part of *The Devils* comes to a climactic conclusion, Captain Lebyadkin suddenly stops dead in his tracks at the threshold to the drawing room, directly in front of Countess Stavrogina's son, "like a rabbit in front of a boa constrictor" (10:155).[110]

But no doubt the most memorable instance of Dostoevskian reptile imagery occurs in *The Brothers Karamazov*, where Ivan is confronted with the very real possibility that the competition being waged between his father and his older brother over Grushenka's affection may well result in the heinous crime of parricide. With regard to this volatile love triangle, Ivan remarks, more with indifference than disgust, "One reptile will devour the other" (14:129), an utterance with significant reverberations throughout the remainder of the novel. For Alyosha, these words are disconcerting mainly because they indicate that Ivan looks upon Dmitry as nothing more than a lowly animal that lacks spirit or humanity.[111] For readers of *The Brothers Karamazov*, however, Ivan's words signal more than a recognition of man's innate carnivorousness and predatory instincts. They also reveal his very real potential for committing the taboo crime of cannibalism: for devouring not simply another species of animal, but one of his own kind. Understood in the terms of insect and arachnid predation, the spider is no longer just eating flies; it is now eating other spiders as well. Dostoevsky broaches this idea of man's cannibalistic nature with just such a metaphor in his *Notes from the House of the Dead* (1860), where the narrator remarks that without work to keep them busy, prisoners at the Siberian prison camp "would eat each other up like spiders shut up in a bottle" (4:17). Likewise in *The Devils* Captain Lebyadkin depicts artistically, in his playful verse allegory *The Cockroach*, how when flies crawl into a glass in summer, they turn into "cannibal flies" (10:141).[112]

It is human cannibalism that serves, of course, as the topic of Lebedev's amusing anecdote in *The Idiot* about the sinful (and hungry) monk from the famine-plagued twelfth century who confesses at last to having survived for many years on a largely "clerical" diet: he admits to having killed and consumed by himself some sixty monks and (for the sake of "gastronomic variety") six lay infants (8:314). Human cannibalism also serves as an important component within the narrative structure of *The Brothers Karamazov*, where the competition between fathers and sons, as Michael Holquist has shown, is built directly upon the Freudian paradigm of the primal horde myth and thus replicates the psychosexual dynamics of the Oedipal complex.[113] According to this primal myth, a despotic father, who for a long time obstructs the sexual desires of his sons as well as their craving for power, is eventually killed and then promptly devoured, in an act of oral cannibalism, by his male offspring. August Strindberg provides a compelling modern statement of this Oedipal myth in his play *The Father* (1887), in which a tyrannical patriarch at one point shouts angrily at his child: "I am a cannibal, you see, and I'm going to eat you. Your mother wanted to eat me, but she didn't succeed. I am Saturn who devoured his children because it was foretold that otherwise they would devour him. To eat or to be eaten—that is the question. If I don't eat you, you will eat me—you've shown your teeth already."[114]

In Dostoevsky's novel, it is Fyodor Pavlovich, of course, who acts out the primal role of the tyrannical tribal despot, "depriving his sons of power, money, and women, better to prosecute his own lusts."[115] Although each of the Karamazov sons has sufficient grounds for hating this despotic father and for desiring his death, Dmitry's case seems best to fit the Freudian psychoanalytical scheme: the eldest Karamazov son competes most overtly with his father both for disputed property (the power of money) and for the enticing Grushenka (carnal desire). It is his brother Ivan, however, who recognizes that the struggle between a tyrannical father and his rebellious sons is an archetypal one, universal in scope and cannibalistic in nature, that all men are fated to share. "Who does not desire his father's death?" Ivan asks rhetorically at his brother's trial. "My father has been murdered and they pretend they are horrified . . . they keep up the sham with one another. Liars! They all desire the death of their fathers. One reptile devours another" (15:117). The Oedipal rivalry Freud describes in the psychoanalytic literature can thus be understood as the repression of a desire for oral cannibalism: it reenacts a mythological fall from grace and harmony in which primal sons seek to eat the original father in an attempt to incorporate his power and authority. "In literature, cannibalism is not anthropological (still less gustatory)," Mervyn Nicholson reminds us, "it is a metaphor for power."[116]

In the works of childhood nostalgia by Gogol, Goncharov, and Kvitka-Osnovyanenko, the orally fixated male characters seek to return to the pre-Oedipal mother and regain the original maternal symbiosis, either by reentering the womb or by suckling at the maternal breast. But in Dostoevsky's psychosexually adult world one seeks Oedipally to attain sexual union with the mother by cannibalizing the father, in the process either eating him or being eaten by him. This Oedipal struggle in Dostoevsky's works can be extended beyond the boundaries of the immediate family to include the socioeconomic dynamics at work in the larger society as well, where empowered groups attempt to cannibalize those who are disenfranchised. Such socioeconomic cannibalism is, after all, the point behind all the predatory imagery that we find in Ostrovsky's *Wolves and Sheep*, Pisemsky's *The Predators*, Leskov's *At Daggers Drawn*, and numerous other literary works from the 1860s and 1870s that dramatize the havoc capitalism was wreaking upon social relations in post-emancipation Russia. Dostoevsky likewise attacks the social, economic, and political ideologies that accompanied the rise of modern capitalism in his homeland, blaming them for having created the ruthlessness of modern secular life. Thus the members of the current generation of Russian nihilists, who have been nurtured on the liberal ideas of atheism, secular humanism, and utopian socialism preached by their fathers, the "European" Russians of the 1840s, are often described as cannibalistic creatures. "Madmen! Conceited creatures!" Mrs. Yepanchin screams at the members of Burdovsky's gang who have come to Prince Myshkin "seeking their rights" in *The Idiot*. "They don't believe in God, they don't believe in Christ! Why, you're so eaten up with vanity and pride that you'll end up devouring each other" (8:238). In the "Necessary Explanation" he reads at Prince Myshkin's name-day party in that same novel, Ippolit conceptualizes the modern secular world as a place that could not exist without the lives of millions of human beings being sacrificed daily: "I agree that otherwise—that is to say, without the continual devouring of one another—it would be quite impossible to organize the world" (8:344). In *The Devils*, when attempting to explicate Shigalyov's paradoxical social theory, Pyotr Verkhovensky (who maintains that "slaves must have rulers" and who advocates a system of "complete obedience, complete loss of individuality") asserts that "once in thirty years Shigalyov resorts to a shock and everyone at once starts devouring each other, up to a certain point, just as a measure against boredom" (10:323).[117]

## Dostoevskyism, Anthropophagy, and the Approaching Apocalypse

As humankind came to discover during the violent twentieth century, it turns out to be but a short step from theory to practice as far as the human capacity for cruelty and tyranny is concerned: in the Russian context, from Shigalyov's philosophical system to Stalinist political reality. Tatyana Tolstaya, who recently characterized the long years of oppressive totalitarian rule in her homeland as "cannibalistic times," compares this barbaric period of twentieth-century Russian history with the reign of Ivan the Terrible during medieval times, when someone is quoted as having said: "We Russians do not need to eat; we eat one another and this satisfies us."[118] Ivan the Terrible himself, in Karamzin's *History of the Russian People* (1816–29), one of Dostoevsky's favorite childhood readings, is shown as being presented with a piece of raw meat during Lent by the holy fool Nikolay, who tells the cruel tsar: "You feed on human flesh and blood, forgetting not only the fast, but even God!"[119]

What underlies such graphic examples of "Asiatic savagery" in Russia's cultural history, Tolstaya explains, is "the sense of sin as a secret and repulsive pleasure," or what she calls "Dostoevskyism."[120] The creator of this "Dostoevskyism" was, of course, simply providing commentary (highly prophetic commentary, if you will) upon the workings of the human mind, especially the darker recesses of the psyche, where our deep-seated urges for cruelty, brutality, and evil lie hidden. Projecting from the prevailing trends of human isolation, social fragmentation, and moral chaos he observed in the mid-nineteenth-century social reality surrounding him, Dostoevsky envisioned a gloomy apocalyptic future for mankind, a dark and somber period of the Antichrist that would be characterized by widespread carnivorousness and cannibalism. "We are approaching materialism," the author warned in an entry for March 1877 in his *Diary of a Writer*, "a blind, carnivorous (*plotoiadnaia*) craving for personal material welfare, a craving for personal accumulation of money by any means" (25:85). The main ethical tenet of the nineteenth century, Dostoevsky insisted in that same entry, proclaims the Hobbesian slogan: "Everybody for himself and only for himself, and every intercourse with man solely for one's self" (25:84). Although, as Malcolm Jones points out, cannibalism in human relations constitutes but one pole in Dostoevsky's vision of humankind, it is nonetheless a highly disconcerting vision.[121]

Dostoevsky's apocalyptic vision of a godless human society, one plagued by widespread anthropophagy, is sometimes communicated symbolically in his novels through microbe imagery. In the epilogue to *Crime and Punishment*, for instance, Raskolnikov has a frightful dream about a devastating pestilence that infects mankind and drives people to cannibalism: "There had appeared a new strain of trichinae, micro-scopic creatures parasitic in men's bodies. But these creatures were en-dowed with intelligence and will. People who were infected immediately became like men possessed and out of their minds. . . . Men killed one another in a senseless rage . . . they bit and ate one another" (6:420).[122] Joseph Frank, commenting upon the "Hobbesian world of Raskol-nikov's feverish nightmare, the war of all against all," observes that this is the world of Western society as Dostoevsky had described it in *Winter Notes on Summer Impressions* (1863): "the plague of a moral amorality based on egoism and culminating in a form of self-deification."[123] A similar plague occurs in the "Dream of a Ridiculous Man," where the narrator contaminates the happy and innocent inhabitants of the har-monious utopian land he visits "much like a filthy trichina or pestilen-tial germ infecting whole countries" (25:115). These once sinless peo-ple, who shared a universal and all-embracing love for one another, used to be free of those impulses of "cruel sensuality" that, according to the narrator, are "the sole source of almost all sin in our human race" (25:113). Indeed, the moral corruption of these people—their fall from grace—involves precisely the genesis and growth among them of carnal sensuality, which generates, in turn, jealousy, cruelty, and the struggle for human individuality: "A struggle began for separation, for isola-tion, for personality, for mine and thine" (25:116).

People are themselves becoming acutely aware of the serious conse-quences that will result from the current "chemical decomposition" of society, Dostoevsky maintained; therefore they are desperately search-ing to find any form of universal solidarity in order to avoid canni-balism. Paraphrasing Dostoevsky's view of this human desire for soli-darity, one critic writes, "Men all clamor for unity and, in default of genuine brotherhood, are all too eager to accept a counterfeit model in the shape of socialism or the Catholic Church, which can offer nothing but the brotherhood of an 'ant-hill.'"[124] In the bleak, apocalyptic de-scription of modern London's urban blight provided in his *Winter Notes on Summer Impressions*, Dostoevsky declares unequivocally that men's craving for even an artificial and synthetic unity of mankind—their yearning to bow down collectively in worship of Baal, the flesh-god of materialism denounced in the Old Testament—arises out of a desperate effort to find an alternative to human cannibalism and mutual annihilation:

> And yet there too [in London] the same stubborn, silent, and by now chronic struggle is carried on, the struggle to the death of the typically Western principle of individual isolation with the necessity to live in some sort of harmony with each other, to create some sort of community and to settle down in the same ant-hill; even turning into an ant-hill seems desirable—anything to be able to settle down without having to devour each other—the alternative is to turn into cannibals. (5:69)

One of the more celebrated of these human "anthills"—to Dostoevsky's mind—was represented by the Crystal Palace, which the Russian author viewed as the embodiment of the utopian dream to build a collective founded on humanistic and socialist principles rather than on religious tenets. "It is a Biblical sight," Dostoevsky wrote in *Winter Notes on Summer Impressions* upon seeing the Crystal Palace for the first time in 1862, "something to do with Babylon, some prophecy out of the Apocalypse being fulfilled right before your very eyes" (5:70).[125]

In *The Brothers Karamazov*, Ivan's Grand Inquisitor recognizes the hidden potential for cannibalism that lies dormant within modern man, a primordial urge that he believes must be restrained through the institution of the Roman Catholic Church. "Oh, ages are yet to come of the confusion of free thought, of their science and cannibalism [*antropofagiia*]," he predicts to a silent Christ. "For having begun to build their Tower of Babel without us, they will end, of course, with cannibalism. But then the beast will crawl to us and lick our feet and spatter them with tears of blood" (14:235). For Dostoevsky, this new "Tower of Babel" constitutes—like the Crystal Palace—yet another misguided attempt undertaken by human beings to construct a harmonious "ant-hill" as a way to satisfy their craving for a community of worship and for universal unity.

Father Zosima, on the other hand, who voices some of Dostoevsky's own most cherished ideas about the messianic role of the Russian Orthodox faith, maintains that the worrisome current tide of modern men's mutual envy and ruthless rivalry can only be stemmed by means of the model Christ has provided us: that is, the Russian Orthodox idea of salvation through a moral brotherhood of man and active Christian love. "They aim at justice," Zosima says of those secular humanists and socialist dreamers who scorn his deeply Christian views of brotherhood and love, "but, denying Christ, they will end by flooding the earth with blood, for blood cries out for blood. . . . And if it were not for Christ's covenant, they would slaughter one another down to the last two men on earth" (14:288). According to Zosima, those who deny Christ "feed upon their vindictive pride like a starving man in the desert sucking blood out of his own body" (14:293). Zosima's final exhortations thus acquire decidedly apocalyptic overtones as he warns prophetically of the cannibalism (even to the point of self-cannibalism) that is certain to visit upon human beings if the affairs of men on earth continue to be dominated by the modern spirit of "isolation" than by "communion," by worldly materialism than by spiritual love. Zosima sadly predicts that today's egoistic "voluptuaries" (*plotougodniki*), who live only in mutual envy, "soon will drink blood instead of wine" (14:285).

A similarly dire apocalyptic prediction is made elsewhere in the novel by Dostoevsky's intellectual paradoxicalist, Ivan Karamazov, who is reported to have argued that

> there is nothing in the whole world to make men love their neighbors. That there exists no law of nature that man should love mankind, and that, if there had been any love on earth hitherto, it is not owing to a natural law, but simply because men have believed in immortality . . . that the whole natural law lies in that faith, and that if you were to destroy in mankind the belief in immortality, not only love but every living force maintaining the life of the world would at once be dried up. Moreover, nothing then would be immoral, everything would be lawful, even cannibalism [*antropofagiia*]. (14:65)

When Smerdyakov at last confesses that it was indeed he who committed the murder of Fyodor Pavlovich (acting upon the belief that Ivan wished him to kill their despicable father), he reminds his brother—whom he idolizes—of those fateful words he had uttered earlier: "You yourself said, 'everything is lawful'" (15:68). However, when Ivan's devil in book 11 quotes back to him excerpts from the poem he had once written, "The Geological Cataclysm," we are presented with a much more hopeful vision of the future. Belief in God and in the immortality of the soul needs to be replaced with a benign and brave humanism, one that in many respects echoes the atheistic notion of the "man-god" that Kirillov had preached in *The Devils*.

There are new men . . . they propose to destroy everything and begin with cannibalism [*antropofagiia*]. Stupid fellows! They didn't ask my advice! I maintain that nothing need be destroyed, that we only need to destroy the idea of God in mankind, that's how we have to set to work. That's what we must begin with. Oh, blind race of men who have no understanding! As soon as men have all of them denied God—and I believe that period, analagous with geological periods, will come to pass—the old conception of the universe and, more importantly, the old morality will fall of itself, without cannibalism, and then everything will begin anew. Men will unite to take from life all it can give, but only for joy and happiness in the present world. Man will be lifted up with a spirit of divine, titanic pride and the man-god will appear. . . and he will love his brother without need of reward. (15:83)

Ivan's message thus recalls the so-called Geneva ideas of freedom, equality, and brotherhood envisioned by Versilov in *A Raw Youth* (13:173) by arguing that the latent cannibalism of humankind can be curbed and moral virtue can be successfully pursued on earth without having recourse to religious faith or belief in the immortality of the soul.[126] The goal of brotherly love, according to Ivan, can indeed be achieved without the necessity of believing in the Christ of Zosima and Alyosha; it can be reached instead through the development of purely human (what Nietzsche would later call "all too human") potential.

Dostoevsky in the novel ultimately discredits Ivan's dream whereby utopian humanism helps people successfully overcome an apocalyptic anthropophagy. For one thing, the author effectively deconstructs Ivan's "Legend of the Grand Inquisitor" through the irony of having it be the devil who—with a highly sardonic reaccentuation—recites the words of this poem back to its half-crazed author later in the novel. Moreover, Ivan's noble, lofty, and highly abstract goal of brotherly love seems quite ludicrous to readers of the novel when it is considered within the context (and against the dialogizing background) of the markedly inimical relationships he has managed to develop with his own flesh and blood, his actual Karamazov brothers Alyosha, Dmitry, and Smerdya-kov. Indeed, in Dostoevsky's notebooks for *The Brothers Karamazov*, Ivan at one point confesses to Alyosha that he is at times tempted "to plunge into the stench of voluptuousness or of ambition or of cruelty" (15:228). "There remains just one thing only," he tells his idealistic younger brother, "bestial voluptuousness, with all its consequences, sensuality taken to the point of cruelty, of transgression, of the Mar-quis de Sade" (15:228).

Through the counterexample provided by Zosima, Dostoevsky strongly implies that the wavering Ivan's dream of a future utopia is destined to fail, because it is based not upon a solid and authentic Christian foundation of love but upon a counterfeit humanist one. As Lebedev, the author's interpreter of the Apocalypse in *The Idiot*, makes clear, without Christian morality even such an ostensible "friend of humanity" as Malthus can just as quickly turn from a putative benefac-tor of mankind into a human "cannibal" (he uses the term *liudoed*, liter-ally "people eater") (8:312). Indeed, the whole point of Lebedev's strange but entertaining anecdote about the conscience-stricken cannibal monk from medieval times seems to be that only the compelling spiri-tual force of a "binding idea," instilled in people during the Christian Middle Ages, could have driven this repentant sinner to make a free confession of his terrible transgression (8:315). Dostoevsky shows quite convincingly in *The Idiot* and his other post-emancipation novels that such a powerful "binding idea" is conspicuously absent in the con-temporary age of growth capitalism in Russia, which is portrayed as a cannibalistic age of railways, banks, and commodity trading.[127] "Lebe-dev tells the tale of a real cannibal," Robin Feuer Miller rightly ob-serves, "to underline the worse horror existing in a spiritual cannibal (Malthus)."[128]

## *Transcending Human Bestiality:* Sobornost', *Polyphony, Communion*

Through his use of predatory, carnivoristic, and cannibalistic imagery, Dostoevsky suggests that in a world that has foresaken Christ and his message of love—an atheistic world that believes instead in Darwin and the laws of science—human beings will behave no differently than arachnids, birds of prey, or reptiles. Deprived of his divine image and reduced to his most primitive animal instincts, man will indeed act in accord with the Malthusian paradigm of violent struggle, conflict, and competition. What then would constitute, to Dostoevsky, the solution? What can possibly curb man's innate carnivorousness, his cruel and apparently insatiable appetite for power, control, and domination? How can man's bestial nature—the insect lust of Karamazovism—be overcome and his truly human face be restored? And what can be done to prevent, in the near future, the apocalyptic nightmare of human cannibalism and mutual annihilation?

Dostoevsky's nonfictional writings suggest that the solution consists in somehow stemming the tendency toward what he called the "chemical decomposition" (*khimicheskoe razlozhenie*) of society (20:83).[129] According to Dostoevsky the journalist, human isolation and social atomization only further aggravate the bestial tendencies within human beings. Modern efforts to reverse the trends toward increasing social fragmentation by means of an ideology that champions human solidarity—be it secular humanism, utopian socialism, or Roman Catholicism—have all been misguided, he argues in such works as *Winter Notes on Summer Impressions* and *Diary of a Writer*. In their neglect of Christ and their rejection of his ethical model they have considered only man's material needs and not his spiritual demands: they have considered mainly man's belly rather than his soul. Because it lacks a firm moral and theological basis for its actions, even the humanistic philanthropy of Malthus (emblematized in Dostoevsky's novels by the rumble of carts bringing "bread" to a starving mankind) is in his eyes inferior to true spiritual peace and harmony.

For Dostoevsky, an authentic utopia can only be the result of a Christian brotherhood—more specifically, a Russian Orthodox brotherhood based on the principle of conciliarism (*sobornost'*)—that is solidly grounded in spontaneous active love and voluntary self-sacrifice rather than in law, calculation, and self-interest (which serve as the foundation for the secular utopias of Western socialism). Love, not conquest, he argued, provided the foundation of the Russian state. Unlike socialism or Catholicism, both of which take away moral freedom, Russian Orthodoxy is a religion that liberates rather than "devours" human beings: it "comforts all, helps all, preserves all personalities, does not swallow them" (24:222). In some of the later entries of his *Diary of a Writer*, where Dostoevsky concerned himself in great part with issues of international politics (especially the so-called Eastern question), the

Russian author repeatedly prophesied the rapidly approaching collapse of Europe and the imminent establishment of an Orthodox utopia, a millennium of Christian brotherhood, just as soon as Russia recaptured the ancient capital of Constantinople from the heathen Turks.[130] Even here, in his discourse about international politics, Dostoevsky makes frequent use of predatory animal imagery, comparing the interests of the reigning European powers in controlling Constantinople, for instance, to five "wolves" surrounding "a choice piece of meat" (23:113). Orthodox Russia, he assures us, "never once during the current century was a wolf, but was always a sheep, true, a voluntary and chivalrous sheep, but a sheep nonetheless" (24:259).

In Dostoevsky's artistic texts, meanwhile, this prophetic and polemical voice from the realm of journalism—the voice that champions a politics of Russian nationalism, messianism, and Panslavism (what Mochulsky calls Dostoevsky's "Christian imperialism")—is considerably muted and modulated; it merges polyphonically within a broad matrix of other dialogized voices.[131] Dostoevsky the artist, in other words, predominates over Dostoevsky the ideologue. Or, as Bakhtin puts it, "the social and religious utopia inherent in his ideological views did not swallow up or dissolve in itself his objectively artistic vision."[132] The way to overcome both human carnivorousness and social atomization, according to Dostoevsky the novelist, is by means of the inner spiritual transformation of individual human beings through imitation of the kenotic model of Christ. As Joseph Frank observes, Dostoevsky's fictional characters are invariably faced with the choice between a Christian doctrine of love and a secular doctrine of power.[133] Or, as Harriet Murav sees it, in Dostoevsky's fiction the discourse of European science and rationalism is countered by the discourse of Russian "holy foolishness" (iurodstvo), a theological and countercultural critique that challenges as well as deconstructs the regnant scientism of his day.[134] The discovery and subsequent liberation of the "human being within man" (as opposed to the "beast" within man) are what compassionate, kenotic Dostoevskian characters—"holy fools" such as Sonya Marmeladova, Prince Myshkin, Marya Lebyadkina, Father Zosima, and Alyosha Karamazov—all seek to effect. Considered metalinguistically, in Bakhtinian terms, all these characters point toward Dostoevsky's dream of attaining a true polyphony by means of their "penetrative" words and their "hagiographic" discourse: "a firmly monologic, undivided discourse, a word without a sideward glance, without a loophole, without internal polemic."[135] They champion a polyphony not of battling and internally divided (dialogized) human voices, but rather of harmoniously reconciled and merged voices. Dostoevsky's ideal, as a religious thinker if not as a literary artist, seems to have been to transform social heteroglossia, with its wide diversity of different speech patterns and tonalities, into one harmonious and melodious chorus in which, as Bakhtin puts it, "the word passes from mouth to mouth in identical tones of praise, joy, and gladness."[136] Christian salvation would thus be achieved through a redemptive polyphony, which would come in the form of a specifically Russian chorus, where the voices of the intelligentsia and the *narod* would merge together at last to sing a joyful hymn to God and to proclaim aloud, "Hosanna!"

The way Dostoevsky believed this choral harmony could be achieved, as noted above, is for each individual to bring about his or her own inner transformation. For Dostoevsky personally, this spiritual change is said to have occurred during his Siberian prison experience, when his humanitarian faith in the essential goodness of the Russian people was shattered by the bestial cruelty and brutishness he initially witnessed there among the convicts and executioners alike. "I am not going to my grave," Dostoevsky had confidently reassured his brother Mikhail on the eve of his departure for Siberia, "you are not accompanying me to my burial—and there are not wild beasts in penal servitude, but people, people who are perhaps better than I am, perhaps worthier than I am."[137] Four years later, however, after he had indeed encountered a number of "wild beasts" (such as the convicts Gazin, Aristov, and Petrov) and sadistic tyrants (such as Major Krivtsov and Lieutenant Zherebyatnikov), Dostoevsky would write his brother about how, soon after arriving at the camp, he felt that the denizens of the Omsk stockade "would have eaten us alive, if given the chance" (28.1: 169). What eventually assuaged the author's disillusionment and restored his faith in human beings during the period of his incarceration, he reveals years later, was the memory that suddenly came to him of an incident from his own childhood, when, while walking alone in the woods near his home, he thought he heard someone shout out "Wolf!" in alarm. The frightened child was comforted by a gentle and kind old peasant, Marey, who assured the nine-year-old boy that no wolf would harm him. This famous episode with the peasant Marey is, of course, often cited as an instantiation of Dostoevsky's abiding belief in the innate moral beauty of the Russian common people. Recalling this scene in the February 1876 entry for *Diary of a Writer*, Dostoevsky expressed admiration for "what deep and enlightened human feeling, what delicate, almost womanly tenderness, could fill the heart of a coarse, bestially ignorant peasant serf not yet expecting, nor even suspecting, that he might be free" (22:49). As Joseph Frank explains,

> Dostoevsky never forgot the tenderness and loving kindness of the peasant serf toward the helpless and frightened son of the masters who held him in bondage. Many years later, the image of Marey rose up before him again in Siberia and helped him inwardly to accept his Russian fellow convicts, despite all their quarrelsomeness and brutality, because he was convinced that the feelings of a Marey were still alive in their souls and could be reawakened.[138]

For our purposes, what is especially significant about the incident with the peasant Marey is the animal imagery that informs it. Read metaphorically, Dostoevsky's conversion narrative tells us that his terrible fright at the threat of being devoured by a wild predatory beast is to be understood as a view of the human world as a cruel Darwinian jungle, where people seek to eat each other. The peasant Marey's kind and gentle words, reassuring the child that there is no wolf and that he will not be devoured, effectively defuses such fears of fairy-tale cannibalism, however, and offers a model of human relations characterized instead by maternal tenderness and gentle care as well as by selfless Christian love.[139]

The gastronomic equivalent to the empathetic, antibestial, anti-Darwinistic episode with the kindly peasant Marey is provided by those rare instances in Dostoevsky's fictional works when food imagery is endowed with positive meaning. Not surprisingly, these brief glimpses of how food can actually bring authentic joy to the lives of human beings (instead of the perverse enjoyment at another's pain and suffering signaled by Lise Khokhlakova's pineapple compote) invariably involve meek, humble Russian types rather than cruel, predatory Western types. In *The Brothers Karamazov*, we find some memorable examples of positive food imagery. First of all, there is Grushenka's fable about the onion (by means of which a guardian angel hopes to lift a wicked sinner out of a burning lake of fire in hell and into God's paradise). When the selfish woman refuses to allow other sinners in the lake to be pulled out along with her, the onion breaks and the woman falls back into the burning lake. "It's my onion, and not yours," she yells at them (14:319), echoing the sadistic peasant husband in the *Diary of a Writer* episode in 1876 who had threatened his abused spouse, "Don't you dare eat this bread: this is *my* bread!" (21:21). Although the "tigress" Grushenka has already shown that she can indeed be a wicked and predatory person (witness how she "shows her claws" at Katerina Ivanovna's home after her rival attempts to win her affection with sweet treats such as hot chocolate, raisins, and candies), in this instance she selflessly "gives an onion" to the crestfallen Alyosha by showing him true love, compassion, and understanding when she learns of the death of his beloved mentor, Father Zosima. Rather than pull off Alyosha's cassock and rapaciously "eat" him up carnally, she instead comforts him, like a loving, merciful sister.[140] Alyosha, for his part, immediately realizes the significance of Grushenka's change of heart. He, too, holds out a metaphorical "onion" to her by looking past her wild, violent reputation as a tigress to see her true soul, recognizing the spiritual treasure hidden within.

A second instance in the novel when food is represented in a favorable light occurs at Mitya's trial. During Dr. Herzenstube's testimony we learn how the kindly doctor performed a gratuitous act of kindness to young Mitya as a child, when, out of pity, he gave the poor, neglected urchin a pound of nuts. Years later, a grown-up Dmitry stops by Dr. Herzenstube's office to thank him for the charitable gesture he had performed years earlier. "You are a grateful young man," the doctor says to him, "for all your life you have remembered that pound of nuts I brought you in your childhood" (15:107). The two embrace, laugh, and weep together in an outburst of emotional agape. Along with the sweet cherry jam that Alyosha so loved as a child (his elder, Zosima, likewise enjoyed eating cherry jam with his tea) and the pancakes eaten by the schoolboys at Ilyushka's funeral, Grushenka's onion and Dr. Herzenstube's pound of nuts are foods that, in the fallen world of destructive predation, carnivorousness, and cannibalism Dostoevsky portrays in his novels, allow us to glimpse what life can be like when Christian love is practiced and human redemption is achieved. As one commentator observes, Grushenka's onion and Dr. Herzenstube's pound of nuts are "two ordinary foods which become transformed into symbols of spiritual nourishment."[141]

## The Brothers Karamazov: *From the Carnal to the Spiritual*

The central concern of Dostoevsky's final novel, one critic has observed, is "collective redemption."[142] If *The Brothers Karamazov* is indeed designed to be read as a parable about human salvation, achieved by means of the Christian transformation of the entire human community (or "family"), then this novel can be said to provide us with the author's vision of how the destructive cycle of psychological, emotional, and physical violence on earth can at last be broken and how human redemption—through Christ—can be attained. In *The Brothers Karamazov*, we see how the sinful lives of two of the Karamazov family's arch-"sensualists"—Fyodor Pavlovich and his bastard son Smerdyakov—both come to violent ends (through, respectively, acts of murder and suicide). Ivan's scientific and rational humanism, meanwhile, ultimately leads him to a philosophical as well as personal dead end, symbolized in the novel by his mental breakdown. The two remaining members of the Karamazov family, however, Alyosha and Dmitry, do seem headed toward success in transcending the human carnivorousness of the earthly "beast pen" (or "stockyard") known as Skotoprigonyovsk. How do these two brothers succeed in overcoming their bestial inclinations, while the other members of the family fail?

Harriet Murav's reading of *The Brothers Karamazov*, which argues for the central role played by "holy foolishness" in the realization of Dostoevsky's utopian vision of human salvation and Christian redemption, provides us with an explanation. Focusing on the religious theme of "katabasis" (a hero's descent into the underworld), Murav shows how both Alyosha and Dmitry are made to experience an edifying—and ultimately transformative—metaphoric tour of hell during the course of the novel. In Alyosha's case, the tour must encompass more than his descent into the verbal and philosophical hell of his brother Ivan's making (that is, the tales of cruelty toward children and the legend of the Grand Inquisitor in book 5). Alyosha's tour of the topography of human sinfulness, as we have seen, also includes his exposure to the sensual temptations provided by food (sausage), drink (vodka), and sex (Grushenka) that the Mephistophelean Rakitin offers him immediately following the death of Father Zosima, when the young novitiate is forced to descend from the heaven/haven of the monastery down into the hell of a highly secularized, sensual, and materialistic world. As a tourist in this modern inferno, Murav notes, the young hero ceaselessly moves among sites of "laceration," temptation, and despair. Alyosha's redemptive ascent out of this metaphorical hell is catalyzed largely by two "miracles" that take place in book 7, both of which involve gastronomic and sexual motifs. The first miracle involves Grushenka's aforementioned onion. Rakitin had brought Alyosha to Grushenka's fully expecting to watch her "devour" and "eat alive" this naive, virginal lamb. "I had the base idea of trying to swallow him up," she herself confesses, comparing herself to a vicious cur ready to "tear the entire world to pieces" (14:318).[143] This sexually predatory "tigress" spares Alyosha, however, by instead showing him sisterly love and Christian compassion upon hearing the disturbing news about the death of his beloved Zosima: in effect, she pulls the hero out of his hell by giving him an onion.[144] "I came here expecting to find a wicked soul," Alyosha admits, "but I found a true sister" (14:318). The second miracle occurs at Father Zosima's wake in the Cana of Galilee chapter, when Alyosha experiences a dream vision of human forgiveness, reconciliation, and harmony that occurs, significantly enough, at a wedding banquet: food, drink, and sex are blessed at this festive celebration of the sacrament of marriage by the presence of Christ and his life-affirming message of active love.

Dmitry's "katabasis," meanwhile, stems from his contentious Oedipal rivalry with his father over money and Grushenka. The wild-goose chase, described at the beginning of book 8, upon which Dmitry embarks in hopes of securing the funds needed to "purchase" Grushenka away from competing male bidders, illustrates this Karamazov brother's misguided search for renewal and resurrection within the sensualist hell-on-earth he inhabits. Fortunately for him, Dmitry's Oedipal rivalry ends not with the expected murder of his father (a crime for which he is blamed and later erroneously convicted), but with his night of revelry at Mokroe. Armed with a pistol as well as with the culinary treats purchased at Plotnikov's grocery store and resolved to end his own life that evening rather than his father's ("I must kill a 'noxious insect' for fear it should crawl out and spoil life for others," he announces ominously [14:366]), Dmitry sets off for one final bout of gastronomic and sexual indulgence with the object of his egoistic, sensual desire, the lascivious Grushenka. "What followed," the narrator informs us, "was almost an orgy, a feast to which the whole world was invited" (14:390). This particular "banquet of life" turns out, of course, to be sensual and demonic rather than spiritual and divine. "The description of the feasting at Mokroe," Murav writes, "corresponds to what Bakhtin calls the folk vision of the underworld, in which earth and the body are reaffirmed. Excessive eating and drinking, gambling, laughter, and buffoonery mark the revelry at Mokroe."[145]

Dmitry's delivery from this hell of sensual indulgence occurs not by means of his planned suicide but as a function of the preliminary police investigation, during which time this "great sinner" is stripped naked—both literally and figuratively—and forced to look critically, as though in a mirror, at his own profaned human image. Confronted with his sinful life's story, Dmitry realizes that he is indeed a loathsome beast who certainly appears capable of murdering his own father.[146] During the questioning, this rapacious "wolf" is now being hunted down by his interrogators. As Dmitry himself acknowledges, "You've got the beast by the tail" (14:427). Readers of the novel are able to surmise that this wild, sensual Karamazovian "beast," who confesses to being the "the lowliest of reptiles" (14:458), by the end of book 9, has finally been tamed and transformed: they witness the deep Christian compassion shown by Dmitry during his dream about the "babe," when he expresses a compassionate, charitable desire to feed this poor starving child and thus alleviate his suffering. "At the risk of allegorizing Dmitry," Murav writes concerning his spiritual transformation, "we can say that he ascends from the earthly feast at Mokroe to the spiritual feast of brotherly love."[147] The sexual dimension of Dmitry's spiritual transformation, meanwhile, which involves a radical change in the nature of his attraction to and desire for Grushenka, follows the same trajectory as does the gastronomic: his romantic passion for her likewise ascends from a carnivorous, bestial appetite for her flesh to a brotherly, Christian concern for her soul.[148]

In The Brothers Karamazov, Dostoevsky thus shows us that a genuine brotherhood of man will come about, in alimentary and sexual terms, only when the wolves lie down peacefully with the sheep, when human beings start to live for their souls rather than their bellies, and when people begin to find joy in the sense of commensalism that results from sharing communally in the banquet of life rather than in the false sense of superiority they derive from egoistic sensuality. A true utopia of universal harmony will be realized only when we finally overcome our carnivorous appetite for power, domination, and violence, when we decide to stop devouring each other (as well as our own selves), and when we turn at last from the individualistic struggle for self-preservation that engenders human cannibalism to a joyful communion through Christ with all other human beings. "In order to break this cycle of violence," Murav observes, paraphrasing Dostoevsky's message, "we must seek to participate in a feast of brotherly love in which we consume not literal but spiritual bread."[149] Darwin's clever theory of natural selection, with its Malthusian notion of the "struggle for existence," may well help to explain predatory human behavior in a modern secular world that is increasingly materialistic, capitalistic, and atheistic.

But Darwinism, Dostoevsky insists, can never impart the more profound spiritual truth that Christ endeavored to teach us and that the peasant Marey embodies: namely, that man can be a brother—rather than a wolf—to his fellow man. Indeed, it is only by learning to share—chorally and communally—in the spiritual banquet of life that Alyosha is beckoned to join in the Cana of Galilee chapter and in the feast of brotherly love that is enjoyed by the pre-adolescent boys attending Ilyusha's funeral at the great stone in the novel's epilogue, that humankind can ever hope to avoid an otherwise inevitable and destructive banquet: the anthropophagic feast of Thyestes.[150]

# Eating as Pleasure
## Tolstoy and Voluptuousness

3

### Tolstoy and the Body: From Hedonism to Asceticism

Whereas it seems rather oxymoronic, as we saw in the previous chapter, to speak about a "culinary" Dostoevsky, it seems entirely appropriate to link gastronomy and literature in the case of Tolstoy, whose fictional works are replete with memorable food imagery, eating metaphors, and scenes of dining. Indeed, the episode where Levin and Oblonsky go to a Moscow restaurant to share a meal in part 1 of *Anna Karenina* has become one of the most celebrated, and most closely scrutinized, scenes of dining in all of world literature.[1] Unlike the orally fixated characters created by "gastronomic Slavophiles" such as Gogol, Goncharov, and Kvitka-Osnovyanenko, however, the people who inhabit Tolstoy's fictional universe do not necessarily regress from genital to oral modes of libidinal satisfaction.[2] Their creator instead allows gastronomic appetite to accompany—and in some cases even to trigger—carnal desire within them. Whereas in the fictional world of Gogol, Goncharov, and Kvitka-Osnovyanenko one must generally choose either food or sex, in Tolstoy's world one can enjoy them both. In his works, eating serves not as a substitute for sexual gratification, but instead as its complement. And unlike Dostoevsky, for whom our physical appetite for food and sex operated according to the paradigm of power and manifested itself as violent aggression, Tolstoy depicts the acts of eating and copulating as human activities through which people seek to satisfy their desire for sensual pleasure.

As we know from his diaries, letters, essays, and literary

works, Tolstoy's attitude toward sensual pleasure was deeply ambivalent. On the one hand, he himself seems to have possessed acute sensual sensibilities and strong physical appetites for the pleasures of the flesh as well as of the palate; at the same time, however, he possessed an equally strong desire for moral and spiritual self-perfection that prompted him to attempt to regulate closely his bodily lusts. Tolstoy's conceptualization of the human body—as an unruly and dangerous "desiring" machine that must be somehow directed and controlled by instructions from the mind and/or the soul—would thus seem to fit perfectly the Cartesian paradigm of ascetic rationalism, whereby corporeal government (regulation of the body) enables the soul to become liberated from its incarceration within the body.[3] His early diaries, for instance, which show him to be what one commentator considers "abnormally sensual," are filled with entries where he admonishes himself for failing to curb his sensuality, usually when he visits prostitutes, gypsies, or serf girls at night and when he overindulges his weakness for rich, stimulating foods.[4] Throughout his life, Judith Armstrong argues, Tolstoy "wages a constant but losing battle with his shameful sexual appetites."[5] "From his youth to his old age," observes another critic, "Tolstoy was body-haunted, obsessed equally by sexual desire and the guilt of sexual satisfaction."[6] In Tolstoy's literary works, the body's strong craving for life's physical pleasures manifests itself in the author's portrayal of characters who enjoy intensely felt bodily sensations. "His earlier novels and stories," G. W. Spence observes in a study of Tolstoy's asceticism, "often express a very vivid awareness of the beauty and richness of sensuous, physical life."[7] Indeed, Dmitry Merezhkovsky recognized in this Russian writer's works such a keen intuitive awareness of—and appreciation for—the instinctive, animal life of human beings that he called Tolstoy a "seer of the flesh," in contradistinction to his most famous contemporary and polar opposite, Dostoevsky, whom Merezhkovsky regarded as a visionary of the spirit.[8] According to Merezhkovsky, Tolstoy was naturally blessed with unusually acute sensory perception, much like a dog's keen sense of smell, a gift that he called "clairvoyance of the flesh."[9] In a similar vein, Thomas Mann argues that Tolstoy's life, like that of the pagan Goethe, recalls the myth of the giant Antæus, "who was unconquerable because fresh strength streamed into him whenever he touched his mother earth."[10] Admiring what he calls Tolstoy's "animalism, his unheard-of interest in the life of the body, his genius for bringing home to us man's physical being," Mann contends that Tolstoy displays in his art "a sensuousness more powerful, more immediately fleshly in its appeal," than does the great German humanist himself.[11] Finally, John Bayley asserts that in the early part of Tolstoy's career his works emit a pagan feeling of optimism about the world, or what the critic labels as "self-sufficiency" (*samodovol'nost'*): that is, a joie de vivre that reflects an innate sense of satisfaction with self, life, and nature.[12]

After the midlife spiritual crisis he experienced in the late 1870s and early 1880s, however, Tolstoy's rich pagan appreciation of earthly delights was eclipsed by deep feelings of moral guilt over the enjoyment of bodily pleasures. He now came to condemn, quite categorically, those pleasures of the flesh he had once celebrated so memorably in his fiction, and he began to advocate instead a rigorous brand of Christian asceticism. According to Mikhaylovsky, the harsh moral code Tolstoy now formulated for himself and others "was aimed chiefly against his own unconquerable fondness for the pleasures of the flesh."[13] During this post-conversion period, Tolstoy's dualistic conception of human beings, as creatures tragically torn between body and soul, between the lure of carnal desire and the promptings of spiritual aspirations, becomes more explicit and prominent in his writings. The author of *The Kreutzer Sonata* (1889) goes so far as to condemn sexual intercourse altogether, advocating instead total celibacy, even for married couples, who, he advised, should live together in conjugal chastity, like brother and sister.[14] This tension between the animal nature and the spiritual nature of human beings, most critics would agree, is present in Tolstoy's works long before his conversion to a radical brand of Christianity in the 1880s. "Among the philosophical questions that tormented Lev Tolstoy throughout his life," Irina Gutkin asserts, "the dichotomy between flesh and spirit in human nature probably ranks second only to the meaning of death."[15] Richard Gustafson, meanwhile, maintains that, as moral and spiritual types, Tolstoy's fictional characters polarize around two extremes: men of the flesh or men of the spirit. "The man of the flesh lives for himself, his own purposes, pleasure, or profit," Gustafson writes. "Often he is represented in pursuit of sex or food."[16] Fleshly characters such as Stiva Oblonsky, he explains, "define themselves by their body, their animal urges."[17] What predominates in Tolstoy's post-conversion period is the strict moral imperative his fictional characters are now made to heed with respect to the body: they are required to subdue the desires of the flesh, to subordinate their physical urges to their spiritual aspirations, and to transcend their base animal natures in order to allow the divine element that lies buried deep within them to emerge. In his later works of fiction as well as in his moralistic essays, it becomes especially clear that Tolstoy condemns sexual passion as an inherently demeaning, degrading, and destructive instinct within human beings, a brutish animal urge that only impedes people in their quest for moral purity and spiritual self-perfection. Where Gogol, Goncharov, and Kvitka-Osnovyanenko reveal in their fiction nostalgia for food and feasting, the late Tolstoy exhibits instead what one critic has characterized as "nostalgia for purity": that is, a desire to ascend to a noncarnal state of chastity, purity, and innocence.[18]

What I explore in this chapter is how the "moral masochism" reflected in the trajectory of Tolstoy's evolving attitude toward the body and human sexuality—his movement from pagan hedonism to Christian asceticism, from vigorous self-enjoyment to rigorous self-denial—is mirrored for the most part by his treatment of gastronomic indulgence. As the pleasures of the flesh come increasingly to be seen as temptations that lure people from the straight and narrow path of moral righteousness and spiritual self-perfection, Tolstoy tends more and more to regard the gastronomic pleasures of the table with a similar feeling of revulsion and disgust—as bodily pleasures that can no longer be considered morally and spiritually palatable. The gluttonous abdomen, in short, had become as much a seductive demon for the ascetic Tolstoy to exorcise as had the lascivious loins. "With the passing years," explains A. P. Sergeeenko, "Lev Nikolaevich became all the more convinced that it was inadmissible to 'get enjoyment' out of food and that one needs to look upon food only as upon a necessary condition of life."[19] What causes gastronomic pleasure to become so distasteful and such a necessary evil for Tolstoy is, in large measure, the belief that eating can lead directly to the arousal of sexual desire. Eating meat and other rich food items, he came strongly to believe, actively stimulates carnal appetite; by removing such culinary luxuries from one's diet, therefore, a person would be able to reduce considerably the incidence and the intensity of concupiscence. As Tolstoy's disenchantment with sexual love, which he came to see as a coarse and brutish animal passion, grew more acute and as his commitment to a strict brand of asceticism intensified, his attitude toward food consumption and eating patterns likewise became less moderate. His later advocacy of such radical ideals in sexual matters as celibacy, chastity, and conjugal continence is thus mirrored by his support of such extreme dietary measures as vegetarianism, abstinence, and fasting. Not unlike Sylvester Graham, John Harvey Kellogg, and a number of other quasi-religious food reformers in nineteenth-century America, Tolstoy late in his life adopted a series of dietary practices that were designed to reduce significantly, if not to eliminate entirely, carnal desire. He thus proceeded, much like these "Christian physiologists" from the diet-conscious United States, to wage an ascetic holy war against the body, launching what was essentially a male purity campaign that operated on the assumption that diet can help shape morality and spirituality.[20]

*Animal Appetites: Sensual Pleasures of the Natural Man*

For those who subscribe to the notion that Tolstoy, at least in his earlier works, was a hedonist who understood life primarily as a "born pagan" and "seer of the flesh," Daddy Yeroshka in *The Cossacks* (1863) would no doubt qualify as the archetypal Tolstoyan character. Endowed with a robust constitution, an earthy nature, and a raw animal vitality, this elderly Cossack appears to epitomize freedom from any moral laws—Christian or otherwise—that might threaten to restrict, constrain, or condemn the gratification of sensual desire. In psychoanalytic terms, Daddy Yeroshka could be said to embody the *id*; he lives mainly according to the ethos that Freud identified as the "pleasure principle": that is, his primitive instincts seek everywhere the immediate satisfaction of an unrestrained animal desire for pleasure, comfort, and happiness. In accord with Yeroshka's hedonistic philosophy, nature ought to serve as the sole moral standard in life: because our animal appetite for food and sex is quite natural, it is therefore right and good that we satisfy that sensual hunger. "God has made everything for the joy of man. There is no sin in any of it," he tries to explain to a skeptical Olenin. "We should take the animal as our model. . . . It eats whatever God gives it!" (6:56). Under Yeroshka's permissive ethic, the moral correctness of appeasing our animal appetites extends, naturally enough, from the gastronomical to the sexual realm. "A sin? Where's the sin? A sin to look at a pretty girl? A sin to make merry with her? Or a sin to make love to her?" he asks rhetorically. "No, my dear fellow, it's not a sin, it's salvation! God made you, and God made the girl too. He made it all, old chap; so it is no sin to look at a pretty girl. That's what she was made for: to be loved and to give joy" (6:47).

It is not difficult to understand the strong attraction that such a "wild beast" (6:46) of a man, with his natural self-absorption and inherent lack of self-consciousness, poses to the more "civilized" and libidinally repressed Olenin, the young Russian officer who has fled Moscow social life in his search for a more authentic way of life in the exotic Caucasus. Indeed, Olenin clearly envies the ability of rugged Cossacks such as Daddy Yeroshka and Lukashka to act freely and instinctually like feral animals, rather than cautiously and cerebrally like domesticated human beings. In the moment of epiphany he experiences while sitting in the stag's lair, Olenin strips away the layers of his oppressive social identity and actually visualizes himself as just such a wild animal, a totally instinctual creature, rather than as the reflective and self-conscious human being he has learned to become as a product of civilization:

> And it became clear to him that he was not in the least a Russian no-
> bleman, a member of Moscow society, the friend and relation of so-
> and-so and so-and-so, but simply just such a mosquito, or such a
> pheasant or deer, as those that were now living all around him. "Just
> as they, just as Daddy Yeroshka, I shall live a while and die." (6:77)

After toying for a time with the idea of finding happiness in a Christian spirit of self-sacrifice and self-abnegation, Olenin later returns to the carpe diem "recipe" for happiness that Daddy Yeroshka swears by; the young hero resolves to follow suit by living like a simple Cossack in harmony with nature.

In living close to nature, of course, free-spirited Cossacks such as Daddy Yeroshka and Lukashka not only hunt and kill; they also liberally indulge their basic animal appetites for both food and sex. "The people live as nature lives," Olenin tries to explain to one of his Moscow acquaintances, "they die, are born, copulate, and more are born—they fight, eat and drink, rejoice and again die, without any restrictions but those immutable ones that nature imposes on sun and grass, on animal and tree. They have no other laws" (6:101–102). Olenin himself, of course, has already experienced a moral freedom of sorts in Moscow, where, we are told, "neither physical nor moral fetters of any kind existed for him: he could do as he liked, lacking nothing and bound by nothing . . . he yielded to all his impulses only in so far as they did not restrict his freedom" (6:7–8). Indeed, Olenin's self-indulgent, immoral lifestyle in Moscow, Gustafson points out, "is captured in the image of his farewell party, the late hours, the abundance of food and drink, the idleness, and the endless conversations about life."[21] Even the fun-loving Lukashka is puzzled as to why Olenin, a wealthy Russian aristocrat, would ever want to leave a comfortable, materialistic playground such as Moscow for the Caucasus. "And why on earth did you want to come here?" he asks Olenin. "In your place I would do nothing but make merry!" (6:85). Like both Daddy Yeroshka and Lukashka, therefore, Olenin already is a man of the flesh; unlike his hedonistic Cossack acquaintances, however, this educated Russian visitor is restrained by a self-consciousness, intellect, and conscience that prevent him from behaving in the same free, instinctual manner as do these primitive "natural" men.

Much of the narrative in the second half of *The Cossacks* concerns itself with describing the holiday festivities that are taking place in this Cossack village in conjunction with the summer solstice and later with the grape harvest. Both of these are festive times during the seasonal calendar, periods of carnival when, as Bakhtin has noted, all the hierarchical rank, privileges, norms, and prohibitions that mark the established order of everyday life within official culture are temporarily suspended.[22] The conscience-stricken Olenin, however, finds it difficult to allow himself to share in the carnival spirit of libidinal release and moral license that reigns in the Cossack village, where few, if any, restrictions are placed upon pursuing the gratification of sensual appetite. Instead, it is his fellow Russian officer Beletsky, a fun-loving type with loose morals, who adapts quite easily to this permissive atmosphere. Indeed, when Olenin balks at the invitation to attend a party at Ustenka's, Beletsky chides him for his puritanical churlishness. "Charming women such as one sees nowhere else, and to live like a monk!" Beletsky exclaims. "What an idea! Why spoil your life and not make use of what is at hand?" (6:94). The "monkish" Olenin occupies himself each day with solitary hunting expeditions that serve largely to mortify his flesh and distract him from his sexual attraction to Maryanka: we are told that he returns home "tired and hungry" from these daily excursions, "with his bag of food and cigarettes untouched" (6:88). Meanwhile, the fun-loving "Granddad," as Beletsky is fondly nicknamed by the Cossack girls, participates very actively in the local party scene, which is characterized by both gastronomic indulgence (the "refreshments" of spice bread and sweets) and sexual license (the "merrymaking" with the girls). This section of the text makes evident an organic connection between food and sex: male characters such as Beletsky and Lukashka seek to "buy" sexual favors by providing tasty comestibles for the young maidens in the village. Out of the two Russian guests, therefore, it is the negative character Beletsky who eagerly follows Daddy Yeroshka's injunction to "make merry," which this amoral libertine does by indulging his animal appetite for both sweet confections and equally sweet young Cossack girls. Restrained by his keen moral sensibilities, meanwhile, the hero Olenin can only ask himself, "What demon has brought me to this disgusting carousal (*pirushka*)?" (6:98).

Despite the apparent celebration of animal vitality and natural appetite that we observe in the portrayal of Daddy Yeroshka in *The Cossacks*, the author's own attitude toward sexual and gastronomic indulgence during this period of his life more closely approximates that of the highly autobiographical Olenin. Like his fictional alter ego, Tolstoy seems to have possessed a healthy fear of his own powerful libidinal urges even during his younger years.[23] It should not surprise us, therefore, to find that the artistic representation of Daddy Yeroshka is pervaded by the same ambivalence toward physical pleasure and man's animal nature that characterized the author's own attitude. Although Olenin may mythologize, exoticize, and romanticize this merry man of the flesh, readers of *The Cossacks* are nonetheless shown that in reality Daddy Yeroshka is, in Gustafson's words, little more than "a liar and a drunkard whose life is based on economic self-interest and personal pleasure."[24] Despite his protagonist's fascination with the primitive vitality of Daddy Yeroshka, Tolstoy makes it clear that there are some serious moral flaws in this ancient warrior, a rather lewd old man who has now been reduced to reminiscing nostalgically about his earlier sexual escapades and military exploits and who behaves in a rather opportunistic fashion toward his wealthy young Russian friend. "The closer we look," writes one critic, "the more clearly we recognize that Eroshka is a very ambiguous figure, indeed—a bundle of contradictions, who epitomizes the incongruous fusion of Christian and Heathen in the Cossack character in general, and whom Tolstoy views with as much irony as admiration."[25] This incongruous fusion of pagan and Christian sensibilities, of course, applies equally well to the author's own spiritual personality: the deep contradictions we find in the author's portrayal of Daddy Yeroshka, as was suggested earlier, seem to mirror Tolstoy's own troubling ambivalence about the tension between the flesh and the spirit in human nature.[26]

### Natasha's Fall: Learning to Restrain Sexual Appetite

During his lifelong search for moral self-perfection, Tolstoy came increasingly to believe that our natural appetites for food and sex must be held firmly in check if our spiritual natures can ever hope to transcend our mere animal personalities. The first step on the path to the morally good life, therefore, is to learn moderation, restraint, and self-control in matters concerning our physical appetites for the pleasures of the flesh and the palate.[27] As A. P. Sergeenko has pointed out, Tolstoy's own diary entries repeatedly indicate the need for moderation not just in sexual activity, but also in eating.[28] This ethos of moderation is precisely the moral lesson that the ebullient young Natasha Rostova is forced to learn in *War and Peace* (1863–69). Like Daddy Yeroshka, the sprightly Natasha is often mentioned as one of those Tolstoyan fictional characters who convey vividly the author's pagan celebration of life and nature. Nicknamed the "Cossack" on account of her wild, free, and uninhibited behavior, Natasha enlivens and rejuvenates nearly everyone who comes in contact with her—especially young male suitors such as Vasily Denisov, Andrey Bolkonsky, and Pierre Bezukhov—with her abundant vitality, an infectious "joy of living" (*zhizneradostnost'*) that manifests itself to some extent in this adolescent girl's emerging sexuality. "Natasha, half grown up and half child," we are told in book 4, "was now childishly amusing, now girlishly enchanting" (10:43). This young "enchantress" personifies the poetic atmosphere of romantic love that permeates the Rostov household early in the novel, embodying a positive affirmation of life that proclaims: "Seize the moments of happiness, allow yourself to love and be loved! That is the only reality in the world, all else is folly" (10:45). Indeed, Natasha seems to personify the life force of Nature itself.

Perhaps no single episode in *War and Peace* better illustrates this joyful spontaneity and acute responsiveness on Natasha's part to the instinctual, intuitive side of life than the scene in book 7 when she extemporaneously performs a lively native folk dance *à la russe* at Uncle's home following the wolf hunt. Natasha, in whose voice "there was originality, freshness, an unconsciousness of her own powers, and an as yet untrained velvety softness" (10:298), usually enchants others like a siren with her singing, but here she captivates everyone with her spirited dance movements.[29] The spirit of earthy sensual pleasure that pervades this scene, as well as book 7 as a whole, is rendered in no small part, however, through the joyful celebration of culinary delights and gastronomic abundance that we find at Uncle's home.[30] Witness in this regard the following description of the sumptuous home-style feast prepared for Uncle and his guests (the Rostov children) by Anisya Fyodorovna, Uncle's domestic partner and cook:

On the tray was some herb vodka, various kinds of liqueurs, mushrooms, rye cakes made out of buttermilk, honeycombs, still mead and sparkling mead, apples, raw and roasted nuts, and nut-and-honey sweets. Afterwards Anisya Fyodorovna brought a freshly roasted chicken, ham, and preserves made with honey or with sugar. All of this was the product of Anisya Fyodorovna's housekeeping, gathered and prepared by her. All of this had the smell and aroma of Anisya Fyodorovna herself; all of it gave off a savory succulence, cleanliness, whiteness, and pleasant smile. (10:263)[31]

"Natasha had a bite of everything," the narrator reports, "and it seemed to her that she had never seen or eaten such buttermilk cakes, such aromatic jam, such honey-and-nut sweets, or such a chicken anywhere" (10:263). Uncle's pickled mushrooms, honey, and cherry brandy seemed to Natasha "the best in the world" (10:265). In this scene Tolstoy thus joyfully extols, in epic fashion, the munificence of the rich natural bounty with which earthly life is blessed. And he allows the reader to witness this joyful celebration of life and nature through the perspective of the lively, "natural" young Natasha.

The author, however, also feels compelled to show readers of *War and Peace* what Ruth Benson refers to as the "dark side" of Natasha's sexual energy: that is, the potentially destructive element implicit in her pagan enjoyment of elemental life.[32] Soon after the scene at Uncle's in book 7, therefore, we are made to witness in book 8 how Natasha's unrestrained passion for life, and her elemental appetite for its rich sensual pleasures, can become truly demonic. While staying in Moscow, this still fairly naive and innocent country girl falls prey to the hypnotic, bewitching spell cast upon her at the opera by the members of the Kuragin family, with their cultivated sexual mystique. Pining for Prince Andrey, her absent fiancé, Natasha quickly becomes intoxicated amid the sexually charged atmosphere of the opera with its sea of alluring, seminude women—in their low-cut dresses with their exposed arms, necks, and shoulders—as well as handsome, attentive men eager to admire this public display of feminine charms and female flesh: "Natasha little by little began to pass into a state of intoxication (op'ianenie) she had not experienced for a long while" (10:325). The true danger of a state of intoxication, as Tolstoy would later make abundantly clear in "Why Do People Stupefy Themselves?" (1888), is that it clouds a person's moral consciousness. And this is precisely what happens to Natasha at the opera, where "in the state of intoxication she was in everything seemed simple and natural" (10:326). Even the operatic performance itself, which had initially struck the young country girl Natasha as "grotesque" and "amazing," suddenly comes to lose all of its defamiliarizing strangeness and artificiality for her: "All that was going on before her now seemed completely natural" (10:330).

In her intoxicated state, Natasha suffers such moral confusion that she takes a liking to Countess Hélène Bezukhova and is pleased by the attention showered upon her by Hélène's brother Anatole, who confesses to being captivated by the young Countess Rostova: "and it did not enter her head that there was anything wrong in it" (10: 327). During her Moscow stay, Natasha soon feels herself being "completely borne away into this strange senseless world" of the Kuragins, a decadent, amoral St. Petersburg world "in which it was impossible to know what was good and what was bad, what was reasonable and what was senseless" (10:338). Initially frightened by the absence of any moral barrier of modesty standing between herself and Anatole, Natasha quickly becomes accustomed to the amoral ways of Prince Vasily's hedonistic family. The young heroine's Kuraginesque state of intoxication culminates in her debilitating fall from moral grace: she suddenly breaks off her engagement to Prince Andrey, impetuously agrees to elope with the already married Anatole, and subsequently falls into such deep despair and unhappiness that she attempts to commit suicide.

Although Natasha eventually recuperates from her illness, her natural vitality is now replaced by feelings of grief, remorse, and a strong desire to serve penance for her sinful actions. She begins to avoid "all external forms of pleasure" and finds that she can no longer sing and laugh:

> As soon as she began to laugh, or tried to sing by herself, tears choked her: tears of remorse, tears at the recollection of those pure times that could never return, tears of vexation that she should so uselessly have ruined her young life, which might have been so happy. Laughter and singing in particular seemed to her like a blasphemy, in the face of her sorrow. (11:68–69)

As the narrator explains, "an inner sentinel strictly forbade her every joy" (10:69). The penitent Natasha rejects her earlier pagan appreciation of life's joys and pleasures, adopting for the time being an overtly religious cast of mind: she rigorously observes the weeklong fast before St. Peter's Day, attends mass, matins, and vespers daily, worships before the icon of the Mother of God, receives communion, and addresses prayers of repentance to God in hopes of finding a new, pure, and happy life. In curbing her appetite for earthly pleasures, Natasha becomes thinner, paler, and sadder, a physical and emotional condition that is only reinforced by the experience of nursing the fatally wounded Prince Andrey before his death. When Pierre finally returns to Moscow following his period of incarceration as a prisoner of the French and goes to visit Princess Mary, he does not at first recognize the lady in the black dress whom he takes to be one of her companions:

> Pierre had failed to notice Natasha because he did not at all expect to see her there, but he had failed to recognize her because the change in her since he last saw her was immense. She had grown thin and pale, but that was not what made her unrecognizable; she was unrecognizable at the moment he entered because on that face whose eyes had always shone with a suppressed smile of the joy of life, now when he first entered and glanced at her there was not the least shadow of a smile; only her eyes were kindly attentive and sadly interrogative. (12:216)

Pierre's return, however, finally does enable Natasha to overcome her grief and sadness. Her eyes quickly begin to shine again and a mischievous smile soon reappears on her face, while some irrepressible force awakens in her soul. "Everything: her face, walk, look, and voice, was suddenly altered," the narrator explains. "To her own surprise a power of life and hope of happiness rose to the surface and demanded satisfaction" (12:231). Love for Pierre, with whom she has always felt the moral barrier that was so conspicuously absent in her relationship with Anatole, thus reawakens at last the power of life in Natasha.

## The Epilogue to War and Peace: Bridling Sexual Appetite through Marriage

Natasha learns to "bridle" her sexual passion and finds spiritual redemption not only through the traditional religious regimen of abstinence, prayer, and penance, but also through her subsequent marriage to Pierre Bezukhov in the epilogue. This conjugal union succeeds in defusing the heroine's bewitching charms and harnessing her sexual energy through the discipline she acquires in fulfilling daily domestic routines in her new roles as a wife and mother. By the time they come to the epilogue, with its nearly suffocating "homey" atmosphere of dirty diapers, noisy children, and prosaic household concerns, many readers feel that the author of *War and Peace* has suddenly brought forth a Natasha who is entirely new, different, and hardly recognizable. "She had grown stouter and broader, so that it was difficult to recognize in this robust, motherly woman the slim, lively Natasha of former days," the narrator informs us,

> The features of her face were more defined and wore a calm, soft, and serene expression. In her face there was none of the ever-glowing flame of animation that had formerly burned there and constituted its charm. Now her face and body were often all that one saw, and her soul was not visible at all. All that struck the eye was a strong, handsome, and fertile female. The old fire very rarely kindled in her now. (12:265–66)

"Confronted with the two Natashas," Benson writes, "Tolstoy mutes the wild sensual Natasha, takes away the primitive power which she displayed in her dance at Uncle's and transforms this 'heavenly creature' into the model mother and wife of the epilogue."[33] Tolstoy, in effect, "de-eroticizes" Natasha by glorifying her newly acquired identity as wife and mother. In a manner not terribly unlike the way Freud, in *Civilization and Its Discontents* (1930), would later describe the civilizing processes of repression and sublimation, Tolstoy shows us how the institution of marriage can be made to fulfill an important regulative function within society with respect to the libidinal urges of human beings. Natasha's marriage to Pierre, as Benson puts it, "exemplifies Tolstoy's attempt to cope with the destructive force of sexuality by controlling and legitimizing it within the framework of marriage."[34] In *War and Peace*, maternity and sexuality are thus kept at a safe, comfortable distance from each other, "neatly compartmentalized," in Evans's words, in order to preserve and protect the existing social order, an order that finds its microcosmic mirror image in the family unit.[35]

Like Natasha, Pierre also learns to curb his robust appetite for food and sex as part of his process of maturation from indulgent bachelor to devoted husband and father in *War and Peace*. Early in the novel, this "untrained bear" of a man is presented to the reader as a natural, if somewhat childish, character who freely indulges his hearty appetite for life's physical pleasures. Although he recognizes that "there is something nasty and vile" (9:251) in the sexual feelings that Hélène Kuragina arouses in him, Pierre allows himself to succumb to this carnal attraction toward her physical beauty, just as he frequently had succumbed to the temptation of joining Dolokhov, Anatole Kuragin, and other young officers in their riotous bachelor carousals. Later in the novel, when he has become the cuckolded husband of an unfaithful wife and a wealthy member of the English Club in Moscow, the stout and indolent Pierre continues to be known for his great "fondness for eating and drinking" (10:295).

Indeed, his transformation as a character in the novel seems to begin in earnest only in book 10, when Pierre leaves Moscow to go visit the Russian army on the eve of the battle of Borodino. "He now experienced a pleasant feeling at the consciousness that everything that constitutes men's happiness—the comforts of life, wealth, even life itself—is rubbish that it is pleasant to throw away" (11:182). Toward the end of that famous battle Pierre joins a small group of soldiers on the road to Mozhaysk around their campfire and finds unexpected joy in the company of these simple men, sharing with them their modest meal of dried bread mixed with the fat drippings of greasy viands heated in a cauldron. "Pierre sat down by the fire and began eating the mash, as they called the food in the cauldron," the narrator writes, "and he thought it more delicious than any food he had ever tasted" (11:289). Upon his return to Moscow, which is being rapidly evacuated as the French army advances upon the city, Pierre feels even more strongly his own insignificance compared with the "truth, simplicity, and strength" (11:356) of this nongentry class of men with whom he has just shared a simple meal and friendly conversation. He abandons his home—as well as the luxury and comfort to which he had become accustomed there—to sleep on a hard sofa and "eat the same food" (11:357) as his servant Gerasim.

Experiencing great joy in renouncing his gentry wealth and power, Pierre finds even more peace and harmony during his period of captivity under the French troops, not only through his acquaintanceship with the archetypal peasant Platon Karataev, but also through the physical privations he must endure as a prisoner. Just like the soldiers' modest meal of mash at Mozhaysk, Platon's simple potatoes seem incredibly delicious to Tolstoy's hero: "It seemed to Pierre that he had never eaten anything that tasted better than this" (12:46). Having grown considerably less stout and become more simple (less pretentious) during his time as a prisoner, Pierre absorbs from the experience the important Tolstoyan life lessons that "a superfluity of the comforts of life destroys all joy in satisfying one's needs" (12:98), that human happiness consists in "the satisfaction of natural human needs" (12:152), and that "all unhappiness arises not from privation but from superfluity" (12:152).

The "moral bath" Pierre emerges from after his release from French captivity makes him worthy at last to wed the now de-eroticized Natasha, whom he has long loved romantically and whom he has now learned to value spiritually as well.[36] It also prepares Pierre to become the faithful husband and devoted father we encounter in the first epilogue, where marriage is presented as a social institution that safely and productively harnesses the instinctual energy of both husband and wife. This regulative function that marriage is designed to fulfill within society, whereby it effectively neutralizes the largely destructive tendencies of the sensual appetites for pleasure within human beings, finds its gastronomical parallel in the author's highly functional attitude toward food and eating. One must eat in moderation, according to Tolstoy, as an unrestrained appetite for food leads to gluttony or overeating, which only leaves one with a feeling of physical, moral, and spiritual dissatisfaction. To make explicit this connection between the need to restrain appetites both sexual and gastronomical, Tolstoy in the epilogue to *War and Peace* resorts to an alimentary analogy—highly anti-gastronomic in nature[37]—that draws a direct parallel between the purpose of marriage (family) and the purpose of a meal (nourishment). "If the purpose of a meal is nourishment of the body," the narrator observes,

> then the person who eats two meals at once perhaps gets greater enjoyment, but he will not attain his purpose, since his stomach will not digest both meals. If the purpose of a marriage is the family, then the person who wishes to have many wives or husbands may perhaps obtain much pleasure, but in no case will he have a family. If the purpose of food is nourishment and the purpose of marriage is the family, then the whole question resolves itself into not eating more than one's stomach can digest and not having more wives or husbands than are needed for the family—that is, one wife or one husband. (12:268)

Natasha, we are told, had no interest in such topical questions as women's rights, the freedom that ought to be accorded a husband and wife in their marital relations, and so on. "These questions, then as now, existed only for those people who see nothing in marriage but the pleasure married people get from one another, that is, only the beginnings of marriage and not its whole significance, which consists in the family," the narrator explains. "Discussions of that kind and today's questions, which are like the question of how to get the greatest enjoyment from one's dinner, did not exist then, just as they do not exist now, for those people for whom the purpose of a dinner is the nourishment it affords and the purpose of marriage is the family" (12:268). For Natasha and Pierre, the purpose of a marriage, like the purpose of a meal, is clearly familial nourishment, not personal pleasure or enjoyment.

It is perhaps worth noting briefly in this regard that Pierre's first wife, the sexually promiscuous and decidedly immoderate Hélène Kuragina, suffers a painful death after contracting an illness that arose, in the narrator's words, "from an inconvenience resulting from getting married to two husbands at the same time" (12:4). The monogamous Natasha, on the other hand, learns to adopt an ethos of moderation, restraint, and self-control that enables her not merely to restrict her sexual appetite by limiting it to just one "meal" (that is, her husband). It also allows her safely to channel her dangerous libidinal energies into the domestic routines that are maintained by the busy wife and mother she becomes by novel's end. Tolstoy's so-called therapeutic view of marriage thus saves his heroine from sensual excess by teaching her moral, emotional, and even visceral discipline: that is, by teaching the wild little Cossack to "bridle" or "harness" her natural animal vitality. Much like the recent bride and young mother Masha in *Family Happiness* (1859), Natasha learns that true contentment, in Tolstoy's fictional world at least, can come only when the "romance" of one's marriage ends (and parenthood begins), when wives become mothers rather than lovers, and when women shift their attention from consuming to nourishing.[38]

### Levin's Ethos of Moderation, Restraint, and Self-Control

Tolstoy's advocacy of an ethos of moderation, restraint, and self-control in matters of sexual and gastronomic appetite—as well as his faith in the institution of marriage and the family as an effective social harness upon human sexual desire—reaches its apex during the period of the writing of *Anna Karenina*, the work that in many ways marks a watershed both in Tolstoy's personal life and in his artistic career. "In the context of Tolstoy's own development," Irene Pearson asserts, "*Anna Karenina* represents a transitional stage between his joy in expressing intensely-felt physical sensations and his urge to asceticism and social reform."[39] "In returning to the theme of the family, marriage, and sexuality in *Anna Karenina*," Amy Mandelker observes, "Tolstoy again reveals his affinities for his beloved Victorian authors Dickens, Eliot, and Trollope, who, while exalting the Victorian ideal of the family, simultaneously, if not always consciously, expose its pathology."[40] In Tolstoy's famous novel of adultery, the largely autobiographical Konstantin Levin embodies not only the author's defense of marriage and the family, but also his highly functional approach to the problem of the strong gastronomic and sexual temptation generated by tasty foods and enticing women.

The most memorable instance in *Anna Karenina* where this ethos of moderation, restraint, and self-control collides with a philosophy of epicureanism and hedonism occurs, of course, in the well-known restaurant scene depicted in part 1 of the novel, when Levin goes to dine with his future brother-in-law, Stiva Oblonsky. From the moment he enters the Moscow restaurant, Levin is immediately made to feel ill at ease by the decadent features of the establishment, by those same elements of urban aristocratic luxury that fill his future brother-in-law with pure delight: the Tartar waiters in their swallowtail coats, the vodka and hors d'oeuvres at the buffet, and the painted Frenchwoman sitting at the counter. "Levin did not take any vodka," we are told, "simply because that Frenchwoman—all made up, as it seemed to him, of false hair, *poudre de riz*, and *vinaigre de toilette*—was offensive to him. He hastily moved away from her as from some dirty place" (18:37). Whereas Stiva feels right at home in this culinary pleasure palace, Levin loses his appetite almost immediately upon entering the restaurant and is greatly discomfitted by the vulgar surroundings, which he seems to fear will profane the sacred image of the virginal Kitty that he faithfully bears in his heart.

During this famous scene of dining Tolstoy conflates the gastronomic and sexual discourses that will be at work throughout his entire novel, exploiting culinary motifs here as an effective way to convey the contrasting attitudes toward sexuality of these two longtime but antipodal friends. The foods they enjoy eating become emblematic not only of their opposing personalities, life values, and moral natures, but also of their diametrically opposed views on sexuality. Stiva Oblonsky, the hedonistic "man of the flesh" whose eyes actually become moist and glisten with delight as he dines, is in ecstasy as he swallows quivering oysters from his silver fork and sips Chablis from his wide-lipped champagne glass. Konstantin Levin, on the other hand, the simple and sober "man of the spirit," can find little pleasure in such exotic culinary fare. To the contrary, he expresses disappointment that there is no buckwheat porridge or cabbage soup at this restaurant (18:38). "Levin ate some oysters, though he would have preferred white bread and cheese," the narrator observes (18:39). The gastronomic dialectic at work here, as Visson has demonstrated, partakes in a wider rivalry within nineteenth-century Russian literature between Russian peasant or "Slavophile" cooking, on the one hand, which features simple and earthy native food items, and elegant Gallic fare, on the other, which the Europeanized gentry imported into Russia from the West. For the Slavophilic Tolstoy, of course, Levin's simple peasant diet of cabbage soup and porridge (*shchi da kasha—pishcha nasha*) is immensely preferable, in moral as well as gustatory terms, to Oblonsky's aristocratic culinary indulgence in oysters and champagne, which represent a decadent Western concern with elegance, luxury, and material values in general.[41]

The contrast in the gastronomical appetites of these two diners in *Anna Karenina* extends well beyond this Westernizer-versus-Slavophile dialectic, however; it encompasses their greatly differing perspectives upon the broader semiotic significance of the very act of eating. As Helena Goscilo observes, Levin and Stiva define for us here the "culinary moral spectrum" that assumes increasing importance in Tolstoy's life and works.[42] For the primitive and rustic Levin, eating is a basic biological act, necessary for the purposes of nutrition by sustaining one's life, strength, and health; for the urbane and sophisticated Oblonsky, on the other hand, eating constitutes, in his words, "one of life's pleasures" (18:38). If we were to borrow the terms suggested by Barthes, we could say that eating for Levin operates within the "realm of necessity" (*l'ordre de besoin*), where food indicates deprivation, while for Oblonsky it operates within the "realm of desire" (*l'ordre de désir*), where food indicates indulgence.[43] Semiotically considered, Levin, with his rustic *appétit naturel*, eats to live, whereas Oblonsky, with his urbane *appétit de luxe*, lives to eat. Stiva, in other words, must artificially stimulate his appetite and create a false hunger in order to generate ever new pleasure out of the act of eating.[44] "It seems ridiculous to me that while we country people try to eat up our meals as quickly as we can, so as to be able to get on with our work, here you and I are trying to make our meal last as long as possible, and therefore we are eating oysters," Levin observes at one point. "Well, of course," Oblonsky replies. "That is, after all, the aim of civilization: to get pleasure and enjoyment out of everything." "Well, if that is its aim," Levin fires back, "I'd rather be a savage." "You are a savage as it is. All you Levins are savages," Stiva exclaims (18:40). As Irene Pearson observes, "the simple way of life in the Russian countryside," where people take a practical, utilitarian approach to food, is contrasted in this scene with what she calls "the French-style civilization of the city," where the aim is to derive as much pleasure as possible from the act of eating.[45] In addition to the geographical contrast between city and country, Oblonsky's and Levin's differing perspectives on food and eating thus reveal to us a whole series of binary oppositions within broader sociological, psychological, and moral categories: for example, enjoyment versus nourishment, luxury versus necessity, nature versus culture, the "ego" versus the "id," the pleasure principle versus the reality principle, urban sophistication versus rural simplicity, the gentry class versus the peasant class, hunger versus appetite.[46]

When the meal has ended and the table conversation switches over to the subject of women, we see that Tolstoy continues to use the gastronomic analogy as a way to illustrate the contrast between Stiva's hedonism and Levin's puritanism. Establishing a setting similar in most respects to Plato's *Symposium*, where, as Gutkin notes, both physical and intellectual pleasures can be enjoyed through the twin activities of dining and discourse, Tolstoy's two male characters proceed to engage in a dialogue about love: more specifically, about carnal versus spiritual love.[47] As we might well expect, each of these men brings to the issue of sexual love the same semiotic code he abides by with respect to the act of eating: for Levin, the sex drive is a dangerous, if necessary, instinctual urge that must be restrained by channeling it within the institution of marriage and the framework of the family; for Oblonsky, sex, like food, constitutes one of life's delicious pleasures and is thus to be enjoyed for its own sake. For the stoical and spartan Levin, sex is merely a means to an end (reproduction), while for the hedonistic and epicurean Oblonsky, sex is an end in and of itself (pleasure).[48] Why a married man would commit adultery is just as incomprehensible to the puritanical Levin as why one would ever go to a baker's shop and steal a roll after having eaten one's fill at a restaurant. "But why not steal a roll (*kalach*)?" the philandering Stiva muses. "After all, a roll sometimes smells so good that you just can't resist it!" (18:44–45).[49] Gluttony and adultery are thus linked together here as pleasurable sensual activities that for Oblonsky, as a member of the rich and idle aristocracy in Moscow, seem to complement and accompany each other.

The lines of verse from Heinrich Heine that Stiva proceeds to quote during this dining scene underscore the semiotic field within which Tolstoy's treatment of sensual pleasure is to be understood throughout the remainder of the novel: "It is heavenly when I have mastered my earthly desires; But when I have not succeeded, I have also had right good pleasure!" (18:45). If the first line (about mastering earthly desires) characterizes Levin's position, then the second line (about the joy of failing to restrain such desire) captures perfectly Oblonsky's attitude. As we see throughout the novel, the epicure Stiva is hardly even trying to master his "earthly desires" (be they gastronomical or sexual in nature); he is seeking only to enjoy "right good pleasure" wherever and whenever he can. For Levin, on the other hand, libidinal restraint does not seem to pose much of a problem. We have seen that he eats for nourishment rather than for pleasure. And, like the tamed, bridled, and domesticated Natasha in the epilogue to *War and Peace*, Levin understands the necessity of harnessing his sexual instincts. He has thus adopted a functional attitude not only toward food but also toward sex, a sensual activity that for him can only be legitimized and justified through the institution of marriage. This attitude is reflected in his comment to Oblonsky that he feels a physical revulsion for "fallen women," sexual creatures whom he considers to be moral abominations (18:45). Indeed, Levin's aversion to erotic women—who are epitomized by the obscenely painted Frenchwoman with her curls—is largely what accounts for his being so "ill at ease and uncomfortable in this restaurant with its private rooms where men went to dine with their ladies" (18:39). He realizes full well, of course, that these private rooms facilitate not only elegant dining, but also amorous trysts.[50] Stiva, with his penchant for marital infidelity, may well feel fully at ease in this realm of eroticism and carnal love, but Levin, who cherishes the idealized picture of the chaste Kitty he carries in his heart, seems much more comfortable in the ethereal realm of platonic love.[51]

*Earthly Desires in* Anna Karenina: *Sins of the Flesh and the Palate*

Throughout the remainder of *Anna Karenina*, Tolstoy continues to identify the satisfaction of gastronomic and sexual desire with a sinful animal appetite for pleasure. The quintessential "man of the flesh" in Tolstoy's famous novel of adultery (perhaps in his entire literary oeuvre) is, of course, the tragic heroine's philandering brother. A reveler whose behavior is governed almost entirely by the pleasure principle, Stiva Oblonsky throughout the novel is shown freely indulging his hearty appetite for both food and women. We learn, for instance, that this "married bachelor" regularly conducts amorous liaisons with young actresses, and we witness how he flirts shamelessly with women of loose morals such as Betsy Tverskaya and the painted hostess at the restaurant. In the gastronomic realm, meanwhile, Oblonsky is shown to derive great pleasure from hosting an elegant dinner party at his Moscow home in part 4 and he enjoys consuming sumptuous repasts, not only at the posh Hotel Anglia restaurant in part 1 but also at Levin's country home when he goes hunting with him in part 2. The hedonistic Stiva, in short, personifies a lifestyle that Levin roundly condemns for its sinful indulgence (*prazdnost'*): that is, he epitomizes all the idleness, luxury, and material comfort of urbane aristocratic life in Russia. When Stiva suddenly shows up at Levin's rural estate in part 6, accompanied by his younger pleasure-seeking partner in sensuality, the amiable bon vivant Vasya Veslovsky, the reader observes once again how in Tolstoy's novel the pleasures of the flesh are invariably made both similar to and contiguous with the pleasures of the palate. Food is here linked closely with sex during the hunting trip: for example, we learn not only that Stiva and Veslovsky spent the first night of the expedition making love to some of the local peasant girls, but also that chubby little Vasya has managed to consume by himself all of the provisions Kitty had prepared as meals for the trio of hungry sportsmen.

The romantic, adulterous relationship between Anna and Vronsky, who combine to create what one commentator calls a "cult of sexuality" in the novel and who may be said to represent "the high point of known and articulated heterosexual desire" in *Anna Karenina*, is likewise associated with images of food and drink.[52] Invariably, however, as Pearson notes, this association is made "in a negative or tainted sense."[53] Like Oblonsky, neither the tragic heroine nor her lover ever really attempts to master their earthly desires. Vronsky, for example, who travels in a fast aristocratic crowd made up of people for whom the most important thing was "to give themselves up unblushingly to every kind of passion" (18:121), is consistently portrayed as a healthy, virile, and carnivorous beast. Witness in this regard, as Goscilo rightly notes, the repeated reference to his strong white teeth and his fondness for beefsteak.[54] Much like Sappho Stolz's young admirer Vaska, who has been nourished on "underdone beef (*goviadina*), truffles, and Burgundy" and who seems to radiate with a "superabundance of health" (18:315), Vronsky is presented as a fine physical specimen. And in much the same manner that the concupiscent Vaska looks ready to "eat up" the

enticing Sappho (18:315), Vronsky's animal passion drives him ultimately to devour the beautiful Anna.

At one point, when he is forced to spend a week serving as the official escort for a foreign prince who is visiting the Russian capital,
Vronsky even experiences an epiphany of sorts and comes to recognize
his own bestial nature. Due to gymnastics and rigorous exercise, the
prince, who epitomizes animal vitality and physical appetite, is able to
maintain a healthy appearance in spite of the sensual excess he indulges in when amusing himself sexually and gastronomically. In search
of a "taste" of distinctively Russian sensual amusements, the prince
is escorted on a round of native popular entertainments: while in
St. Petersburg, he experiences, among other things, horse racing, bear
hunting, troika riding, crockery smashing, gypsy girls, pancakes, and
champagne. Vronsky, however, soon finds this escort duty both weari-
some and maddening. "The main reason why the prince's presence especially oppressed Vronsky," the narrator explains, "was that he could
not help but see himself reflected in the prince, and what he saw in that
mirror was not flattering to his vanity. The prince was a very stupid,
very self-assured, very healthy, and very clean man—and nothing more"
(18:374). To Vronsky's mind, however, the prince is not even a human
being; instead he is merely a "stupid hunk of beef" (*goviadina*) (18:374).
"Can I really be like that myself?" muses a perplexed Vronsky, who is
not normally given to reflection of this kind. He later characterizes the
prince to Anna as "a finely-bred animal like those that get first-place
prizes at cattle shows," the sort of creature who despises "everything
except animal pleasures" (18:378). To this unflattering characterization, a pregnant, jealous, and thoroughly unsympathetic Anna responds sarcastically, "But don't all of you love those animal pleasures?"
(18:378).[55]

Anna, the St. Petersburg adulteress who relinquishes her domestic
identity as wife and mother by abandoning her husband and young son
to pursue her sexual passion for Vronsky (thus reversing the pattern of
development followed by Natasha Rostova in *War and Peace*), likewise
is closely identified throughout the novel with food imagery that serves
mainly to reinforce the reader's image of her as a fleshly creature. As
Evans notes, Anna is depicted as "a female creature for whom sexual
passion is as much a part of the fabric of everyday life as food and
drink."[56] In Anna's case, however, unlike Stiva's, it is the language of

gastronomy that is frequently invoked when she wishes to express her spiritual state or her emotional needs. "I unhappy?" she says to her lover soon after they consummate their love affair. "I am like a hungry person to whom food has been given. He may be cold, his clothes may be ragged, and he may be ashamed, but he is not unhappy" (18:201). By equating her sexual appetite with such a basic human need as physical hunger, Anna seeks to justify the necessity, and hence the morality, of indulging her sexual passion. "I am alive and I am not to blame that God made me such that I need to love and live," she says later in another attempt to rationalize her adultery. "I cannot repent of breathing, of loving" (18:308–309).[57] It is significant, as Goscilo notes, that "Anna resorts to food imagery only after she succumbs to Vronsky and her own desires."[58] Indeed, as the story progresses, and the heroine's moral, emotional, and psychological deterioration becomes ever more painfully evident to the reader, we see that Anna's sexual desire is actually more an "appetite" she has chosen to indulge liberally (and thus inflame) than a basic, essential "hunger" she has no choice but to appease.[59] In sexual matters, therefore, Anna seems to possess an *appétit de luxe* (like Stiva's), although she strives to convince herself that her erotic desire is actually an *appétit naturel* (like Levin's). If, as Isaiah Berlin once asserted, Tolstoy is a hedgehog who thinks he is a fox, then Anna is a glutton who thinks she is starving.

"The key to understanding Anna," Gary Saul Morson boldly maintains, "is that she is Stiva's sister, Anna Oblonskaya."[60] This Oblonskian family resemblance, this genetic commonality of sensual traits and physical appetites, becomes especially prominent in part 7, when Anna takes her final carriage ride through Moscow prior to her suicide. During that ride, Anna confesses that, while she may not know any longer who she is, she does, as the French say, know what her "appetites" are. She proceeds to generalize about the nature of human desire, using a gastronomic metaphor for her sexual lust that sounds distinctively Oblonskian:

"Here they want some of that dirty ice cream; they know that for a certainty," she thought, as she watched two boys stopping at an ice cream vendor, who lifted down a tub from atop his head and wiped his perspiring face with the end of the cloth. "We all want something sweet, something tasty; if we can get no bonbons, then we'll take dirty ice cream. And Kitty is just the same: if not Vronsky, then Levin." (19:340)

Like Stiva's *kalach*, Anna's ice cream and bonbons are here shown to represent much more than merely some sweet and tasty comestibles; these gastronomic objects of desire are also metaphors for the sexual appetite of a now jaded libertine. Moreover, Anna realizes that she has herself become that dirty ice cream: she openly expresses here the fear that, as an object of carnal desire for Vronsky, she no longer has in her "the right flavor" to suit the tastes of her lover (19:343). Like her pleasure-seeking brother, therefore, Anna comes increasingly to identify human desire with basic animal lust, with a purely physical appetite for food and sex.

As Pearson correctly notes, Anna by the end comes to view life in Darwinian terms as "a battle between individuals for the satisfaction of their appetites."[61] Not unlike Vronsky, Anna has reduced all of human existence essentially to the satisfaction of one's animal urges; as a result, living has become a meaningless activity from which she can no longer derive any true lasting pleasure. As she herself puts it (significantly, in English), "the zest is gone" (19:343).[62] "In *Anna Karenina*," one critic has observed, "to be good means to be able to resist the impulses of nature, not, as in *War and Peace*, to give in to them."[63] Tolstoy's tragic heroine, unfortunately, learns this lesson either too late or not at all.

The author's condemnation of the sinful pleasures of the flesh and the palate in *Anna Karenina* culminates with the brief conversation Levin has in part 8 with Fyodor, a peasant from the village where Levin had once leased out land to be worked cooperatively. Fyodor makes a sharp distinction between those people, like Fokanych, who live rightly, "in God's way," by acting selflessly for the betterment of their "soul" (*dusha*), and those who, like Mityukha, instead live selfishly for the benefit of their "belly" (*briukho*) (19:376). At first sight, one would think that the cast of characters in Tolstoy's novel supports this distinction: there seems to be such a clear dichotomy between egoists (such as Anna, Vronsky, Oblonsky, and Veslovsky), on the one hand, and more altruistic and spiritual creatures (such as Levin, Kitty, Dolly, and Varenka), on the other. The novel's parallel plot lines—one focused on Anna, the other on Levin—likewise seem to support this polarity:

whereas the heroine, a "man of the flesh" who lives largely for the gratification of her senses, ultimately perishes in despair, the hero, a "man of the spirit" who lives mainly for the benefit of his soul, ultimately finds spiritual peace. A difficulty with this polarized scheme, however, is that the author's masterly artistic portrayal of Anna mitigates much of our moral condemnation of her sinful behavior. "We are so moved by compassion for her suffering," Edward Wasiolek observes about Tolstoy's heroine, "that we tend to overlook the fund of sheer nastiness in her by the end of the novel."[64] Not all readers, perhaps, are so willing as Wasiolek to overlook Anna's serious failings, but most of them do seem to believe that Tolstoy did not wish for this graceful, charming, and passionate creature to be categorically condemned.[65]

*Levin's Intoxicated Consciousness: Eating, Drinking, Whoring*

Another difficulty with this over neat opposition between sensual and moral characters in *Anna Karenina* is that Levin is not without problems and shortcomings of his own by novel's end. In part 8, for instance, he is contemplating suicide and experiencing marital difficulties of his own with Kitty. Worse yet, the narrative events depicted in part 7, when Levin and Kitty move to Moscow during the final period of her confinement, show us that the hero's ethos of moderation, restraint, and self-control in matters involving sensual pleasure is severely tested—if not, in fact, defeated—by the same infectious spirit of aristocratic *prazdnost'* that Stiva and Veslovsky had brought with them from the city to the countryside when they invaded Levin's rural estate in part 6. Compared with part 1, Levin's activities in Moscow during this section of the novel now closely resemble the immoral behavior of Stiva Oblonsky: the former country bumpkin pays a number of meaningless social calls, attends the theater, and even dines at the infamous English Club in the company of such merry sybarites as Oblonsky, Vronsky, and Yashvin. Where the scene of dining at the Hotel Anglia depicted in part I had illustrated Levin's moral puritanism, the scene of dining at the English Club depicted in part 7 reveals how Levin's characteristic restraint has now given way to a desire for a variety of sensual pleasures. We witness our hero eating and drinking out in public, seemingly without restraint, while his wife, nine months pregnant, lies home confined in bed. Caught up in the holiday atmosphere reigning at the club, Levin now partakes quite willingly and enthusiastically in a number of those leisure activities that—either explicitly or implicitly—he had condemned so categorically in part 1: eating, drinking, gambling, and socializing. Essentially Levin has been seduced by the charms of aristocratic life in Moscow. The noble "savage" from the Russian countryside, the rustic who once prided himself on his simple peasant ways, appears to have been effectively "civilized" as he comes to realize his inherent kinship with his gentry brethren in the city. "He had grown hungry, and so he ate and drank with great pleasure," the narrator says of the previously abstemious Levin, "and with still greater pleasure he took part in the simple merry conversations of his companions" (19:267).

As the evening progresses, Levin's behavior more and more resembles that of Stiva Oblonsky; indeed, the puritanical Levin seems to have been transformed suddenly into an Oblonskian playboy and hedonistic "man of the flesh." When Prince Shcherbatsky, in the midst of the evening's festivities at the English Club, asks his favorite son-in-law, "Well, and how do you like our temple of idleness (khram prazdnosti)?" (19:268), we ought to be struck by the delicious irony. The Levin we remember from part 1 would have been appalled by this den of iniquity; the Levin we now observe in part 7 seems to be thoroughly at home. Levin's "seduction" here bears analogy with the way the virginal Natasha Rostova allows her rustic naïveté and innocence to be corrupted when she attends the opera in Moscow in book 8 of War and Peace. The sense of estrangement, the defamiliarizing ostranenie that Levin feels initially, when he is thrust into an alien milieu (that is, urbane Moscow where aristocrats revel in sensual pleasure), has passed by part 7, and he, like Natasha, now finds such indulgent behavior quite normal and natural. Both of these characters seem to lapse into a state that Richard Gustafson has characterized as the "intoxicated consciousness."[66] The evening spent at the English Club could thus be said to serve as the objective correlative of the general intoxication of Moscow social life—with its ethos of idleness and comfort—that has now overtaken the previously sober and industrious Levin.[67] It is no doubt this intoxicating feeling of prazdnost' that prompts him to break his promise to Sviazhsky: rather than attend, as planned, the meeting of the Agricultural Society with him that evening, Levin opts instead to go with Oblonsky to visit his sister Anna. The significance of this step should not be ignored or overlooked: Levin, the morally upright gentry farmer, is passing up a meeting of the Agricultural Society in order to go with a hedonistic and philandering friend to pay a visit to a "fallen woman" in the city he once characterized as an immoral Babylon.[68]

Levin's visit to Anna's home, when examined within this context, shares many of the structural characteristics as trips to brothels depicted in works of Western literature. A typical pattern that emerges from the nineteenth-century European novel involves a group of men going to a restaurant or a club to dine and drink, and then, in post-prandial lethargy, either retiring to private rooms or setting off for a brothel where they pair off with the prostitutes working there. "Nineteenth-century French novelists in particular," writes James Brown, "fully exploited the relationships between food and fornication in their depictions of tête-à-tête meals, and, in the novel as in contemporary society, the co-occurence of the culinary and the sexual acts was made explicit in public dining houses where the *cabinet particulier* was designed specifically for amorous diners."[69] The satisfaction of gastronomical desire in the novels of Balzac, Flaubert, and other nineteenth-century French writers seems to generate, in turn, the need to satisfy sexual desire.[70] In such works, eating generally serves as a stimulant for fornication, with food and drink invariably whetting the men's sexual appetite for women. Perhaps the most memorable instance within nineteenth-century Russian literature of this pattern of dining, drinking, and whoring occurs, as we saw in the previous chapter, in part 2 of Dostoevsky's *Notes from Underground* (1864). Following the farewell dinner arranged at the Hôtel de Paris by Trudolyubov, Ferfichkin, and Simonov in honor of their friend, the officer Zvertsov, who will soon be leaving St. Petersburg, the gastronomically sated revelers then go "there" (5:147): an establishment that, the narrator explains, serves as a *millinery emporia* by day; at night, however, if one had an introduction, one might visit it "as a guest" (5:151). It is of course as "guests," and thus for the sole purpose of enjoying carnal pleasure, that these three young men, with the underground man in hot pursuit, have now come to the brothel.

In *Anna Karenina*, it is Levin's wife Kitty who identifies for us this pattern of dining, drinking, and whoring, a pattern she associates with the urbane playboys of Oblonsky's ilk. "She already knew now what consorting with merry males of Oblonsky's sort meant," the narrator reports early in part 7, "it meant drinking and then driving somewhere. She could not think without horror of where men drove to in such cases" (19:248).[71] Of course, her husband, as we know, has been consorting this very evening not merely with "merry males of Oblonsky's sort," but with Oblonsky himself, and now, after dining and drinking, the two of them are driving off to visit a fallen woman. Intoxicated (in a metaphorical if not actual sense) after his evening spent eating, drinking, and socializing at the English Club, Levin himself has second thoughts about the propriety of going with Oblonsky to visit Anna, both while en route to her place (19:271) and after they arrive (19:273).[72] As Joan Grossman has pointed out, the physical description of the interior decor of Anna's home that Tolstoy provides at this point in the narrative strongly suggests the "seductive" atmosphere of a brothel: specifically, the portrait of Anna ("the painting of an alluring woman strategically placed and illuminated by a reflector lamp"), the dim lighting, the luxurious rooms, the soft carpets, the exclusively male visitors.[73] When Levin finally does meet Anna in person, Tolstoy's heroine immediately makes a strongly favorable impression upon him, captivating him by her beauty and her personality. Levin feels a surprising amount of tenderness, affection, and compassion for Anna as he observes her in animated conversation with her brother Stiva (19:276). Indeed, the narrator leaves little doubt in our minds that in a very short time Anna has succeeded in thoroughly charming, if not actually seducing, her already slightly intoxicated visitor.[74] Reluctantly taking his leave of Anna late in the evening, Levin never ceases to think of this "wonderful, sweet, pathetic woman" all the way home, "recalling every detail of the expression of her face, entering more and more into her situation, and feeling more and more sorry for her" (19:279). Thus Levin's memories of this evening betray a closeness, a tenderness, and an empathy characteristic of sexual intimacy.

In the immediate aftermath of this visit, two narrative events occur that encourage the reader to view it as comparable to a trip to a brothel. First of all, there is the jealous outburst by Kitty once she learns where her husband has just spent the evening. "You have fallen in love with that vile, nasty woman!" Kitty screams when her husband finally returns home late that evening and describes his visit to Anna's. "She has bewitched you! I can see it in your eyes. Yes, yes! What can come of this? You were at the club drinking and drinking, and gambling, and then you went . . . to see whom?" (19:281). The insinuation in Kitty's last question suggests, of course, the very pattern of dining, drinking, and whoring she herself had alluded to earlier when speaking about the idle lifestyle of the young aristocratic playboys in Moscow ("merry males of Oblonsky's sort"). Now that same pattern is explicitly associated with her husband's recent trip to Anna's. Even Levin himself comes to admit that this had been an "unsuitable" trip to see someone "who could only be called a fallen woman" (19:284). A second indication that Levin, at a symbolic level, has visited a brothel that evening is the testimony provided by Anna herself, who confirms that she had indeed attempted to seduce Kitty's husband, whom she sought to attract spiritually and emotionally, if not sexually. "She had unconsciously done all in her power to awaken in Levin the feeling of love toward her," the narrator explains, adding parenthetically that Anna now did this to all the young men she met (19:281). It is almost as if Levin's visit merely afforded Anna yet another opportunity to exercise her considerable powers of attraction and seduction, "sexual" powers she now seems increasingly called upon to invoke as she seeks more and more desperately to retain Vronsky's love and affection.[75] "If I produce such an effect on others, on this married man who loves his wife," Anna muses after Levin's departure, "why is *he* [Vronsky] so cold toward me. . . . He wishes to give me proofs that his love for me must not interfere with his freedom. But I don't need proofs; I need love!" (19:281–82).

One inference readers are invited to make at this point in the narrative is that Anna has become as addicted to sexual love as she has to morphine, opium, and tobacco.[76] The moral abyss into which adultery has thrown Anna—the smoking, the drugs, the maternal negligence, the obsessive flirting—contributes to the reader's image of her as having indeed become a loose (albeit pathetic) "fallen" woman. Trapped like a prisoner in the Moscow house she and Vronsky have rented, Anna is unable to go out into society; conversely, respectable people are either unable or unwilling to come visit her. Dolly and Kitty, for instance, are hesitant to call upon Anna. Worse yet, the promiscuous Betsy Tverskaya refuses to pay Anna a visit for fear that it will injure her reputation in society circles. From the psychological and emotional standpoint, therefore, Anna is hardly better off than a lowly harlot; she is essentially a "kept" woman, who leads an isolated existence in a luxurious but insulated brothel-like setting, where she is only allowed to have male visitors and is forced to live off her seductive charms. Her compulsive flirting with young men like Levin likewise exposes the mentality and behavior of a courtesan. Even Anna's suicide, when seen as an act of retribution against Vronsky, can be said to parallel the action of the prostitute who enters her profession as a way of seeking vengeance against the man who first precipitated her fall from chastity.

## Radical Measures for Sweet Pleasures: The Need for Abstinence

Although Levin's social activities in Moscow suggest a sybaritic pattern of eating, drinking, and whoring, most readers of *Anna Karenina* are no doubt inclined to dismiss the hero's sensually indulgent behavior in part 7 of the novel as nothing more than a temporary aberration.[77] Even Levin himself admits that Moscow life, where there is "nothing but talk, food, and drink," had made him a bit crazy (19:281). Once he leaves that "immoral Babylon" and returns to the safety and tranquillity of his estate in the Russian countryside in part 8, he is able to regain his moral composure. Upon completing *Anna Karenina*, however, Tolstoy does not seem able to regain his earlier moral equilibrium and to continue abiding by his earlier principles. As he reveals in his *Confession* (1879), the author had now become thoroughly disenchanted with his conventional mode of life, calling into question the basic values and beliefs that had guided his conduct up to this point in his life. Sounding more like Anna than Levin, Tolstoy's narrator in *Confession* claims that once his eyes had at last been opened to all the evil in life and to the meaninglessness of human existence, he could no longer deceive himself: in the face of inevitable death, all of life's charms are revealed as merely a cruel and stupid hoax perpetrated upon man.

To illustrate his point, the narrator recounts an ancient Eastern fable whose central metaphor is gastronomic. Surprised by a wild beast that threatens to kill him, a traveler seeks refuge in a dried-up well, at the bottom of which he sees a dragon with gaping jaws eagerly waiting to devour him. The man grabs hold of a wild bush growing in the cracks of the well and he clings desperately to its branch, even as he sees that two mice (one white, the other black) are gnawing away at it. "Soon the branch will give way and break off, and he will fall into the jaws of the dragon," the narrator explains. "The traveler sees this and knows that he will surely die. But while he is still hanging there, he looks around and sees some drops of honey on the leaves of the bush, and he stretches out his tongue and licks them" (23:14). For Tolstoy, this gastronomic image—of a man licking tasty drops of honey as he awaits certain death—captures perfectly what he now considers our basic existential predicament as human beings:

> Thus I cling to the branch of life, knowing that inevitably the dragon of death is waiting, ready to tear me to pieces; and I cannot understand why this torment has befallen me. I try to suck the honey that once consoled me, but the honey no longer brings me joy. Day and night the black mouse and the white mouse gnaw at the branch to which I cling. I clearly see the dragon, and the honey has lost all its sweetness for me. I see only one thing—the inescapable dragon and the mice—and I cannot avert my eyes from them. This is no fable, this is the naked truth, irrefutable and understood by everyone. (23:14)[78]

Just like his tragic heroine, who finds at the end of *Anna Karenina* that she has lost her appetite for living ("the zest is gone"), Tolstoy now finds that the two drops of honey he had formerly considered so delicious and tasty in his own life—his love for his family and for his writing—have lost all their flavor for him. They no longer console him or bring him any joy: all their sweetness is now gone.[79]

This parable about the human condition, however, seems to apply exclusively to the members of the privileged gentry class, and not to the impoverished peasantry, whose lives, according to the narrator, are marked "more by deprivation and suffering than by pleasures" (23:32). The conditions of luxury, idleness, and epicurean indulgence under which the "parasites" from the upper classes live in late imperial Russia, Tolstoy now realized, make it virtually impossible for them ever to understand the true meaning of life. Already in *Anna Karenina*, Donna Orwin argues, the author had shown his readers that the peasant way of life is the only truly moral way. "As Tolstoy perceived a split between nature and moral goodness," she explains, "he turned from nature to culture—and peasant culture became his new standard for morality."[80] In order to live a moral life, in accord with the ways of God, one must therefore renounce entirely the gentry way of life—as well as the sensual pleasures traditionally associated with it—and adopt instead the

more genuine and morally authentic lifestyle of the hardworking peasants, who have never strayed from their religious faith.

In keeping with his view of gentry epicureanism as a pervasive and
infectious pathological condition, however, Tolstoy advocates more than
simply eating and living like a peasant. He also comes to recognize that
gastronomic appetite and sexual desire are powerful libidinal drives
that cannot be successfully restrained or moderated through sheer
willpower. The physical pleasures of the flesh and the oral delights of
the palate must instead be avoided entirely; they are, by their very nature, debasing, dangerous, and destructive for any human being who
wishes to rise at all above the level of gratifying his or her basic animal
inclinations. Like alcohol, tobacco, and other addictive drugs, food
and sex "stupefy" people: first, they stimulate the desire for sensual
pleasure; second and more important, they blur the demands of moral
conscience and thus deaden the spiritual or divine part of one's human
nature.[81] Levin's ethos of moderation and libidinal restraint with regard to food and sex in *Anna Karenina*, much like his anachronistic
defense of the rural gentry, conventional marriage, and traditional
religious belief, simply could no longer constitute a viable code of
moral behavior for the deeply disillusioned Tolstoy, who emerges
from his spiritual crisis of the late 1870s and early 1880s as a man
fully at war with the physical pleasures that tempt the human body.[82]
He now regards both food and sex as intoxicating and addictive sources
of pleasure whose despotic power over man's will and debilitating effect upon his life call for more radical measures than mere moderation
and restraint.[83]

This shift to more radical measures for dealing with the allure of
physical pleasures appears to have stemmed largely from Tolstoy's
evolving view of the self. In his essay "On Life" (1888), Tolstoy delineated clearly two very different aspects of the self within each human
being: (1) an "animal personality" that strives instinctively for the
gratification of one's egoistic desires (especially the desire for bodily
pleasure), and (2) a "rational consciousness" that aspires toward the
morally good, concerning itself especially with the welfare of others.
As Henrietta Mondry points out, there is a long-standing European
philosophical tradition, particularly within Christianity, of equating
animality with mere physiology. "European thought has separated animals and humans into binary categories, with the animal as the stig-

matized Other," she explains.[84] Tolstoy's model of the self perpetuates these Cartesian dualisms of flesh and spirit, body and soul, animal and divine. The aim of human life, Tolstoy explains in his essay, ought to consist in bringing about "the subservience of our animal body to the law of reason" (26:348): that is, we should be seeking to transcend the physical pleasure and corporeal well-being sought by our lower animal self and striving to practice a compassionate Christian love that places concern for others above concern for oneself. As Nikolay Ivanovich puts it in the play, *Light Shines in the Darkness* (1902), "the flesh inclines to live for itself while the spirit of enlightenment yearns to live for God, for others" (31:129). In one of his religious essays, *The Kingdom of God Is Within You* (1893), Tolstoy acknowledges that divine perfection is an ideal that human beings can strive for but never actually attain (he calls it "the asymptote of human life" [28:77]); yet the striving after divine perfection nonetheless "deflects the direction of man's life from its animal condition" (28:78). According to Tolstoy, we should therefore be seeking in our lives to replace animalistic "desire" (*zhelat'*) with humane "pity" (*zhalet'*), selfish egoistical lust with selfless compassionate love, eros with agape.[85] We should likewise be striving, as the peasant Fyodor had advised Levin in part 8 of *Anna Karenina*, to live not for our belly, but for our soul.[86] As Tolstoy had noted as early as 1852 in a diary entry, "The yearning of the flesh is for personal good, while the yearning of the soul is for the good of others" (46:133–34).

The male protagonists in many of Tolstoy's post-conversion works of fiction—such as Ivan Ilyich (*The Death of Ivan Ilyich*, 1886), Stepan Kasatsky (*Father Sergius*, 1898), Vasily Brekhunov ("Master and Man," 1895), and Dmitry Nekhlyudov (*Resurrection*, 1899)—are thus portrayed at various stages of the process of discovering this divine aspect within themselves, trying to renounce their base animal personalities and coarse sensual appetites.[87] In each case, the addictive quality of those intoxicating vices that characterize the idleness and luxury of upper-class life is shown to have inured these men to what Tolstoy considered to be the debasing animal activities from which they derive sensual pleasure and enjoyment (especially eating and copulating), activities that are condoned, if not implicitly encouraged, by the customs, mores, and values of their social milieu. Tolstoy depicts how the fear of death, which so paralyzes such moral philistines as Ivan Ilyich and Vasily

Brekhunov, suddenly disappears once they renounce the kind of life where the sole object is to attain as much physical comfort, material well-being, and personal enjoyment as possible.

The moral philistinism Tolstoy was condemning through his portrayal of such fictional chacracters was, to his mind, widespread in contemporary society. The social milieu that existed in late-nineteenth-century Russia for aristocrats like Tolstoy was marked by a significant broadening of access to the cultural and material privileges that had traditionally been the exclusive domain of the nobility under earlier tsarist regimes. The Age of Reform, inaugurated with the emancipation of the serfs in 1861, witnessed the launching of a state-sponsored process of rapid industrialization and modernization of the country, where an enlarged public sphere and increased social mobility hastened the growth of a middle class (consisting largely of merchants, professional people, and industrialists) eager to share the newfound affluence. New restaurants and department stores appeared in a growing number of Russian cities, along with other forms of retail sales and popular mass entertainment.[88] With the beginnings of a consumer society finally taking root in Russia, however, there also arose a moral backlash generated by anxieties about the public's increasing desire for—and widespread consumption of—these new commodities. Fears about the negative effects that commercialization might have upon Russian society, especially in the sphere of traditional high culture where "boulevardization" (or vulgarization) of art was purportedly taking place, were expressed mainly by members of the intelligentsia, whose ascetic commitment to public service was seriously offended and even threatened by the philistine pursuit of personal comfort, luxury, leisure, and sensual indulgence they were now observing all around them. Medical and pedagogical literature in Russia from the 1890s and early 1900s, as Laura Engelstein observes, was marked by a preoccupation with male sexual desire, teaching the public the self-restraint and internalized control deemed necessary for fulfilling one's civic responsibility.[89]

Tolstoy was among those educated Russians of his generation who feared the disorder and perhaps even destruction that the desire for pleasure—especially sexual and gastronomical pleasure—could engender. In 1881, when he moved with his family to live in Moscow, Tolstoy volunteered to serve as a census-taker in the capital city's very worst slums; it was an eye-opening experience that many scholars believe radically changed his view of the existing social order. "Town life was a great trial for Tolstoy," writes one of his biographers,

> the crying contrast between city beggars and the insolent opulence of the rich, at every street corner hungry beggars with hands stretched out for alms, and gluttons gorging themselves in brilliantly lighted restaurants, coachmen shivering on their boxes whilst their masters enjoyed the music of the theatres or churches—all this made his heart ache, imbued as he was with the Christian spirit and seeking for its manifestation around him.[90]

Tolstoy's bitter disillusionment with the existing social order found expression in the scathing essay *What Then Must We Do?* (1886), in which the author bemoans the fact that tens of thousands of cold, hungry people are forced to suffer while "We, I and thousands of others like me, overeat ourselves with beefsteaks and sturgeon" (25:190). The seemingly perpetual holiday enjoyed by the materially wealthy (whom Tolstoy refers to disdainfully as the "ever-feasting" ones) was held directly responsible for the abject misery of the poor. Feelings of guilt about enjoying membership in the privileged classes of late imperial Russia prompted Tolstoy to confess that he is a "parasite" and a "louse" (25:246) who feeds upon the labors of others and thus indirectly causes them to die of starvation. In the immediate wake of his census experience in Moscow, Tolstoy endeavored to reform radically his own personal life, ultimately renouncing all superfluous pleasures (hunting, smoking, drinking alcohol, eating meat, indulging in sex, and so on) and dedicating himself to productive labor on behalf of the general welfare of others.

### Fatal Attraction: Carnal Love, Madness, and Murder

At this point in Tolstoy's life, as Aileen Kelly notes, "his intellect presented the process of self-perfection to him as one of self-mastery and self-denial, the control or elimination of instinctive drives in the name of norms and prescriptions advanced by reason and the conscious moral will as answers to the question of how human beings should live."[91] The body's instinctual drives needed to be controlled or eliminated, Tolstoy indicates in the works of fiction he writes after *Anna Karenina*, because the stupefying effects of physical pleasure are so despotic and debilitating. As far as the sex drive is concerned, Tolstoy exposes the addictive and fatal attractions of this carnal pleasure quite graphically in "The Devil" (1889). The author goes to great lengths to point out that the central character, Yevgeny Irtenev, is by no means a pathologically debauched libertine. Like all the other healthy young men of his age, class, and station, Yevgeny has had sexual relations with a variety of women since reaching the age of puberty, but he has engaged in these sexual acts only insofar as they are necessary to maintain his physical health and to keep his mind sharp and clear. "The main thing was that he now felt at ease, tranquil, and cheerful" (27:485), the narrator comments on Yevgeny's emotional state after the hero has had sexual intercourse for the first time with the healthy and alluring Stepanida, whose main function, as a peasant woman living on his estate, is to satisfy the young master's sexual needs. Before long, however, Yevgeny becomes painfully aware that he is no longer free to control his own will (or master his id); he finds, to his great chagrin, that he cannot resist Stepanida's sexual allure, even after his marriage, when his new bride arrives and begins to live with him on his estate. Carnal desire continues to raise its now ugly head and torments this devoted young husband who loves his wife and does not wish to be unfaithful to her. It seems that only death—whether murder or suicide—can free the increasingly disturbed and distressed Yevgeny from the terrible torment of his insatiable appetite for sexual pleasure.

Tolstoy's fear and distrust of erotic desire, as well as his all-out Victorian assault upon the pleasure principle, undoubtedly receive their most explicit artistic expression in his highly controversial novella *The Kreutzer Sonata*, a work of unprecedented sexual honesty and explicitness that seems in large measure to have grown out of the author's own disillusionment with married life.[92] The tale's central character, Pozdnyshev, is a jealous, murderous husband who confesses that his swinish animal nature overpowered his more human side. Like Yevgeny Irtenev and other male members of his social class, Pozdnyshev is taught sexual debauchery at a very young age "for health's sake." The carnal relations he experiences with other women even before courting, marrying, and then living conjugally with his unnamed wife—who is characterized in an early draft of the novella as being "a sweet, tasty morsel" that Pozdnyshev enjoyed eating (27:367)—reinforce his society's view of women not as actual human beings, but as mere objects of male sexual desire. His real crime, as he himself admits, is not so much the murder of his wife as his carnal desire for her. Indeed, one of the important lessons the hero learns as a result of his own unhappy marriage is that true altruism (selfless love of one's neighbor) should replace the kind of selfish, pleasure-seeking sexual love that so intoxicates men. In his attempt to deromanticize his society's idealized notions of love, Pozdnyshev thus manages to strip carnal love of any positive emotional or spiritual value it might have, reducing it to mere sexual passion and a brutish animal lust that dominates, controls, and eventually ruins those who engage in it.[93] The exacerbated concupiscence that results from an unregulated animality, Tolstoy's hero asserts, is not only destructive, but also highly addictive. "I had become what is called a fornicator [*bludnik*]," Pozdnyshev confesses about his purported sexual addiction,

> To be a fornicator is a physical condition like that of a morphine addict, a drunkard, or a smoker. As a morphine addict, a drunkard, or a smoker is no longer a normal human being, so too a man who has known several women for his pleasure is no longer a normal human being but is a man perverted forever, a fornicator. . . . A fornicator may restrain himself, may struggle, but he will never have those pure, simple, clear, brotherly relations with a woman. . . . And so I had become a fornicator and I remained one, and it was this that brought me to ruin. (27:19)

In addition to condemning carnal love as a disgustingly swinish activity, Tolstoy's hero condemns the institution of marriage as a moral fraud perpetrated by the members of his decadent social class: he exposes it as a gentry sham whose main purpose is actually to legitimize man's wanton sexual desires. For Pozdnyshev, marriage turns out to be nothing more than mutual enslavement: men enslave women by enjoying them as sexual objects, while women retaliate by enslaving men through their sexual attractiveness. Wives, consequently, are not essentially different from prostitutes. Pozdnyshev, as one critic observes, is "virtually driven mad by the inevitability of the man's enslavement to carnal desires, woman's enslavement as an object of pleasure for man, and the concomitant abasement of self for both."[94] Wishing to leave no doubt in the reader's mind that the extreme opinions on sexuality, love, and marriage expressed by his deranged protagonist accurately reflect the author's own views, Tolstoy wrote "Afterword to *The Kreutzer Sonata*"(1890), in which he categorically condemns carnal love and asserts that sexual continence, "which constitutes an indispensable condition of human dignity in the unmarried state, is still more essential in the married one" (27:81). Husbands and wives are thus exhorted to live together chastely, like brother and sister, in their conjugal union.

If, as one commentator has suggested, "*Anna Karenina* ends as a 'cry of despair,' with the foundations of marital and family relations eroded," then *The Kreutzer Sonata* may be said to deliver a nearly primal scream that quickly obliterates whatever remaining hopes readers of Tolstoy may have entertained about the viability of romantic love, marriage, and the family.[95] By questioning the validity of marriage as a Christian institution, by appealing for a noncarnal, compassionate form of love in the relationship between the sexes, and by championing chastity and sexual continence as an ideal for young couples (whether single or married), *The Kreutzer Sonata*, as we shall see in the following chapter, launched heated debate in Russia during the 1890s over the question of sexual morality.

For our purposes here, what is particularly illuminating about the highly negative views on carnal love and marriage expressed by Pozdnyshev in *The Kreutzer Sonata*, and later by Tolstoy in "Afterword to *The Kreutzer Sonata*," is how, in both instances, excesses of sexual debauchery are linked directly and causally with gastronomic indulgence. The young males of Pozdnyshev's social class, for instance, are said to be fed the types and quantities of food that inflame their sensuality. "The men of our circle," Pozdnyshev asserts in one variant version of the text, "are kept and fed like breeding stallions" (27:303). The same seems to be true of gentry women, whose main (perhaps even sole) function, we are told, is to bewitch men with their sexual allure. Describing his own wife's animal sexuality, Pozdnyshev says that "she was like a well-fed, harnessed horse, who had been standing for too long and whose bridle has now been removed" (27:47). The libidinal connection between diet and sex, according to Pozdnyshev, is one of direct cause and effect: eating rich and fleshly foods leads directly and ineluctably to the arousal of sexual desire. "You see, our stimulating superfluity of food, together with complete physical idleness, is nothing but the systematic excitation of sexual lust," he explains.

The usual diet of a young peasant lad is bread, kvas, and onions; he keeps alive and is vigorous and healthy; his task is light agricultural work. When he goes to perform railway work, his rations are buckwheat porridge and a pound of meat a day. But he works off that pound of meat during his sixteen hours wheeling around thirty pound barrow-loads, so it's just enough for him. But we, who consume two pounds of meat every day, and game, and fish, and all sorts of warming foods and strong drinks—where does all that go? Into excesses of sensuality. And if it goes there and the safety-valve is open, everything turns out all right; but close the safety-valve a bit, as I closed it temporarily, and at once a stimulus arises which, passing through the prism of our artificial life, expresses itself in utter infatuation, sometimes even platonic. (27:23–24)

Pozdnyshev thus extends into the realm of diet and sexuality the fundamental moral contrast Tolstoy had described in *Confession* between the authentic peasant way of life (based on hard work and simplicity) and the decadent gentry way of life (based on idleness and luxury). The industrious peasant, who subsists on a basic diet of healthy, wholesome foods, works off his sexual energy in exhausting manual labor; the idle rich, meanwhile, who indulge their aristocratic appetite for all sorts of tasty and stimulating foods (served in immoderate amounts), are plagued by sexual excitation and carnal lust.

"The point is that we should rid ourselves of that criminal view on life that says I am to eat and sleep for my own pleasure," Tolstoy writes in *What Then Must We Do?*

And we should adopt that simple and correct view, which the working man grows up with and lives with: that man is before all else a machine which is loaded with food in order to be nourished and that it is therefore shameful, oppressive, and impossible to go on eating without doing any work, that to eat without doing any work is the most shameless, unnatural, and therefore perilous condition, a kind of sin of Sodom. (25:388)

In the decadent bourgeois society depicted in *The Kreutzer Sonata*, it is, of course, this "criminal" aristocratic view of the body as a site for pleasure (rather than the "simple" and "correct" peasant view of the body as a machine designed for labor) that prevails within Pozdnyshev's social milieu. Rich foods, as a result, only further fuel the flames of that middle-class crowd's insatiable desire for sexual pleasure. When he accounts for the origins of his own fatal infatuation with the woman he would later wed, grow to hate, and subsequently murder, Pozdnyshev asserts that his carnal love for her was the result, in large part, of "the excess of food I consumed while living an idle life" (27:24). The direct cause-and-effect connection between gastronomic excess and sexual excitation is reiterated when Pozdnyshev claims that, had he lived in circumstances normal to man, "consuming just enough food to suffice for the work I did," he would not have fallen in love and "none of all this would have happened" (27:24).

In a variant version of *The Kreutzer Sonata* that circulated privately in manuscript form, Pozdnyshev states bluntly, "All of our love affairs and marriages are, for the most part, conditioned by the food we eat" (27:303).[96] In "Afterword to *The Kreutzer Sonata*," Tolstoy would voice a similar sentiment, castigating upper-class parents for raising their children to behave like animals: that is, the children are concerned only with their physical appetites and well-tended bodies. "And in pampered children, as in all sorts of overfed animals," Tolstoy writes, "there is an unnaturally early appearance of an irresistible sensuality, which is the occasion of the terrible sufferings of these children in adolescence." As a consequence, he adds, "the most terrible sexual vices and diseases are the normal condition for children of both sexes, and they often persist even into adulthood" (27:82). In "Afterword," Tolstoy further links food and sex as sinful pleasures: "the attainment of the goal of union with the object of one's love, whether in marriage or outside of marriage, no matter how poeticized that union might be, is a goal unworthy of man, just as is unworthy of man the goal of procuring for oneself sweet and abundant food, which many people imagine to be the highest good" (27:82). In light of the direct causal connection Tolstoy makes between food and sex, it seems not insignificant, therefore, that in *The Kreutzer Sonata*, when Pozdnyshev returns to his home early from his business trip, fully expecting to catch his wife and Trukhachevsky in the act of adultery, he finds them not in the bedroom, engaged in sexual intercourse, but rather in the dining room, where they are finishing a romantic meal together.

## The First Step: *Gluttony, Abstinence, and Fasting*

Given Tolstoy's representation of food in *The Kreutzer Sonata* and in several of his other post-conversion works of fiction as a dangerous stimulant,[97] it should not surprise us terribly to find that among the extreme measures the author comes to advocate late in his life (such as his renunciation of hunting, drinking, smoking, and fornicating) he would also include vegetarianism: that is, the renunciation of meat from one's diet. After all, if the moral and spiritual ideal Tolstoy believed we should all be striving to attain is absolute sexual continence, then it follows that we should avoid eating meat: fleshly food, he came to believe, arouses in us sexual passion and carnal desire.[98] Tolstoy for much of his adult life could be said to fit perfectly the profile of those social and moral heretics who, according to Colin Spenser, find the society they live in to lack moral worth and are thus psychologically drawn to vegetarianism as a way of life.[99] In any event, we know that Tolstoy gave up eating meat during the course of the 1880s, not long after suffering the spiritual crisis recorded in his *Confession*, and he remained a vegetarian throughout the last twenty to twenty-five years of his life.[100]

One of the pro-vegetarian works that made a very strong and favorable impression on Tolstoy was *The Ethics of Diet: A Catena of Authorities Deprecatory of the Practice of Flesh-Eating* (1883) by the British vegetarian, Howard Williams. Tolstoy, who first received a copy of Williams's book from Chertkov in April 1891, arranged to have *The Ethics of Diet* translated into Russian (by his daughters) and agreed to write the preface for this first Russian edition. This preface or introductory essay, which Tolstoy finished a year later, is titled *The First Step* and originally appeared in the journal *Questions of Philosophy and Psychology* in 1892.[101] It constitutes by far Tolstoy's best-known piece of writing on the issue of vegetarianism. Characterized as one of "the most thorough, soul-searching modern treatments of the moral reasons for vegetarianism," this essay is invariably cited whenever Tolstoy's vegetarian beliefs are discussed.[102] *The First Step* consists of two unequal parts: (1) a rather lengthy sermon preaching against the sin of gluttony, and (2) a brief narrative account of a recent visit Tolstoy made to a local abattoir in Tula. It is the second part of the essay especially that helped to establish Tolstoy's reputation as "the father of organized Russian vegetarianism"; it provided an eloquent and compelling indictment of the unjustifiably cruel, violent, and inhumane exploitation of animals necessitated by the widespread use of meat in the human diet.[103]

It is the lengthier first part of the essay, however, that reveals how Tolstoy's initial motivations for becoming a vegetarian were as much ascetic and religious as ethical and humanitarian.[104] Eating fleshly foods is morally wrong, Tolstoy argues in this part, and not only because it perpetuates cruelty and brutal violence to animals. Meat-eating is also to be condemned, he writes, because it "serves only to develop animal feelings, to excite lust, to promote fornication and drunkenness" (29:84). Tolstoy contends, in other words, that a carnal diet stimulates a carnal appetite: that eating animal food arouses animal passions. He argues, in fact, that one should abstain from eating not just meat, but any rich and tasty food item from which one might conceivably derive gustatory enjoyment. After all, gastronomic pleasure, in Tolstoy's chain of reasoning, leads directly and ineluctably to sexual pleasure. Accordingly, he inveighs strongly in this essay against the sin of gluttony (overeating) and he encourages his readers to practice abstinence and fasting, rather than mere moderation, in matters concerning food and drink.

In the opening sections of *The First Step*, where he refers to some of the ancient Greek philosophers as well as to the early church fathers, Tolstoy asserts that it is impossible for one to lead a good and moral life—whether as a Christian or as a pagan—unless one begins with abstinence (*vozderzhanie*) and self-abnegation (*samootrechenie*). Well in advance of Michel Foucault's argument in his *History of Sexuality* (1984), Tolstoy thus draws our attention to the direct continuities that exist between the first Christian doctrines on the body and the moral philosophy of classical antiquity. But where Foucault conceptualizes sexuality in ancient Greece as part of a series of dietetic practices—a "technique of the self," as he puts it—that turned desire into a matter of the proper use of pleasure, Tolstoy seeks instead to subordinate desire to a very rigid moral code.[105] The indispensable "first step" up the ladder of moral virtues, Tolstoy writes, involves the renunciation of our basic physical appetites and our liberation from the animal lusts that plague us.

Although the abstract language Tolstoy employs in the early part of this essay might lead one to think that he is speaking about our sexual appetite and our lust for the pleasures of the flesh, it soon becomes clear that the author has in mind mainly our gastronomical appetite and our oral lust for the pleasures of the palate. When he finally does specify the three basic "lusts" (*pokhoti*) that torment human beings, Tolstoy identifies them as "gluttony, idleness, and carnal love" (29:73–74). Not unlike Pozdnyshev in *The Kreutzer Sonata*, Tolstoy in his essay on vegetarianism posits a direct cause-and-effect link between food and sex. "The gluttonous person is not equipped to struggle against laziness," he writes, "nor will the gluttonous and idle person ever be strong enough to struggle against sexual lust. Therefore, according to all moral teachings, the striving for abstinence commences with the struggle against the lust of gluttony; it commences with fasting" (29:73–74). In the same way that the first condition for a morally good life is abstinence, Tolstoy explains, "the first condition for a life of abstinence is fasting" (29:74). Just as gluttony is the first sign of a morally bad life, so is fasting "the essential condition for a good life" (29:74).

What lends particular urgency to this need to fast, according to Tolstoy, is the fact that the main interest of the vast majority of people in society is to satisfy their craving for food.[106] "From the poorest to the wealthiest levels of society," he writes, "gluttony is, I think, the primary aim, the chief pleasure of our life" (29:74). Even destitute working-class people, Tolstoy sadly notes, seek to follow the example of the decadent upper classes; they too seek to acquire "the tastiest and sweetest foods, and to eat and drink as much as they can" (29:74).[107] In a letter he wrote during this same period, Tolstoy explained to a correspondent: "I think that one of the principal sins, the most widespread and perhaps even the fundamental sin, the one out of which a whole series of other sins develop, is gluttony [*obzhorstvo*]—gourmandism [*gortano*] and worship of the belly [*chrevobesie*]—the desire to eat well, to eat at length, and to eat as much as possible." "I also think," he adds, "that the lust for food [*pishchevaia pokhot'*] is closely tied to sexual lust [*polovoiu pokhot*] and serves as its basis" (65:292).

Anton Chekhov, who openly acknowledged that Tolstoy's moral philosophy had informed his own thinking for a number of years, seems to have recognized this ascetic connection Tolstoy makes between abstinence from sex and abstinence from fleshly food. By way of explaining his eventual disenchantment with the life-denying morality of Tolstoyism, Chekhov observed that he personally found "there is more love for mankind in electricity and steam than in chastity and abstention from eating meat."[108] It is precisely this commitment to a rigid brand of Christian asceticism—more than any humane compassion he may have felt for creatures from the animal kingdom—that initially prompted Tolstoy to adopt a vegetarian diet. Although *The First Step* was written as a preface to a book on vegetarianism, it turns out that Tolstoy's introductory essay is hardly about vegetarianism at all. It is essentially a moral tract that warns about the dangers of gluttony and preaches the need to practice abstinence.[109] "I will try to write it [*The First Step*] in the way it seems to me that it ought to be written and in the way that I want to write it," Tolstoy explains to Chertkov in a letter of June 23, 1891, "not about vegetarianism, but about gluttony" (87:98). And this is exactly the way that Tolstoy himself refers to the essay—as a moral tract about gluttony and abstinence—in his diary and correspondence during the summer of 1891 while he was fully engaged in writing *The First Step*.[110] It is thus his condemnation of gluttony and his advocacy of abstinence, rather than his support of vegetarianism, that served as his primary concern and motivation in writing the essay. Much like Vladimir Solovyov, who in his essay "On Fasting" conceives of abstinence (*vozderzhanie*) in its widest possible sense as transcendence of our base animal nature and the egoistic urges of what he refers to as our "sensual soul" (*chuvstvennaia dusha*), Tolstoy seems to understand vegetarianism primarily as one of the means of diminishing our lustful appetite for the sensual pleasures of the flesh.[111]

"What is wrong and therefore impoverished in the relationship between the sexes," Tolstoy wrote to a correspondent in March 1890, "is due to the view shared by people of our class that the sexual relationship is a source of pleasure" (65:61). The only effective way to change this view and succeed in curbing our voracious sexual appetite, Tolstoy suggests in his "Afterword to *The Kreutzer Sonata*," is to eliminate any pleasure we might possibly derive from the act of sexual intercourse. Only in this way can we succeed in our efforts to make ourselves what he elsewhere calls voluntary "eunuchs" and thus conquer our carnal lust.[112] The same anti-hedonistic, anti-epicurean reasoning seems to inform the masochistic solution Tolstoy advances in *The First Step* for curbing our basic animal craving for food: that is, one should strive as much as possible to remove all the pleasure out of the act of eating.[113] As long as a person continues to enjoy the pleasure that eating provides, Tolstoy maintains, there can be no limit to the increase of the desire or appetite for gustatory pleasure. One can keep the lust for tasty food under control, he notes, only when one does not eat except in obedience to necessity. "The satisfaction of a need has limits," he writes, "but pleasure does not have any limits. For the satisfaction of one's needs, it is necessary and sufficient to eat bread, kasha, and rice. While for the augmentation of pleasure, there is no end to the flavorings and seasonings" (29:77). In the lengthy passage that ensues, Tolstoy proceeds to illustrate in considerable detail how, if we continue to eat rich and spicy comestibles, our appetite for gustatory pleasure will never be satisfied but will instead keep growing exponentially: that is, we will be seduced into piling one more delicious entrée on top of another at a meal.[114] Because eating rich and tasty foods stimulates our desire for additional physical pleasures (both gastronomical and sexual), Tolstoy's solution is thus for us to practice gastronomic abstinence by striving as much as possible to make "unpalatable" the pleasures of the palate, to make "disgusting" the delights of the stomach. Our main purpose in eating, after all, ought to be to provide healthy nourishment for the body, not to derive pleasure, enjoyment, or stimulation for our taste buds and digestive tract. Nourishment, rather than gustation, ought to be the primary physiological aim of the activity of eating, and a sort of gastronomic "chastity" ought to be the spiritual ideal toward which we strive in matters concerning the palate.[115] Food addiction, like sexual addiction, thus requires that we adopt austere measures of regulation over what we ingest into the body.

After spending more than twenty pages of this twenty-eight-page essay sermonizing about the sin of gluttony and the virtue of abstinence, Tolstoy turns at last to the topic of vegetarianism per se. He mentions how reading Williams's *The Ethics of Diet* implanted in him the desire to go visit a slaughterhouse in order to see firsthand what it was that propelled the vegetarian movement: "in order to see with my own eyes the point of the matter when people speak about vegetarianism" (29:78). For the next five pages Tolstoy switches from his homiletic mode of discourse as a moral preacher to his incomparable narrative style as a verbal artist, depicting for the reader in gruesome naturalistic detail the manner in which innocent, suffering cattle are brutally slaughtered at the modern abattoir in Tula. Finally, on the last two pages of the essay, Tolstoy directly addresses the issue of the fledgling vegetarian movement. "What is it that I wish to say? That for people to be moral they need to stop eating meat?" the author asks rhetorically.

"Not at all," he continues. "I simply wished to say that for a good life a certain sequence of good actions is necessary" (29:84). The indispensable "first step" in this sequence of steps leading to the morally good life, he reiterates, is abstinence from meat:

> If he earnestly and sincerely strives to lead a good life, the first thing that a man will abstain from, while fasting, will always be the use of animal food, because, not to mention the arousal of passions produced by the food, its use is directly immoral since it necessitates killing, an act that is repugnant to moral sensibility, and it is provoked only by avarice and the desire for gourmandism. (29:84)

As we see, even here Tolstoy condemns the use of fleshly food in one's diet on ascetic as well as humanitarian grounds: eating meat is wrong not merely because it involves the slaughter of animals, but also because it stimulates in human beings their base animal personalities and excites their sinful sexual lust. "It was the moral principle—the constant striving to perfect oneself as a member of mankind, as a summons to humanity to strive toward self-perfection," Vladimir Porudominsky observes, "that was the main impetus behind Tolstoy's conversion to vegetarianism."[116]

## Christian Physiology: Food Reform as Male Purity Crusade

Tolstoy's belief that diet can help shape sexual morality (by diminishing the intensity of our carnal urges) echoes the view promulgated earlier in the nineteenth century by key figures in the American health reform movement, men such as Sylvester Graham, William Alcott, and John Harvey Kellogg—all of whom warned of the highly disturbing influence, and even debilitating effect, that meat and other rich food products have upon the male sexual organs. Vegetarianism was regarded by these American health reformers, much as it was by Tolstoy, mainly as a cure for what they considered to be dangerously uncontrollable male libido: the absence of meat in one's diet was promoted as a way of bringing about male sexual abstinence. In his history of the American health reform movement, Whorton refers to Graham, Alcott, Kellogg, and other purity advocates in the United States from this period as "Christian physiologists," as they sought to promote godliness by teaching their followers how to suppress their animal appetites and sexual passions mainly through a strict regimen of diet, exercise, and hygiene.[117] These health reformers are generally regarded as founders of "the male purity movement" in nineteenth-century America because their Victorian fears about male orgasm and their obsessive concern with sexual purity led them to advocate behavioral reforms that involved bodily as well as social control.[118] Although Tolstoy appears not to have been personally acquainted with the writings of American health reformers such as Alcott, Graham or Kellogg (other than through the brief biographical sketches provided in Williams's *The Ethics of Diet*) and although his argument for converting to a vegetarian diet may well lack the scientific grounding and coherence of the physiological rationale they provided, he too associates abstinence from animal food very closely with abstinence from sexual activity.[119]

Tolstoy shares another important trait with these purity crusaders from nineteenth-century America: a disdain for the civilizing process of socioeconomic modernization. All four of these men—Graham, Alcott, Kellogg, and Tolstoy—developed their rather eccentric views on diet and chastity during a period in the history of their respective societies when the pressures and artificial conditions of modern civilized life made the public extremely apprehensive about human sexuality. Graham's food theories, as Nissenbaum has convincingly argued, emerged during the Jacksonian era largely as a way to deny the power of the new values of the capitalist marketplace, which was rapidly replacing the traditional family household as the primary locus for economic activity and social relationships in early-nineteenth-century America.[120] The traditional homemade bread baked with unadulterated whole wheat flour that Graham championed so passionately in his writings (what came to be known as "Graham bread") was itself mostly a symbolic attempt to protest against the growing commercialization of grain agriculture in the United States during a period of vanishing economic self-sufficiency. "The transformation of American sexual ideology and behavior," Jayme Sokolow points out, "coincided with the modernization process. During the nineteenth century, urbanization, commercialization, industrialization, and increased geographical mobility made antebellum America appear disorderly and dangerous to many reformers."[121]

Later in the century Dr. Kellogg would likewise crusade against the artificial conditions and enervating effects of urban life in modern-day America, urging the well-to-do patrons at his Battle Creek Sanitarium not only to adopt a more natural diet, but also to incorporate a daily regimen of exercise into their largely sedentary and sybaritic lives. "Kellogg's advocacy of extreme self-denial," Sokolow writes, "was related to his vision of the city, the center of luxury, corruption, and sexual indulgence. His books and sanitarium were designed to counteract urban civilization by re-creating rural life and habits, which were synonymous with natural health and sexual restraint."[122] In the case of Tolstoy, his countrymen only began to voice their anxieties about human sexuality and the perceived decline of morality in Russian society somewhat later in the century, when the modernizing process accelerated sharply following the reforms of Alexander II. As recent studies devoted to this topic have shown, the debate on sexual morality in Russia intensified greatly during the 1890s and 1900s, when public discourse began to occupy itself with such controversial social and moral issues as rape, divorce, abortion, venereal disease, prostitution, homosexuality, and masturbation.[123] Tolstoy's own literary output during this period—works such as "The Devil," *Father Sergius*, and *Resurrection*—reflect this general anxiety over male sexual desire felt within Russian society at the turn of the century, when the ideology of extreme sexual moderation came to the fore.[124] As Laura Engelstein notes, "the Russian adoption of a (modified) Victorianism coincided with the revolt against Victorianism in the West."[125] Tolstoy, in short, was living during a time in Russian cultural history when he was certainly not alone in experiencing (and voicing) deep anxieties about the deleterious impact a modern urban environment was having upon the moral and spiritual health of his countrymen.

## Tolstoy's Ethics of Diet: Health, Hunger, and Hypocrisy

Understood within the context of Tolstoy's ongoing battle against the body (and specifically his campaign against the physical pleasures that tempt the body), *The First Step*, as we have seen, reads less like the "Bible of vegetarianism" his Tolstoyan followers made it out to be, than as a moral diatribe against epicureanism in general and gluttony in particular. In his *Confession* Tolstoy had observed that most people of his social class pursue an epicurean lifestyle as a means of escaping the realization that human life is meaningless. A little more than a decade later, in *The First Step*, he details the gentry's obsession with gastronomic excess—their daily pattern of gluttony—that constitutes, as he put it, "the first sign of a bad life" (29:74). "The educated classes," he writes, "imagine that happiness and health (as medical men assure them, stating that the most expensive food, meat, is the healthiest) reside in eating savory, nourishing, easily digestible food" (29:74–75).[126] Indeed, the wealthy may pretend that lofty interests and elevated concerns mainly occupy their attention, but all this is really a sham, according to Tolstoy:

> All this occupies them in the intervals of business, real business, between lunch and dinner, while their stomachs are full and it is impossible for them to eat any more. The one real, living interest for the majority of both men and women is eating food, especially after the first years of youth: How to eat? What to eat? When? Where? (29:75)

Two years earlier, in his play, *The Fruits of Enlightenment* (1889), Tolstoy—through the members of the Zvezdintsev family—had savagely satirized the gluttony of the Russian gentry. According to the peasant cook for the Zvezdintsevs, these indolent aristocrats are expert at "stuffing themselves" with all sorts of rich and tasty comestibles. "They don't just sit down, eat, cross themselves, and then get up," she explains to a fellow peasant:

> They eat nonstop. Scarcely do they get their eyes open in the morning, God bless, then right away comes the samovar, tea, coffee, and hot shchicolate. As soon as they have drunk up two samovars, then it's "put on a third." And then there's breakfast, and then it's dinner, and then there's coffee again. As soon as they've stuffed themselves, then they have tea again. Then they're eating little snacks: sweets and jam, and there's no end to it. Even lying in bed they're still eating! (27:157–58)

When the young ladies in the family have eaten too many sweets, the servants are ordered to retrieve sauerkraut from the larder to be used as a purgative. "As soon as there is a little room [in their stomach]," explains the cook, "they are at it again" (27:163). Even the family's pet dog is indulged and pampered in the epicurean fashion characteristic of the gentry: the cook must prepare a special cutlet to be served to her at dinnertime. Tolstoy's play strongly suggests that the Zvezdintsevs—like many other gentry families in Russia—have quite literally "gone mad with fat" (*besilis' s zhirom*): that is, they have become spoiled and corrupt as a result of living a pampered life of luxury, idleness, and comfort.[127]

In his own life, Tolstoy had by now long rejected the obscene and insane practice of epicureanism. In *What Then Must We Do?* Tolstoy had roundly condemned the idle aristocratic life of luxury and comfort that he and his family had long enjoyed, identifying it synecdochically with the excessive amounts of rich foods they consumed at their five-course meals. In addition to the poverty and misery this opulent lifestyle caused for others, the rich foods served at their superfluous meals ruined gentry stomachs by whetting an appetite not for truly nutritious fare, but rather for the types of food that only further irritate one's digestive system. In an angry outburst aimed against the new culture of modern conveniences, pleasantries, and artificial cures that was gaining wide currency in Russia, Tolstoy points to a recent advertisement he had seen for stomach powders designed for the rich, a product whose name, *Blessings for the Poor*, merely confirms his view that only the poor people in Russia (that is, the peasants) have proper digestion, while the rich need help (25:393). Rather than continue to eat like an aristocrat himself, Tolstoy sought instead to follow a bland and modest vegetarian diet of simple, largely unappetizing foods (mainly basic peasant fare such as kasha and cabbage soup) that would sufficiently nourish his body while not pleasuring it or arousing its sensual appetites unnecessarily. In his quest to remove all the pleasure out of the consumption of food and the practice of sex, Tolstoy strove to follow what he perceived to be the admirable example of the Russian peasant, adopting and then maintaining throughout the remainder of his life a highly "functional," utilitarian approach toward these two most basic of the physical appetites. "Instead of the sweet, fatty, refined, complex, and spicy foods to which I used to be attracted," Tolstoy proudly declares in 1884,, "the simplest foods—cabbage soup, oatmeal porridge, black bread, and tea—have now become what I need and enjoy most of all" (25:384). Like the traditional Russian peasant, Tolstoy came to view food mainly as a source of fuel for the body, rather than as a source of pleasure for the senses.

One culinary barometer that tracks this shift in conceptualization and perspective during his lifetime is provided by Tolstoy's changing attitude toward Ankovsky pie. Named after the Swedish doctor (Professor Anke) who first provided the Tolstoys with the recipe, this sweet confection was for many years a favorite dessert in the Tolstoy home, a culinary treat that Lev Nikolaevich, it seems, was particularly fond of. Ankovsky pie, in the words of one critic, served as "an indispensable attribute of the festive table in the Tolstoy household" and became for Tolstoy himself "a symbol of a life put right and sanctified once and for all."[128] After his spiritual conversion, however, and by the time he wrote *The First Step*, Ankovsky pie, according to one frequent visitor to Yasnaya Polyana (his brother-in-law, S. A. Behrs), had become a term Tolstoy now pronounced in a sarcastic tone to express "his disapproval of our undue hankering after comfort and luxury."[129] Porudominsky explains the demise of Ankovsky pie later in Tolstoy's life as follows: "Whereas earlier it signified for Lev Nikolaevich the joyful stability of the family hearth, it became for him an image of an earlier stagnant, idle, and unjust way of life, one that was incompatible with the goals and ideals which he would like to serve."[130] Tolstoy's resolve to live simply, chastely, and austerely, "in God's way" (as the peasant Fyodor had advised Levin in part 8 of *Anna Karenina*), thus found itself in direct conflict with Ankovsky pie and all that it came to represent for his aristocratic family, as is comically illustrated in the following anecdote related by S. A. Behrs: After helping Lev Nikolaevich sweep out his upstairs study one day, Behrs was seen standing on the balcony with his host, both of them with brooms in hand, by his younger sister, who teased him about apparently having converted at last to Tolstoyism. Seeking good-naturedly to extend the joke, Tolstoy proceeded to make the sign of the cross over this new "convert" to his radical brand of Christianity and, raising his eyes up toward the heavens, he solemnly asked Behrs: "Dost thou renounce Ankovsky pie and all its evil works?"[131]

This anti-epicurean orientation, according to Tolstoy, ought to apply not just in our diet, but also in our appreciation of art. Tolstoy's all-out Victorian attack upon the pleasure principle in connection with both sex (*The Kreutzer Sonata*) and food (*The First Step*) enters the realm of aesthetics when, in his essay *What is Art?* (1896), he challenges the notion that "taste" can ever serve as the arbiter of what constitutes good art. Any theory that defines art on the basis of the pleasure derived from an aesthetic object will necessarily be a false one, he argues. To substantiate this claim, Tolstoy makes use of the following gastronomic analogy:

> If we were to analyze the question of food, it would not occur to anyone to see the importance of food in the pleasure that we receive from eating it. Everyone understands that the satisfaction of our taste can in no way serve as the basis for our determination of the merits of food, and that we therefore have no right to suppose that the dinners with cayenne pepper, Limburger cheese, alcohol, and so on, to which we are accustomed and which please us, constitute the very best human food. . . . To see the aim and purpose of art in the pleasure we get from it is like assuming . . . that the purpose and aim of food consist in the pleasure derived from consuming it." (30:60–61)

"People came to understand that the meaning of food resides in the nourishment of the body only when they ceased to consider that the aim of that activity is pleasure," Tolstoy continues. "And the same is true with regard to art. People will come to understand the meaning of art only when they cease to consider that the aim of that activity is beauty, that is, pleasure" (30:61). In art as in life, therefore, one must judge the quality of an object not in terms of the pleasure it may give, but rather of the nutritive purpose—moral or physiological—that it serves.[132] Counterfeit art, like carnal love and rich foods, succeeds only in "stupefying" people; it debilitates their moral constitution and weakens their spiritual strength. In his later years, Tolstoy quite frequently drew analogies between art and food, using gastronomic tropes to describe the processes of intellectual, moral, or spiritual ingestion. "We eat sauces, meat, sugar, sweets—we overeat and think nothing of it. It doesn't even occur to us that it's bad," he writes in 1890. "And yet catarrh of the stomach is an epidemic ailment of our way of life. Isn't the same true of sweet aesthetic food—poems, novels, sonatas, operas, romances, paintings, statues? The same catarrh of the brain. The inability to digest or even to take wholesome food, and the result—death" (51:45).[133] In the second of his "Three Parables" (1895), meanwhile, Tolstoy uses an extended metaphor about adulterated food to convey his point about the counterfeit nature of the art and science he had been "fed" in his day (31:60–62).[134]

Ironically, however, Tolstoy's renunciation of tasty dishes and his strict adherence to a bland vegetarian diet of simple peasant foods (which he claimed never consciously to have betrayed during his later years and which he alleged never cost him any effort or deprivation) coincided almost exactly with the exacerbation of the chronic digestive problems that had plagued him since 1865.[135] Although Tolstoy boasted about the inexpensive yet nutritious meatless diet he followed, his wife complained of the burden such a special diet placed upon her as a homemaker (by forcing her to have two menus prepared for every meal instead of just one). She also lamented that this "abominable" and "senseless" diet was having quite a ruinous effect upon her husband's once robust health.[136] In Sophia's opinion, Lev's vegetarian diet did not give him nearly enough nourishment; indeed, she believed that it was directly responsible for his rapidly deteriorating physical condition and his constant bouts with digestive ailments (the doctors diagnosed him in the 1880s as having severe catarrh of the stomach). Moreover, she deplored what might be termed his "misdemeanors at table" (*zastol'nye prostupki*): the immoderate portions he ate, the incompatible combinations of dishes he selected, and the haste with which he ate those large servings. "Again Lev Nikolaevich is complaining about his stomach: heartburn, headache, sluggishness," she writes in her diary on February 24, 1898:

> Today at dinner I watched with horror as he ate: to start with he had some pickled mushrooms (milk-agarics), all glued together from being frozen, then four large buckwheat toasts with soup, and some fermented kvass, and some black bread. And all of this in enormous quantities.[137]

"An old man of sixty-nine," she objected, "really shouldn't eat this sort of food, which just bloats him up and doesn't give him any nourishment at all!" (1:359).[138] In accord with Tolstoy's utilitarian approach to food, the purpose in following a rather bland vegetarian diet, of course, was to obtain the basic nutritional value of food rather than any pleasing taste. Such an austere, unappetizing diet was also designed to reduce sexual appetite. His wife's testimony, however, asserts that, in strictly alimentary and physiological terms at least, his "functional" diet had proved after all to be quite "dysfunctional."[139]

In light of what we know today about the nutritional benefits of a vegetarian diet (not to mention Tolstoy's relative longevity), Sophia's concern for her husband's health may seem rather misplaced. Indeed, Lev's vegetarianism was repellent to her mainly because it was paradigmatic of what she considered the many eccentric ideas her husband had begun to entertain after his midlife crisis, when he seemed to have abandoned nearly all of his earlier values, beliefs, and practices. "Sofia Andreevna's arguments with her husband about food issues possess a culinary character only in outward appearance," explains Porudominsky. "These were actually arguments about [competing] worldviews."[140] Tolstoy's abandonment of a normal diet, therefore, struck his wife as but another behavioral eccentricity she could only hope would prove short-lived. "I should be happy to see him healthy again—instead of ruining his stomach with all this (in the doctor's words) harmful food," she noted sadly in 1891. "I should be happy to see him an artist again—instead of writing sermons which masquerade as articles. I should be happy to see him affectionate, attentive, and kind again—instead of this crude sensuality, followed by indifference" (1:192–93).

As this diary entry strongly suggests, Sophia considered her husband's advocacy of vegetarianism, much like his sexual ideal of celibacy and his religious ideal of brotherly love, not merely counterproductive; to her mind, it was also patently hypocritical. Indeed, she seemed to derive special pleasure out of noting those occasions when the "saint" and "prophet" of Yasnaya Polyana failed—with respect to food and sex— to practice what he preached. With regard to sex, Sophia records in her diary how the physical side of love continued to be inordinately important to her elderly husband, who seems to have remained quite concupiscent even though he had already passed the age of sixty-five and was publicly preaching absolute marital chastity.[141] "If only those who read *The Kreutzer Sonata* with such reverence could catch a glance of the voluptuous life he leads, and realized that it was only this that made him happy and good-natured," she wrote in 1891 following one of her husband's sudden outbursts of sexual passion, "then they would cast their deity down from the pedestal on which they have placed him!" (1:163).[142] Sophia likewise questioned the authenticity of his Christian love, as it was practiced by a man who seemed to show so little compassion for the members of his own family—especially his long-suffering wife. "Oh, this sham Christianity, founded on malice toward those closest to you, instead of simple kindness and honest, fearless candor," she exclaimed angrily amid all the legal wrangling over her husband's will and the personal quarrels that went on with Chertkov and other of Tolstoy's followers (whom she called the "dark people") in the period just prior to his death (2:152).

This purported sexual and religious hypocrisy on her husband's part, Sophia insisted, was matched by his gastronomic insincerity as well. Although in his essayistic writings he preached moderation in food consumption, abstinence from meat, and simplicity as well as blandness in diet, Tolstoy apparently continued in his private life to succumb to the sinful temptations presented by the pleasures of the table.[143] In her diary, where she chronicles the persistent digestive troubles Tolstoy experienced during the last part of his life, Sophia repeatedly upbraids her husband for eating enormous amounts of food—often at the wrong time of day and usually on a weak stomach. "Just before he left, he greedily gulped down some treats we had purchased for little Andryusha's sixth birthday—some dumplings, grapes, a pear and some chocolates," she writes soon after her husband's recovery from a bout with stomach pain in December 1901. "And now look what happens. The moment he gets a little better he undoes it all with his intemperate appetite and excessive activity" (2:30). On more than one occasion Sophia claimed that she had to take steps to guard against her husband upsetting his stomach through bouts of overeating and unleashing his generally immoderate eating habits. As was true with so many other aspects of his life, Tolstoy's indulgent gastronomic behavior in the privacy of his own home seemed to her greatly at variance with the rigid principles of abstinence he preached in public. Even during the final year of his life, she would lament the glaring discrepancy she saw between his ethical tenets on the one hand and his actual conduct on the other.

> How much more spiritually inclined he was a few years ago! How sincerely he aspired to live simply, to sacrifice all luxuries, and to be good, honest, and open; to be sublimely, spiritually inclined! Now he enjoys himself quite openly, loves good food, a good horse, cards, music, chess, cheerful company, and having hundreds of photographs taken of himself. (2:190)

Her husband's attempt to improve himself morally and spiritually, through a rigorous brand of Christian asceticism, thus seemed undermined by what she considered the relatively sybaritic lifestyle he continued to maintain on his gentry estate. In her opinion, his radical "diet" had turned out to be detrimental not only for his physical health, but for his moral and spiritual health as well.[144]

## Gastronomic Inequities and the Guilt-Ridden Aristocrat

Sophia's perspective on Tolstoy's dietary practices—and, indeed, on his radical Christian beliefs in general—is not without bias, of course. Yet Tolstoy himself confessed on a number of occasions during his post-conversion years to being deeply troubled by the deep chasm that existed between the luxurious way of life he and his aristocratic family enjoyed at Yasnaya Polyana and the terrible hunger, poverty, and deprivation that characterized the life of the peasants who lived nearby. As early as 1879, in his *Confession*, Tolstoy pointed out that he, like the other "parasites" of his social class, was guilty of "devouring the fruits of the peasants' labor" (23:5). And in *The Kingdom of God Is Within You* he noted that humankind is divided into two very separate castes: "one, which labors, is oppressed, in need, in suffering, and the other, idle, oppressing, and living in luxury and pleasure" (28:91). The whole gentry life of luxury, Tolstoy observed, is nothing other than unjust exploitation and parasitism. "Thus they live," he writes disdainfully, "devouring each day for their pleasures hundreds and thousands of workdays of the exhausted laborers" (28:269).

As we have seen, Tolstoy's growing social consciousness developed even further as a result of his experience as a participant in the Moscow census conducted in 1881–82. As he later recorded in his essay *What Then Must We Do?* Tolstoy was appalled by the miserable living conditions—the abject poverty, hunger, disease, and so on—he observed when visiting working-class neighborhoods and city slums in the capital. The full extent of the human misery he witnessed there—as well as the ultimate complicity and culpability he felt in helping to cause it—was painfully brought home to him each day when he returned in the evenings to enjoy the luxurious five-course meals served in his Moscow house:

> Upon seeing this hunger, cold, and degradation suffered by thousands of people, I understood—not with my mind and my heart alone, but with my entire being—that the existence of tens of thousands of such people in Moscow at the same time when I, along with

thousands of others, gorge myself with steak filets and sturgeon . . . is a crime, a crime that is committed not just once, but is constantly being committed, and that I, with my luxury, not only tolerate this crime, but directly participate in it. (25:190)

He would continue to feel guilty about his complicity, Tolstoy added, "as long as I will have an excessive amount of food to eat while another has none at all" (25:190). Tolstoy was so disgusted and distressed by what he witnessed in the city, in fact, that he claimed that "all those joys of a life of luxury, which used to seem like joys to me before, now caused me suffering" (25:191). It was particularly painful for Tolstoy to ob-serve, for instance, how a poor twelve-year-old orphan named Seryo-zha, whom he had placed in his own kitchen, was soon corrupted by the lazy, indulgent lifestyle he observed in the Tolstoy household, espe-cially among the author's children, who "gorged themselves on tasty, fatty, and sweet foods" and "threw to their dogs the kind of food which constituted a tasty delicacy for this young boy" (25:214). He even re-ferred to his youngest son as a "fatted calf," alluding to the upper-class practice of overfeeding and gastronomically indulging their children.[145]

For Tolstoy, the socioeconomic inequity that lay at the basis of the entire class structure in Russia gave rise to this sharp division between the wealth of the upper classes and the poverty of the lower classes, a contrast that for him repeatedly found expression in gastronomic terms: food came to serve in his writings as one of the chief measures of a life lived either rightly or wrongly. The idle, luxurious life of the aristocratic Tolstoy family was thus frequently emblematized by what he considered the excessive gorging that went on at their dinner table, where a large number of relatives, friends, and guests would regularly sit down to a veritable orgy of eating and drinking. Alongside all this shameless feasting, meanwhile, there lived hungry, ill-clad servants who were oppressed by the endless toil required to feed these comfort-able social parasites. "I had no dinner," Tolstoy records in his diary in April 1910, "I felt a tormenting anguish from the awareness of the vile-ness of my life among people who are working so that they can just barely save themselves from a cold, hungry death, save themselves and their families. Yesterday there were fifteen people gorging themselves with pancakes, while five or six domestics were running about, barely managing to prepare and then serve the fodder" (58:37).[146]

In addition, as a result of his volunteer work with famine relief in the early 1890s, during which time he helped to set up free food kitchens in various parts of the country, Tolstoy became well aware of the terrible hunger that afflicted thousands of peasants daily throughout Russia. Despite the charitable relief efforts he and some other members of his privileged class undertook to help feed these starving people, Tolstoy realized full well that in socioeconomic terms, as he put it, "we live by devouring the labors of thousands of people" (68:244).[147] By participating in the perpetual holiday, the incessant Lucullan "orgy" that was being lived each day by the ever-feasting members of Russia's privileged class, Tolstoy felt that he and his family were guilty of leading the kind of life that "takes bread and labor away from people who are tormented by work" (25:312). "The common people are starving," Tolstoy reasoned, "because we are excessively sated" (29:106). As one of his biographers has observed, Tolstoy "reached the conclusion that only a radical change in the whole social order could abolish the dreadful, bitter, and savage poverty created by the opulent and idle life of the privileged classes."[148] It is the duty of enlightened people, when looking at the miserable life of the common folk, to remove the blinders, the ardent conscientious objector Boris proclaims in *The Light Shines in Darkness*, "so as to comprehend the connection between their sufferings and our pleasures" (31:148).

Tolstoy's feelings of shame and embarrassment at the wide disparity between rich and poor in his country were only exacerbated, therefore, by the knowledge that he himself continued to succumb at times to the gastronomic indulgence he condemned so roundly in the Russian gentry.[149] Indeed, the shame and embarrassment were intensified in light of Tolstoy's well-publicized views on abstinence, fasting, and diet. "I am sensual and I lead an idle, well-fed life," he reproaches himself in a letter to Chertkov in 1884 (85:80). As late as 1908 he would still find himself unable to keep from drinking excessive amounts of coffee: "Always too much—I can't restrain myself" (56:110). In the secret diary that he began to keep in 1908, Tolstoy would even admit that Sophia was right to taunt him about eating asparagus on the sly while preaching culinary simplicity (56:173). Meanwhile, in one of the more telling entries in her diary, Sophia expresses the torment she felt, while reading drafts of *Resurrection*, by the idea that her husband, already an old man of seventy, should describe with such extraordinary gusto, "like a gastronome savoring some particularly delicious piece of food," the scenes of carnality between the chambermaid and the officer depicted in Tolstoy's final novel (3:81). While food and sex may well have become socially, morally, and spiritually unpalatable for Tolstoy after his conversion, Sophia's testimony and his own writings suggest that these objects of desire had lost few of their sensual charms and little of their physical attraction for the puritanical old apostle of Yasnaya Polyana.[150] "All life is a struggle between the flesh and the spirit," Tolstoy had written in 1895, "and gradually the spirit triumphs over the flesh" (52:26). Such existential optimism is tempered, however, by the more candid remark he reportedly made to Gorky: "The flesh ought to be a well-trained dog for the soul, running wherever the soul sends it. But just look at us, how do we live? The flesh rushes about and acts unruly, while the soul follows after it helpless and pitiful."[151] For this "born pagan" and "seer of the flesh," who, according to Merezhkovsky, sought during the second half of his life "to subordinate his elemental nature to his consciousness," the war against the body and its carnal appetites was not an easy one.[152] "And the harsh moral code he promulgated," explains a more recent commentator, "was aimed chiefly against his own unconquerable fondness for the pleasures of the flesh."[153] Although Tolstoy may have sought in his later years to follow a rigid ascetic diet, and although his followers like to mythologize his purportedly strict adherence to (and deep fondness for) bland peasant food, he never did lose entirely his hearty appetite for both food and sex.[154] He never completely ceased to crave those pleasures of the flesh and delights of the palate that gratified his body rather than nurtured his soul. In his *Confession*, Tolstoy had acknowledged the Socratic truth that one must strive "to be free of the body, of all the evils that result from the life of the body" (23:22–23), and he had begun during the early 1880s, both in his life and in his writings, to wage a full-scale war against the physical pleasures that mercilessly tempt the human body. Tolstoy in his later years thus epitomized the paradigmatic Christian view of the body as an unruly, passionate, animal, and alien Other that requires strict regulation through the iron discipline of diet and self-denial. But even extreme dietary practices, as we have seen, were not enough to silence appetite in Tolstoy's case. The full-scale war he waged upon his body apparently continued right up to the time of the author's death, with no clear victor on either side.

# Carnality and Morality in Fin de Siècle and Revolutionary Russia

## 4

## Dostoevsky, Tolstoy, and the Zoological Self

The shadow cast by Dostoevsky and Tolstoy, the two giants of the great nineteenth-century Russian novel, on the literature, culture, and intellectual life of late imperial Russia is indisputably enormous. Although their influence may have been felt most strongly in quite different cultural and philosophical spheres (Dostoevsky's upon turn-of-the-century religious philosophers, for example; Tolstoy's upon social activists and cultural dissidents), both left a lasting imprint—as writers as well as thinkers—on generations of Russians to come. The memorable characters who populated their novels, as well as the provocative ideas that informed their nonfiction, took on a life that extended long after their authors' deaths (Dostoevsky in 1881, Tolstoy in 1910). Their immediate influence on the subsequent generation of Russian writers and thinkers, however, is especially pertinent to many of the issues in this book: one's attitude toward the desiring body, the nature of physical appetite, the relationship between carnivorousness and sensuality, the purported remedies of asceticism and vegetarianism, and so on. As the process of modernization accelerated in late imperial Russia and as traditional conceptualizations of human nature began to be more seriously challenged, the twin corporeal concerns of food and sex assumed an even more prominent position in public and artistic discourse in Russia. The legacy of Dostoevsky and Tolstoy in matters involving carnality and morality, as we shall see in this chapter, made itself felt in a number of ways in turn-of-the-century and revolutionary Russia.

An especially significant area involved discussions of the human animal, especially his sexual nature. The wide dissemination within Russian society of Darwin's theories in particular and of materialist philosophy in general, along with the appearance of works of literary "naturalism" by writers such as Emile Zola, helped to generate a lively debate about the animal nature of human beings. Darwin's theories contributed to the public conversation about the so-called zoological self, largely by calling into question the uniquely human (if not divine) properties of man. They also prompted the use of animal metaphors—especially metaphors of predatory animals—in works of literature by writers who sought to emphasize the instinctual and elemental aspects of human behavior, both in the private sphere (sexual life) and the public sphere (socioeconomic relations). Different writers, of course, conceived of man's animal nature in different ways and used different animals to characterize human beings. Where Dostoevsky's human bestiary, as we saw in an earlier chapter, is populated by predatory creatures who "devour" others by ensnaring and then eating up their defenseless prey, Tolstoy's notion of human appetite focuses instead on what he calls our "animal personality" (26:347): that part of our inner self that strives instinctively for the gratification of egoistic desires, particularly the basic physical pleasures provided by food and sex. Where Dostoevsky's human animals are invariably wild beasts of prey (wolves, reptiles, spiders, tarantulas), Tolstoy's are more likely to be domesticated but still selfish, greedy, and pleasure-seeking creatures, such as cattle, horses, dogs, and pigs, who live only to fill their own bellies and to satisfy the urges of their loins.[1] If Dostoevsky's views on gastronomical and sexual desire were largely reduced in fin de siècle and revolutionary Russia to a bestial, bloodthirsty "Dostoevskyism," then those of Tolstoy were associated with a much less feral "Tolstoyism," which advanced a hyper-Christian ethos advocating pacifism, vegetarianism, celibacy, and nonresistance to evil. Although there were some contemporaries who voiced a clarion call for a "Red Tolstoy" to appear upon the impoverished literary scene in early Soviet Russia, most Bolshevik leaders and moral commentators during the 1920s were much less concerned about Tolstoy as a novelist, than about Tolstoy as a moral-religious ideologue whose followers had created a movement that now competed quite vigorously with Bolshevism in the contest to win over the hearts and minds of the idealistic young.[2] The "revolutionary asceticism" and "revolutionary sublimation" that early Bolshevik commentators advocated for Communist youth stood the very real risk of being preempted (and thus trumped) by the Tolstoyan message of sexual abstinence he and his radical Christian followers preached.[3]

In this chapter we shall be examining how one or the other of these two opposing conceptualizations of the human animal—the Dostoevskian notion of predatory "bestiality" (*zverstvo*) or the Tolstoyan idea of hedonistic "animality" (*zhivotnost'*)—was appropriated by a number of writers in fin de siècle and revolutionary Russia who were concerned with the nature of human sexual desire. The choice these writers made depended mainly on their respective view of the zoological self and the desiring body. The juxtaposition of "bestiality" and "animality" did not originate with Dostoevsky and Tolstoy, of course, even though these two Russian writers did revive quite memorably for their contemporaries two views of the inner self that had been delineated long ago in Greek antiquity. In Plato's *The Republic*, for example, where a distinction is made between a "rational" and a "desiring" part of the human soul, Socrates notes that it is the responsibility of the "rational" part to control the "desiring" part (which is by far the largest part of every soul) and thus to keep it from "gorging itself on the so-called pleasures of the body."[4] Indeed, the true philosopher, according to Socrates, will be concerned with the pleasures of the soul and will recede from "the pleasures that come through the body" (148). This Platonic view of the human self—structured on the divide between reason and instinct, between spirit and body—certainly seems to agree with the Tolstoyan notion of "animality" (*zhivotnost'*), whereby the desiring body, with its lust for the physical pleasures provided by food and sex, must be bridled so as not to impair the soul's aspiration for spiritual love and sublime knowledge.

Socrates also makes mention, however, of the "tyrant": that is, the type of person who, as illustrated in the legend about the shrine of Lycaean Zeus in Arcadia, "tastes of human flesh" and "necessarily turns into a wolf" (224). An advocate of the people whose sacrilegious mouth has once tasted kindred blood, Socrates warns, "becomes a tyrant and a wolf instead of a man" (224). A tyrant of this sort gives himself up to "lawless" desires, allowing "the wild, bestial part" of his soul to "gratify its instincts" irrationally and shamelessly (229). In this condition, a man "abandons all shame and good sense and dares anything," including acts of murder and incest (229). "All we want to know is that there's a class of wild, terrible, lawless desires in each of us," Socrates explains; a man succumbs to these lawless desires and becomes a tyrant, he adds, "whenever his nature, habits or both makes him amorous, demented, or drunk" (231). According to Socrates, carnal love—or sexual desire—is what turns people into shameless tyrants: they become lawless "wolves" who are destined to live out their lives "as friends to no one, but always as either masters or slaves" (233). This view of the self as being susceptible to (and capable of) irrational tyranny seems to accord with the Dostoevskian notion of "bestiality" (*zverstvo*), whereby sexual desire manifests itself as a wolfish instinct for shameless, lawless, bloody violence. Where Tolstoyan *zhivotnost'* reflects a view of the sex drive as a libidinal appetite for pleasure, Dostoevskian *zverstvo* reflects instead a view of the sex drive as brutal, violent aggression.

Dostoevsky's view of human desire appealed primarily to those Russian writers who understand our appetite for food and sex as operating according to the paradigm of power rather than pleasure. Dostoevsky's carnivorous male heroes were closely linked in the Russian consciousness at the turn of the century not only with the predatory beasts invoked by Darwin's notion of the struggle for existence, but also by the "blonde beast of prey" celebrated in the philosophical writings of Friedrich Nietzsche (1844–1900). In sensationalized works of Russian boulevard fiction—such as Mikhail Artsybashev's *Sanin* (1907), Evdokia Nagrodskaya's *The Wrath of Dionysus* (1910), and Anastasia Verbitskaya's *The Keys to Happiness* (1913)—a perverse erotics of violence, dominance, and subordination was pursued by male characters seeking to exercise a vulgarized Nietzschean will-to-power in their sexual relations. The fin de siècle's "new barbarism," energized in large part by the Dostoevskian trope of alimentary violence, experienced a resurgence soon after the Bolshevik Revolution as well, when several early Soviet writers— such as Boris Pilnyak, Yury Olesha, and Lev Gumilyovsky—likewise resorted to predatory imagery in their efforts to portray the unleashing of violent bestial instincts within human beings during this time of social and political upheaval.

Tolstoy's view of human desire (as an insatiable and ultimately crippling appetite for the bodily pleasures provided by food and sex), on the other hand, found no home in turn-of-the-century Russian literature where advocates of the "new sensualism" challenged the abstinence, self-denial, and Christian asceticism preached by the puritanical Tolstoy and his zealous followers. Indeed, Artsybashev's controversial young hero, Vladimir Sanin, directly challenges the Tolstoyan imperative that one should seek to deny and transcend (rather than indulge) the animal appetites of the desiring body. Yet by the time of early Soviet Russia, Tolstoyan renunciation of the pleasures of the flesh found a much warmer reception. Writers in the 1920s—such as Aleksandr Tarasov-Rodionov and Lev Gumilyovsky—created heroes who practice "revolutionary asceticism" by striving to overcome the allure of bodily pleasures and dedicate all their energies instead to the construction of a socialist society. In Gumilyovsky's *Dog Alley* (1926), the author even "Tolstoyanizes" the predatory animal imagery he invokes in the text—transforming Dostoevskian *zverstvo* into Tolstoyan *zhivotnost'*—by portraying the sex drive itself as an ensnaring, devouring desire that is at the same time intoxicating, addictive, and debilitating.

## The Legacy of Tolstoy: Fear of the Flesh

Tolstoy's conceptualization of the human animal as a pleasure-seeking creature rather than a power-hungry beast established its legacy in fin de siècle Russia largely in the championing of asceticism and abstinence, both sexual and gastronomical, voiced by those who feared the effects that modernization was having upon traditional moral values in their homeland. As Peter Ulf Møller has charted masterfully in *Postlude to The Kreutzer Sonata: Tolstoj and the Debate over Sexual Morality in Russian Literature of the 1890s* (1988), Tolstoy's controversial 1889 novella, and especially the radical Christian asceticism that undergirded it, was instrumental in propelling a heated debate on sexual morality in late imperial Russia, problematizing the sexual instinct—the "animal within man"—as a cause of human suffering.[5] While Tolstoy's Victorian, if not medieval, brand of asceticism certainly found a receptive audience among conservative moralists, it managed to provoke what we might call an *influence de rebours* among contemporary advocates of erotic liberation and rehabilitation of the body, such as Zinaida Gippius, Dmitry Merezhkovsky, and Vasily Rozanov. These modernist writers reacted strongly against the puritanical trend in Russian literature and culture at this time by celebrating physical pleasure and sexual exploration rather than moral virtue in one's personal life. Indeed, it was the reaction *against* Tolstoy's puritanism, where issues of food, sex, and carnality are concerned, that constitutes his primary legacy at the turn of the century.

As Laura Engelstein has pointed out in *The Keys to Happiness: Sex and the Search for Modernity in Fin-de-Siècle Russia* (1992), the sexual question first became a self-consciously defined moral, social, and cultural issue in Russia only in 1889, the year when *The Kreutzer Sonata*, Tolstoy's controversial novella about the fatal consequences of male sexual desire, began to circulate among educated Russian readers.[6] Conservative moral commentators, often relying upon the biological findings of physicians and other public health officials, contributed to the barrage of popular literature that suddenly appeared in print in the wake of Tolstoy's text. They actively promoted sexual abstinence as a prophylactic measure to guard against the numerous sociosexual ailments—such as masturbation, prostitution, and venereal disease—that were now said to be appearing in unprecedented numbers within Russian society. The process of modernization, which was resulting in the rapid growth of cities, the increasing complexity of socioeconomic life, and the widespread questioning of traditional moral values and social conventions, helped to turn sexual promiscuity into a hotly debated topic within Russian society. For the conservative voices contributing to this debate, the ways to deflect our natural appetite for sensual gratification echoed the measures promulgated by Tolstoy (examined in the previous chapter): sexual restraint as facilitated by an increase in hard physical labor and a commensurate decrease in indulgence in such private luxuries and material comforts as rich foods, strong drinks, and soft beds. The conservative voices that spoke out in favor of libidinal repression and sexual abstinence found philosophical support in the writings of religious thinkers such as Tolstoy, Nikolay Berdyaev, Vladimir Solovyov and other enemies of the modern urban environment.

While the conservative supporters of traditional morality in fin de siècle Russia inveighed mightily against what they perceived to be declining moral standards within their society, there were many who greeted modernization—as well as modernism—quite enthusiastically and who reacted strongly against the ascetic puritanism that emerged in the wake of Tolstoy's *Kreutzer Sonata*. Avant-garde artists, such as the "Decadent" writers Valery Bryusov, Konstantin Balmont, Zinaida

Gippius, and Fyodor Sologub, actively promoted an erotic trend in literature—what James Billington has called a "new sensualism"[7]—that sought to destigmatize and thus rehabilitate the human body, to reintroduce a pagan appreciation for the natural joys of human life, and to liberate carnality from the life-denying moral philosophy of Tolstoy, whose teachings were perceived as shackling the productive energies of human nature. For Dmitry Merezhkovsky in particular, Tolstoy's evolution during his life and career—from a pagan sensualist (a "seer of the flesh") to a Christian moralist who preaches a monkish asceticism—epitomized the decidedly ruinous course that results from denying the impulses of one's flesh.[8] Vasily Rozanov likewise decried Tolstoy's assault upon eros, promoting carnal love as a healthy form of human expression and advocating the refashioning of the family through a new brand of religious sensuality. Waxing lyrical about the erotic pleasures of carnality, the "erotomaniac" Rozanov denounced those who, like Tolstoy, sought to pathologize the joyful naturalness of sex and render it a disease, disorder, or sickness of which human beings needed somehow to be "cured."[9] "Rozanov's main psychic concern is indulgence, not abstention," writes Renato Poggioli, "he is an orgiast rather than an ascetic; he aims not to mortify the flesh, but to glorify it; he wants to satisfy man's urges, not to restrain them."[10]

Within popular culture, meanwhile, the sacrifice of moral values for aesthetic pleasure and the advancement of an ideology of personal fulfillment advocated by the modernists were echoed in the tabloid press and boulevard fiction, where questions of physical pleasure and sexual desire were given special prominence. What is particularly edifying for our purposes here, however, is that these questions were often phrased in the language and imagery of food and eating. One of the advertised cures for "sexual neurasthenia" (impotence) that Engelstein includes in her study, for instance, carries the headline "sexual hunger" (*polovoi golod*) and suggests that Dr. William Manken's remedy will, like any alimentary nourishment, eliminate the "weakness" and "nervousness" that plague sexual neurasthenics.[11] Similarly, the January 1906 issue of the satirical periodical *Satira* carries a graphic illustration that portrays members of the ruling class feasting and whoring at table while the common people toil, suffer, and starve: wealthy aristocrats are shown imbibing champagne and consuming rich foods while they consort with prostitutes (a naked woman in silk stockings is depicted in a reclining position on top of the dinner table amid all the plates, goblets, and revelers).[12]

## The Competing Sexual Moralities of Tolstoyism and Saninism

One of the most interesting turn-of-the-century advocates of carnal rehabilitation and sexual liberation who reacted strongly against Tolstoy's ascetic puritanism is Mikhail Artsybashev (1878–1927). A subtext of anti-asceticism and anti-Tolstoyism can be found in Artsybashev's "pornographic" best seller *Sanin*, whose eponymous hero preaches a hedonistic philosophy of personal pleasure where issues of sexual desire are concerned. Indeed, *Sanin* can be read very productively as an intertextual response directed at Tolstoy: a response directed not to any one particular literary text written by Tolstoy, but rather to the views on sexuality, pleasure, and the body that the sage of Yasnaya Polyana espoused during his later years through his moralizing essays and his didactic tales. As we saw in the previous chapter, after the midlife spiritual crisis he experienced during the late 1870s and early 1880s, Tolstoy turned from being a pagan sensualist to a Christian moralist. "The body with its carnal desires ceased to be the subject of ecstasy and became the target of scorn," one critic has noted. "Tolstoy, who had once glorified the body, now preached that the flesh had to be forcibly broken to bring about the liberation and salvation of the soul. He demanded the mortification of the body."[13] Although Artsybashev seems to have greatly admired the author of *War and Peace* and *Anna Karenina* as a literary artist whose realist aesthetic he sought to emulate in his own writing, the author of *Sanin* appears to have had very little respect for Tolstoy as a moralist and philosophical thinker—or for Tolstoyism as a moral code.[14] Through the hedonistic ethos of "Saninism," the new morality of sexual libertinism advanced by the eponymous hero in *Sanin* that champions the human body, physical pleasure, and sexual passion, Artsybashev is challenging not Tolstoy the writer but rather the ascetic Christian creed of Tolstoyism. In particular, he is challenging Tolstoy's denigration of the body, along with its attendant carnal appetites, as something inherently base and unredeemably animalistic.

Tolstoy, for his part, had little to say about Artsybashev, his novel, or its main hero that is positive. In February 1908 Tolstoy received a letter from M. M. Dokshitsky, a gymnasium student from Ukraine, who expressed fascination both with the philosophy of Artsybashev's charismatic young protagonist and with Tolstoy's own Christian worldview. Unable to decide whether "Saninism" or Tolstoyism was the better philosophical outlook for him to pursue in life, Dokshitsky asked for Tolstoy's opinion about Sanin's ideas and beliefs. In his reply, Tolstoy confessed that he was horrified by the "stupidity, ignorance, and smug self-assurance" (77:58) of the disgusting filth Artsybashev's hero had preached in the novel. Tolstoy proceeded to lament both the pernicious influence that Artsybashev's novel was exerting upon many young people in Russia and the author's egregious lack of knowledge about what some of the world's greatest minds have had to say in regard to the essential questions of human life. In an effort to help Dokshitsky decide correctly which of the two philosophies of life—Saninism or Christianity—is the better one to follow, Tolstoy promised to send him a copy of *A Circle of Readings* (1904–1908), the collection of uplifting moral thoughts from various writers and thinkers Tolstoy had compiled for Posrednik Press. In addition to *A Circle of Readings*, he also advised Dokshitskii to read the Gospels.

Tolstoy likewise makes some highly disparaging remarks about the author of *Sanin* in a short essay, titled "On Insanity" (1910), in which he expresses deep concern over the increasing number of suicides that are being committed by young Russians. Tolstoy blames this wave of contemporary "insanity"—the veritable epidemic of despair and depression he has been observing among members of the younger generation in Russia—in large part on the diet of lurid works of contemporary literature by decadent modernist writers (such as Artsybashev) that so many young Russian readers were greedily consuming. Tolstoy identifies the leading ideologues for the current "lost generation" as Darwin, Haeckel, Marx, Maeterlinck, Hamsun, Weininger, and Nietzsche; it is their godless ideas, he insists, that are driving more and more young people in Russia to despair and ultimately to suicide. This moral decline, this widespread "insanity," Tolstoy asserts, appears to be the terribly steep price that is now being paid in turn-of-the-century Russia for the material and scientific "progress" that has been advocated as part of the process of modernization (38:401).

Tolstoy's angry reaction to *Sanin*—precisely the kind of nihilistic literature that was, in his opinion, poisoning the minds of young Russians—seems entirely understandable, especially when we consider that much of Artsybashev's novel is a refutation of some of Tolstoy's most cherished ideas, beliefs, and teachings. Indeed, Otto Boele asserts that Tolstoyism—along with socialism, asceticism, and Christianity—is one of the primary targets of the author's criticism in *Sanin*.[15] Among the more obvious of the "Tolstoyan" targets one finds in the novel is, of course, Tolstoy's signature doctrine of nonresistance to evil, which is preached rigorously in, among other places, *The Kingdom of God Is Within You* (1893), and which came to serve as a central tenet of Tolstoyism.[16] In *Sanin*, the author explicitly attacks Tolstoy's doctrine through his satiric portrayals of two secondary characters: Captain Von Deitz, a tall, skinny army officer, who explicitly purports to be—and is widely considered by other characters in the novel to be—an "admirer of Tolstoy" (*poklonnik Tolstogo*), if not in fact an actual "Tolstoyan disciple" (*tolstovets*), and Yakov Adolfovich Soloveychik, the son of a Jewish mill owner who professes to be a Tolstoyan and is deeply troubled by Sanin's violent attack upon a man (Zarudin) who had injured him.[17] Soloveychik's suggestion that Sanin should have adopted a turn-the-other-cheek reaction to his injury prompts Artsybashev's hero to inveigh mightily against Tolstoy's Christian notion of nonresistance to evil. Sanin relates how there once was a time in his own life when, under the influence of a fellow student named Ivan Lande, he himself had seriously considered pursuing the Tolstoyan ideal of a selfless Christian life. But Sanin soon became thoroughly disenchanted with Lande's Tolstoyan way of life, which—with its Christian quietism and monkish asceticism—merely robbed life of all its beauty, richness, and vitality.

The strongest criticism of Tolstoyan moral-religious ideas in *Sanin*, however, is expressed through the portrayal of Yury Svarozhich, a former student at the technical institute who was recently exiled to his hometown because of his political activities in Moscow. Determined to pursue a path toward moral self-perfection by leading a life of self-sacrifice and by waging a constant war against his animal impulses, Svarozhich sounds very much like one of the young male heroes who can be found in Tolstoy's fiction, even like Tolstoy himself during his post-conversion years. Sanin, one critic notes, "recognises his natural foe in Christianity, in the person of Jesus Christ, and in His Russian interpreter, Leo Tolstoi."[18]

Tolstoy's main complaint about *Sanin* was that one finds no restraint of animal appetite—no abstaining from immediate sensual gratification—in the novel's eponymous hero, who appears to fetishize the instinctual reflexes of human beings. "Enjoy yourself to the utmost, and don't worry about anything," is how Tolstoy paraphrased Sanin's credo.[19] Indeed, one of Artsybashev's main complaints against Tolstoy's Christian philosophy of self-denial is that such a repressive mentality sought "unnaturally" to extinguish all the natural pagan joy to be found in life. "Nothing that gives pleasure can ever be degrading," one critic writes, paraphrasing Sanin's hedonistic doctrine, "what is natural cannot be wrong."[20] The opposition between Artsybashev's pagan philosophy of life-affirmation and Tolstoy's Christian philosophy of life-abnegation is made particularly evident in the contrasting views, actions, and fates of Sanin, the author's ostensible mouthpiece, and Svarozhich, the surrogate for Tolstoyan sexual morality in the novel.

### Yury Svarozhich and the Futility of Tolstoyan Abstinence

The narrative structure of Artsybashev's novel, with its central romantic competition being waged over the voluptuous Zinaida Karsavina, reads in large part as a contest between these two fictional characters (Sanin and Svarozhich) as well as the opposing ideologies (Saninism and Tolstoyism) that each represents. Artsybashev's protagonist is characterized throughout the narrative as a "natural" man whose formative years of childhood upbringing and adolescent education were spent apart from his family and without the normal mechanisms of socialization. This circumstance, we are told, allowed his soul to develop in a distinctively independent, original, and natural way, "like a tree growing in a field" (1:35). In social terms, Sanin, as an uninhibited "natural" man, is unfettered by the demands of his society's conventions or by traditional moral constraints. In terms of his personality and character, Sanin's naturalness manifests itself primarily in an open, accepting attitude toward the physical urges and sensual desires of the human body: Artsybashev's hero champions what Laura Engelstein terms "the cult of happy physicality."[21] Indeed, Sanin seems to possess a nearly unquenchable thirst for the corporeal pleasures of life, a hearty, lustful appetite that is fully justified (even mandated) by his philosophy of sensual indulgence. What distinguishes a natural man from mere animals, Sanin explains, is the human need for, and understanding of, sensual gratification:

> The more animalistic an animal is, the less it understands gratification and the less able it is to secure it. It merely satisfies its needs. We all agree that man isn't created to suffer and that suffering isn't the goal of human aspirations. In other words, gratification is the goal of life. . . . Yes, by nature man is not adapted to abstinence, and the most sincere people are those who don't hide their physical lusts. (1:62)

To live life to its fullest and, in the process, to avoid pain, suffering, and misery, the hedonistic Sanin reasons, "it is necessary to satisfy one's natural desires. Desire is everything: if desire dies in a person, life dies; and if he kills desire, he kills himself" (1:130). Compare this passionate defense of libidinal desire as the very essence of human happiness with the ascetic sentiment expressed by Seryozha Popov, a well-known Tolstoyan of that era: "Not to desire anything—that is happiness."[22]

The polarity between Tolstoyan self-abnegation (which seeks to overcome, even extinguish entirely, carnal desire) and Saninian self-affirmation (which seeks everywhere to satisfy and enjoy it) is especially evident in their sharply contrasting views on the morality of drinking alcoholic beverages. Sanin's unbridled lust and passion for life lead him to endorse the use of alcohol; intoxication, to his mind, liberates a person from repressive emotional, psychological, and moral fetters. "In my opinion, only a drunkard lives life as it should be lived," Sanin states. "A drunkard does only what he feels like doing: if he feels like singing, he sings; if he feels like dancing, he dances; and he doesn't ever feel ashamed of his joy and merrymaking" (1:84). To the ancient Roman adage (from which his surname may well derive), *mens sano in corpore sane*, Artsybashev's hero would thus add another: *in vino veritas*. This endorsement led one contemporary critic to condemn the hard-drinking Sanin as nothing more than "an amoral alcoholic."[23]

Tolstoy, on the other hand, adamantly condemned the use of alcohol; to his mind, strong drink kills human reason and deadens one's moral sensibilities. In his essay "Why Do People Stupefy Themselves?" (1890), Tolstoy writes: "People drink and smoke not to keep their spirits up, not for gaiety's sake, and not because it is pleasant, but in order to stifle conscience within themselves" (27:282). Beyond all of its addictive qualities, the use of alcohol is a destructive habit, according to Tolstoy: it leads directly to sexual debauchery by eliminating the moral restraints that are normally in place to harness libidinal desire. "Dissoluteness does not lie in anything physical—no kind of physical misconduct is debauchery," explains Pozdnyshev, speaking for the author in *The Kreutzer Sonata*. "Real debauchery lies precisely in freeing oneself from moral relations with a woman with whom you have physical intimacy" (27:17). Where Sanin's followers in contemporary Russia purportedly established "free love" leagues, where binge drinking, group sex, and other forms of moral libertinism were said to take place, Tolstoy advised his followers instead to create temperance leagues that encouraged abstinence from alcohol (and thus from sexual promiscuity).[24]

The counterpoint to the Saninian mixture of egoism, eroticism, and epicureanism in the novel, as noted above, is provided by Yury Svarozhich, whose adherence to Tolstoyan ideas, beliefs, and teachings runs much deeper than that of either Von Deitz or Soloveychik.[25] Such is especially true with respect to the Tolstoyan fear of, and disdain for, the human body with its attendant carnal appetites. Generalizing from his own personal battle against the pleasures of the flesh, Tolstoy late in his life had declared war on the human body as a site of irresistible physical temptations that are highly addictive and seriously debilitating. As a consequence, a key moral notion for the post-conversion Tolstoy, as we saw in the previous chapter, was "abstinence" (*vozderzhanie*), which he considered the necessary first step along the long and arduous path to moral and spiritual self-perfection. Thus Svarozhich, as the epitome of the Tolstoyan moral man, seeks to sublimate and transcend the bodily desires that obstruct him in his quest for moral and spiritual self-purification.[26]

That Yury Svarozhich adheres to the Tolstoyan ideology of renunciation of the pleasures of the flesh is evident in one of the novel's earliest scenes, when Yury ventures off into a dark, imposing cave together with the beautiful young schoolteacher Karsavina during a picnic outing. He quickly finds himself sexually aroused by her physical nearness but feels that he must resist his sexual impulses. In accord with the tenets of Tolstoyan sexual morality, Yury endeavors to sublimate the sinful carnal passion and libidinal excitation he is experiencing for Karsavina with a more spiritual feeling of compassion and sympathy.

Throughout the remainder of the novel, however, sexual desire continues to raise its ugly head for Yury whenever he happens to encounter Karsavina. Svarozhich is deep in a state of denial as far as his true feelings for this young woman are concerned. As the narrator explains, "Everything he [Yury] thought about her [Karsavina's] attractiveness, purity, and spiritual depth was conveyed through her physical beauty and tenderness, but for some reason Yury did not admit this to himself; he tried to convince himself that he found the young woman attractive not because of her shoulders, bosom, eyes, or voice but rather because of her chastity and purity" (1:93–94). Yury's denial of the undeniable sexual attraction he feels toward Karsavina, the narrator explains, leads directly to the repression of his sexual desire for her—evidenced in the text by the "voluptuous" and "sunny" images of beautiful naked women that begin to visit him at night in his dreams, when the contents of his subconscious mind are able to emerge more freely (1:103). Svarozhich even starts to daydream, fantasizing about how Karsavina would look if she were stripped naked: "Yury thought that if suddenly she were to throw off her clothes and then, bare, light, and gay, run through the dewy grass into the mysterious green grove, it wouldn't be at all strange, but splendid and natural; instead of destroying the verdant life of the dark garden, it would only enhance it" (1:110).

For the most part, however, Yury manages to dispel such erotic pagan fantasies, even if at times he clearly envies Sanin's ability to trust his bodily urges and to indulge them rather freely.[27] Placing his trust in the judgment of his rational consciousness over the promptings of his animal personality, Svarozhich justifies his fear of bodily pleasure by dismissing Sanin's pagan enjoyment of life as mere "animalism" (zhivotnost'). "Life is sensation," Yury reasons, "but people aren't senseless beasts; they must direct their desires toward the good, and not allow those desires to gain control over them" (1:150). To Svarozhich's mind, therefore, the libertine Sanin is nothing but "a repulsive, vulgar man" (1:141), while the philandering Ryazantsev, his sister's fiancé, is similarly dismissed as "a filthy animal" (1:143).

Despite what Svarozhich's rational consciousness might tell him about the need to sublimate his libidinal energies and channel them toward a higher moral good, his sexual repression has led to his emotional life becoming increasingly gray, lifeless, and empty. "There was no spark in his life," the narrator comments. "He was on fire only at those times when he felt healthy and strong, and was in love with a woman" (1:198). Although Yury prides himself on the fact that he is unlike the other young men in his social milieu, he also realizes that the ideas and behaviors of Sanin, Ryazantsev, Novikov, and other robust young males in his hometown are having an unwholesome effect upon him. "They're far removed from tragic self-flagellation," he muses. "They're as content as triumphant swine. Zarathustras! Their whole life is contained within their own microscopically small ego; and they're even infecting me with their vulgarity. Doesn't he who keeps company with wolves learn to howl like a wolf? It's only natural" (1:203). In the face of the hedonistic thinking that surrounds him, Yury stubbornly struggles to preserve his core Tolstoyan beliefs. "To live and sacrifice!" he tells himself. "That's genuine life!" (1:204). All it seems to take, however, is physical proximity to the alluring Karsavina to erode Yury's already waning enthusiasm for Tolstoy's teachings (especially as Karsavina's reciprocal attraction has now become evident). In the end, Yury abruptly ceases his sexual pursuit of Karsavina, expressing disgust one evening at his desire "to defile this pure, holy young woman" (1:320) "It would've been so repulsive," he thinks to himself, "thank God I turned out to be incapable of it! It's all so vile: on the spot, almost without words, like a beast!" (1:320).

## Sanin's Paganism: The Ethos of Unbridled Animal Passion

Sanin quickly avails himself of Yury's lost sexual opportunity with Karsavina when he offers to escort her home—initially on foot and subsequently by boat—later that same night. Many critics have interpreted as a rape scene the episode of sexual seduction in the rowboat when Karsavina submits to the power of Sanin's carnal yearning for her. They may well be correct, yet the narrator makes it quite clear that Karsavina had remained sexually excited and unsatisfied following her interrupted, unconsummated tryst with Svarozhich earlier that same day. "And for the hundredth time she recalled with the most profound rapture the incomprehensibly enticing sensation she had experienced in submitting to Yury for the first time," the narrator reports (1:330). During her trip home with Sanin, whose mere physical closeness produces "a sense of unfamiliar excitement" within Karsavina (1:333), her state of unfulfilled sexual longing persists, growing even stronger: "She felt an irresistible but only dimly conscious desire to let him know that she was not always such a quiet, modest young woman and that perhaps she was altogether different, both naked and shameless. She felt excited and elated as a result of this unfulfilled desire" (1:334-35). As she listens to Sanin while he shares his unorthodox views about such issues as the denigration of the body and the stigmatization of physical desires one observes within contemporary Russian society (as well as the possibility of young people enjoying the kind of love that is free of fear, jealousy, or slavery), Karsavina suddenly realizes that "before her lay an entire world of original feelings and sensations previously unknown to her; all of a sudden she felt like reaching out to it . . . a strange excitement overcame her body and manifested itself in nervous trembling" (1:338). When the carnal seduction at last does take place, we are told that Karsavina felt and understood with her entire being Sanin's strong sexual yearning for her and that she was "intoxicated" by it (1:338). "She was suddenly submerged in an incomprehensible loss of will," the narrator explains. "She relaxed her arms and lay back, seeing and recognizing nothing; with both burning pain and agonizing delight she surrendered to another's strength and will—those of a man" (1:339).

Although genuine tears will subsequently be shed and bitter regret will be felt at the loss of her virginity (as well as at her betrayal of Yury's love), Karsavina is shown to lack the strength of will to push Sanin away during their sexual encounter in the rowboat. "She did not defend herself when he began kissing her once again," the narrator informs us.

> She welcomed this burning new delight almost unconsciously, with half-closed eyes receding ever deeper into a new and enigmatically enticing world that was still strange to her. At times she seemed not to see or hear or feel anything, but each of his movements, each force exerted on her submissive body she perceived with extraordinary piquancy, with mixed feelings of humiliation and eager curiosity. (1:340)

This scene of purported sexual assault, Boele argues, "is intended to suggest that Karsavina enjoys the experience and is initiated into a new, more 'natural' way of life. Functionally speaking, Sanin is only an instrument designed to demonstrate the superiority of a higher truth. His unpretentious enjoyment of life is clearly presented as an example to all."[28] Engelstein interprets the scene similarly: "In the soothing lull of a warm summer night, with no desire for commitment or sense of remorse, Sanin enjoys a momentary connection with another man's sexually frustrated sweetheart." "Indeed, his special role in the narrative," she notes, "is to convince young women who have succumbed to desire that their impulses have improved rather than degraded them."[29] The sexual aggressiveness Sanin exhibits in this scene is thus intended for the edification not merely of the novel's male readers but for its female ones as well; as Engelstein observes, Artsybashev seeks in his novel to vindicate "women's capacity for sexual pleasure."[30] Like so many of the other young people in the town who fall under the spell of Sanin's charismatic personality, Karsavina views the events of this fateful night as "some powerful intoxication" (1:344) that suddenly overcame and transformed her. Later, when she finds herself in a more sober and reflective state, she will return to her conventional morality and feel guilty that she, "a vile, depraved creature" (1:351), surrendered herself carnally to Sanin that night. Thus, if one of Sanin's most important roles is to propagandize a new, more genuine and individualistic way of being in the world, then in the case of Karsavina his efforts have not been entirely successful. "However great Sanin's desire to propagandize his fellow-men in the way of true being," Luker writes, "his words have no more than a temporary effect on them, and to a man they fail to emulate him."[31] The same is true, of course, for the female characters in the novel. As Phelps notes, "It is clear that Artsybashev believes that for some time to come women will not accept the gospel of uncompromising egoism."[32] Although female characters like Zinaida Karsavina and Lida Sanina can be true to themselves temporarily, one critic notes, they cannot "be so for good, because like the vast majority they eventually succumb to the flabby mediocrity of their convention-bound lives."[33]

Yury Svarozhich, we soon learn, fatally shoots himself, not because Karsavina has betrayed him (he appears not to have been aware that she submitted to Sanin's sexual advances in the rowboat that fateful night), but because he has become increasingly alienated and depressed as a result of leading a loveless, celibate life. According to Sanin, brooding intellectuals like Yury Svarozhich, who are deeply dissatisfied with life, are simply "afraid to live" and "afraid to feel" (1:337). They spend their lives in emotional prisons of their own making, slavishly subordinating the body to the spirit and stigmatizing their natural, physical desires as shameful bestial urges. For Sanin, man is—or ideally ought to be—not a repressed, fearful moralist like Svarozhich, but rather "a harmonious combination of body and spirit" (1:336). As Luker observes, "by making spontaneous, passionate love to Karsavina, he [Sanin] has implicitly passed sentence on the vacillating, introspective Iurii."[34] In a novel whose appeal to contemporary Russian youth seems to have been predicated less on its eroticism per se than on what Naiman calls its "pretense to ideological coherence,"[35] the eponymous hero of *Sanin* offers a radically new sexual ethos designed to supplant the Tolstoyism of self-abnegating moralists such as Yury Svarozhich.

Although there are other textual elements in *Sanin* that could be read as critiques of Tolstoyan ideas (most notably, his doctrine of non-resistance to evil), it is Tolstoy's ascetic Christianity and his deep-seated Cartesian attitude toward the human body and its carnal appetites that are the main targets of Artsybashev's critique. Just as Tolstoy made clear his disapproval of the "stupidity, ignorance, and smug self-assurance" of the hero Sanin and the moral bankruptcy of Saninism, so too did Artsybashev proclaim his disdain for Tolstoyism. Indeed, this disdain is spelled out in "About Tolstoy" (1911), which Artsybashev included in his *Notes of a Writer*, a collection of essays that, according to P. V. Nikolaev, "were initiated by the argument with Lev Tolstoy about human nature."[36] In his essay, Artsybashev openly acknowledges the enormous debt he owes to Tolstoy as a writer and creative artist; he also leaves no doubt, however, about the low opinion he holds of Tolstoy's moral and philosophical teachings. "As a thinker, if by this word we mean a person who has discovered a new idea and brought forth a new revelation," Artsybashev writes,

> Tolstoy is not worth a brass farthing. Alas, this is a fact. Compared to Christ, Tolstoy was the same, for example, as Pisarev compared to Darwin or a mediocre professor compared to Newton. Not a single one of his numerous writings on philosophical and religious themes is worth even three pages out of the Gospels. The weakness of his interpretation of Christian morality is startling. He got so muddled in trivialities, he so weighed down an idea with trifling nonsense that, as a way to hoist the truth about the corruption of the spirit by the flesh, he demonstrated the indecency of ladies' jerseys and the indubitable harm of tobacco. (3:690)

Tolstoy's moral-religious beliefs, according to Artsybashev, are "short-sighted" and "bankrupt" (3:697, 698). Artsybashev considers the post-conversion Tolstoy to be "a narrow-minded dogmatist who based everything on one single point, who deprived his mind of the freedom of any further searching, and who rested in a blissful calm, believing that the truth had been found!" (3:690). To Artsybashev's mind, Tolstoy's code of morality is impracticable and unrealizable: "He himself was unable to live with it, and not because he was weak, as he tried to argue in justifying himself, but rather because it was impossible to live with this code" (3:690).

It is a curious irony of Russian literary history, as D. S. Mirsky long ago reminded us, that Tolstoy himself—as one of the first writers to lift the aesthetic taboos of Russian realism and portray the physical side of life without the "genteel" and "puritanical" conventions that had previously characterized literary depictions of love, sex, and death—turns out to be the one who provided much of the impetus for the "new sensualism" that permeates the works of Gorky, Andreev, Artsybashev, and other neo-realists at the turn of the century. The moralistic works Tolstoy produced in his later years, beginning with *The Kreutzer Sonata* (1889), constitute, in Mirsky's words, "a step in the direction of *Sanin*."[37] With his taboo-lifting brand of realism, his creation of metaphysical and moral problem stories, and his intense consciousness of the elemental verities of life (especially sex and death), Tolstoy the literary artist served as a trailblazer and model for the younger generation of Russian neo-realist writers like Artsybashev. Even the didactic element in the latter's prose, Mirsky points out, can be traced back to Tolstoy's poetics. "Artsybashev's preaching proceeds directly from Tolstoy," he asserts, "only it is Tolstoy the other way around."[38] Indeed, his hedonistic, paganistic hero Sanin, as we have seen, sought specifically to puncture the idea Artsybashev himself once characterized as the "eternal mirage" human beings invariably construct and that Tolstoy indefatigably preached: that the human body, with its sensual desires as well as its sensuous appropriation of the natural world, is something that must be sacrificed for the good of the spirit.[39] As a direct response to Tolstoy's puritanical teachings, *Sanin* aims instead to restore lost value to the human body and its attendant carnal appetites. Despite the considerable artistic influence Tolstoy may have exerted upon Artsybashev as a writer, Saninism, as a radically new moral-sexual ethos being advocated in early-twentieth-century Russia, directly challenges the Tolstoyan sexual morality that may actually have spawned the erotic novel in the first place.

Perhaps the legacy of Tolstoy extends beyond literary aesthetics, however, and influences sexual morality as well. Arkady Gornfeld, for instance, alleges that the "sexual realism" one encounters in *Sanin* (which he claims is designed to appeal to the "dark sexual instincts" of the novel's readers) reveals something persistently nightmarish about the narrative, "like the sadistic dream of an ascetic who is struggling with the flesh."[40] Artsybashev's text, in short, seems to have reminded the critic of the carnally tormented Tolstoy himself. Aleksandr Zakrzhevsky, meanwhile, asserts that "the imperious and stupefying fate of Tolstoy's *The Kreutzer Sonata* hangs over Artsybashev with an immobile and irrepressible heaviness."[41] It may well be the case, as these interpretations suggest, that *Sanin* is merely a variation on *The Kreutzer Sonata*: that is, a literary work in which carnal desire is all-pervasive and human beings are portrayed as essentially animalistic in their sexual passion.[42] "In his pessimistic Orientalism," complained one contemporary critic, "he [Tolstoy] sees nothing but the purely animal, carnal, brutal, and, in his own words, 'hoggish,' in passionate love."[43] Sanin himself, in this vein, could be considered merely a new Pozdnyshev, albeit one who lacks, in Zakrzhevsky's words, "Tolstoy's redemptive idea."[44]

It could be argued, in short, that Artsybashev, who advocates in *Sanin* an indulgence in sexual pleasure that the author of *The Kreutzer Sonata* categorically condemns, may well be proceeding directly from his famous predecessor in sexual morality as well as literary art. In the end, the Saninism proselytized in Artsybashev's novel may be simply another kind of Tolstoyism; only here too it is Tolstoyism turned "the other way around."

## Bolsheviks and Bonbons: Gustatory and Sexual Temptation in Chocolate

Tolstoy's Christian credo of renunciation of the pleasures of the flesh found a much warmer reception in the immediate aftermath of the October Revolution of 1917, especially among Soviet proletarian writers, such as the novelist Aleksandr Tarasov-Rodionov, and Bolshevik moralistic commentators, such as the sexologist Aron Zalkind. Both Tarasov-Rodionov and Zalkind subscribed to the notion, promulgated by the Party during the 1920s, that the pursuit of private, personal pleasure needed to be subordinated to the greater common good served by advancing the class interests of the proletariat. Tarasov-Rodionov's novella *Chocolate* (1922) provides us with an edifying example of what Eric Naiman has called the "ideological poetics" that would come to dominate Soviet fiction during the decade immediately following the Bolshevik Revolution, when food, sex, and the body figured prominently in discourses about War Communism, NEP (New Economic Policy), and socialist construction.[45] More specifically, Tarasov-Rodionov's novella illustrates how chocolate, a luxury food item, becomes highly politicized and ideologized as a result of the decadent life values attached to it. The sweet confection in *Chocolate* reflects the deep anxieties being experienced in Soviet Russia during the 1920s by loyal communists such as Tarasov-Rodionov: anxieties about preserving the ideological purity of Bolshevism amid a socioeconomic environment that threatened to infect members of the young socialist society with corrupt capitalist and bourgeois values. In many ways, the anxieties experienced by Tarasov-Rodionov and other loyal Bolsheviks bear close affinities with the fears of a generation earlier about the negative impact that modernization (and modernism) was having upon moral standards. Indeed, chocolate—as a food item as well as a literary and cultural sign—becomes highly politicized and ideologized in Tarasov-Rodionov's Soviet novella, reflecting the lingering influence of Tolstoy's ideas about carnal desire and gastronomical pleasures.

The central figure in *Chocolate* is Aleksey Ivanovich Zudin, the chairman of a regional Cheka headquarters.[46] A Bolshevik of proletarian birth and a true believer in the goals of the Revolution, Zudin is unflinching in fulfilling his duty of combating sabotage and counterrevolution wherever they may appear, and matter-of-factly sentencing people to be executed on a daily basis. But troubles begin for Comrade Zudin soon after he decides to show uncharacteristic mercy toward Yelena Valts, a former ballet dancer accused of engaging in illegal activities and participating in a counterrevolutionary conspiracy. During her interrogation, Zudin becomes convinced that Yelena is telling the truth when she claims she was present at the apartment of a White Guard conspirator for sexual rather than political purposes. Yelena tearfully confesses to Zudin that she was reduced to selling her body to "dirty, sweaty men" only to avoid starving to death.[47] Feeling sorry for this rather pathetic social parasite, Zudin hires her to work as a member of his own secretarial staff at Cheka headquarters, hoping that some honest work will reform the petit bourgeois whore. Not long afterward, however, Yelena tries to show Zudin her loving gratitude in the only way she knows: by giving his wife nylon stockings, his two young children tasty chocolate ("real, imported chocolate," his wife points out [286]), and Zudin himself her body, which he staunchly refuses to accept.

Although the Cheka chief is self-disciplined enough to resist the sexual allure of his new secretary, he does not quite have the heart to force his wife and children to return the luxurious gifts they have received from kind and generous "Auntie Yelena." Feeling guilty about the many years of material privation his wife and children have been forced to endure, as well as about his long-standing neglect of his family because of the many hours he must work each day at the Cheka office, Zudin allows them to keep the gifts, even though he realizes that, by accepting such gifts, his wife and children are not maintaining the "proletarian grade" in their standards of behavior.

As a committed Party member, he holds himself to a much higher level of self-denial, of course. Indeed, in an earlier scene the author demonstrates the stark contrast between Zudin and his wife over the issue of material comforts. When at lunch one day Zudin gently reproves his wife, Liza, for having prepared such a "holiday feast" (soup that has meat in it) and reminds her that it is rather awkward for him to ask for more than their normal ration of meat, she expresses concern that their two young children are not getting enough fat in their meager diet ("Look at how pale they are, just skin and bones," she observes [279]), imploring her husband to take advantage of his government position and demand some extra rations. It seems unfair to her that he should deprive himself and his family of an adequate diet when everybody else in positions of power within the Soviet leadership seems to be receiving more than their fair share. "You work like an ox, night after night, yet you eat like a bird, feeding on lentils," she says to him, noting that he looks more emaciated now than he did in those prerevolutionary days when he was living in political exile (279). Zudin, for his part, reminds his wife that they are not alone in suffering such privations. "Hundreds of thousands do not see any extra food either," he points out. "What will they say if you start to butter your pies? As it is, in the factories they are already grumbling that the commissars are living like kings as far as food and heat are concerned!" (279). Liza, of course, strongly disagrees with his perception of the situation: "One might think we were indulging in unnatural appetites, to listen to you!" (279).[48] The issue of class struggle implicit in the couple's argument about physical self-denial and material indulgence surfaces when Zudin and his wife engage in a semijocular name-calling exchange: she accuses him of being a "bourgeois" when he asks whether there is any mustard to go with the horsemeat she has cooked, while he questions whether she is truly a "communist" after she complains about the unprecedented shortage of butter they are now experiencing in the food shops (278).

An ensuing scene, in which Zudin is shown successfully resisting Yelena's sexual advances, demonstrates not only his high degree of self-restraint, but also the way in which sexual and gastronomical pleasures are closely associated with chocolate throughout the novella. Zudin is working late, and Valts happens to be the sole staff member on duty that evening. When the two find themselves alone in his office, Yelena sits down beside him on his divan and confesses her deep love for him. Yelena's physical beauty, elegant attire, and aromatic scent have increasingly aroused Zudin's interest. On several occasions, he has been mesmerized by her dark, "chocolate-colored" eyes,[49] and he feels troubled whenever he finds himself close to—or even just thinking about—the delectable secretary. On this particular evening, as he sits close to Yelena on the soft divan in front of a warm fire burning in the stove, Zudin suddenly feels overwhelmed by feelings of sexual longing: "Reclining his body back on the cushions, he noticed with amazement how his temples were throbbing strongly, and how it felt as if someone were squeezing his heart so tightly and yet so sweetly. And powerful threads of current, forming into a mighty wave, flooded over him, dragging him toward the dear Valts, the longed for and enticing Valts, the warm Valts" (293).[50] The warm touch of Yelena's tender hand on his own causes his heart to skip a beat "in joyful terror" (293). And her ardent declaration of love causes Zudin to feel uncontrollably languid, desirous, and yielding.

"He was melting like wax," the narrator informs us. "It seemed to him as if a flood of soft, fragrant, warm, sticky lava of tasty milk chocolate was spreading all over him, pouring into his mouth and choking his throat to the point of spasms" (294). Clearly, sexual and gastronomical connotations are suggested here in this colorful and erotic image of milk chocolate visualized as an eruption of flowing liquids and spasmodic bodily excitation. Yet Zudin manages somehow to regain his emotional equanimity and succeeds in resisting Yelena's allure. He calmly explains to her that, tempted as he is, he simply cannot and must not yield to what he characterizes as "the indulgence of a carefree passion" with her. "I am not a saint, of course," he tells her.

> All sorts of tender and coarse feelings, all the instincts that are natural to man, are not alien to me either. But all the same there is also something within me, Yelena Valentinovna, something that you will not understand—how can I explain it to you?—I have within me class feeling! It is a wondrous, ever-living, and powerful spring. I derive from it all of my strength, from it alone do I drink all of my personal, sublime happiness. . . . It weaves crowns of wondrous delights for us; before it the dreams in our heart and the thoughts in our head about women are but mere trifles. It resounds in our heart with a mighty upsurge. Both reason and emotion are held in its joyous power. (295–96)

"So should I suppress this feeling, or exchange it for something else, or forget it?" Zudin asks her rhetorically. "And all for the sake of experiencing the delicate love of a woman?" (296). Tarasov-Rodionov's politically and ideologically correct hero concludes his didactic little speech to Yelena by telling her, "There are many places where there is a great deal of sweet chocolate, but that is alien to us. We are not at all accustomed to it. With its softness it only hinders us in our cruel struggle, and since that is the case, we have no need for it" (296). Real Bolsheviks, in other words, do not eat chocolate. Nor, by implication, do they indulge in sexual pleasure.

## Bread Versus Chocolate: Politicizing and Ideologizing Food

Despite his ascetic victory this evening in resisting the sweet pleasures promised by sex and chocolate, Zudin's problems with Yelena are far from over. It does not take very long before Valts manages to get caught misusing her staff position to extort gold from a bourgeois family desperate to have its wrongly imprisoned son released from jail. A full-scale investigation reveals that the imported chocolate Yelena gave to Zudin's children had been provided by one of her lovers, an Englishman named Edward Hackey, who is deeply involved in espionage activities against the Soviet regime. As Hackey puts it in a letter to Yelena that seeks to recruit her loyalty, he has not forgotten "how my little kitten loves to nibble chocolate" (281). Because Zudin originally hired Yelena to work at Cheka headquarters and because he appears to have accepted bribes from her in return for protecting her and covering up her illegal activities, he is now arrested and placed under interrogation. In addition to receiving contraband chocolate, silk stockings, and gold, engaging in sexual relations with a White Guard conspirator (Valts), participating in orgies that involved alcohol and whores, and collaborating with a class enemy (all of these being trumped-up charges), Zudin stands accused of having violated the trust of the working masses by abusing the power and authority accorded him as a high-ranking Cheka official and Party member.

At first, Zudin is fully confident that his innocence will be established and that he will be exonerated. After all, his only crime was showing compassion for the unfortunate Yelena Valts, with whom he never did enter into sexual relations and from whom he never did knowingly accept any bribes. If he is guilty of anything, it is only of a lack of prudence and good judgment in his attempt to reform her.[51] He candidly explains to the chief investigator: "I thought that an honest job would help to get her back on her feet as a human being, and would help her to shake off the cobwebs of the despicable bourgeois mode of life. But apparently I made a mistake: chocolate proved to be stronger" (340). During the period of his incarceration and interrogation, however, Zudin reflects critically upon his past life and career; he comes to see that he too has perhaps fallen short of what he calls "proletarian standards" of ethical conduct. He now realizes that the mere appearance of misconduct on his part may well be enough to discredit both himself as a Bolshevik and the Party as a whole. Workers at the local factory are already expressing cynicism about the behavior of these Bolshevik leaders. "And where were you before?" they ask derisively when they are approached by Party officials about helping to defend their town against nearby White Guard units. "Were you out devouring chocolate?" (363). "Where is that Zudin of yours?" they add:

Bring him here and hand him over to us: we'll straighten him out! We're not even being given our daily allotment of one-eighth of a pound of bread every day, while he gets chocolate?! Our children are dying in the cold from starvation, while he keeps company with a ballet dancer dressed in silks?! Why do you protect him? Or are you just as guilty as he is? Until you uproot and exterminate this foul scum, we won't believe what you say any more. We don't believe you! We don't believe you! And we won't go anywhere for you. Go eat your chocolates! (363–64)

By the end of the investigation, Zudin has become convinced that his execution is necessary in order to mobilize worker support for the Revolution, especially during the current White Guard military offensive when enemy troops are rapidly advancing upon the city. He believes that his execution will serve as an edifying example to other Bolshevik leaders who, because of the nature of their work and their mode of living, find themselves similarly distanced from the lives of the starving masses. Such men, he muses, continue to consider themselves Communists even as they puff on Havana cigars, cool their chocolate in delicate porcelain cups, and play with the heavy watch chains on their vests. In short, Zudin now realizes that his tragic story can be read as a cautionary tale by those Party members who might be tempted to let their desire for personal pleasures and material comforts pervert their sense of public duty and devotion to the revolutionary cause.

What helps Zudin to accept the necessity of his own execution are two allegorical dreams he experiences during his incarceration; both of these dreams, significantly enough, involve the political and ideological importance of chocolate. In the first dream, Zudin convinces a gigantic old peasant to share his last piece of bread with him (rather than hoard it). But the peasant soon discovers that Zudin is hiding a huge, fragrant piece of chocolate in his pocket. "What is this?" exclaims the peasant. "Have you deceived me?! . . . You have taken my last piece of bread when you already have sweets!" (346). Confused and embarrassed, Zudin tries to continue walking forward, but finds that he keeps falling down into the mud. "He was covered all over with a sticky brown mass," the narrator observes. "Was it clay? Or was it chocolate? . . . How could he tell?" (346). Zudin suddenly awakens, startled by this disquieting dream, and asks himself: "Really, what is this damned chocolate, this chocolate that follows me so importunately? Where did it come from?" (347).

The answer seems to be provided by his second dream, where the action takes place initially in a Russian chocolate factory and then in a rather primitive colonialist sweatshop, located somewhere in the developing world, where scantily clad black slaves are melting bean pods down into cacao. Zudin attempts to raise the consciousness of these exploited black workers, but just as in his earlier dream about the peasant, his promise to lead these poor downtrodden laborers to a chocolate-free future, to a workers' utopia without any capitalist exploitation, rings hollow when the slaves find that there is chocolate hidden in Zudin's pocket. "This is a master!" they shout upon their discovery. "He has deceived us! . . . He has chocolate!" (359).

These two lengthy dreams, both of which crudely allegorize Marxist-Leninist doctrine, reflect Zudin's deep-seated fear that he may unwittingly have corrupted his ideological purity as a result of direct contact with capitalist and bourgeois elements (that is, the alluring Yelena Valts with her chocolate). They help Zudin to understand why his own execution is necessary: after all, how can those who serve in the vanguard of the Revolution expect to command the trust of workers and peasants when they are seen stuffing themselves with a luxury food item, such as chocolate, which is currently in very short supply or is too expensive for anyone but the privileged few to be able to afford? Early in his interrogation, Zudin had stated, " *My* fate is not of much interest to me. What I am concerned about is *our* fate" (324). Now, after the revolutionary tribunal has reached its verdict and ordered his execution, Zudin continues to maintain that the interests of the Party, of the Revolution, and of the workers' future must take precedence over his own personal fate: "After all, only one thing, in truth, is important: that the cause—the cause of bringing about as soon as possible the happiness of all people—not perish. That is the only thing that matters" (382).

The distinction between purity and depravity is also reified in the novel's opposition between "bread," which represents the basic staff of life, and "chocolate," which symbolizes excess and luxury. Whether it be the giant peasant in Zudin's first dream (who is willing to share with others his last crust of bread), the factory bosses in his second dream (who try to economize on costs by importing chocolate from the colonial world rather than producing bread at home), the actual local factory workers (who often fail to receive their daily ration of bread, while Zudin and other Party officials are believed to be devouring chocolate), or the elegant and alluring Yelena Valts (who likes to nibble on chocolate bars during her walks), the author of *Chocolate* repeatedly and consistently encodes these two opposing food items with social, moral, and ideological values that categorize the social-class affiliation of the people who do or do not eat them. If Valts, as a petit bourgeois whore who becomes involved in an espionage ring, plans an extortion scheme, and participates in other forms of counterrevolutionary activity, is the sexual demon who must be resisted and destroyed, then the chocolate that is so closely associated with her throughout the novella is the gastronomical demon that must likewise be exorcised.

## Bolshevik Saints, Revolutionary Asceticism, and Tolstoyism

Zudin's rigid ideological thinking and strict asceticism are characteristic of many positive heroes of Soviet proletarian fiction during the 1920s and early 1930s, literary characters who believe that social duty and class loyalty must triumph over their personal feelings and physical needs. This type of narrative championed a puritanical code of ethics that was apotheosized in works of Socialist Realism, particularly in the portrayal of Pavel Korchagin, the ascetic hero of Nikolay Ostrovsky's *How the Steel Was Tempered* (1934).[52] In a study titled *Saints and Revolutionaries: The Ascetic Hero in Russian Literature* (1993), Marcia Morris examines how, as a character type, the ascetic hero in Russian literature can be found both in medieval saints' lives and in many formulaic, didactic novels from the Bolshevik 1920s. In these works of early Soviet fiction, she points out, the asceticism is no longer a religious phenomenon; it now stems from apocalyptic expectations and millenarian thinking on the part of the revolutionaries.[53] The ascetic hero of early Soviet fiction thus girds and disciplines himself—through physical self-denial and emotional self-abnegation—in order to render himself capable of fulfilling the revolutionary tasks that await him. "It became characteristic for Soviet prose of the 1920s," explains Mikhail Zolotonosov, "to feature a positive hero: the Communist who seeks to overcome the criminal call of the flesh."[54]

In historical and cultural terms, this Bolshevik brand of puritanism was not without precedent in tsarist Russia. A central tenet of late-nineteenth-century Russian political culture, after all, had been "an idealized notion of abnegation of the self in favor of the social whole," whereby dedication to the common good, it was believed, could help deflect an appetite for personal gratification that seemed to be growing stronger as the forces of modernization took hold at all levels of Russian society.[55] Historically considered, the Bolshevik campaign during the 1920s to suppress sexual desire and subordinate it to the advancement of proletarian class interests finds perhaps its primary source in Nikolay Chernyshevsky's seminal novel *What Is To Be Done?* (1863).[56] For many young Russian radicals, the character Rakhmetov is an exemplar of secular asceticism, illustrating how—through labor, self-discipline, and the denial of bodily pleasures—libidinal energy could successfully be diverted and channeled into purposeful revolutionary activity. In fact, as an ascetic model, Rakhmetov "was being fervently promoted as an ideological goal for every conscientious young Soviet citizen in the 1920s."[57]

The prerevolutionary roots of this Bolshevik strain of asceticism can be found not only in Tolstoy's writings, but also in writings by Nikolay Fyodorov, Nikolay Berdyaev, and other influential turn-of-the-century religious thinkers. Indeed, their message of physical self-denial, renunciation of pleasure, and sexual sublimation was revived and ideologically recontextualized in early Communist Russia.[58] Messages advocating sexual self-restraint in Soviet Russia during the 1920s, as Sheila Fitzpatrick has argued, came mainly in the form of advice from Party authorities to Communist youth: "The authorities—most of them Old Bolsheviks, who saw the revolutionary cause as a vocation requiring sacrifice—recommended self-discpline, abstinence, fidelity to one partner, and sublimation of sexual energies in work."[59] One of the most extreme and dogmatic Bolshevik champions of this puritanical message of spartan self-denial was the self-styled sexologist Aron Zalkind, whose twelve "sexual commandments" spelled out quite clearly how revolutionary youth could divert their sexual energy away from personal pleasure and sublimate it instead into productive labor and meaningful class-oriented activity.[60]

If Zudin's inner struggle between his sense of social duty and his personal desires seems psychologically unconvincing for modern readers, it does nevertheless reflect accurately the vigorous campaign against personal pleasure that was launched in Soviet Russia during the 1920s.

As Zudin makes clear in a short speech he gives to Valts early in the novel while attempting to raise her political consciousness, he firmly believes that the greatest threat to the cause of the Revolution is posed not by some external power (such as foreign interventionists or White Guard elements); our greatest enemy, he explains, resides inside each and every one of us. "Yes, within us ourselves," he insists, "in our inner yearning for the past: for the everyday life of the past, for the rags of the past, for the habits of the past. That's where our real enemies are!" (283). For old-guard Bolsheviks like Zudin, defense of the Revolution is likely to entail sacrificing love, marriage, and family, as those remnants of bourgeois private life promise only to sap one's social energy and thus weaken one's dedication to the common cause. As one enthusiastic supporter of revolutionary asceticism in early Soviet Russia noted at the time, "sex is the soul of the bourgeoisie."[61]

The Bolshevik campaign against personal pleasure during the 1920s was expressed through a rhetoric of asceticism that was not only sexual, but also gastronomical in nature. "Protecting one's ideological purity during NEP," Naiman points out,

> entailed not only controlling sexual urges but also refraining from overeating and, in general, from surrounding oneself with opulence. However, just as the dictate to sublimate sexual desires quickly developed into the recommendation that young communists abstain entirely from sexual intercourse (and from all noncollective physical pleasures), so vigilance against gastronomic indulgence and rich living was transformed by reductive logic into a dictate to survive on the minimum quantity of food, sleep, and shelter necessary to sustain human existence. In the puritanical discourse of the 1920s, sexual excess could be equated with the consumption not only of rich foods but of as little as a small piece of bread.[62]

Because sexual lust had become linked closely in the Bolshevik mindset with gluttony and the desire to eat rich foods, excesses in eating and sexual behavior were noted throughout the NEP period to distinguish the morally corrupt and sensually depraved bourgeois from the physically malnourished but ideologically pure proletarian. "Oral as well as genital asceticism," Naiman explains, "functioned as behavioral identity cards for the ideologically committed builders of communist society."[63] This distinction finds instantiation in the contrast between the celibate Bolshevik Zudin and the promiscuous ballet dancer Valts. Indeed, Zudin's tragic fall proceeds directly from the fact that in his attempt to reform Valts he has created the impression that he belongs not to the proletariat, but to the bourgeoisie.

Tarasov-Rodionov's two-pronged attack upon the pleasure principle, whereby his proletarian characters are warned of the sexual and gastronomical dangers that lurk ominously around them, closely resembles the ascetic orientation of Tolstoy, who once proclaimed that "the alpha and omega of a morally good life is the constant battle against luxury" (88:19–20).[64] The debate over sexual morality Tolstoy helped to inspire in late tsarist Russia found new presentation in this Bolshevik obsession with purity as part of the war against privilege. Indeed, one can hear distinct echoes of several Tolstoyan teachings in *Chocolate*: the view of women as demonic seductresses ("She is a devil, not a woman," Zudin at one point thinks of Valts [292]), the distinction between luxury and necessity (in diet as well as in other spheres of daily life), the preference for peasant-produced bread over gentry-imported chocolate, the need for austerity in sexual and gastronomical matters, the belief that certain types of food can weaken one's resolve to avoid sensual pleasures, the call to share our food fraternally and unselfishly with others, and so on.

What is perhaps most "Tolstoyan" about Zudin's revolutionary asceticism, however, is the striving for moral self-perfection that inspires it. Like Tolstoy, Zudin believes that our greatest challenge is to eradicate or at least silence the enemy that lies buried within each and every one of us. The identity of that inner "enemy" is, to quote Valts,

> our intimate feeling of self-love, of egoism, and our yearning for various comfortable . . . well, let's say, habits, which have come down to us as a legacy from thousands of ancestors—in a word, all of this pleasant culture, this comfort that you so despise. . . . All of this culture—it is, after all, a part of our "I," of our body, and to kill it . . . No, it's impossible! (284)

Although the motivation for Tolstoy's Christian asceticism was moral and religious, whereas Zudin's ideology is based instead on Bolshevik doctrine and proletarian class consciousness, they both seek to make themselves spiritually pure by resisting and renouncing bodily pleasure. "It seems to me," Valts observes to Zudin, "that both in the Gospels and in your words one hears the same idea about perfecting the very essence of man: the enemy is within us. How then is one to reach self-perfection?!" (284).[65] The answer for Zudin, as it had been for Tolstoy and his followers, is by resisting both sexual and gastronomical temptations. What happens in early Soviet Russia is that this Tolstoyan ideal of moral purity and spiritual self-perfection—this ascetic striving for freedom from sinful luxury by overcoming one's base egoistic desires—now acquires unprecedented ideological significance as a rigorous set of behavioral commandments for members of the working class to obey.[66]

Tarasov-Rodionov's novella takes this connection between ideological purity and a religious-style asceticism one step further, however, suggesting that even the mere *appearance* of indulgence in sexual and gastronomic pleasure is enough to compromise proletarian standards of ethical conduct. During the Stalinist era, as we shall see in the following section, the Bolshevik campaign against private life and personal pleasure was halted during the mid-1930s, when the government reversed its earlier official policy toward love, marriage, and the family, and reintroduced middle-class values, leading to a retreat from the fundamental tenets of Communism.[67] Under Stalin the practice of providing special benefits (such as additional food rations, access to exclusive stores, restaurants, and hospitals, subsidized housing, chauffeured cars, and so on) to high-ranking Party officials, as part of a hierarchical system of privilege known as *nomenklatura*, became firmly established in Communist Russia.[68] Soviet commentators during the Stalinist and post-Stalinist years were careful, therefore, to point out that although Tarasov-Rodionov should be commended for having raised the theme of the pernicious influence bourgeois mores and manners can have upon members of the proletariat, he is nonetheless guilty of committing serious ideological errors in *Chocolate*. "In particular," notes one Soviet-era critic, "he yielded to the 'sacrificial' philosophy of the irreconcilability of personal interests with social duty."[69]

## Stalinist Triumphalism: Rise of Consumerism, Demise of Tolstoyism

The years from 1933 to 1937 have been called a "time of triumphalism" in Soviet Russia, a period when socialism was declared to have achieved its irreversible victory.[70] In a policy shift that some have characterized as a "great retreat" from—even an outright "betrayal" of—the basic principles and core values that had guided the October Revolution, the Soviet leadership in the mid-1930s suddenly abandoned the ascetic puritanism, sublimation of desire, and rhetoric of sacrifice and self-denial that had dominated War Communism and the early years of Bolshevik rule. Proclaiming that the transitional period from capitalism to socialism had now been successfully completed, Stalin signaled a new ideological orientation that celebrated—rather than condemned or stigmatized—images of abundance, pleasure, and personal well-being. These images of prosperity were designed to offer graphic proof that the Communist utopia had now been achieved in Soviet Russia, thus vindicating Stalin's famous declaration: "Life has become better, comrades. Life has become more cheerful." By the mid-1930s, as one scholar has pointed out, "food, drink, and consumer goods came to be celebrated with a fervor that even Madison Avenue might have envied."[71] Chocolate, which had been categorically condemned as a marker of bourgeois decadence and venality during the 1920s, now became one of the symbols of a newly achieved material well-being and economic prosperity in Stalinist Russia. "This was *la vie en rose*, Soviet style," notes Sheila Fitzpatrick in her discussion of how a relaxation of social mores and the promotion of leisure culture came to characterize the Stalinist rhetoric used by government officials and Party leaders during this period. "To some people," she writes, "it looked like embourgeoisement or 'a second NEP.'"[72] As Randi Cox observes, "what had been decried as bourgeois decadence during NEP was now redefined, with the help of advertising, as cultured and worthy of desire."[73]

What Soviet citizens living under Stalinist rule during the mid-1930s were witnessing, of course, was the birth of a consumer society and a culture of consumption in Communist Russia. "The New Soviet Man and Woman were not only engineers, Stakhanovites, and kolkhozniki," one critic reminds us, "they were also shoppers, customers, and consumers."[74] In an effort to validate Comrade Stalin's assurance that the severe material scarcities that had plagued the Soviet Union during the postrevolutionary period—and especially during the first Five-Year Plan (1928–32)—had now been overcome and the long-awaited socialist utopia of prosperity had at last been established, Soviet authorities exerted tremendous effort and committed manifold resources toward dramatically increasing the production and distribution of new consumer goods.

This dramatic shift in the direction the centrally planned economy was taking (from heavy industry to light industry, from production to consumption) is particularly evident in the area of food products, which were now ordered to be produced and distributed in unprecedented quantities. Luxury food items, such as caviar, cognac, champagne, and chocolate, which had been unavailable just a few years earlier, suddenly became the focus of intensive economic planning. As Jukka Gronow explains in his study, *Caviar with Champagne: Common Luxury and the Ideals of the Good Life in Stalin's Russia* (2003), Stalin believed that success in revolutionizing the consumer goods industry in the USSR (by increasing the quantity and improving the quality of luxury items) so that it could rival Western standards would validate the socialist state and demonstrate that the Soviet Union could compete economically on a world stage. Foodstuffs, clothing, and household items that had been conspicuously absent from store shelves during the final years of collectivization and the first Five-Year Plan were now suddenly advertised as being available for purchase. "The history of the rebirth of the Soviet chocolate industry is particularly revealing," writes Gronow, "within a couple of years its product variety jumped from just a dozen to several hundred."[75] Where chocolate during the 1920s was a highly stigmatized luxury item that only the rich beneficiaries of private trading under NEP could afford—either financially or ideologically—to purchase and consume, by the mid-1930s that stigma had been entirely removed and intensive efforts were undertaken to make chocolate as widely available as possible to the Soviet population through increased production and improved distribution. From the perspective of the Soviet leadership, the availability of a new luxury consumer good such as chocolate acted as a visible sign that the happy and prosperous way of life promised by the Revolution had indeed been reached.

The report on the Soviet food industry, delivered in January 1936 by Anastas Mikoyan, Stalin's food minister, provides a clear indication of just how drastically the Party's and the government's official attitude toward consumption—and consumption of luxury food items in particular—had changed.[76] Noting that historically tsarist Russia had had no need for a food industry, because the more cultured segments of the country's bourgeois and aristocratic population could get the luxury food items they wanted at chic import shops located in both Petersburg and Moscow (such as the famous Eliseev store on Tverskoy Boulevard), Mikoyan boasted that these food items no longer needed to be imported from abroad as they were now beginning to be produced at home (7). And whereas only a very few Russian confectionery factories had even existed in tsarist days (Mikoyan mentions specifically the "George Borman" chocolate factories in Petersburg and Kharkov), and these produced chocolate bonbons exclusively for the upper crust (what Mikoyan calls the "cream" of bourgeois society in Russia), the nine Soviet-era chocolate factories that had been newly built during the 1930s under Stalin's first two Five-Year Plans were now said to be able to provide the average Soviet consumer with sufficient amounts and a wide assortment of high-quality chocolate (12). Comrade Stalin and the Party's Central Committee, it was also announced, had decided to allot 900,000 rubles toward the importation of more cocoa beans into Soviet Russia. "Thank you, Central Committee," Mikoyan says to loud applause,

> Now we will have delicious chocolate bonbons in abundance. We no longer need to import tractors, and we do not import automobiles. We are now wealthy enough to be able to spend a modicum of our foreign currency on cocoa beans for chocolate. We possess a confectionery industry that is technologically well-equipped and we possess qualified personnel: we can produce high-quality chocolate bonbons in enormous quantities. (48)[77]

This optimistic 1936 Soviet food industry report reflects a strong feeling of national pride in the country's newfound economic self-sufficiency as well as a Marxist-Leninist concern for the more widespread—as well as more egalitarian and equitable—distribution of a food item that in tsarist Russia had been exclusively produced for, distributed to, and consumed by the privileged classes. It also reveals the startling change of direction that had occurred in the official policy concerning the consumption of food products. The minister concludes his report on the state of the Soviet food industry optimistically: "Under the banner of Lenin and Stalin, we will move ahead toward an abundance of food products, toward an abundance of consumer goods, and toward a cultured life for every member of our society!" (63).

"The Soviet citizen was meant to be and look happy, to dress better and to enjoy life—especially in the sphere of material culture," notes Gronow when describing Stalin's new cultural policy.[78] Revolutionary asceticism and Tolstoyan self-denial were no longer fashionable, of course, in this changed ideological, moral, and cultural climate of conspicuous consumption. As Cox notes, the insistence by some left-wing commentators that "domestic comfort was inherently counterrevolutionary and self-indulgent no longer carried any weight by the mid-1930s. Revolutionary asceticism had been supplanted by an entirely proper striving for a cultured life."[79] Where the cultural politics of the 1920s had been dominated by "the conception of proletarian culture and the ideal of the ascetic self-sacrificing worker," the official rhetoric of the mid-1930s was instead characterized by a spirit of material indulgence, hedonism, and consumerism.[80] Julie Hessler, who in her study of the Stalinist turn to consumerism during the mid-1930s concentrates mainly on the government's campaign for "cultured trade" during this period, likewise notes the seismic shift in Party thinking that accompanied this policy change. "In the 1920s," she observes, "an interest in material possessions was portrayed in official publications as a sign of bourgeois decadence, a deviation from the ascetic values of the socialist revolution."[81] By the mid-1930s, however, that attitude had been reversed. "During these years," she points out, "asceticism gave way to cultured consumerism as the recognized relation of the individual to material possessions."[82] The regime's public valorization and official sanction of material values meant that the populace need no longer eschew consumer goods, including luxury items such as chocolate, as decadent bourgeois indulgences. "In the mid-1930s," writes Gronow, "the former ideals of revolutionary asceticism and social egalitarianism gave way to the emergence of a new hierarchy and a new system of social order, one that allowed for a more hedonistic and individualistic way of life."[83]

Like so many other utopian dreams from the Soviet 1920s, revolutionary asceticism—along with the Tolstoyan struggle against hedonism and bodily pleasure it had mandated—was destined to disappear suddenly and irrevocably from the discourse that surrounded the construction of socialism in the USSR under Stalin and his successors. Stalin's Second Five-Year Plan was merely the first of many official directives signaling this new focus on "the joys of consumption," "the enjoyment of life," and "a new lifestyle of pleasure" that would come to dominate Party rhetoric throughout the remainder of the Soviet period.[84] Tolstoy's conceptualization of the human animal as a creature that strives instinctively for the gratification of its physical desire for pleasure seems to have been implicitly shared by the Party leadership in the Soviet Union both during and after Stalin's reign. Unlike Lenin and the early Bolsheviks, however, who eschewed self-indulgence in bodily pleasures, Stalin and his successors encouraged, at least in their official rhetoric, an ethos of consumption that pandered to the inherently hedonistic animality (*zhivotnost'*) that Tolstoy instructed his followers to restrain, control, and ultimately overcome.

## *Dostoevsky's Legacy: Human Bestiality in Prerevolutionary Fiction*

If in matters concerning carnality and morality Tolstoy left his imprint on fin de siècle and revolutionary Russia mainly through his championing of asceticism, abstinence, and moral puritanism, Dostoevsky's legacy was felt most strongly by those writers and thinkers who subscribed to the modern idea of the zoological self championed in the late nineteenth century by the Social Darwinists. By the 1890s and 1900s, Darwinism had begun to give way to—or, more accurately, merge with—Nietzscheanism as the ideology of metaphysical and moral nihilism that best captured the spirit of emergent capitalism and the materialist values of the nascent bourgeoisie in Russia. Where Darwin had become closely identified with such notions as the "struggle for existence" and the "survival of the fittest," Nietzsche was seen as adding an elitist element to this predatory and carnivoristic philosophy.[85] "Nietzsche thinks a people is created only so that five or six outstanding individuals should exist," writes V. V. Chuyko. "These are the tigers and lions born to devour the sheep."[86] What was perceived to be Nietzsche's joyful, Dionysian affirmation of the dark and cruel psychic urges in human nature (a perception shaped in large measure by Max Nordau's unflattering characterization of Nietzsche's ideas in his book *Degeneration* [1892]) led many Russian critics and readers at the time to identify this new amoral philosophy closely with Dostoevsky's "cruel talent."

More specifically, they linked Nietzscheanism with the sadistic hedonism and violent aggressiveness of Dostoevsky's "nihilist" heroes, who were seen to have liberated themselves from the slave morality of the weak and mediocre herd surrounding them.[87] Svidrigaylov, Stavrogin, and other "master" personality types from Dostoevsky's novels were now perceived as Russian incarnations of the fierce and fearless "blond beast of prey" (*blonde Bestie*) of vulgar Nietzscheanism, the "laughing lion" who, in liberating his primordial instincts, abandons himself to cruel and violent pleasures with no concern for the effect his behavior has upon others. The critic Nikolay Grot, for example, considered Nietzsche a Social Darwinist who views people as "beasts whose only purpose in life is the struggle for existence, power, and strength."[88] Nikolay Mikhaylovsky, meanwhile, asserted that Nietzsche's moral views (and his nihilistic conceptualization of human nature) bear close affinities with those despicable values shared by both Darwin and Dostoevsky. "There is no doubt," writes Mikhaylovsky, "that those gloomy depths of cruelty, limitless love of power and malice, into which Dostoevsky loved to look and which have become the basis for Nietzsche's theory, really exist and are a subject of great interest for the student of the human spirit, that is, the sick, unbalanced spirit; these are pathological cases."[89] As Edith Clowes explains, Mikhaylovsky "finds in Nietzsche's writing the same 'cruelty' he had condemned in Dostoevsky" and believes that both the Nietzschean superman and the Dostoevskian underground man share "the same insight that cruelty and love of power are at the root of human nature."[90]

This close identification of Dostoevsky's demonic male heroes with a popularized and vulgarized version of Nietzscheanism in turn-of-the-century Russia helped to link the Russian writer's poetics, in the minds of many contemporaries, with a perverse erotics of violence, dominance, and subordination. In largely distorted form, some of Nietzsche's central notions—in particular, his belief, espoused in such works as *The Genealogy of Morals* (1887) and *The Antichrist* (1895), that the legacy of Christian culture has been the unfortunate reduction of the strong, aggressive, and daring beast of prey within human beings to a tame, domesticated, civilized animal—were now voiced by a number of fictional characters in Russian literary works. Matvey Prispelov, the central character in Pyotr Boborykin's *The Cruel Ones* (1901), for example, is a self-proclaimed Nietzschean who, in imitation of Dostoevsky's amoral "man-god," seeks to assert his dominance over others through sexually aggressive behavior.[91]

Brutish sexual aggression of a predatory nature likewise characterizes the behavior of the strong, rapacious male figures one finds romanticized in many of the sensational Russian boulevard novels that were popular during the immediate prerevolutionary period, when the search for pleasure and the quest for self-determination by many literary characters were frequently accompanied by the exercise of a Nietzschean will-to-power, especially in the portrayal of sexual relations. In the realm of sexuality, as Clowes observes, there seem to be no equal partners among the literary characters in Russian boulevard fiction, only "masters" and "slaves."[92] In the popular fiction of fin de siècle Russia, where, according to conservative moral commentators at least, an ethos of self-love and a cult of the individual personality were quickly replacing the traditional Russian moral values of self-abnegation, Christian compassion, and civic duty, egoistic thinking and rapacious behavior almost invariably characterized the search for sexual liberation and personal self-discovery.

The very title of Evdokia Nagrodskaya's *The Wrath of Dionysus*, with its explicit allusion to the Roman god of sensualism, eroticism, and hedonism (whom Nietzsche had lionized in his writings), signals to readers that they can expect to find in this boulevard novel a vulgarized Nietzschean erotics of dominance, pain, and humiliation. The "Wrath of Dionysus," it turns out, refers more immediately to the title of an important painting that is being undertaken by the novel's heroine, Tanya Kuznetsova, a Russian artist living and working in Rome, whose confused sexual identity (her friend Latchinov theorizes that she is a man—with male sensibilities, characteristics, and desires—who is trapped in the body of a woman) propels the central story line in the novel. In a text where art is thrown into conflict with personal life and where romantic love is constantly threatened by sexual passion, the "bestial" element manifests itself mainly as the dark power of sexual instinct aroused in the heroine by her lover Stark, whose obsession with Tanya seriously jeopardizes her commitment to art as well as her marriage to a kind, loving husband. "It's the body!" Tanya exclaims in exasperation at one point. "When the body cries out, there is nothing to be done: neither reason nor intellect can help."[93] After the heroine finally surrenders to Stark's insistent sexual advances and they at last enjoy mad, passionate love together, he confesses to her: "I'm a savage beast . . . a crude animal" (96). Despite all the vulgarized Nietzschean rhetoric of Dionysian frenzy that surrounds discussion of Tanya's painting, however, there is not actually any of the carnivoristic discourse or cruel erotics of dominance and humiliation that the reader has been led to expect. Tanya's lover Stark, it turns out, is himself a woman trapped in a man's body, and his main concern is not to inflict pain and suffering upon the heroine, but rather to win her affection, to get her to marry him, and then to raise their child together as a family.

Anastasia Verbitskaya's *The Keys to Happiness*, meanwhile, features at least two male characters (both of them are competing for the heart of the novel's heroine, the dancer Manya Yeltsova), who embody the rapacious sensuality that during this era came to be vulgarly identified with Dostoevsky, Darwin, and Nietzsche. The two are Baron Mark Steinbach, a wealthy Jewish industrialist who financially supports progressive social causes and the arts, and Nikolay Nelidov, a reactionary anti-Semitic aristocrat who believes that the ferocious natural law of the jungle (survival of the fittest) is what will prevent humankind from suffering the biological degeneracy that is currently being hastened by women and Jews.[94] Steinbach, whose teeth are "sharp like those of a predator" (1:141), whose eyes are "wild" (like those of a dog when it is about to bite someone) (1:164), and whose smile is "predatory" (1:147), openly acknowledges that he has been endowed genetically with a "monstrous sensuality" that is the curse of his Jewish blood (1:158). The obscurantist Nelidov, meanwhile, looks at Manya with eyes that are "cruel and full of desire, the way savages look at a woman they are about to carry off as spoils of conquest" (2:26). "Ah, I'd so love to take her into my embrace, to melt into one with her! And destroy her in a single upsurge of passion!" Nelidov thinks to himself upon meeting Manya for the first time. "How hard it is to control myself!" (2:28). And control himself is precisely what he fails to do the very next day with young Manya, who can clearly sense his savage intent right from the beginning ("You're cruel. You're a beast of prey," she tells him [2:29]):

He kissed her silently, greedily, rapaciously, like a wild man. Crudely, painfully, and somehow primitively, he caressed her shoulders, breasts, and knees, and with a single blow of his blind and mighty desire destroyed all that had separated them just yesterday, even just a moment before. What did it matter to the dark force ruling his behavior that one week ago he hadn't even known that this girl existed? (2:36)

The submissive Manya, for her part, can offer only feeble resistance to Nelidov's rape attempt: "She hadn't expected this. She hadn't wanted it. She was crushed by these stormy, crude, unfamiliar caresses. . . . He'd taken her into his arms like booty, and made off into the woods. She, like a slave, had succumbed to his desire. . . . She felt that he'd wanted to destroy her in his embrace, that this wasn't even love, but some kind of blind hatred" (2:36).

Although Nelidov may well be the character in the novel most in possession of what the narrator characterizes as "a cruel and triumphant desire" (3:141), it is sexual passion itself—especially male sexual passion—that constitutes the truly dark and demonic force of carnivorousness at work in *The Keys to Happiness*. Indeed, when, near the novel's end, we learn that, at long last, passion no longer predominates within the visibly aged Nelidov, we are told that this "master" personality was now "free of cruelty and the elemental thirst for destruction" (6:272).

*Vulgarized Nietzschean Erotics in Artsybashev's* Sanin

Vladimir Sanin is usually included among those characters in early twentieth-century Russian boulevard fiction who exhibit the sadistic hedonism of the Nietzschean "beast of prey." Compared by some commentators to Dostoevsky's "bestial" Dmitry Karamazov,[95] Artsybashev's hero was considered by many contemporary critics to be a Russian incarnation of the Nietzschean *Übermensch*, a "beast of prey" whose erotomania presents readers with a highly sexualized instantiation of the German philosopher's defense of extreme individualism, preoccupation with self, and will-to-power. Even present-day scholars continue to characterize Sanin as "a kind of Nietzschean superhero."[96] Unlike the stereotypical "beast of prey" that circulated in turn-of-the-century Russian boulevard fiction, however, Artsybashev's hero does not revel in the sadistic, elitist erotics of cruelty, violence, and savagery. To the contrary, Sanin's hedonistic credo—that human beings should avail themselves of the numerous physical pleasures and libidinal enjoyments that life has to offer the human body—is one that is advocated equally for all people (including members of both genders) and that should not be pursued at the expense of pain and suffering in others. "While exalting the purity of natural desire," Engelstein writes, "Artsybashev condemns sexual conquest for the sake of domination, along with language and actions degrading to women."[97] Indeed, Artsybashev's "erotics of parallel status for men and women," she explains, contrasts quite sharply with the conventional Nietzschean erotics of dominance and subordination that one usually encounters in boulevard fiction.[98] Despite all its sexual suggestiveness, argues another critic, *Sanin* imposes "its own scale of sexual values," one that roundly condemns a vulgarized Nietzscheanism.[99]

Where one does find an erotics of cruelty, violence, and savagery at work in *Sanin*, however, is in the thinking and behavior of two highly negative male characters: the misogynistic military officer Zarudin and his debauched friend Voloshin. Zarudin's attitude toward women—potential victims of the free exercise of his male sexual prowess—is vividly illustrated in an early scene, where he has just learned that the virginal Lida Sanina (the hero's sister) intends to give herself to him sexually. We find him fantasizing about what her carnal "fall" from grace will entail:

> But after her promise today, uttered in a strangely faltering and submissive voice, one that Zarudin recognized from his experience with other women, all of a sudden he unexpectedly felt his own strength and the imminent proximity of his goal, and he understood that it could turn out in no other way than the one he desired. And this sweet, langorous feeling of voluptuous anticipation was combined with a slight and unconscious trace of spite, that this proud, clever, pure, cultured young woman would lie beneath him, just like all the others, and that he would do with her exactly as he wished, just as he had done with all the others. His bitter, cruel mind began vaguely to conceive of imaginatively humiliating, lascivious scenes in which Lida's naked body, dishevelled hair, and astute eyes were woven into some wild bacchanalia of voluptuous cruelty. He suddenly had a clear picture of her lying on the floor; he heard the swish of a whip, saw the pink stripe on her tender, naked, submissive body, and shuddering, he staggered at the rush of blood to his head. Golden sparks flashed in his eyes. (1:59–60)

Lida, for her part, realizes soon after she agrees to sleep with Zarudin that her male seducer subscribes to a vulgarized Nietzschean erotics of dominance and humiliation: "All of a sudden Lida was horrified to realize how far she'd gone in giving herself to Zarudin. For the first time she felt that, from that irretrievable and incomprehensible moment, the obviously fatuous and shallow officer, so far beneath her, enjoyed some kind of humiliating power over her" (1:89).

The lecherous Voloshin, who is visiting Zarudin from the capital, obviously shares his provincial friend's cruel, sadistic, and misogynous attitude:

> A dissipated human body, like the raw edge of an exposed nerve honed to the point of pain by violent pleasures, reacted painfully to the very word "woman." Immutably naked, immutably available, she stood before Voloshin at every moment of his life; every woman's dress, draped around the lithe, full figure of a female body, aroused him to a state in which his knees began to tremble dreadfully. When he left Petersburg, where he had relinquished a multitude of luscious, sleek women who tormented his body nightly with frenzied, naked caresses, and when he had to attend to a complicated, important matter on which depended the lives of many people who worked for him, Voloshin was preoccupied by the unconcealed fantasy of young, fresh females reared in the provincial wilderness. He imagined them as shy, frightened, and as firm as forest mushrooms; even from a distance he could detect the enticing fragrance of their youth and purity. (1:234–35)

Voloshin's lascivious talk about women's breasts and about his own naked lust soon inspires his host Zarudin, who is overcome by "the male instinct to boast" and who is "tormented by an unbearable desire to surpass Voloshin," to begin bragging about Lida's magnificent body:

> And she [Lida] arose before Voloshin's eyes completely naked, shamelessly exposed in the most profound mysteries of her body and passions, debased like some animal to be traded at a fair. Their thoughts crawled all over her, licked her, mauled her, mocked her body and her feelings; a stinking poison trickled onto this splendid young woman, who was capable of giving pleasure and love. They did not love the woman, they were not grateful to her for the pleasures she afforded; instead they tried to humiliate and insult her, to cause her the vilest, the most indescribable pain. (1:239)

In keeping with the "scale of sexual values" operative in Artsybashev's text, which everywhere eschews sexual conquest merely for the sake of exhibiting male power and masculinist dominance, the ravening Zarudin and Voloshin are consistently characterized by the narrator as "beasts" (*zverei*), "frenzied beasts" (*osatanevshikh zverei*), or "wild beasts" (*dikikh zverei*), whose fantasies of male aggrandizement and female humiliation are categorically condemned.[100]

The visit paid to Zarudin by his debauched friend from the capital, Luker rightly notes, shows just how different—in the sexual sense—these two bestial characters are from the novel's hero. "However desirous of women Sanin may be," Luker points out, "he is never lascivious."[101] When the narrator observes that Zarudin and Voloshin did not love Lida as a woman and were not grateful to her for the carnal pleasures she afforded, the reader is strongly encouraged to infer that Sanin would have acted much differently toward a woman he desired carnally. Indeed, Sanin's behavior toward Karsavina immediately following their sexual intimacy in the rowboat is very instructive in this regard: we are told that "he was comforting and addressing her in a familiar way" and that "his voice was full of tenderness, subdued strength, and gratitude" (1:340). Karsavina, for her part, is rather surprised to find that the normally strong and self-assured Sanin now seems "so pitiful and intimate" (1:342). The very next evening Sanin feels compelled to go visit Karsavina and to tell her directly about the "enormous happiness" (1:349) she had afforded him the night before:

> I so want you to understand me . . . and not to harbor any loathing or hatred for me. What was I supposed to do? There came a moment when I felt that something between us had disappeared and that if I let the moment pass, it would never be repeated in my life . . . that you would go by and I would never experience the delight and happiness I could have. You're so lovely, so young. . . . You're suffering, but yesterday was so good! But this suffering is only because our life is arranged so atrociously; people themselves determine the price of their own happiness. But if we lived differently, this night would remain in both our memories as one of our most valuable, interesting, and splendid experiences, the sort that make life worth living. (1:348–49)

These sentiments are not those of a vulgarized Nietzschean superman or rapacious Dostoevskian predator. As Luker notes, Sanin here "is sincerely grateful to his mate for a unique experience that has brought him incomparable joy"—unlike Zarudin, who revels sadistically in his male sexual prowess and in his capacity to dominate and humiliate submissive female victims.[102]

## Dostoevskian Carnivorism in Early Soviet Fiction

The Bolshevik takeover in 1917 may well have ushered in a vastly different moral climate for early-twentieth-century Russia, especially where the issue of sexual relations is concerned, but Dostoevskian tropes of alimentary violence and images of sexual predation continued, nonetheless, to appear in the aftermath of the October Revolution. Much as Mikhaylovsky, Gorky, and other radical democrats had done before them, Bolshevik commentators during the immediate postrevolutionary period assailed the cynical evaluation of human beings as bloodthirsty and power-hungry beasts of prey. Nonetheless, World War I, the October Revolution, and the ensuing civil war helped to provoke a resurgence of the turn-of-the-century's "new barbarism" and to revive the ethos of human carnivorism throughout the 1920s, when "eating" others expressed metaphorically the nature of social life in the modern world. In his study of Bolshevik Nietzscheanism, Mikhail Agursky notes, "Revolution and revolutionary violence were seen through the Nietzschean prism by many pro-Bolshevik intellectuals as a manifestation of Dionysian ecstasy which would also continue after the Revolution."[103]

Revolutionary violence during this period was portrayed in zoological terms by anti-Bolshevik commentators as well. Prince Yevgeny N. Trubetskoy, for example, wrote a pamphlet, *The Kingdom of the Beast and the Coming Rebirth of Russia* (1919), that discusses some of the country's recent historical events—principally World War I, the rise to power of the Bolsheviks, and the civil war—from an anti-Bolshevik perspective, using beast metaphors that demonstrate just how thoroughly the language, imagery, and ideas of Dostoevsky, Darwin, and Nietzsche had permeated the consciousness and the discourse of the Russian intelligentsia. Trubetskoy, who laments the overall collapse of moral and spiritual values in the postwar world, accuses the Western allies, gathered around the negotiation table at the peace conference in Paris after the armistice, of being just as "predatory" and having just as "wolfish" an appetite for power as the German militarism they had fought so hard to defeat (4–5). "In general, this is the politics of a cowardly beast," inveighs Trubetskoy, "this is that elementary method of protecting one's own security to which dogs have recourse in a fight: if you're going to devour, then do it to the death" (3–4). The First World War, in Trubetskoy's opinion, was from the very start a manifestation of "the zoological principle in humankind" (4), whereby a number of nations fought out of a fear of being "eaten up" by other "predator-nations" (6). The war not only "unbridled the wild beast in international relations," Trubetskoy notes sadly; it "unbridled the wild beast in man" and created the type of the "man-tiger," who returned from the front transformed into "blood-thirsty Bolsheviks" (7).

This "image of the beast," which had lived in the hearts of men long before the war, became especially manifest in Bolshevism, which renounces the spirit, bases all human relations exclusively on a materialistic (mainly, an economic) foundation, and views the relations between social classes according to "the naked zoological principle of the struggle for existence" (10). As Trubetskoy explains,

> The proletariat is becoming the sole possessor of all material goods, not on the strength of any demands for justice, but exclusively according to *the right of might*. From the Bolshevik point of view, what is being fulfilled in the class war is not any higher truth, but solely the right of big fish to swallow up little fish. Previously the bourgeoisie exercised this right, but now it is the proletariat's turn. And no humane considerations should mollify or restrict this right of the large beast to enjoy its booty. The class war, as the Bolsheviks understand it, is just as cruel and merciless as the struggle for existence in the animal kingdom: it can end only with the total annihilation of one of the adversaries. (10)

Invoking dire apocalyptic imagery drawn from the Book of Revelation, the author warns that Bolshevism, which represents "not the simple unbridling of human passions, but the worship of the beast [*zveropoklonstvo*], the subordination of the human to the bestial" (11), is luring humankind into the claws of "the beast from out of the abyss" (13). The new society being constructed by the Bolsheviks, he asserts, "is not a human kingdom, but a bestial kingdom" (11), one where the law that governs social life is "the interminable, intransigent dispute of dogs fighting over a tossed bone" (12). "Society is being transformed into a herd of wild beasts," he intones. Trubetskoy concludes his harangue by noting that humankind needs to chose between the Bolshevik path, which leads to "the kingdom of the beast," and the Orthodox Christian "path of resurrection" (21). By following the latter path, people will find their basic humanity returned, the essential sacredness of human life restored, and the evil "beast" of the Apocalypse vanquished by God's merciful love.

As Trubetskoy's anti-Bolshevik pamphlet makes abundantly clear, the predatory language and carnivorous imagery that Dostoevsky had invoked were revived following the Bolshevik takeover in 1917 and continued to circulate in both intellectual and literary spheres. The Dostoevskian trope of alimentary violence is encountered frequently during the 1920s, for instance, in the prose works of Boris Pilnyak, as it appealed so strongly to this writer's abiding interest in the biological and instinctual nature of human beings. Even in Pilnyak's earliest stories, many of which allegorize the life of animals, one finds a "celebration of the primitive, sensual, unreasoning life—of birds, beasts, and the animal man."[104] *Naked Year* (1922), however, is the text where the author most memorably reveals his fascination with the deep-seated, primitive, elemental urges of human beings, which he believed had been unleashed by the forces of revolution and civil war in early Soviet Russia. "Like Pil'nyak's other fiction of the early 1920s," writes Naiman, "it portrays the Revolution as an exhilarating destructive force that strips away centuries of civilization, leaving man in the clutches of paganism, violence, and sexuality. For Pil'nyak, the Revolution returns man to a nearly animal, sexually charged, state of existence."[105]

Thus Irina Ordynina, a character in *Naked Year* who serves as a particularly vocal adherent of the Darwinist notion of the survival of the fittest and the Nietzschean idea of the superman, champions the belief that might makes right and that only the strong and the free will prevail: only those "masters" whose muscles are strong, whose will is resilient, whose mind is free, and whose beauty is godlike will succeed in vanquishing life during these primitive and troubled "Varangian" times. "I wish to drain the entire cup that freedom and intellect and instinct have given me," Irina proclaims. "Instinct, too, for are not these present days, after all, a battle of instinct?!"[106] Words such as "rape" (*nasilovat'*), "beast" (*zver'*), and "instinct" (*instinkt*) become refrains in Pilnyak's novel. Indeed, "beast" actually becomes "a word with positive value" in *Naked Year*: it reinforces the author's emphasis on the biological basis of human life, where violence and cruelty constitute a vital, inherent component.[107]

This emphasis is especially true during the disturbing scene of primitive brutality and violence at the Mars loop station, an episode where, as Gary Browning writes, "all human pretensions crumble into bestiality as man combats both the elements and his fellow man in a brutal battle for survival."[108] In *Machines and Wolves* (1925) as well, Pilnyak captures vividly the savage inclinations of human beings during this chaotic time in revolutionary Russia, when the collapse of stable governance and the disappearance of humane values implicitly encouraged people to behave (and to treat each other) like beasts, particularly like wolves. One of the characters, Yury Roschislavsky, openly admits, "I lived through those years behaving like a wolf," while his brother Dmitry confesses: "I became a wolf toward other people."[109] Pilnyak's narrator likewise asserts that during this time of great upheaval men had indeed "become lupine" (*liudi ovolchilis'*).[110] The naturalistic Pilnyak was castigated for his biocentric view of human life by Yury Dobranov, a contemporary critic, who objected to the way the author glorified "the voice of sperm and blood."[111]

Like the primitivist Pilnyak, a number of other independent-minded writers during the 1920s portrayed the unleashing of violent animal instincts within human beings that accompanied the Revolution and civil war in Russia. Most writers in the early Soviet period, however, seem to have preferred to employ beast metaphors and tropes of alimentary violence along the lines of social class rather than individual personalities, depicting the conflict between the Old World and the New World—in Marxist terms, the class warfare between the proletariat and the bourgeoisie—in terms of animal predation. Yury Olesha's *Envy* (1927) provides an instructive example. Olesha manages to organize the alimentary and sexual motifs in his text in such a way as to help advance the story's central power struggle: the conflict between the romantic old-world values of heroic individualism, free imagination, and personal glory championed by Ivan Babichev and his disciple Nikolay Kavalerov on the one hand, and the new Soviet ethos of science, industrial progress, and collectivism preached by Andrey Babichev and his protégé Volodya Makarov on the other. As the two Babichev brothers vie against each other to enlist the ideological and personal loyalties of the members of their country's younger generation, represented in the novella by Kavalerov, Makarov, and especially Valya Babicheva, the socioeconomic and political ramifications of this competition are conveyed largely in sexual, gastronomical, and alimentary terms. For the homeless, unemployed Kavalerov, power and success in the new Soviet society are embodied (quite literally) in the person of Andrey Babichev, the "remarkable man" whom Agursky characterizes as a "Bolshevik superman."[112] The sheer physicality of power that Kavalerov perceives in this "big man" manifests itself in such gastronomical and alimentary terms: the food commissar possesses not merely a voracious appetite for food, but also—like the gigantic food-processing machines in the meat factories of the Food Industry Trust he oversees—the capacity to "devour" slaughtered animal parts. The corpulent Andrey exhibits the capacity to consume what Elias Canetti terms the "food of power."[113]

Ivan Babichev, whose "Conspiracy of Feelings" has emerged out of his rebellion against his powerful, gluttonous brother's Communist plan to eradicate all the old-world emotions associated with the bourgeois epoch, likewise grasps intuitively Canetti's notion of the "food of power"; he repeatedly describes power relationships in masticatory and alimentary terms that emphasize the destructive and violent aspects of oral ingestion. Unlike Bakhtin, who views the act of eating in a rather benign and bloodless way as a "joyful," "exultant," and "triumphant" encounter between man and his world,[114] Olesha recognizes the inherently aggressive and violent nature of our biological need to feed ourselves. A Dostoevskian semioticization of eating as an act of devouring occurs in Olesha's novella, where Ivan refers to himself as a "devourer" (*pozhiratel'*) of crayfish. "Look: I don't eat them," Ivan points out, "I destroy them."[115] Olesha proceeds to pun on the word *zhrat'* (to devour) when he has Ivan say that he devours crayfish "like a high priest" (*kak zhrets*) or, literally, "like one who devours" (57).

Predatory animal imagery is frequently invoked in *Envy* to communicate the bestial nature of gastronomical and sexual power. When Ivan tries to impress upon Kavalerov the necessity of waging an ideological "battle of the epochs" against Andrey Babichev and Volodya Makarov, for instance, he recounts for his newfound disciple an anecdote about how he, as an adolescent, had once "torn to pieces" (*terzal*) a haughty twelve-year-old girl who was threatening to eclipse Ivan's superiority and popularity among his peers through her ability to get whatever she wanted and to have everyone worship her. Jealous of the magnetic powers of attraction this popular girl possessed, the thirteen-year-old Ivan tore the clothes as well as scratched the physiognomy of this poor sacrificial "victim" whom he, much like a wild beast, had "caught" in his claws (60).

Projecting these same primitive predatory instincts outward toward his brother and the whole new Soviet world Andrey represents, Ivan imputes to them a similarly bestial appetite for power, violence, and destruction. "They are devouring us like food," he complains, when explaining to Kavalerov the nature of the current ideological struggle. "They are ingesting the nineteenth century into themselves, like a boa constrictor ingests a rabbit. . . . They chew and digest. What's of use—they imbibe, what's injurious—they throw away. . . . Our feelings they throw away, our technology—they imbibe" (73).[116] What is also "gnawing" (*glozhet*) at both Ivan and Kavalerov, the self-proclaimed "king of the vulgarians" here realizes, is a feeling of envy that threatens to destroy the two of them unless they act soon. They must either find a way to kill the predatory "beast" of Bolshevik ideology or resign themselves to being eaten up and thus ingested into the "collective body" that some advocates of proletarian culture during the 1920s—most notably, Aleksey Gastev—envisioned as the incarnation of Soviet society.[117]

As we learn from the letter he composes in part 1, Kavalerov has likewise declared war against Andrey and had already agreed to join Ivan's conspiratorial army even before meeting Andrey's older brother (41). Unlike Ivan, however, Kavalerov seems motivated to launch a military campaign against Andrey less for ideological reasons than for personal ones.[118] Bitterly resentful at his recent displacement from Andrey's divan—and thus his rejection, in favor of Volodya Makarov, as the salami-maker's spiritually adopted son—Kavalerov has also grown increasingly angry that this fat, powerful monster seems to stand in his way romantically as well, blocking his pursuit of the young and beautiful Valya. For the ideologically naive Kavalerov, Andrey's power—his ability to devour and destroy—is understood as a threat not so much to this romantic dreamer himself or even to the old-world values he embodies. The perceived threat, rather, is that the gluttonous Andrey will swallow up the object of Kavalerov's sexual desire: his beloved Valya. In his letter to Andrey, Kavalerov accuses the director of the Food Industry Trust of viewing his own niece as nothing more than a "tasty little morsel" (*lakomyi kusochek*) (39) to which this unrestrained libertine wishes to "treat himself" (*polakomit'sia*) (40).[119] Later, when he finally musters enough nerve to return to Andrey's apartment and confront both Babichev and Makarov face-to-face, Kavalerov tells his young rival that Andrey had lived with Valya during Volodya's absence and that he plans further to "amuse himself" (*pobalovat'sia*) with her during those four years that will elapse before Volodya finally marries Valya (47).

In both of these instances, Kavalerov seems to be projecting onto Andrey his own hedonistic desires. He depicts the latter's putative gastronomical and sexual consumption of Valya primarily in terms of the code of pleasure: Andrey is portrayed more as a refined epicure who wants to "taste" the delicate sexual charms of this appealing young girl, than as gluttonous brute who threatens to "devour" a rather defenseless creature. More often than not, however, Kavalerov is inclined to understand Andrey's lustful pursuit of Valya in terms of power rather than pleasure: more specifically, he views this pursuit in terms of gastronomical and sexual violence. Not unlike Ivan, Kavalerov resorts to the language of hunting and the imagery of predatory animals when he seeks to describe the ravening nature of Andrey's sexual and ideological designs upon Valya. Babichev is accused, for example, of wanting to "subdue" (*pokorit'*), to "tame" (*priruchit'*), and to "control" (*zavladet'*) this vulnerable young creature (39). "You are a glutton (*obzhora*) and a gourmandizer (*chrevougodnik*)," Kavalerov exclaims. "Will you not stop at anything for the sake of your physiognomy? What will deter you from debauching (*razvratit'*) the girl?" (39). Just as Ivan Babichev is afraid that the powerful Andrey will "devour" him, along with all the other disenfranchised remnants of the dying bourgeois epoch he represents, so too does Kavalerov fear that the gluttonous director of the Food Industry Trust will "make use of" Valya in the same way that the ferocious food-processing machines at his factory utilize animal parts: "You want to use (*ispol'zovat'*) her," Kavalerov writes, "as you use (I purposely apply your own words here) 'the heads and hooves of sheep with the aid of cleverly applied electric spiral drills' (from your brochure)" (39). Because Andrey's alleged debauchery and devouring have become nearly synonymous in the narrator's mind, Kavalerov can be seen as promising to protect Valya against both gastronomical and sexual harm when he vows boldly in his letter that he will not allow Andrey either to "get" Valya or to "use" her. Kavalerov believes that Valya must be defended against what one critic calls "the hungry lusts" of the carnivorous Andrey Babichev, "who would like to eat her."[120]

## Dog Alley *and the Bolshevik Debate on Sexual Morality*

The ethos of human carnivorism that became closely associated with Dostoevsky, Darwin, and Nietzsche in revolutionary Russia was not entirely at the service of the Marxist concern with class warfare, however. It also figured prominently in the heated debate that erupted in Bolshevik public discourse during the late 1920s over the so-called sexual question. The debate, which reached its peak near the end of the NEP era (1921–27), focused mainly on the question of what role love, marriage, and the family should now play in the lives of those who were currently engaged in the process of dismantling the old bourgeois order and creating a new communist society in Russia. Two diametrically opposed positions toward the *polovoi vopros* quickly emerged: (1) an open, liberal, even radical, attitude that viewed sexual energy in a positive way as a liberating force that would free people from the stultifyingly repressive, hypocritical, old-fashioned morality that had regulated life within bourgeois society (an attitude that for a long time was closely, yet erroneously, associated with the purported "free-love" advocate, Aleksandra Kollontay); and (2) a repressed (and repressive), conservative, puritanical attitude that considered libido a dangerous and damaging force in private life that must somehow be restrained and subordinated to the public interest of advancing the class struggle of the proletariat.[121] It is this later attitude of spartan self-disciplie and puritanical self-restraint in the sexual sphere—that is, the "revolutionary asceticism" exhibited by Zudin and other Bolshevik puritans—that eventually came to dominate the discussion of the sexual question in Soviet Russia during the 1920s.[122]

One of the works of Soviet fiction from the 1920s that contributed most directly to this Bolshevik debate over sexual morality was Lev Gumilyovsky's *Dog Alley*. This controversial novel was vilified by some at the time as a vicious slander upon the purportedly depraved sexual mores of contemporary Soviet youth; others viewed it as a cheap pornographic work that unnecessarily depicted a number of sexual scenes merely to arouse the reader's more prurient interests. However, *Dog Alley* can (and should) be read today as essentially a sensationalized tale that warns of the grave dangers that may result from not strictly regulating one's sexual desires.[123] "Intended to scare Soviet youth into personal reformation," explains Gregory Carleton, " *Dog Alley* recalls the best of nineteenth century anti-masturbation fright literature: repent now or you will destroy yourself and others."[124] One of the distinctive features that characterizes Gumilyovsky's cautionary tale—and that distinguishes it from the typical anti-masturbation fright literature Carleton mentions—is the extensive use the author makes of spider imagery to help dramatize the pernicious consequences sexual dissipation can have upon Communist youth. Resorting to the spider trope (a favorite beast metaphor of the time) to scare young Soviet readers away from the temptation of sexual promiscuity, Gumilyovsky at the same time invokes the views on human bestiality and sexuality promulgated by Dostoevsky and Tolstoy. Gumilyovsky's approach in warning of the dangers of sexual desire is to take a Dostoevskian predatory beast image (the spider) and turn it into a Tolstoyan trope. More specifically, the author of *Dog Alley* employs Dostoevskian "bestiality" (understood as "brutality" or *zverstvo*), in the form of the spider as a predatory beast, but he casts it semiotically as Tolstoyan "animality" (*zhivotnost'*): as a brutish (rather than brutal) animal appetite for sensual gratification of physical desire that ignores the spiritual dimension of human beings.[125]

The story's principal male character, Khorokhorin, is a Party cell leader at a provincial university in the lower Volga region who strongly believes that casual sex is necessary for him if he wishes to maintain normal health: that is to say, regular sexual activity enables him to preserve his mental equilibrium and work productively. For Khorokhorin, the sex act is performed on a regular basis merely as a way to satisfy a simple and "natural" biological need. In a slightly modified version of the infamous "glass-of-water" theory of casual sexual relations that gained wide currency in revolutionary Russia during the early 1920s, Khorokhorin subscribes to the crudely reductive materialist and physiologist notion that a young person performing the sex act is equivalent to a thirsty or hungry person satisfying his or her physical appetite by drinking water or eating food. Just like his progressive-minded female comrade Anna Ryzhinskaya, who two to three times a week agrees to satisfy her male friend's sexual hunger, Khorokhorin is a sexual liberationist and champion of unfettered sexuality. He prides himself on the way the "new people" in Soviet Russia—such as he, Anna, and the other members of the "Down with Shame" circle they have organized locally—are waging an ideological battle against those apologists for bourgeois philistinism who claim that there is more to sex (like romance, love, affection, and spiritual affinity, for instance) than mere physiology. "We don't acknowledge any love!" Gumilyovsky's protagonist proclaims categorically. "All of that is a bourgeois trick that hinders the cause! It's a diversion for the sated!" (16). As one contemporary critic complained, Khorokhorin seems to acknowledge "only naked physiology" where matters of love and sex are concerned. According to the sexual philosophy of Gumilyovsky's protagonist, "Instincts have to be satisfied since they are natural."[126] Khorokhorin thus interprets the triumph of the Bolshevik Revolution mainly as "the emancipation of the body, the 'instinctual' and the 'natural,' from the fetters of the psyche and the spiritual."[127] Korokhorin is, in many ways, the Bolshevik incarnation of Artsybashev's prerevolutionary, hedonistic libertine Sanin.

Khorokhorin's libertinist philosophy of sexual permissiveness, however, is painfully demolished during the course of the novel as a result of his growing infatuation with, and subsequent obsession over, an enticing female student named Vera Volkova, who resides in an apartment on a side street named Dog Alley and whose sexual charms eventually propel the young Communist leader down a slippery slope of mental, moral, and physical degeneration. Initially, Khorokhorin views the prospect of a sexual union with Vera as "a useful, reasonable, and necessary diversion" (17). But upon hearing the sobering account by the promising young university lecturer Burov of his ill-fated affair with Vera (he is one of her earlier male victims), Khorokhorin becomes terrified, not just for himself and the neurasthenic Burov, but "for all those who, like him [Burov], had become enmeshed in the snares of an enormous, white, sated sexual spider who had drunk up not merely his blood, but also his brain, the most important part of a person—his brain" (63). Khorokhorin ultimately blames Vera for ruining his life: to his mind, she is the one who initially lured him into the dark abyss of unrestrained sexual promiscuity. It is as a direct consequence of his infatuation with her, Khorokhorin believes, that he now finds himself immersed in a veritable swamp of degeneracy that includes carnal addiction, venereal disease, and sexual psychopathology. As a way out of his dire predicament, Khorokhorin contemplates murdering the coy vixen, who alternately seduces and resists him, but he eventually decides to commit suicide instead. He miraculously recovers from a self-inflicted gunshot wound, however, and at story's end we are told that he had left the university to go live in a small town in Siberia where he is never again seen with any woman. Khorokhorin, whose name derives from the Russian verb *khorokhorit'sia* (to swagger, to boast), is thus made to experience a very painful cure for the hubris he had demonstrated in preaching that sexual promiscuity and moral libertinism should be endorsed as positive modes of behavior for revolutionary youth in Bolshevik Russia.

In sharp contrast to the ill-fated, libidinous Khorokhorin, the ostensible heroes in Gumilyovsky's novel—"positive" characters and model Communist youth such as Semyon Korolyov and Zoya Osokina—preach what during the mid-1920s was fast becoming the Party line: the need to practice rigorous self-restraint in sexual matters and to regulate strictly one's biological instincts. "Sexuality had become a key arena for class struggle in the Bolshevik moralistic discourse," Igal Halfin observes about this period, a time when "a good revolutionary was a proletarian who put loyalty to his class before the satisfaction of his instincts."[128] As the vigorous Korolyov declares proudly at one point, "We must nurture within ourselves a class, Party, and Komsomol brand of virtue" (123). A disorderly and dissipated sex life, he and Osokina insist, violates Communist morality: it weakens one's physical and mental strength, and thus diminishes one's fitness for waging the class struggle against the bourgeoisie. Like the promising young microbiologist Burov before him, Khorokhorin, in succumbing to the sexual charms of Vera Volkova, is becoming fatally entangled in the web of a greedy sexual spider that, as we saw above, is allegedly sucking out not only his lifeblood and vital energy, but also his mental stability. Indeed, the none-too-subtle author of *Dog Alley* makes little, if any, effort to disguise his arachnoid imagery: one of the book's chapters is titled "The Spider," while another is called "The Spider Weaves Its Web."[129]

## Spiders and Flies: The Nature of the Beast Within

Although E. B. White's endearing children's story *Charlotte's Web* (1952) attempts to provide arachnids with a more positive image, traditional spider lore has historically presented these crawly creatures in a decidedly negative light: as foul, loathsome, and evil beasts to be feared and detested. "With every spider you kill," runs a New England folk saying, "you kill an enemy!"[130] In Russian folklore, meanwhile, the belief is held that whoever kills a spider will have forty sins forgiven.[131] In the wake of Darwin's theories and their reception in late-nineteenth- and early-twentieth-century Europe and America, as Bram Dijkstra has demonstrated in his provocative study, *Evil Sisters: The Threat of Female Sexuality and the Cult of Manhood* (1996), this traditional arachnophobia merged with modern misogyny. Many male writers, artists, and thinkers at the time demonized women by identifying them with images of a predatory voluptuary from the arachnid world: that is, with various incarnations of the voracious female spider—such as the black widow, the tarantula, the praying mantis—whose main characteristic was seen to be her sexual/reproductive cannibalism.[132]

In late imperial Russia, as Laura Engelstein points out, conservative social critics, such as Vasily Rozanov, added a racist, anti-Semitic dimension to this misogyny by portraying Jews as bloodsucking "spiders" who prey upon the "flies": that is, Russian Orthodox believers.[133] "The spider is but one, yet there are ten flies caught in his web," writes Rozanov. "Here we have the story of Russians and Jews: one hundred million Russians and seven million Jews." Describing the logic of the pogrom as "a convulsion in response to suffering and misery," Rozanov explains: "The spider sucks the fly. The fly buzzes. Its wings tremble convulsively—and they brush against the spider, they feebly tear at the spider's web in one spot. But already the fly's leg is caught in the noose. And the spider knows this." "We need to free ourselves from the spider," Rozanov concludes, "and sweep all the cobwebs out of the room."[134] Mikhail Zolotonosov has demonstrated how an entire subculture of Russian anti-Semitism flourished at the turn of the century, not just in the writings of a philosopher and social critic like Rozanov, but also in pulp fiction and the popular press, which attracted a broad mass audience during this period.[135] A close association was being made between wealthy Jews and predatory spiders, he notes, in boulevard novels such as N. Ponomarev's *Petersburg Spiders* (1888) as well as in the caricatures that appeared on the pages of popular anti-Semitic magazines such as the aptly named *The Spider* in St. Petersburg and of conservative newspapers such as *The Two-Headed Eagle* in Kiev.

By the time of the October Revolution, however, it had become fairly standard Bolshevik practice to foreground a Marxist—as opposed to a misogynist or anti-Semitic—semantics of the spider image in cultural texts by portraying the proletariat's class enemies, especially the bourgeoisie, as subhuman vermin and parasites. This imagery was invoked so that the use of violence and terror against these class enemies would be seen as not only justified but also necessary. In left-wing revolutionary rhetoric, the rich were portrayed as the powerful political and socioeconomic "spiders," while the poor were metaphorized as the hapless "flies" that they lured, trapped in their sticky web, and then devoured.[136] Indeed, Wilhelm Liebknecht's widely disseminated pamphlet, *Spiders and Flies* (1917), divided the Russian population precisely into these two warring zoological species: the disgustingly monstrous, insatiably rapacious "spiders" were all those gentry landowners, bourgeois landlords, and other capitalist exploiters who sucked the lifeblood out of the working poor.[137] Like vulnerable "flies," members of the urban and rural proletariat fall into the traps set to catch all those who are desperately needy, hungry, and thus extremely susceptible to falling victim to socioeconomic predation.[138] During the NEP period, of course, it would be the unscrupulous Nepmen who, as predatory speculators, would be characterized as constituting a species of creatures that were "feeding" on the economic organism—on the body politic that was constructing socialist society in early Soviet Russia.

What Gumilyovsky does in his novel, however, is apply this predatory spider imagery not directly to the bourgeoisie, the main class enemy of the proletariat, but to sexuality itself, with whose potential for evil the pleasure-seeking bourgeoisie was already closely associated. In this respect, Gumilyovsky was embodying in a work of fiction the ideas about "revolutionary sublimation" and "spermatic economy" that were being disseminated in the mid-1920s by Bolshevik moralists such as Aron Zalkind, a self-styled psycho-neurologist who was one of the most prominent early Soviet commentators on sexual issues. This architect of the notorious "twelve commandments" for avoiding sexual stimulation simply inserted the bourgeoisie into the place that had traditionally been reserved for the algolagnic female by misogynistic nineteenth-century critics, who portrayed woman as the threatening incarnation of sexuality.[139] Zalkind thus tended to characterize sexuality in predacious terms, describing the sex drive as "a spider, greedily and mercilessly sucking out an enormous amount of the body's energy."[140]

However, as was noted earlier, the extensive use Gumilyovsky makes in *Dog Alley* of spider imagery extends the Bolshevik debate over sexual morality during the 1920s to include the views of both Dostoevsky and Tolstoy on the sexual nature of the human animal. Their opposing conceptualizations of the human animal—both the Dostoevskian notion of predatory "bestiality" (*zverstvo*) and the Tolstoyan idea of hedonistic "animality" (*zhivotnost'*)—reverberate throughout the text of *Dog Alley*. The very title of Gumilyovsky's novel, one commentator has pointed out, provides an obvious allusion to the "animal origins of the human instincts."[141] Indeed, one of Gumilyovsky's contemporaries complained that *Dog Alley* reads much like a "treatise on zoology."[142] What is not quite so obvious from the title, however, is whether the author's allusion to the zoological self—to the animal nature of human beings—refers to a wild Dostoevskian dog (perhaps rabid) that threatens to bite, maul, and devour others, or to a more domesticated, but still greedy, Tolstoyan dog that seeks immediate gratification of its instinctual urges for food and sex. In *Dog Alley*, of course, the reader quickly realizes that the dominant animal metaphor is not the dog at all, but rather the spider: a preying and carnivorous creature that would normally be assumed to inhabit the Dostoevskian bestiary, with its sexual entrapment-predation ethos, rather than the Tolstoyan one, with its sexual intoxication-addiction syndrome. Gumilyovsky's innovation is that he transforms the predatory Dostoevskian spider into a Tolstoyan trope: human sexuality in *Dog Alley* turns out to be not only an ensnaring, devouring desire, but an intoxicating and addictive one as well.

## *Dostoevskian Bestiality and Tolstoyan Animality in* Dog Alley

In *Dog Alley*, the libidinous and promiscuous Khorokhorin is surrounded by spider imagery that recalls the entrapment-predation trope for sexual desire found in Dostoevsky's fiction and that was closely associated at the time with so-called Karamazovism. When Khorokhorin first meets Vera, the novel's demonic femme fatale, for instance, we are told that her riveting, nearly hypnotic gaze envelops him "like a spider's web" (17). The same image is repeated a little later in the story, but this time the narrator adds that Vera's "spider's web" of a gaze envelops not just Khorokhorin, but "all his desires, thoughts, and feelings" (46) as well. Following his initial conversation with Burov, during which he learns about Vera's alleged predatory sexual behavior in the past, Khorokhorin comes to find that "to think about Vera meant to think about Burov, about the spider, about the attic, about everything that now blended together into one nightmarish image of a sated spider hanging in its web" (67). When Khorokhorin openly confronts Vera with his contention that she is a predatory creature, shouting angrily at her, "Spider! . . . Spider! Spider! Sexual spider!" (85), she throws the accusation right back into his face, asking him pointedly, "Are you not a spider yourself? Are you not a spider?" (85).

In a later scene, where Khorokhorin and his new girlfriend, the naive and innocent Varya Polovtseva, are out strolling at night through a moonlit forest grove and he is suddenly overcome with lustful urges (at this point in the story he still foolishly believes that sexual intercourse with a nice young girl like Varya could return to him "his emotional equilibrium, peace, and joy" [96]), the natural setting that surrounds them is described in arachnoid terms. The moonlight, we are told, "was weaving a bright spider's web" (96) amid the entangled tree branches and twigs. Indeed, "the spider's web of moonlight above his head" (96), along with the presence of other young couples who are engaged in lovemaking in the woods that romantic evening, is said to be responsible for casting Khorokhorin into the terrifying swamp of sexual desire from which he finds it impossible to extricate himself. The nocturnal scene is, in the narrator's words, "a spider's web of branches, moonlight, darkness, and last year's rotting mold crunching underfoot" (98–99). When Varya runs ahead of Khorokhorin along the path through the trees, it was as if she were severing "the terrifying spider's web" all around them (99). This scene thus strongly suggests that the promiscuous Khorokhorin, a sexual libertine who is now suffering the effects of neurasthenia and erotomania, has simply projected his own carnal desires and perverse fantasies onto the outside world of nature and the people who surround him.

In this dark, foreboding, Gothic setting, Khorokhorin—just like a hapless fly caught in a sticky spider's web—"felt himself stuck to something from which it was impossible to free his feet" (100). Moreover, one of the two chapters depicting this scene is titled "Tengli-fuut" (Tanglefoot), the name of a popular brand of flypaper that was produced in North America and widely used in Europe and Russia at the time.[143] The narrator explains that the most terrifying thing about flypaper is that there is really nothing sweet about it, as it is made out of rosin. "It is useless to buzz with one's limpid wings, struggling to break free toward the light," he observes, "when one's feet are so firmly stuck to a fatal deception!" (97). The clear implication here is that the object of sexual desire, like a spider and like flypaper, makes itself appear "sweet" in order to attract into its sticky, fatal snares hapless victims—both male "flies" (such as Khorokhorin and Burov) and female "flies" (such as the sexually active Vera Volkova and the virginal Varya Polovtseva) alike.

Like Dostoevsky, Gumilyovsky thus uses the spider to serve as a symbol of sexual evil, but here the spider is made to represent not so much another person as the sex drive itself. Gumilyovsky's spider represents "not just the snares of a single villainous type," Naiman points out, "but the much larger Gothic enemy of universal sexuality."[144] Although Khorokhorin, for his part, may insist that Vera Volkova is a "sexual spider" (her surname alone, which derives from the word for wolf, bespeaks her predatory and carnivorous nature), the true spider in this story—as both the narrator and Burov remind the reader on more than one occasion—is sexual attraction itself; it can suck all the vitality, reason, and strength out of those human beings, male and female alike, who fall prey to its fatal allure. Spider imagery is thus used to reinforce the author's message that sexual freedom leads one not upon the road to health, well-being, and happiness, but rather upon a downward spiral to mental degeneration, erotic violence, and moral perdition.

The mental, emotional, and physiological pain and suffering both Khorokhorin and Burov are made to suffer as a result of their obsessive sexual desire for the purportedly predatory Vera Volkova recall not so much the entrapment-predation pattern of Dostoevsky, however, as the intoxication-addiction motif found in Tolstoy's later writings. As we saw in the preceding chapter, many of the male protagonists in Tolstoy's post-conversion fiction, such as Irtenev and Pozdnyshev, are driven to insanity, murder, and/or suicide as a result of their intoxication by, and subsequent addiction to, an insatiable desire for sexual gratification. Gumilyovsky's characters come to subscribe to the same puritanical views on sexual morality many of Tolstoy's fictional heroes and ideological followers uphold.[145] As Carleton notes, although Gumilyovsky himself would later claim that Lenin served as the main inspiration for the views on sexual morality the author espouses in *Dog*

*Alley*, it may be more appropriate to see Tolstoy as the one playing that role.[146] Like the cynical Pozdnyshev, for example, the highly disillusioned Burov comes to believe that "pure" sexual feeling is a fiction (57), that there cannot be any true romantic love between a man and a woman (60), and that there is instead only "naked animal attraction" (61). Carnal desire, as portrayed in Gumilyovsky's novel, amounts to what Korolyov later calls "a naked animal feeling" (150), one whose wild, primitive nature marks, for civilized and cultured people of the modern age, a regressive step toward the Stone Age.

This view about sexual degeneration is reaffirmed near novel's end in Burov's suicide note, in which he asserts, when analyzing the "zoological drama" (164) that has just unfolded in *Dog Alley*, that "the ruinous effect of sexual debauchery, from a psychological and cultural perspective, lies above all else in the disintegration of the complex of sexual feeling, in the recidivistic relapse into wildness, into our animal condition" (163). Worse yet, for Gumilyovsky's characters, this primal "animal" urge, once unleashed and indulged, becomes an addictive intoxicant. Like Tolstoy's Irtenev, Gumilyovsky's Khorokhorin initially decides to act upon his sexual attraction toward Vera Volkova primarily for reasons of health (to maintain his mental and emotional equilibrium); he soon finds himself, however, so mesmerized by her attractive body parts (her exposed legs, knees, and arms) that he is unable to think of almost anything else. "At first, all this is justified as a natural need, and that's fine," Khorokhorin reasons. "But then it becomes an end in itself, an amusement, a form of entertainment, a diversion. It's disgusting" (101). Khorokhorin comes to learn the sobering Tolstoyan lesson that sex, like alcohol, tobacco, and other dangerous intoxicants that promise physical pleasure, "seizes the entire person and drags him down into the abyss" (101). It is no doubt for this reason that Khorokhorin, like Tolstoy's tragic heroine, Anna Karenina, contemplates laying his head down upon railroad tracks in order to put an end to all the misery and suffering unrestrained sexual desire has brought upon him (102). Just as the sexual addiction—the feeling of enslavement to their own sexual passion—Tolstoy's Irtenev and Pozdnyshev experience eventually brings them to a troubling loss of control over their bodily appetites and drives them both to the brink of insanity, so too do Gumilyovsky's Khorokhorin and Burov betray clear signs of mental degeneration and neurasthenia.[147]

Much like Tolstoy, Gumilyovsky makes his characters come to the realization that what appears "natural" and "instinctual" in human beings (namely, the sex drive) is in fact what is basely "animalistic" in them. The primitive sexual creature within them must be overcome and transcended if they are ever to become truly human. Animal desires, in short, should not be mistaken for natural human needs. When, early in the novel, Khorokhorin insists to one of his female comrades (Babkova) that satisfying one's sexual appetite is as natural as eating if one is hungry, she provides a distinctively Tolstoyan reply. Reminding Khorokhorin that he would never have developed this urgent sexual need if he had not allowed himself to get out of hand and become undisciplined, Babkova points out to him that sexual activity is as necessary to a young person as vodka is to a chronic drunkard. Like alcohol, sex seems to become a necessity—just as tobacco, morphine, and cocaine do—only if one allows oneself to indulge one's appetite for those stimulants. "Yes, people do become ill and die from hunger and starvation," she reminds him, "but no one has yet fallen ill and died from the lack of gratification of the kind of animal needs you have!" (33). When Khorokhorin complains that he is "starving" from lack of sexual release, his peasant-born colleague, Borovkov, who is forced to live separately from his wife while he is enrolled at the university, advises him to follow his example and work out at the gym. Physical exercise, Borovkov explains, has enabled him to go more than two years without sex (34).

The pro-abstinence sentiments expressed by Babkova and Borovkov echo Pozdnyshev's assertion in Tolstoy's *The Kreutzer Sonata* that although eating is the most natural of biological functions, indulging one's sexual appetite is decidedly unnatural. "It is natural to eat," Pozdnyshev insists. "And to eat is, from the very start, enjoyable, easy, pleasant, and not shameful; but this [copulation] is horrid, shameful, and painful. No, it is unnatural! And an innocent, uncorrupted girl, as I have become convinced, always hates it" (27:29). The fear of enslavement to one's own sexual appetites, which torments such male protagonists as Tolstoy's Irtenev and Pozdnyshev, is clearly reflected in Gumilyovsky's novel, where the recent events that occurred in Dog Alley are said to have found artistic representation in a play called *Slaves of Love* (10) and a film titled *Victims of Sensuality* (11).

Echoes of Tolstoy's puritanical views on sexual morality can also be heard in Gumilyovsky's novel in the distinction Burov draws between two separate spheres within the human psyche: a higher consciousness where reason prevails and a subconscious realm where instincts rule. Like the "rational consciousness" and "animal personality" that compete against each other in Tolstoy's binary model of the human self, consciousness and instinct, according to Burov, are in a state of constant battle within human beings (57). He considers the naked animal act of sexual intercourse to be highly negative and dangerous because it causes serious internal disharmony and psychic distortion, leading us to commit acts that escape the control of our higher consciousness (58). Thus there is not any good that can result from sexual attraction, Burov concludes. It only leads, in fact, to "a vicious circle, a spider's web" (60), into which we stand in danger of falling and becoming fatally trapped. Like Tolstoy's Irtenev and Pozdnyshev, Gumilyovsky's Burov was schooled to believe, as a young student at the gymnasium, that it is beneficial for one's health to visit a house of prostitution and lose one's virginity during adolescence. The general sentiment among members of his social class was that sexual debauchery was actually a virtue, not a vice.[148] Compare this with Pozdnyshev's confession that he practiced debauchery in a steady, decent way for health's sake beginning at age sixteen. "I fell not because I surrendered to the natural temptation of a particular woman's charm," Pozdnyshev hastens to explain his loss of virginity as an adolescent:

> No, I was not seduced by a woman—rather I fell because, in the social set around me, what was really a fall was regarded by some as a most legitimate function that was beneficial for one's health, and by others as a very natural and not only excusable but even innocent amusement for a young man. I did not understand that it was a fall, but simply began to indulge in those half-pleasures, half-needs, which, as was instilled within me, were natural at a certain age. I began to indulge in debauchery as I began to drink and to smoke. (27:19)[149]

Burov's adolescent experience with sexual indulgence is strikingly similar. He even relates the instance of one classmate whose mother hired an attractive maid to take care of her son's sexual needs and thus spare him the need to go visit prostitutes (62).

Perhaps the quintessentially Tolstoyan view on sexual morality espoused in *Dog Alley*, however, is the insistence that sexual abstinence and sublimation of libido should everywhere characterize the relations between the sexes. Tolstoy advocated the renunciation of our animal self and the transcendence of our egoistic desires, both of which are necessary if people are to achieve the Christian ideal of love toward God and service for one's neighbor. Semyon Korolyov provides a Bolshevik version of this sexual ideal in the speech he delivers at Vera Volkova's gravesite during the funeral ceremony near the end of *Dog Alley* (Vera dies from a gunshot wound suffered at the hands of the mentally deranged Burov, who proceeds to kill himself). He reminds those in attendance that the new socialist way of life they are working so diligently to construct must be based upon mutual respect and the "comradely equality" of women (149). A disorderly and dissipated sex life, he warns them, will only lead Communist youth down a path directly antithetical to the goals of the Revolution, largely because sexual license objectifies and enslaves women, encouraging men to treat women merely as a means for attaining their own pleasure. "Sexual restraint and a comradely relationship toward a beloved woman," he proclaims, "this is the higher, Communist type of sexual relations, this is the foundation of our sexual morality, which is as distant from the sexual morality of putrid bourgeois society as the sky is from the earth" (152).[150] "Abstinence was declared the key to proletarian health around the time Gumilyovsky embarked on writing his novel," Halfin observes. "It was a 'prerequisite' to the very important mechanism of 'sublimation' (*zameshchenie*), 'the transformation of a lower form of energy into a higher one.'"[151]

Korolyov's didactic funerary speech, with its call for a Bolshevik version of Tolstoy's Christian asceticism, echoes at novel's end what has been described as the "Razinism" voiced earlier in the story by Zoya Osokina: the desire to imitate Stenka Razin, the iconic and iconoclastic figure from tsarist times, who was now resurrected for young Bolsheviks as the personification of an ascetic willingness to forsake all personal pleasures (such as sexual gratification) in order to fulfill the greater social duty of advancing the revolutionary struggle against the forces of political oppression.[152] It is while listening to the historical folk song about Stenka Razin that Zoya Osokina suddenly comes to understand what she—and other Communist youth—must now do: "renounce all carnal joys for the sake of duty and for the struggle" (90).

The private pleasures of "sexual feeling" and "sexual ecstasy," she now realizes, must give way in devoted young Communists like herself to a collectively shared "revolutionary ecstasy" (43). The Tolstoyan ideal of a Christian brotherhood of man, based on a compassionate, noncarnal brand of love, appears to have become transformed here into the Bolshevik myth of a sexless, male comradeship (*tovarishchestvo*) that many hoped would eventually prosper under Communism.[153]

In concluding this discussion of how in *Dog Alley* Gumilyovsky may be said to have "Tolstoyanized" the spider imagery he appropriated from Dostoevsky, I should point out that Tolstoy did make occasional use of spider imagery himself. But the symbolism that attaches to the arachnoid imagery in Tolstoy's writings is radically different from the type we find in the works of either Dostoevsky or Gumilyovsky. Whereas both of these writers, in their depiction of human bestiality, identify the spider with an evil, Gothic dynamic of predatory entrapment and fatal destruction (rape, or even the threat of rape, one critic reminds us, constitutes "the quintessential moment in the Gothic"),[154] Tolstoy invokes the image of "a sticky web of love" to describe his positive ideal of an altruistic, compassionate, noncarnal kind of love, a truly Christian brand of agape that can catch and embrace everything and everyone that comes in contact with it. "In order to be happy," Olenin thinks to himself in *The Cossacks*, "one thing is necessary: to love, and to love in a self-sacrificing way, to love everyone and everything, to throw out a spider's web of love on all sides and to catch in it everyone who comes along" (6:105).[155] The spider's web that Tolstoy envisions people weaving is thus a benign web of love and kindness, one that emanates from the divine aspects of the human self rather than from its base and egoistic animal personality.[156] This benevolence may well explain why Gumilyovsky, when presenting his puritanical, neo-Tolstoyan views on sexual morality in *Dog Alley*, felt nonetheless compelled to borrow the image of the spider not from the apostolic Tolstoy, but from the Gothic Dostoevsky.

## The Dostoevskian Legacy in Post-Soviet Literature

Although Dostoevskian beast metaphors and tropes of alimentary violence occasionally make an appearance in Soviet literature of the Stalinist and post-Stalinist years—especially in beast allegories such as

Fazil Iskander's *Rabbits and Boa Constrictors* (1982) and in the literature of exposure written by some of the more ecologically minded writers (such as Valentin Rasputin and Chingiz Aytmatov)—the Socialist Realist aesthetic tended to make the artistic depiction of beastly cruelty, conflict, and struggle obsolete. After all, if Soviet literature's task is to portray exclusively the positive aspects of socialist society in its imminent development, then images of violence and aggression would seem to be categorically out of place. The advent of *glasnost'* and *perestroika* during the Gorbachev years and the subsequent collapse of Communist rule in 1991, however, witnessed not only the emergence of pornography, pulp fiction, and the "dark literature" of morbidity (*chernukha*), but also the return of tropes of alimentary violence. The purported romanticization of violence that many critics observe in post-Soviet literature, film, and culture has, in fact, been attributed by some directly to the legacy of the "cruel talent" of the recently rediscovered Dostoevsky.[157] Despite the Supreme Soviet's April 1991 resolution calling for urgent measures to curb the propagation of pornography and dismantle the new "cult of violence and cruelty" in Russia, images of violence (especially sexual violence against women) have greatly proliferated not only in post-Soviet film and fiction, but in daily life as well.[158] Contemporary Russia has become, according to Viktor Erofeev, "a paradise for sadists." "I do not know of another country," he explains, "where women would be so strongly aroused by the prospect of rape and where men would so naively confuse the sexual act with fighting."[159] As Igor Kon puts it, "the beast has broken loose" in post-Communist Russia, where the end of censorship and the advent of a market economy have led to sex becoming grotesquely deromanticized, commercialized, and commodified. One can only hope that Kon, who continues to insist that "Russia is not a zoo," ultimately proves correct in his assertion that "the beast is not as terrible as it is made out to be."[160]

One postmodern writer whose work exemplifies the Dostoevskian brand of human bestiality that has reemerged in the New Russia is Viktor Pelevin. In his novel *The Life of Insects* (1994), which one scholar has interpreted as a polemic—against such works as Karel and Josef Čapek's play, *From the Life of Insects* (1921), and Franz Kafka's "Metamorphosis" (1916)[161]—characters morph back and forth between human and various insect forms, taking the shape of mosquitoes, flies, dung beetles, flying ants, moths, hemp bugs, cockroaches, and so on. One of the more prominent predatory characters in the novel is an American entrepreneur, Sam Sucker, a human mosquito who is visiting the Crimea in hopes of setting up a joint business venture with a pair of Russian investors. All three of these venture capitalists, of course, are really doing nothing other than "sucking" Russian blood. "We suck everybody's blood," one of them openly acknowledges.[162] Another central character, the female ant Marina, marries an Army major in hopes of attaining a comfortable, middle-class existence for herself. But during the intermission of Glinka's opera *A Life for the Tsar*, her husband trips on the stairway, strikes the back of his head against one of the steps, and dies without regaining consciousness. Some of his fellow officers proceed to gnaw off and devour parts of his torso with their mandibles, saving a few of the choicest portions for his pregnant widow, who is soon driven by poverty, hunger, and dire need to cannibalize not only her dead husband's body parts, but also some of her own unhatched eggs. "Life is a struggle," she later instructs her surviving daughter Natasha, "and in this struggle the strongest win."[163]

The earlier, nineteenth-century Darwinian notion that "man is a wolf to his fellow man" (*chelovek cheloveku—volk*) is thus transformed in Pelevin's late-twentieth-century novel into the insect idiom: "the ant is a beetle, cricket, and dragonfly to his fellow ant" (*muravei murav'iu—zhuk, sverchok i strekoza*).[164] "Pelevin's evocation of a Russia confronted by the first pangs of capitalism," one scholar correctly observes, "seems to recall—and perhaps not accidentally—Dostoevsky's polemics with the popular Darwinist ideas of society as composed of predators and prey that accompanied Russia's initiation into capitalism during the 1860s and 1870s."[165] Eating and drinking, this scholar notes, emerge as "the ultimate act of predatory power" in Pelevin's insect novel about post-Communist Russia, which portrays a grotesque world where "one's relationship to the Other is predicated entirely on the act of eating or devouring."[166]

Another postmodern writer who portrays the New Russia as a grotesque world where Dostoevskian "devouring" (*plotoiadnost'*) dominates the dynamics of human interactions is Vladimir Sorokin. Unlike Pelevin, however, who depicts human beings as predatory insects, Sorokin portrays people as monstrous cannibals whose appetites are perversely carnivorous. The author, who has been characterized as a highly nihilistic writer and criticized for actively cultivating a "poetics of monstrosity," was vilified as a sick, sordid pornographer and even prosecuted in 2002 in an ugly public campaign against his morbid art that was launched by the pro-Putin group Marching Together—mainly because in his controversial novel, *Blue Lard* (1999), he had portrayed Khrushchev and Stalin as sodomites engaged in homosexual acts of oral and anal intercourse inside the Kremlin.[167] Sorokin acknowledges that, as a writer, he is mystified by the question, Why are human beings unable to do without violence? In an interview with *Der Spiegel* in February 2007 he openly declared: "Yes, violence is my main theme."[168] Many of his prose works reflect a "cruel" Dostoevskian talent he possesses for portraying the violence he observes in the world around him. Indeed, violence of a specifically alimentary nature is a central theme in the thirteen stories that compose the collection *The Feast* (2001).[169]

The opening story, "Nastya," for example, tells the tale of Anastasia Slavina, a young provincial miss who, as she dutifully records in her diary entry for August 6, 1899, is overjoyed that "The Most Important Day" of her young life has finally arrived: on this day she is celebrating her sixteenth birthday. "Lev Ilyich arrived last evening," she writes, "and after supper I sat with him and Papa in the large gazebo. Papa was arguing with him again about Nietzsche, insisting that in one's soul one needs to overcome one's very self. Today I am supposed to do this."[170] In Nastya's case—as in the case of several other local maidens whose parents seem to belong to an odd enclave of Russian Nietzscheans—the way to "overcome one's self" and "surmount all boundaries" is for her to submit to a bizarre rite of passage on the occasion of her coming of age: she will be cooked alive inside a stove and then served at a banquet table, where her roasted body will be consumed by family, friends, and a few invited guests.[171]

For the purposes of our study, what is particularly relevant about this perverse tale of ritual cannibalism is the way Sorokin makes reference in it to Dostoevsky and some of his carnivorous male heroes. Dmitry Mamut, one of the guests in attendance at Nastya's sixteenth birthday party, accuses her father of being "an incorrigible Nietzschean" (39) who, like many other members of the Russian intelligentsia at the turn of the century, has allowed himself to become blinded by the German philosopher's demagoguery. "Nietzsche," Mamut asserts, "has not added a single thing that is essentially new or original to philosophical thought in the world" (40). Even Nietzsche's signature idea of the superman, he insists, was broached by several other thinkers and writers before him, including Dostoevsky. "All of your Nietzsche can be found in the little article Raskolnikov wrote!" he tells his host. "Lock, stock, and barrel! And what about Stavrogin and Versilov? Are they not supermen?" (40). Sorokin thus seems to be suggesting that the Dostoevskian notion of predatory "bestiality" (*zverstvo*) that had thrived among followers of Darwin and Nietzsche in fin de siècle Russia, has now reemerged in his homeland at the turn of the twenty-first century.[172]

In concluding this discussion of the Dostoevskian legacy of human bestiality in the Soviet and post-Soviet periods, we should bear in mind that comparing human beings to beasts of prey who seek to swallow up and devour weaker creatures is patently unfair to the animals so depicted. After all, predatory creatures such as wolves, lions, and boa constrictors are merely following their natural instincts of self-preservation and obeying the law of survival of the fittest. "People talk sometimes of bestial cruelty (*zverskuiu zhestokost'*), but that's a great injustice and insult to the beast; a beast can never be so cruel as a man, so artistically, so artfully cruel," Dostoevsky's Ivan Karamazov reminds us:

> The tiger only tears and gnaws, that's all he can do. He would never think of nailing people by the ears, even if he were able to do it. These Turks took a pleasure in torturing children, too; cutting the unborn child from the mother's womb, and tossing babies up in the air and catching them on the points of their bayonets before their mother's eyes. Doing it before the mother's eyes was what gave zest to the amusement. (14:217)

The intoxication of cruelty that inflames the blood in some human beings, Dostoevsky would insist, is, in the final analysis, a pathologically human trait, not a natural animal one. Ivan Karamazov is perhaps not telling us anything radically new when he asserts that "in every man a beast lies hidden"; significantly, however, he adds that it is "the beast of rage, the beast of lustful heat at the screams of the tortured victim, the unrestrained beast that has been let off the chain" (14:220). This inner beast, Dostoevsky is telling us, is the cruel, sadistic, "artistic" face of the dangerously sensual and instinctual creature that only human beings are capable of becoming.[173]

## The Portrayal of Animals in Dostoevsky and Tolstoy

In this study of carnal desire, as it is represented in works by Dostoevsky, Tolstoy, and other writers in nineteenth-century and early-twentieth-century Russia, our discussion began with the oral regression and infantilism exhibited by the gluttonous gourmands who inhabit the prereform worlds of Gogol, Goncharov, and Kvitka-Osnovyanenko. It soon moved to the erotic perversities contemplated by Dostoevsky's predatory carnivores and the sexual temptations visited upon Tolstoy's pleasure-seeking hedonists. As the main focus of this study gradually shifted from the table to the bed, however, such gustatory notions as tasting, savoring, chewing, and swallowing slowly ceded place of prominence to such libidinal notions as arousal, passion, lust, debauchery, abstinence, and rape. What began as a book largely about food and appetite thus mutated into a book largely about sex and passion. As the society Dostoevsky and Tolstoy inhabited in late tsarist Russia was increasingly "becoming modern," the desiring human body that they and some of their contemporaries portrayed in their writings began more and more to be characterized in terms of what the followers of Darwin, Nietzsche, and Zola posited as the "zoological" self: that is, the instinctual "animal" or "beast" that is said to dwell inside every human being. As a result, Tolstoyan "voluptuousness" (*sladostrastie*) eventually morphed into "animality" (*zhivotnost'*), while Dostoevskian "carnivorousness" (*plotoiadnost'*) was transformed into "bestiality" (*zverstvo*). As we saw in the preceding chapter, male sexual desire in Rus-

sian literature written in the immediate aftermath of Dostoevsky and
Tolstoy is expressed not so much by the language of food and the imagery of eating as by analogy with creatures from the animal kingdom.
Beast metaphors and animal similes, in short, have come to replace the
gastronomical and alimentary conceptualizations of carnal desire on
which this study was initially structured.

Dostoevsky and Tolstoy did more than compare the somatic desires
of human beings to the instinctual urges of creatures from the animal
kingdom, however; they also portrayed animals artistically as fictional
characters. In the case of Dostoevsky, whose works of fiction feature
relatively few actual animals, one of the most memorable depictions
occurs in part 1, chapter 5 of *Crime and Punishment*, when Raskolnikov,
on the eve of his bloody axe-murder of the pawnbroker Alyona Ivanovna and her sister Lizaveta, dreams what the narrator characterizes
as "a terrible dream" (6:46). He dreams that he is a seven-year-old
child again and is witness to a disturbing scene of graphic violence as a
drunken peasant inflicts a brutal physical beating upon "a small, lean,
decrepit old dun-colored mare" (6:46). The drunken peasant, named
Mikolka, is lashing the old mare mercilessly about the head and eyes
with his whip, trying unsuccessfully to get her not only to pull the cart
she was harnessed to (it is filled with rowdy people who have been ca-
rousing all day long at a local tavern), but also to gallop off with the
heavy human load. When the pitiable old creature, grunting and flinch-
ing under the painful blows she is receiving from her cruel master's
whip, proves unable to pull the load, Mikolka flings away his whip and
begins to strike her repeatedly with a long, thick wooden shaft, then
later with an iron crowbar, until she is at last beaten to a bloody death.
Throughout this episode of brutal violence being inflicted by a frenzied
human being upon a poor, defenseless animal, during which time several of the bystanders voice their objection to the drunken peasant's
savage treatment of the horse he owns, Mikolka repeatedly insists that
he is free to do as he pleases with her because she belongs to him. "You
keep out of this!" he shouts angrily at one of the people in the crowd.
"She's mine, isn't she? I can do what I like with my own." "She's my
property," he yells at some one else. "My own property!" (6:48).

This dream scene is similar in many respects, of course, to the scene
of brutality from peasant life that Dostoevsky will later describe in the
essay "Environment" (1873), in his *Diary of a Writer*, where an abusive

peasant husband insists that his starving wife not touch his bread. "Don't you dare eat this bread," he warns her, "this is *my* bread!" (21:21). The husband, as we recall from chapter 2, feels fully justified in whipping his spouse when she does indeed touch some food that belongs to him. He even goes so far as to hang her upside down by her heels (like a chicken) and force her to watch him as he eats his porridge. The physical, emotional, and psychological torments she suffers at the hands of her brutish husband, who curses, beats, and maims her, drive her eventually to commit suicide. The peasant husband's extreme possessiveness and egoism is thus anticipated by Mikolka's exhibition of cruelty toward the female horse he possesses—and beats to death—in *Crime and Punishment*. Both of these scenes remind us that in Dostoevsky's writings the body invariably serves as a site of violence, power, and aggression, while possession is understood to grant license to torment, abuse, and injure the things one ostensibly "owns," whether it be a human being (a wife) or an animal (a horse).

Perhaps the most memorable portrayal of an animal in Tolstoy's fiction is likewise that of a horse: the title character in "Kholstomer: The Tale of a Horse" (1885), the first work of fiction Tolstoy wrote following the profound spiritual crisis he experienced during the late 1870s and early 1880s. But Tolstoy's fictional horse, significantly enough, is male rather than female; and the manner in which his story is told is characterized not by Dostoevskian violence, brutality, and sadism, but rather by Tolstoyan hedonism, libidinal enjoyment, and sensual indulgence. Much like the Houyhnhnms in Jonathan Swift's *Gulliver's Travels* (1726), Kholstomer is an anthropomorphized horse designed largely to show the serious shortcomings of "civilized" human life.[1] When the story opens, Kholstomer is already an old piebald gelding who is resigned to leading a bland existence with few pleasures or delights. Living among younger, more playful colts and fillies, he is not so impatiently hungry as they are, he shows no strong emotions like they do, and he derives no "flavor" from licking an oak post or his bit (26:4). "Suffering for the pleasure of others is nothing new to me," he reflects quite soberly and stoically. "I have even begun to find a certain equine pleasure in it" (26:5). Although the expression of his face is now one of "stern patience, thoughtfulness, and suffering," it is apparent that he had once been "a remarkably fine horse" (26:7). Indeed, when Kholstomer finally relates the story of his life to the young horses that have been mercilessly tormenting the old gelding, we learn that he had once been a very swift and strong thoroughbred. He was so swift, in fact, that he soundly beat the speedy Swan in a two-horse race. This victory, however, results in Kholstomer being sold and eventually becoming the property of the Hussar officer, Nikita Serpukhovskoy, with whom the horse goes on to spend what he claims were "the best years of my life":

> Although he was the cause of my ruin, and although he never loved anyone or anything, I loved him and still love him precisely for that reason. What I especially liked about him was the fact that he was handsome, happy, and wealthy, and therefore he did not love anyone. You understand that lofty equine feeling of ours. His coldness, his cruelty, and my dependence on him gave special strength to my love for him. "Waste me, drive me to exhaustion," I used to think to myself during those good times we had together, "I'll only be the happier for it." (26:23)

What this horse so admires about his human owner, it appears, is not only his beauty and wealth, but also his egoism, hedonism, and narcissism.

One of the most important structural elements of the story, critics have pointed out, is this central opposition between the life of Kholstomer, a moral creature whose life is devoted to laboring for humans, and that of his owner Serpukhovskoy, a lascivious man of the flesh who leads a highly amoral existence.[2] As one might well expect, Kholstomer, the ugly piebald horse whose "mad passion" (26:17) for Vyazapurikha leads to his being castrated at a young age and developing a wise stoicism in the face of life's many injustices, is favorably contrasted to the handsome young Hussar officer whose life of luxury, decadence, and self-indulgence (especially self-indulgence in the pleasures offered by food, drink, and women) leads to his eventually becoming a "flabby old man." One scholar has noted that Kholstomer's castration "frees the hero from the animal desires of the flesh, thereby allowing him to direct his energies toward more virtuous contemplations."[3] In contrast, it has become painfully obvious that Serpukhovskoy, by the time he reaches age forty, has already "let himself go and sunk physically, morally, and financially" (26:29). Although as a middle-aged man he waxes nostalgically about his earlier wastrel ways,[4] the narrator makes it clear that this sybarite's entire earthly existence has been one long wasteful, purposeless exercise in pleasuring a bovine body that eventually will decline, die, and decay.

The sharp contrast Tolstoy establishes in the story between an anthropomorphized horse, who possesses not only native intelligence but also a firm moral compass, and an animalistic human being, who seems to live only to gratify the pleasure-seeking impulses of his body, is made particularly evident in the way each of these creatures faces death and gives up the "spirit." Kholstomer, who becomes infected with a virus after licking a peasant horse (while waiting outside a tavern all night for the groom Vaska to return), has his throat cut in a poignant scene that is told largely from the horse's perspective. In the final chapter of the story the reader is given direct access to Kholstomer's stream of consciousness: we witness both his thoughts (the horse mistakenly believes that the stranger in a bloodied coat who has suddenly shown up at the stable yard is there to cure him of the itch) and his final sensory impressions ("he felt that something had been done to his throat . . . then he felt something liquid streaming profusely down his neck and chest" [26:36]). The noble horse proceeds to confront death with great dignity: "He heaved a deep sigh. And he suddenly felt much better. The whole weight of his life had been lifted" (26:36). Even following his death, Kholstomer's body parts are put to good use: in a natural, sustainable way his skinned carcass provides food not only for some local dogs, hawks, and crows, but also for a family of wolf cubs.

The former Hussar officer's death, on the other hand, is not even mentioned, let alone described. At story's end the reader is simply told: "Serpukhovskoy's dead body, which had walked about the earth, eating and drinking, was buried in the ground much later. Neither his skin, nor his meat, nor his bones were of use in any way" (26:37). Dressed up in a fine new military uniform with finely polished boots, Serpukhovskoy's "plump," "rotting," "maggot-ridden" human body (26:37) is lowered into the ground and covered over with earth, in conformity with an absurd social ritual whose wastefulness and meaninglessness are laid bare by the narrator.[5] By using a gelding to argue for what one scholar has characterized as "the *spiritual* castration of human lust and passion," this story illustrates clearly how, in accord with Tolstoy's conceptualization of the human animal, man is invariably represented as a pleasure-seeking creature who must learn to transcend his bodily appetites if he wishes to attain spiritual fulfillment.[6]

## Becoming Modern: Body, Spirit, and Carnality

We should bear in mind that when Dostoevsky and Tolstoy characterize human beings as "beasts" or "animals" and when they portray anthropomorphic creatures as characters in their fiction, they are not seeking to advocate a zoological conceptualization of the self. Darwin (whose theories collapsed the essential distinctions between animal and human) and Nietzsche (whose philosophy championed the liberation of the beast of prey trapped inside human beings) are generally regarded as the chief sources at the turn of the century of those self-reflexive animal metaphors that reinforced the perception of man as a natural, physical being. The writings of these latter two thinkers have deeply permeated the modern consciousness, which today maintains, as one contemporary scholar has put it, "We are not just rather like animals; we *are* animals."[7] In *Beasts of the Modern Imagination: Darwin, Nietzsche, Kafka, Ernst, and Lawrence* (1985), Margot Norris examines the "biocentric" spirit that Darwin and Nietzsche infused into the modern imagination. Positively valuing the sensual, passionate body—and what she calls its "instinctual epistemology"[8]—for the effusion of power it is capable of manifesting, these biocentric thinkers viewed human aggression as a healthy discharge of the animal vitality, energy, and vigor that had for too long been repressed within human beings, whether by the spirituality of religious belief, the rationalism of Enlightenment thought or the humanism of civilized life. Biocentric ideas that seek to devalue religion, reason, and humanism, Norris points out, are especially prominent in the art and thought of D. H. Lawrence, who once proclaimed: "My great religion is a belief in the blood, the flesh, as being wiser than the intellect. We can go wrong with our minds. But what our blood feels and believes and says is always true. The intellect is only a bit and a bridle. . . . The real way of living is to answer to one's wants."[9] Lawrence is, in the words of Kenneth Inniss, "a priest of *eros* rather than *agape*. On the whole he seems far more benevolent towards most types of wild animal than toward man."[10] In Lawrence's moral universe, Norris writes, "there would be power and splendor in proclaiming, 'I *am* an animal.'"[11] In turn-of-the-century Russia, meanwhile, the biocentric tradition is perhaps best represented by Vasily Rozanov, a philosopher who is said to have emerged out of Karamazovism and who is often referred to as the "Russian Nietzsche."[12] Like

Lawrence, Rozanov strongly insists that man ought to surrender to the secret knowledge possessed by the human body and its animal instincts. Both of these thinkers may thus be said to subscribe to the brand of "militant carnivorism" that is promulgated so memorably in Nietzsche's *Thus Spoke Zarathustra* (1885), where the author proclaims, "man does not live by bread alone, but also by the flesh of good lambs."[13]

Dostoevsky also reminds us that man does not live by bread alone. His invocation of Christ's words, however, is not designed to mock the purported docility of those who would follow the religious credo espoused in the New Testament. Dostoevsky seeks instead to reinforce the essential Christian (and Neoplatonic) idea that there is a spiritual and moral dimension in human beings that ought to transcend the merely physical and carnal. When explaining to a correspondent in June 1876 what he meant by "stones turned into bread," a phrase he had used in a recent issue of *Diary of a Writer* (and a phrase he would soon reprise so memorably in the Grand Inquisitor legend), Dostoevsky referred to the devil's temptation of Christ during his forty days spent in the wilderness (that is, his urging Christ to assuage his hunger—and reveal his divinity—by turning the stones surrounding him into bread):

> To this Christ responded: "Man does not live by bread alone," that is, he stated an axiom about man's spiritual origin too. The devil's idea could only apply to man as an animal [*chelovek-skot*], but Christ knew that you cannot vivify man with bread alone. . . . Christ replied with the unmasking of a secret of nature: "Man does not live by bread alone" (that is, like animals). . . . Without entering into any theories, Christ announces straight out that in addition to the animal world there is a spiritual world in man as well. (19.2:85)

Dostoevsky, in short, stands on the side of Christ and the spiritual aspect of man in the face of the scientific theories of Darwin and the biocentric ideas of Nietzsche, both of whom privileged the animal nature of human beings and the desiring body as sources of knowledge. Although Dostoevsky's militant carnivores—the Underground Man, Svidrigaylov, Stavrogin, and several other of his male fictional characters—would later be lionized by some fin de siècle critics as the forerunners of Nietzsche's blond beasts of prey, they were intended primarily as warnings about the dire consequences that would ensue if man's base animal instincts and bestial urges were allowed to be unleashed. Dostoevsky recognized our human capacity for cruelty; he did not, in the manner of Nietzsche, call for its liberation.

Like Dostoevsky, Tolstoy felt a deep aversion for the biocentric ideas promulgated by followers of Darwin and Nietzsche. With respect to such Darwinian theories as the struggle for existence and the survival of the fittest, Tolstoy maintained that these laws pertain to animals and do not apply to humans. "Man absolutely ought to obey that law which follows from his spiritual attributes," he insisted.[14] Darwin's theories, according to Tolstoy, operated exclusively within the material realm, not the spiritual. As his close friend and colleague Vladimir Chertkov once put it (in a book chapter titled, appropriately enough, "Man or Animal?"),

> There can be two completely different views on the nature of man: either we are merely the most highly developed of animals, the final creatures in the order of creation, in which case our single law is instinct, our single purpose in life is the struggle for existence, or we are spiritual creatures, endowed with bodies that can be subordinated to our spirit.[15]

Nietzsche's pagan philosophy, which discredits the idealist conception of life (the ontological view that assigns spiritual depth to human beings and thus separates them from animals), likewise failed to impress Tolstoy. Characterizing Nietzsche as a "clever feuilletonist," an amoral "madman," and a "preacher of egoism" rather than a bona fide philosopher, Tolstoy most likely had the German thinker largely in mind when he wrote:

> Buddha and Christ spoke a truth that is as true today as it was six thousand years ago. This truth only becomes more comprehensible in larger and larger measure through time. But we no longer pay attention to what great minds were saying a thousand years ago. And what today's thinkers are saying will not be known in a hundred years.[16]

One of the eternal truths Tolstoy seems to have learned from Buddha and Christ is that in our earthly lives the spirit should occupy a position of ascendance over the body and its animal instincts. "The source of everything is the soul," Tolstoy once wrote (in regard to the adage *mens sana in corpore sano*). "When the soul is weak, then a healthy body will overeat and engage in debauchery. But it does not work the other way around: the body does not exert a similar influence upon the soul. The source of everything is the soul. This is where Christianity distinguishes itself from paganism."[17] Where Nietzsche called for the rehabilitation of our desiring bodies and the liberation of our animal instincts, Tolstoy instead preached the need for us to allow the ascetic promptings of our spiritual self to bridle the carnal urges of our zoological self. "The essence of life," he writes in his diary in February 1908, "is the liberation of the soul from the body, from the errors of the body, from the sufferings identified with the body" (56:108). Man's immortal soul and mortal body, Tolstoy believed, are engaged in an eternal struggle. And, he feared, it was becoming increasingly difficult during the modern age for the spirit eventually to triumph over the body.

In a decidedly old-fashioned, premodern way, both Dostoevsky and Tolstoy regarded the gratification of our carnal appetites as constituting "sins" of the flesh. Although their respective conceptualizations of animal desire differed quite markedly (Dostoevskian "carnivorousness" and "bestiality" being juxtaposed, as we have seen, to Tolstoyan "voluptuousness" and "animality"), they do share the belief—almost medieval in its religiosity—that carnality is something inherently sinful. Much in the tradition of Catholic bookmen from the Middle Ages, such as St. Augustine and St. Thomas Aquinas, these two famous Russian novelists continued to subscribe to the Christian postlapsarian view that carnal lust is the unfortunate legacy of an original sin that has blighted the human condition ever since Adam and Eve were expelled from a paradise free of concupiscent desire.

In light of the long-standing Russian cultural tradition of moral puritanism (discussed in the opening chapter of this book), it should not surprise us to find that Dostoevsky and Tolstoy, both of whom are regularly invoked as forerunners of twentieth-century existentialism, adopt such a medieval attitude toward food, sex, and the body. Despite the influx of forces of modernization that were beginning to transform life in their native land, nineteenth-century Russia remained a largely feudal country with an autocratic ruler, an essentially nonstratified social hierarchy of aristocrats and serfs. Perhaps most important, the country was still much under the sway of the Russian Orthodox

Church. As Dostoevsky's final novel, *The Brothers Karamazov*, vividly illustrates, Orthodox monasteries (and the holy men who dwelled inside them) continued to play an active role in the moral and intellectual life of Russian society. Carnal appetites, consequently, tended to be perceived by many educated Russians at the time not as normal features of the desiring body, but rather as profane, sinful desires emanating from an unruly animal nature inside man that must be forcibly restrained and tamed. And indeed, Dostoevsky and Tolstoy, both of whom were writers with a pronounced religious bent, considered carnality indecent, immoral, and offensive. As Emil Draitser has noted, "Tolstoy and Dostoevsky refer to sex either as something highly despicable that evokes revulsion (e.g., in Tolstoy's *The Kreutzer Sonata*) or as a destructive force (e.g., in Dostoevsky's *Idiot*)."[18]

The ascetic tendencies of Russian Orthodoxy, however, extended even farther in their influence than to the consciousnesses of the spiritually inclined Dostoevsky and Tolstoy. They also infiltrated the mentality of the radical nihilists of the 1860s, such as Nikolay Chernyshevsky and Nikolay Dobrolyubov, those zealous political activists and militant atheists whom Berdyaev once characterized as "the monk-ascetics" of a new utopian social order.[19] The ascetic denial of bodily pleasures is thus an ethos, redolent of a medieval brand of Christianity that permeated nineteenth-century Russian culture to an extent that was not generally the case in the more advanced European countries during this time.

The main contributions Dostoevsky and Tolstoy made to the discourse on carnality and the desiring body consist in their contrasting conceptualizations of the animal instincts within man. As far as Dostoevsky was concerned, the "sins of the flesh" pose an especially grave danger to human beings, considered as creatures with a spiritual dimension, because they unleash the aggressive instincts inside man. Food and sex, as they are portrayed in his writings, serve as triggers for the bestial violence, cruelty, and brutality that can erupt when human beings pursue their carnal appetites for power and domination. The language and imagery Dostoevsky consistently uses to represent the desiring body are invariably predatory, carnivorous, and rapacious. For Tolstoy, on the other hand, the "sins of the flesh" are manifestations of the pleasure-seeking instincts of the human animal. Food and sex in his works arouse concupiscence rather than aggression, libidinal enjoyment rather than blood lust, sensual delight rather than conquest or destruction. The contrasting gastropoetics and sexual dynamics of these two famous Russian writers—pitting "devouring" against "tasting," carnivorousness against voluptuousness, power against pleasure—help us to understand the broad range of carnal appetites experienced by the desiring body. Their respective conceptualizations of the zoological self, meanwhile, help us more fully to appreciate the deep anxieties felt by idealistic and/or religious thinkers at the turn of the century: that the forces of modernization were contributing to the de-spiritualization of man.

Both Dostoevskian "bestiality" and Tolstoyan "animality" remind us that the process of "becoming modern" during the second half of the nineteenth century in Russia put into question what it meant to be a human being. The irony here, as we have seen, is that both Dostoevsky and Tolstoy, in their efforts to defend the notion that our humanity consists in large measure in our spiritual and moral nature rather than our animal and carnal nature, became closely linked in the minds of many contemporaries with those modern thinkers—most prominent among them, Darwin, Nietzsche, and Freud—who gave birth to the biocentric idea of the zoological self. These two Russian writers did not consider the "sins of the flesh" to be merely quaint religious notions, relics left over from an earlier Age of Faith, that had outlived their usefulness in a modern, secular world. To the contrary, Dostoevsky and Tolstoy remind us that food and sex still appeal to those devilishly carnal appetites—appetites that not only challenge and threaten our human nature, but also help to define it.

# Notes

*1. Introduction: Food and Sex in Russian Literature*
(pages 1–39)

1. Tom Stoppard, *Arcadia* (London: Faber and Faber, 1993), 1–2.
2. Ibid., 3.
3. See, for example, George Steiner, *Tolstoy or Dostoevsky: An Essay in the Old Criticism* (New York: Dutton, 1971) and *Tolstoi ili Dostoevskii? Filosofsko-esteticheskie iskaniia v kul'turakh Vostoka i Zapada*, ed. V. E. Bagno (Saint Petersburg: Nauka, 2003).
4. D. S. Mirsky, *A History of Russian Literature: From Its Beginnings to 1900*, ed. Francis J. Whitfield (New York: Vintage Books, 1958), 279.
5. Nicholas Berdyaev, *Dostoievsky*, trans. Donald Attwater (New York: Meridian Books, 1957), 216.
6. Ibid., 217.
7. "No English novelist is as great as Tolstoy—that is to say has given so complete a picture of man's life, both on its domestic and heroic side," wrote E. M. Forster. "No English novelist has explored man's soul as deeply as Dostoevsky." See Forster, *Aspects of the Novel* (New York: Harcourt, Brace, and World, 1954), 7.
8. Dmitry Merejkovski, *Tolstoi as Man and Artist; with an essay on Dostoïevski* (Westport, Conn: Greenwood Press, 1970).
9. See Steiner, *Tolstoy or Dostoevsky*, 7, 9.
10. Mikhail Bakhtin, *Problems of Dostoevsky's Poetics*, trans. Caryl Emerson (Minneapolis: University of Minnesota Press, 1984). "Tolstoy's world is monolithically monologic," writes Bakhtin, "the hero's discourse is confined in the fixed framework of the author's discourse about him" (56).
11. Joseph Brodsky, "Catastrophes in the Air," in Brodsky, *Less Than One: Selected Essays* (New York: Farrar, Straus, and Giroux, 1986), 277. Galya Diment takes issue with Brodsky's rather bold assessment in her article, "'Tolstoy or Dostoevsky' and the Modernists: Polemics with Joseph Brodsky," *Tolstoy Studies Journal* 3 (1990): 76–81.
12. Ronald Tobin, "Les mets et les mots: Gastronomie et sémiotique dans *L'Ecole des femmes*," *Semiotica* 51 (1984): 133–45.
13. Although the closest Russian-language equivalents for the verb "to eat" (*est'* and *kushat'*) cannot match the same range of semantic difference Tobin finds between the French verbs *manger* and *goûter*, Dostoevskii frequently uses one lexical item that does convey quite effectively the sense that eating (as well as copulating) functions as an act of violence and aggression in his fiction. That

word, *plotoiadie*, a compound noun made up of *plot'* (flesh) and *iad* (to eat), has two primary meanings: it can denote either "carnivorousness" or "voluptuousness" and "lustfulness."

14. Gian-Paolo Biasin, *The Flavors of Modernity: Food and the Novel* (Princeton, N.J.: Princeton University Press, 1993). Biasin provides here his own English translation of *I sapori della modernità: Cibo e romanzo* (Bologna: Il Mulino, 1991).

15. Claude Lévi-Strauss, *Structural Anthropology* (Garden City, N.Y.: Doubleday, 1967), 85.

16. Mary Douglas, "Deciphering a Meal," *Daedalus* 101, no. 1 (1972): 61–81.

17. Pierre Bourdieu, *La Distinction* (Paris: Le Minuit, 1979) and Jack Goody, *Cooking, Cuisine and Class* (Cambridge: Cambridge University Press, 1968). For an anthology of seminal anthropological and sociological writings on food, see *Food and Culture: A Reader*, ed. Carol Counihan and Penny Van Esterik (New York: Routledge, 1997).

18. Roland Barthes, *Elements of Semiology,* trans. Annette Lavers and Colin Smith (New York: Hill and Wang, 1967), 27–28.

19. Jonathan Culler, *Roland Barthes* (New York: Oxford University Press, 1983), 72–73.

20. Roland Barthes, "Pour une psycho-sociologie de l'alimentation contemporaine," *Annales* 16 (1961): 77–86.

21. Ronald Tobin discusses the nature and the parameters of "gastrocriticism" in his essay, "Qu'est-ce que la gastrocritique?" *XVII siècle*, no. 217 (2002): 621–30.

22. See, for example, *Literary Gastronomy*, ed. David Bevan (Amsterdam: Rodopi, 1988); *Diet and Discourse: Eating, Drinking and Literature*, ed. Evelyn J. Hinz (Winnipeg: University of Manitoba Press, 1991) (special issue of *Mosaic: A Journal for the Interdisciplinary Study of Literature* 24, nos. 3–4 [Summer/Fall 1991]); *Littérature et gastronomie*, ed. Ronald W. Tobin (Paris and Seattle: Papers on French Seventeenth-Century Literature, 1985); *Cooking by the Book: Food in Literature and Culture*, ed. Mary Anne Schofield (Bowling Green, Ohio: Bowling Green State University Popular Press, 1989); *Littérature et nourriture*, ed. James W. Brown (special issue of *Dalhousie French Studies*, 11 [1987]); *Le roman et la nourriture*, ed. André-Jeanne Baudrier (Paris: Presses universitaires de France-Comté, 2003).

23. James W. Brown, *Fictional Meals and Their Function in the French Novel, 1789–1848* (Toronto: University of Toronto Press, 1984). See chapter 5, "Balzac: The Meal as Metonym and Index of Social and Economic Spheres," 23–54.

24. Ronald W. Tobin, *Tarte à la crème: Comedy and Gastronomy in Molière's Theater* (Columbus: Ohio State University Press, 1990).

25. Mikhail Bakhtin, *Rabelais and His World,* trans. Hélène Iswolsky (Cambridge, Mass.: MIT Press, 1968).

26. Biasin, *Flavors of Modernity*, 27.

27. Louis Marin, *La parole mangée et autres essais théologico-politiques* (Paris: Librairie des Méridiens–Klincksieck, 1986). The English translation is Louis Marin, *Food for Thought*, trans. Mette Hjort (Baltimore, Md.: Johns Hopkins University Press, 1989).

28. Michel Jeanneret, *Des mets et des mots: banquets et propos de table à la Renaissance* (Paris: Librairie José Corti, 1987). The English translation is *A Feast of Words: Banquets and Table Talk in the Renaissance*, trans. Jeremy Whiteley and Emma Hughes (Chicago: University of Chicago Press, 1991).

29. Tatiana Tolstaia, "The Age of Innocence," *New York Review of Books* (October 21, 1993), 24.

30. Ibid., 24.

31. See his introductory essay, "Poetika kukhni," in Petr Vail' and Aleksandr Genis, *Russkaia kukhnia v izgnanii* (Los Angeles: Almanakh, 1987), 88.

32. Jocelyne Kolb examines this neoclassical legacy during the Romantic era in her book, *The Ambiguity of Taste: Freedom and Food in European Romanticism* (Ann Arbor: University of Michigan Press, 1995).

33. P. A. Viazemskii, *Zapisnye zapiski (1813–1848)*, ed. V. S. Nechaev (Moscow: Akademiia nauk, 1963), 23. "Izmailov is the Russian Krylov," Viazemskii adds, "just as Krylov is the Russian LaFontaine" (35).

34. F. F. Vigel, *Zapiski* (Moscow: Krug, 1928; repr. Oriental Research Partners, 1974), 362.

35. W. E. Brown, *A History of Russian Literature of the Romantic Period* (Ann Arbor, Mich: Ardis, 1986), 1:121.

36. P. N. Polevoi, *Istoriia russkoi slovesnosti s drevneishikh vremen do nashikh dnei* (Saint Petersburg: A. F. Marks, 1900), 3:428.

37. V. G. Belinskii, *Polnoe sobranie sochinenii* (Moscow and Leningrad: Akademiia nauk, 1953–59), 4:148.

38. *Literaturnye listki*, part 4, nos. 19–20 (1824): 49.

39. Jean Chopin, "Oeuvres de Basile Naréjny," *Revue Encyclopédique*, 44 (1829): 118–19.

40. Ibid.

41. See *Sochineniia Barona A. A. Delviga* (Saint Petersburg, 1895), 128. For critical studies that examine Narezhnyi's Teniersism, see Vladimir Danilov, "Ten'er v russkoi literature," *Russkii arkhiv* 53, no. 2 (1915): 164–68, and, more recently, Ronald D. LeBlanc, "Teniersism: Seventeenth-Century Flemish Art and Early Nineteenth-Century Russian Prose," *Russian Review* 49 (1990): 19–41.

42. John Mersereau, Jr., *Russian Romantic Fiction* (Ann Arbor, Mich: Ardis, 1983), 71.

43. Pavel Mykhed, "O prirode i kharaktere smekha v romanakh V. T. Narezhnogo," *Voprosy russkoi literatury*, 2 (1983): 90.

44. Mikhail Bakhtin, "Rable i Gogol' (Iskusstvo slova i narodnaia smekhovaia kul'tura)," in Bakhtin, *Voprosy literatury i estetiki* (Moscow: Khudozhestven-

naia literatura, 1975), 487. For a study that examines the satiric and come-dic representation of food and eating in Narezhnyi's novel (from a largely Bakhtinian perspective), see my "The Monarch as Glutton: Vasily Narezhny's *The Black Year*," in *Diet and Discourse: Eating, Drinking and Literature*, ed. Evelyn J. Hinz (Winnipeg: Mosaic, 1991), 53–67.

45. Bakhtin, *Rabelais and His World*, 18.

46. Ibid., 281. For studies of Rabelais's poetics of grotesque realism, especially as it pertains specifically to images of food and drink, see (in addition to Bakhtin) Françoise Charpentier, "Le symbolisme de la nourriture dans le *Pantagruel*," in *Pratiques et discours alimentaires à la Renaissance*, ed. Jean-Claude Margolin and Robert Sauzet (Paris: Maisonneuve, 1982), 219–31; Michel Jeanneret, "Ma patrie est une citrouille: themes alimentaires dans Rabelais et Folengo," in *Littérature et gastronomie*, ed. Tobin, 113–48; Samuel Kinser, *Rabelais' Carnival: Text, Context, Metatext* (Oxford: Oxford University Press, 1990); and Louis Marin, "Utopic Rabelaisian Bodies," in Marin, *Food for Thought*, 85–113.

47. Bakhtin, "Rable i Gogol," 487.

48. See Ronald D. LeBlanc, "Teniers, Flemish Art, and the Natural School Debate," *Slavic Review* 50, no. 3 (1991): 576–89.

49. That critic was the notorious Faddei Bulgarin. See *Severnaia pchela*, no. 22 (1846): 86.

50. See Nils Åke Nilsson, "Food Images in Čechov. A Bachtinian Approach," *Scando-Slavica*, 32 (1986): 27–40. Svetlana Boym discusses what she calls the "literary charms" of *poshlost'* in works by Gogol and Chekhov in her book, *Common Places: Mythologies of Everyday Life in Russia* (Cambridge, Mass.: Harvard University Press, 1994); see esp. 48–56.

51. Lynn Visson, "Kasha vs. Cachet Blanc: The Gastronomic Dialectics of Russian Literature," in *Russianness: Studies on a Nation's Identity*, ed. Robert L. Belknap (Ann Arbor, Mich.: Ardis, 1990), 60–73.

52. Ibid., 66.

53. Linda Wolfe includes this famous scene in her book, *The Literary Gourmet* (New York: Random House, 1962), a collection she describes as "The Pleasure of Reading about Wonderful Food in Scenes from Great Literature," 196–204.

54. Quoted in Nikolai Barsukov, *Zhizn' i trudy M. P. Pogodina* (Saint Petersburg, 1890), 3:73. For a recent historical study that explores this tension between East and West (and native and foreign) in the nineteenth-century Russian culinary domain, see Alison K. Smith, *Recipes for Russia: Food and Nationhood Under the Tsars* (DeKalb: Northern Illinois University Press, 2008).

55. Richard N. Coe, *When the Grass Was Taller: Autobiography and the Experience of Childhood* (New Haven, Conn.: Yale University Press, 1984), 64.

56. Ibid.

57. Benedict Anderson, *Imagined Communities: Reflections on the Origin and Spread of Nationalism* (London: Verso, 1991).

58. Vissarion Belinskii, who had high praise for Kvitka-Osnov'ianenko's literary talents, deplored this provincial writer's unfortunate tendency to continue to caricature European (especially French) people and ways in Russia: "According to Mr. Osnov'ianenko's conception of things, all foreigners are scoundrels and bastards. From them comes all the evil on earth—both the cold in winter and the heat in summer, both the rheumatism in old age and the illiteracy in youth." See the review of Kvitka-Osnov'ianenko's *Zhizn' i pokhozhdeniia Petra Stepanova syna Stolbikova* in V. G. Belinskii, *Polnoe sobranie sochinenii* (Moscow: Akademiia nauk, 1953–59), 5:597.

59. For more discussion of "gastronomic Slavophilism" in the works of Gogol, Goncharov, and Kvitka-Osnov'ianenko, see my "Food, Orality, and Nostalgia for Childhood: Gastronomic Slavophilism in Midnineteenth-Century Russian Fiction," *Russian Review* 58 (1999): 244–67.

60. Raymond Williams, *The Country and the City* (New York: Oxford University Press, 1973); see esp. chapter 4, "Golden Ages," 35–45.

61. Maggie Kilgour, *From Communion to Cannibalism: An Anatomy of Metaphors of Incorporation* (Princeton, N.J.: Princeton University Press, 1990), 20.

62. Jeanneret, *Feast of Words*, 25.

63. Cited in David Magarshack, *Gogol: A Life* (New York: Grove Press, 1957), 267.

64. Commenting upon the ruthless peasant milieu that surrounded him in the Russian countryside during the post-emancipation years, Aleksandr N. Engelgardt describes this rapacious socioeconomic climate in terms of animal predation. "Kulak ideals reign there," he writes, "everyone is proud of being a pike and strives to eat up the carps. Every peasant, if the circumstances are favorable, will exploit anyone else in the most splendid fashion, it is all the same whether it be a peasant or a lord, he will squeeze the juice out of him, will exploit his need." See Engelgardt, *Letters from the Country, 1872–1887*, trans. and ed. Cathy A. Frierson (Oxford: Oxford University Press, 1993), 223. For a detailed account of this predatory behavior among the Russian peasants, see "Kulak: The Village Strongman," chapter 7 of Frierson's *Peasant Icons: Representations of Rural People in Late Nineteenth-Century Russia* (Oxford: Oxford University Press, 1993), 139–60.

65. Peter V. Marinelli, *The Pastoral* (London: Methuen, 1971), 75.

66. In *The Battle for Childhood: Creation of a Russian Myth* (Stanford, Calif.: Stanford University Press, 1990), Andrew Wachtel discusses Saltykov-Shchedrin's *Old Times in Poshekanie* (1887–89) rather than *The Golovlev Family*, considering the former "the most thoroughgoing refutation of the gentry myths of childhood" (95).

67. Andrew Durkin describes the Golovlev family as a "death-oriented, self-

devouring matriarchy" in *Sergei Aksakov and Russian Pastoral* (New Brunswick, N.J.: Rutgers University Press, 1983), 244–45.

68. Darra Goldstein discusses the Golovlev family's gluttonous appetite for power, and the devouring imagery it inspires, in "The Myth of Nourishment in *Gospoda Golovlevy*," paper delivered at the annual meeting of the AAASS in Washington, DC, in October 1990. See also her "Domestic Porkbarreling in Nineteenth-Century Russia, or Who Holds the Keys to the Larder?" in *Russia—Women—Culture*, ed. Helena Goscilo and Beth Holmgren (Bloomington: Indiana University Press, 1996), 139–44. The terrifying jaws of the devil, who threatens to eat sinners alive, are especially prominent in medieval paintings that depict the tortures of hell. "Representations of Hell before 1400," Allen J. Grieco observes, "often concentrated on an imagery of devouring in which the damned were roasted and boiled as if they were nothing more than food for the devil." See *Themes in Art: The Meal* (London: Scala Books, 1991), 10–11. Some of these medieval paintings are reproduced by Alice K. Turner and Anne L. Stainton in their essay, "The Golden Age of Hell," *Arts and Antiques* 1 (1991): 46–57.

69. Hugh McLean, "Gogol's Retreat from Love: Toward an Interpretation of *Mirgorod*," in *Russian Literature and Psychoanalysis*, ed. Daniel Rancour-Laferriere (Philadelphia: John Benjamins, 1989), 101–22.

70. Ibid., 112.

71. Ivan Yermakov, "The Nose," in *Gogol from the Twentieth Century: Eleven Essays*, ed. and trans. Robert A. Maguire (Princeton, N.J.: Princeton University Press, 1974), 169.

72. As Julian Graffy observes, the world of Afanasii Ivanovich and Pulkheriia Ivanovna is one where "marriage is more like the relationship of mother and son than that of husband and wife." See "Passion versus Habit in *Old World Landowners*," in *Nikolay Gogol: Text and Context*, ed. Jane Grayson and Faith Wigzell (New York: St. Martin's Press, 1989), 38.

73. James Woodward interprets Pulkheriia Ivanovna's motherly nurturing and feeding of Afanasii Ivanovich as a sign of his emasculation. See *The Symbolic Art of Gogol: Essays on his Short Fiction* (Columbus, Ohio: Slavica, 1981), 53. Darra Goldstein, meanwhile, reads Afanasii Ivanovich's interest in the secret "treasure" (*klad*) hidden inside of the larder (*kladovaia*) as an indicator of his sexual desire, as this is a literary text where food has become highly eroticized. See "Domestic Porkbarreling," 135. It is entirely possible, however, that the "interior" (*vnutrennost'*) of the larder that arouses Afanasii Ivanovich's desire is, in metaphorical terms, not the woman's sexual cavity but rather the mother's womb to which he wishes psychologically to return.

74. Renato Poggioli, "Gogol's 'Old-World Landowners': An Inverted Eclogue," *Indiana Slavic Studies* 3 (1963): 66.

75. See, for example, Janko Lavrin, *Goncharov* (New Haven, Conn: Yale University Press, 1954), 47, and Leon Stilman, "Oblomovka Revisited," *American Slavic and East European Review* 7, no. 1 (1948): 64.

76. François de LaBriolle, "Oblomov n'est-il qu'un paresseux?" *Cahiers du monde russe et soviétique* 10, no. 1 (1969): 47.

77. Milton Mays, "Oblomov as Anti-Faust," *Western Humanities Review* 21, no. 2 (1967): 51.

78. Ibid., 144. See also my "Oblomov's Consuming Passion: Food, Eating, and the Search for Communion," in *Goncharov's Oblomov: A Critical Companion*, ed. Galya Diment (Evanston, Ill.: Northwestern University Press, 1998), 110–35.

79. Goldstein, "Domestic Porkbarreling," 130.

80. See, for example, Stilman, "Oblomovka Revisited," 68; Renato Poggioli, *The Phoenix and the Spider: A Book of Essays About Some Russian Writers and Their View of the Self* (Cambridge, Mass.: Harvard University Press, 1957), 43; Alexandra Lyngstad and Sverre Lyngstad, *Ivan Goncharov* (New York: Twayne Publishers, 1971), 96–97; Kenneth E. Harper, "Under the Influence of Oblomov," in *From Los Angeles to Kiev: Papers on the Occasion of the Ninth International Congress of Slavists*, ed. Vladimir Markov and Dean S. Worth (Columbus, Ohio: Slavica, 1983), 116; Faith Wigzell, "Dream and Fantasy in Goncharov's *Oblomov*," in *From Pushkin to Palisandriia: Essays on the Russian Novel in Honor of Richard Freeborn*, ed. Arnold McMillin (New York: St. Martin's Press, 1990), 101; LaBriolle, "Oblomov n'est-il qu'un paresseux?" 48–50; and Mays, "Oblomov as Anti-Faust," 152. For a sustained Freudian analysis of Oblomov's regression wish, see John Givens, "Wombs, Tombs, and Mother Love: A Freudian Reading of Goncharov's *Oblomov*," in *Goncharov's Oblomov: A Critical Companion*, ed. Galya Diment (Evanston, Ill.: Northwestern University Press, 1998), 90–109.

81. Givens, "Wombs, Tombs, and Mother Love," 92.

82. Natalie Baratoff, *Oblomov: A Jungian Approach (A Literary Image of the Mother Complex)* (New York: Peter Lang, 1990), 106.

83. "Agafya is the true object of Oblomov's regression wish," writes Givens, "for she alone, as his nanny-surrogate, can undo 'the traumatic experience of weaning' and satisfy his needs—libidinal and otherwise—according to the pleasure principle, which governs his id-driven existence just as it did the mythical world of the Oblomovka he reconstructs from his childhood. His dream of Oblomovka, of course, was the source of his regression wish in the first place." See "Wombs, Tombs, and Mother Love," 100.

84. Ibid., 99.

85. This interpretation seems to accord with Freud's understanding of regression: "the neurotic is in some way tied to a period in his past life; we know now that this period in the past is one in which his libido could attain satis-

faction, one in which he was happy. He looks back on his life-story, seeking some such period, and goes on seeking it, even if he must go back to the time when he was a suckling infant to find it according to his recollection or his imagination of it under later influences." See Freud, *A General Introduction to Psychoanalysis*, trans. Joan Rivière (New York: Pocket, 1971), 374.

86. Writing about Pieter Brueghel's famous canvas *Land of Cockaigne* (1567), which depicts a trio of peasant farmers lying around with unbuttoned pants after eating all the food on a maypole, Grieco notes that Brueghel's painting "visualizes a dream of repletion which the lower classes fulfilled only on rare occasions." Chronic lack of food in medieval culture, Grieco explains, "gave rise to a myth of a land in which all was abundance and in which food literally begged to be eaten." See Grieco, *Themes in Art: The Meal*, 30–31.

87. Grigorii Kvitka-Osnov'ianenko, *Pan Khaliavskii. Roman* (Kiev: Dnipro, 1984), 68. All further citations from *Pan Khaliavskii* come from this edition of Kvitka-Osnov'ianenko's novel and will be cited parenthetically in the text.

88. It seems no accident that on at least two different occasions Pan Khaliavskii's mother refers to her favorite child as her "womb" or "belly" (*utroba*); see 65, 212.

89. Roman Koropeckyj, "Desire and Procreation in the Ukrainian Tales of Hryhorii Kvitka-Osnov'ianenko," *Canadian Slavonic Papers* 44, nos. 3–4 (2002): 165–73.

90. Sigmund Freud, *Three Essays on Sexuality*, trans. James Strachey (New York: Basic Books, 1962), 64.

91. Joanna Hubbs, *Mother Russia: The Feminine Myth in Russian Culture* (Bloomington: Indiana University Press, 1988), 208.

92. Williams, *Country and the City*, 30.

93. Jeanneret, *Feast of Words*, 2.

94. N. V. Gogol, *Sobranie sochinenii v shesti tomakh* (Moscow: Khudozhestvennaia literatura, 1978), 2:8. All further citations from "Old World Landowners" come from this edition of Gogol's works and will be cited parenthetically in the text by volume and page number.

95. Poggioli, "Gogol's 'Old-World Landowners,'" 58.

96. A host's duties and responsibilities toward his guests were spelled out quite clearly in the gastronomical writings of Grimod de la Reynière, Brillat-Savarin, and other authorities on the art and science of fine dining in early nineteenth-century Europe. For examples, see the various selections included in *Gusto: Essential Writings in Nineteenth-Century Gastronomy*, ed. Denise Gigante (New York: Routledge, 2005).

97. V. P. Meshcheriakov, "Lukavyi letopisets pomestnogo byta," in Kvitka-Osnov'ianenko, *Proza* (Moscow: Sovetskaia Rossiia, 1990), 13.

98. Richard Peace, *Oblomov: A Critical Examination of Goncharov's Novel* (Birmingham, Eng.: University of Birmingham, 1991), 31.

99. I. A. Goncharov, *Sobranie sochinenii v vos'mi tomakh* (Moscow: Khudo-

zhestvennaia literatura, 1953). All further citations from *Oblomov* come from this edition of Goncharov's works and will be cited parenthetically in the text by volume and page number.

100. Iurii Loshchits, *Goncharov* (Moscow: Molodaia gvardiia, 1977), 169.

101. Ibid., 172–73.

102. M. V. Otradin, "'Son Oblomova' kak khudozhestvennoe tseloe," *Russkaia literatura*, no. 1 (1992): 7.

103. Mikhail Bakhtin, *The Dialogic Imagination: Four Essays*, ed. Michael Holquist, trans. Caryl Emerson (Austin: University of Texas Press, 1988), 227. Agaf'ia Matveevna's brother seems to represent the counterforce to this commensal and communal spirit at table. Early in part 4 it is pointed out that Ivan Matveevich dined alone, eating at a later time, separately from his sister and her children, mostly in the kitchen (4:388).

104. Mays, "Oblomov as Anti-Faust," 147.

105. Lyngstads, *Ivan Goncharov*, 78.

106. From the brief humorous exchange that takes place between Oblomov and Zakhar in part 2, chapter 8, the reader gets the sense that Olga—much like Stolz—is given to teasing the hero about his rather hearty appetite. "I said, sir, that you had dinner at home, and supper at home, too," Zakhar reports back about a conversation he had with Olga. "'Why,' the young lady asks, 'does he have supper?' Well, sir, I told her you had only two chickens for supper." "Well, what did she say?" Oblomov asks nervously. "She smiled, sir. 'Why so little?' she asked" (4:236–37). As Peace notes, Olga "coaxes him [Oblomov] out of eating supper (a provincial custom frowned on in St. Petersburg, as we learn from *A Common Story*)." See Peace, *Oblomov*, 48.

107. Eliot Borenstein, "Slavophilia: The Incitement to Russian Sexual Discourse," *Slavic and East European Journal* 40, no. 1 (spring 1996): 142.

108. Jane T. Costlow, Stephanie Sandler, and Judith Vowles, introduction to *Sexuality and the Body in Russian Culture*, ed. Jane T. Costlow, Stephanie Sandler, and Judith Vowles (Stanford, Calif.: Stanford University Press, 1993), 10.

109. Igor Kon, *The Sexual Revolution in Russia: From the Age of the Czars to Today*, trans. James Riordan (New York: Free Press, 1995), 13–14.

110. Eve Levin, *Sex and Society in the World of the Orthodox Slavs, 900–1700* (Ithaca, N.Y.: Cornell University Press, 1989).

111. Eve Levin, "Sexual Vocabulary in Medieval Russia," in *Sexuality and the Body in Russian Culture*, ed. Jane T. Costlow, Stephanie Sandler, and Judith Vowles (Stanford, Calif.: Stanford University Press, 1993), 42.

112. Eric Naiman, "Historectomies: On the Metaphysics of Reproduction in a Utopian Age," in *Sexuality and the Body in Russian Culture*, ed. Jane T. Costlow, Stephanie Sandler, and Judith Vowles (Stanford, Calif.: Stanford University Press, 1993), 262.

113. For studies that examine the mythification and idealization of the maternal in Russian culture, see Adele Marie Barker, *The Mother Syndrome in the Russian Folk Imagination* (Columbus, Ohio: Slavica, 1986), and Joanna Hubbs, *Mother Russia*.

114. Kon, *Sexual Revolution in Russia*, 28.

115. Ibid., 29.

116. James H. Billington, *The Icon and the Axe: An Interpretive History of Russian Culture* (New York: Vintage Books, 1970), 492. Billington asserts that "the early years of the twentieth century brought about a preoccupation with sex that is quite without parallel in earlier Russian culture" (492).

117. Richard Stites refers to this conservative turn under Stalin and his successors as the "sexual thermidor." See Stites, *The Women's Liberation Movement in Russia: Feminism, Nihilism, and Bolshevism, 1860–1930* (Princeton, N.J.: Princeton University Press, 1978), 376.

118. Brown, *Fictional Meals and Their Function in the French Novel*, 14.

119. See, for example, Peter Farb and George Armelagos, *Consuming Passions: The Anthropology of Eating* (Boston: Houghton Mifflin, 1980).

120. Paul R. Abramson and Steven D. Pinkerton discuss the bifurcation of human sexuality in *With Pleasure: Thoughts on the Nature of Human Sexuality* (New York: Oxford University Press, 1995).

121. Aristotle, *The Nicomachean Ethics*, trans. by David Ross, revised by J. L. Ackrill and J. O. Urmson (New York: Oxford University Press, 1998).

122. Plato, *The Republic*, trans. Raymond Larson (Arlington Heights, Ill.: Harlan Davidson, 1979), 98, 107–109.

123. Ibid., 244.

124. Ibid., 3: "Once I was with the poet Sophocles when someone asked: 'How's your sex life, Sophocles? Are you still able to enjoy a woman?' 'Hush!' said Sophocles. 'The greatest happiness of my life was escaping from that cruel and raging tyrant.'"

125. Tobin, *Tarte à la crème*, 2.

126. Pierre J. Payer discusses the views of Aquinas and other influential Catholic churchmen on food and sex in *The Bridling of Desire: Views of Sex in the Later Middle Ages* (Toronto: University of Toronto Press, 1993).

127. Levin, *Sex and Society in the World of the Orthodox Slavs*, 57.

128. Freud, *A General Introduction to Psychoanalysis*, 232–33.

129. Bakhtin, *Rabelais and His World*, 281.

*2. Eating as Power: Dostoevsky and Carnivorousness*
(pages 40–97)

1. Richard Brautigan, *The Abortion: An Historical Romance 1966* (New York: Simon and Schuster, 1971), 28. A real library of this sort (named, appropriately enough, the "Brautigan Library") was actually established in Burlington, Vermont, in 1990.

2. Simon Karlinsky, "Dostoevsky as Rorschach Test," *New York Times Book Review* (June 13, 1971), 23. The "neurotic young girl" (who dreams of eating pineapple compote while witnessing the suffering of a crucified child) whom Karlinsky alludes to here is, of course, the pathological Lise Khokhlakova in *The Brothers Karamazov* (15:24). She also tells Alesha: "Let me be rich and all the rest poor. I'll eat candy and drink cream and not give any to anyone else" (15:21). Another memorable example of the pathology of eating that we sometimes encounter in Dostoevskii's fiction is provided by Arkadii's friend Lambert in *A Raw Youth* (1875), who claims that when he becomes rich he will derive the greatest pleasure from feeding his dogs bread and meat while the children of the poor starve to death (13:49).

3. Karlinsky, "Dostoevsky as Rorschach Test," 23. Dostoevskii's novels, according to one early-twentieth-century critic, cannot bear comparison with the novels of Tolstoi, Turgenev, or even Borborykin "as reflections of life by means of which one might study social types and the moods of one or another historical moment in Russian life." See the introductory essay by Ch. Vetrinskii (pseudonym for Vasilii E. Cheshikhin), "Fedor Mikhailovich Dostoevskii: zhizn', lichnost' i tvorchestvo," in *F. M. Dostoevskii v vospominaniiakh sovremennikov, pis'makh i zametkakh*, ed. Ch. Vetrinskii (Moscow: Sytin, 1912), xli.

4. While there may not be any "culinary Dostoevskii," Louis Szathmary has written an article on "The Culinary Walt Whitman." See the *Walt Whitman Quarterly* 3, no. 2 (1985): 28–33.

5. Dostoevskii is generally seen as being, as Alex De Jonge puts it, "more interested in mental states than in physical reality." See *Dostoevsky and the Age of Intensity* (New York: St. Martin's Press, 1975), 66. "Dostoevsky does not portray the world of nineteenth-century reality," De Jonge explains, "he reveals the myths upon which that reality is founded" (2).

6. Bruce K. Ward, *Dostoyevsky's Critique of the West: The Quest for the Earthly Paradise* (Waterloo, Ontario: Wilfred Laurier University Press, 1986), 128.

7. Mikhail Lermontov, *Sobranie sochinenii v chetyrekh tomakh* (Moscow and Leningrad: Akademiia nauk, 1958–59), 4:401, 438. Stavrogin, like Pechorin, is referred to in the novel as a "vampire" (10:401).

8. Nina Pelikan Straus discusses this male sexual violence and cruelty toward women (what she calls the "masculinist disease" that afflicts a number of Dostoevskii's fictional men) from a feminist perspective in *Dostoevsky and the Woman Question: Rereadings at the End of a Century* (New York: St. Martin's Press, 1994).

9. For a study of the influence of Dickens on Dostoevskii, see N. M. Lary, *Dostoevsky and Dickens: A Study of Literary Influence* (London: Routledge and Kegan Paul, 1973).

10. "Being so strong and healthy," the narrator tells us, the Yepanchin girls

"sometimes liked to have a good meal, which fact they had no desire to conceal" (8:32). Their mother, we are told, "sometimes looked askance at the frankness of their appetites" (8:32).

11. For a study of this theme in the works of one of Dostoevskii's British contemporaries (and a putative literary influence), see Gail Turley Houston, *Consuming Fictions: Gender, Class, and Hunger in Dickens's Novels* (Carbondale, Ill.: Southern Illinois University Press, 1994).

12. In his correspondence, Dostoevskii often complained about how debts had eaten up his meager financial resources. See, for example, his letter to Emiliia Dostoevskaia of October 11 (23), 1867 (28.2:231–33). He also lamented that he felt pressured to write for deadlines to eke out an existence, "selling my pen for a piece of daily bread." See his letter to Eduard Totleben of October 4, 1859 (28.1:342–44).

13. "You were hungry!" Sonia Marmeladova declares as she seeks desperately for an explanation as to why Raskol'nikov would have murdered the pawnbroker. "No, Sonia, no," he replies. "I'll tell you what: if I'd killed simply because I was hungry, then I should be . . . *happy* now!" (6:317–18).

14. Roland Barthes, "Lecture de Brillat-Savarin," in Jean-Anthèlme Brillat-Savarin, *Physiologie du goût* (Paris: Hermann, 1975), 8. "The question confronting most of the characters in Sue's *Les Mystères de Paris* and Hugo's *Les Miserables*," James Brown notes, "is not how well they eat but rather whether they will eat at all. The very acquisition of food becomes the primary concern for characters in their novels because it is at a premium. These poor souls subsist at the absolute *degré zéro alimentaire*." See *Fictional Meals and Their Function in the French Novel, 1789–1848* (Toronto: University of Toronto Press, 1984), 91.

15. This image, according to Joseph Frank, derives from Aleksandr Gertsen's correspondence with Pecherin. See *Dostoevsky: The Miraculous Years, 1865–1871* (Princeton, N.J.: Princeton University Press, 1995), 201.

16. Daniel Rancour-Laferriere discusses this desire for suffering (what he calls "moral masochism") as a Russian cultural trait in *The Slave Soul of Russia: Moral Masochism and the Cult of Suffering* (New York: New York University Press, 1995).

17. "Through Father Ferapont," Robin Feuer Miller correctly points out, "Dostoevsky ridicules the assumption that simple abstinence from earthly bread is itself an indication of an abundance of spiritual bread." See *The Brothers Karamazov: Worlds of the Novel* (New York: Twayne Publishers, 1992), 50.

18. Natalia Kolb-Seletski, "Gastronomy, Gogol, and His Fiction," *Slavic Review* 29, no. 1 (1970): 46.

19. Although his purpose is ostensibly to impress Father Ferapont with the rigor and austerity of the fasts kept by the monks at his monastery, the monk who visits Father Ferapont in book 4, chapter 1, provides us, in effect, with a gastro-

nomic list that likewise stimulates the appetite—if not the reader's, then at least the speaker's (and perhaps also his listener's). "Our dietary regime is arranged according to the ancient monastic rules," he explains to Father Ferapont.

During all forty days of Lent there are no meals provided on Monday, Wednesday, and Friday. On Tuesday and Thursday, we have white bread, stewed fruit with honey, wild berries, or salt cabbage and oatmeal gruel. On Saturday we have white cabbage soup, noodles with peas, and kasha, all with oil. On Sunday we have dried fish and kasha as well as cabbage soup. During Holy Week, from Monday until Saturday evening, for six whole days, we have only bread and water and uncooked vegetables, and that sparingly; eating is permitted, but not every day, just the same as is ordered for the first week in Lent. On Good Friday nothing is eaten. In the same way on Good Saturday we have to fast until three o'clock and then take a little bread and water, and drink a single cup of wine. On Holy Thursday we drink wine and have something cooked without oil or not cooked at all. . . . This is how we keep the fast. (14:153)

20. Eve Levin discusses Eastern Orthodox views on sins of the flesh in *Sex and Society in the World of the Orthodox Slavs, 900–1700* (Ithaca, N.Y.: Cornell University Press, 1989). See especially chapter 1, "The Ecclesiastical Image of Sexuality," 36–78.

21. As Bruce Ward notes, Ivan's "Legend of the Grand Inquisitor" effectively contrasts man's base physical and lofty spiritual appetites by juxtaposing lowly "earthly" bread (which satisfies our physical desires) with sublime "heavenly" bread (which satisfies our spiritual desires). See *Dostoyevsky's Critique of the West*, 106.

22. The same seems to be true for the audience in *The Idiot* that has gathered to celebrate Prince Myshkin's name day. When they are told that Ippolit is prepared to begin the reading of his "Necessary Explanation," one of the guests snacking at the hors d'oeuvre table observes, "What reading? It's time to eat appetizers!" (8:319).

23. Joseph Frank, *Dostoevsky: The Stir of Liberation, 1860–1865* (Princeton, N.J.: Princeton University Press, 1984) 204.

24. Ibid., 205.

25. Kilgour, *From Communion to Cannibalism*, 52.

26. In addition to the masculinist psychology of sexual cruelty that is exhibited by Fedor Pavlovich through his participation in the gang rape of Stinking Lizaveta, Diane Oenning Thompson asserts that the elder Karamazov's conjugal life with his second wife, Sof'ia Ivanovna, essentially amounted to "legalized rape." See *"The Brothers Karamazov" and the Poetics of Memory* (Cambridge: Cambridge University Press, 1991), 131.

27. De Jonge, *Dostoevsky and the Age of Intensity*, 179. Dostoevskii, according to De

Jonge, would share Baudelaire's contention that "cruelty and sexual pleasure are essentially identical" (179).

28. A. Kashina-Evreinova, *Podpol'e geniia (Seksual'nye istochniki tvorchestva Dostoevskogo)* (Petrograd: Tret'ia strazha, 1923), 34. "What sharply strikes one's attention in Dostoevskii's writings," observes another early-twentieth-century commentator, "is the author's indication—persistently reiterated—of the degree of suffering at which point a person at last finds an acute feeling of pleasure in that very suffering. One can hardly consider this peculiarity of the human psyche to be somehow unconditionally characteristic of all people at all times. It is necessary to recognize this peculiarity as a trait that is especially characteristic of Dostoevskii himself and that comes close to being a sadistic perversity." See Ch. Vetrinskii, "Fedor Mikhailovich Dostoevskii," xxv.

29. See Strakhov's letter to Tolstoi of November 28, 1883, in *L. N. Tolstoi– N. N. Strakhov: Polnoe sobranie perepiski*, ed. A. A. Donskov (Ottawa and Moscow: Slavic Research Group at the University of Ottawa and Gosudarstvennyi muzei L. N. Tolstogo, 2003), 2:652, 653.

30. Ibid., 2:652–53.

31. Robert L. Jackson addresses this issue (the veracity of Strakhov's assessment of and accusation against Dostoevskii) in "A View from the Underground: On Nikolai Nikolaevich Strakhov's Letter About His Good Friend Fyodor Mikhailovich Dostoevsky and on Leo Nikolaevich Tolstoy's Cautious Response to It," in Jackson, *Dialogues with Dostoevsky: The Overwhelming Questions* (Stanford, Calif.: Stanford University Press, 1993), 104–20.

32. Geir Kjetsaa, *Fyodor Dostoyevsky: A Writer's Life*, trans. Siri Hustvedt and David McDuff (New York: Viking Penguin, 1987), 153.

33. T. Enko, *F. Dostoevskii—intimnaia zhizn' geniia* (Moscow: MP Teleos, 1997), 134.

34. Kashina-Evreinova, *Podpol'e geniia*, 69.

35. Enko, *F. Dostoevskii—intimnaia zhizn' geniia*, 135.

36. Ibid.

37. Konstantin Mochulsky, *Dostoevsky: His Life and Work*, trans. Michael A. Minihan (Princeton, N.J.: Princeton University Press, 1967), 110.

38. Ibid., 318.

39. Commenting on the perverse sexuality (and skewed power gradient) that Dostoevskii is prone to portray in his novels, Susanne Fusso observes that the author's post-Siberian fiction is replete with "scenes of erotically intense and even sexually abusive relations between grown men and young girls ranging in age from five to sixteen." See *Discovering Sexuality in Dostoevsky* (Evanston, Ill.: Northwestern University Press, 2006), 17.

40. "For the most part," writes R. L. Jackson, "sexuality in Dostoevsky's novelistic universe is disclosed in its negative, or destructive, manifestations." See

Jackson, "In the Darkness of the Night: Tolstoy's *Kreutzer Sonata* and Dostoevsky's *Notes from the Underground*," in *Dialogues with Dostoevsky*, 213.

41. Kashina-Evreinova, *Podpol'e geniia*, 65.

42. Kilgour, *From Communion to Cannibalism*, 16.

43. Ibid., 5.

44. Straus argues that the novel initially seems structured as a regression to fantasies of destroying symbolic maternity. See *Dostoevsky and the Woman Question*, 23. Louis Breger likewise examines Raskol'nikov's matricidal urges in *Dostoevsky: The Author as Psychoanalyst* (New York: New York University Press, 1989).

45. I understand the term "romantic realist" in the sense that Donald Fanger uses it in his seminal book, *Dostoevsky and Romantic Realism: A Study of Dostoevsky in Relation to Balzac, Dickens, and Gogol* (Chicago: University of Chicago Press, 1965).

46. Mervyn Nicholson, "Eat—or Be Eaten: An Interdisciplinary Metaphor," in *Diet and Discourse: Eating, Drinking and Literature*, ed. Evelyn J. Hinz (Winnipeg, Canada: Mosaic, 1991), 200.

47. Kilgour, *From Communion to Cannibalism*, 145. Kilgour sees this change as having taken place during the Renaissance, when individualism became a leading cultural value in the West.

48. This dictum stands at the center of Norman Brown's treatment of food in his book, *Love's Body* (New York: Vintage, 1966); see esp. 162–65. Mervyn Nicholson examines eating as power in a number of modern works of fiction in "Eat—or Be Eaten," 191–210.

49. In his review of Fred Kaplan's biography of Dickens, John Bayley writes, "'I could eat you' is the unspoken wish of Dickens' liveliest characters." See "Best and Worst," *New York Review of Books* (January 19, 1989), 11. For a more detailed study of Dickens's purported obsession with human carnivorousness, an obsession rooted in his earliest childhood days and stimulated in large part by his boyhood reading of fairy tales, travel accounts, and "penny dreadfuls," see Harry Stone, *The Night Side of Dickens: Cannibalism, Passion, Necessity* (Columbus: Ohio State University Press, 1994).

50. Gail Turley Houston, *Consuming Fictions*, 4, 46. James E. Marlowe concurs that Dickens's fiction is dominated by themes of metaphoric cannibalism. See "English Cannibalism: Dickens After 1859," *Studies in English Literature, 1500–1900* 23, no. 4 (1983): 647–66.

51. Frank, *Dostoevsky: The Miraculous Years*, 22.

52. See, for example, Ronald Hingley's introduction to *Memoirs from the House of the Dead*, by Fyodor Dostoevsky, trans. Jessie Coulson (New York: Oxford University Press, 1983), xvi, where he writes, "*House of the Dead* played a significant role in the evolution of Dostoevsky's social and political views. It stands half way between the early, confusingly documented socialism of his

twenties and the very different system of hard-and-fast dogma which he was to champion from his mid-forties onwards. He then began to emerge as an extreme Russian nationalist; as a fanatical conservative; as a devotee of the Russian Orthodox Church; as an idolator of the Russian common people."

53. Edward Wasiolek, *Dostoevsky: The Major Fiction* (Cambridge, Mass.: MIT Press, 1964), 24.

54. Ibid., 25.

55. Witness, for example, the description of the kind widow, Nastas'ia Ivanovna, at the opening of part 1, chapter 6 of *Notes from the House of the Dead*: "All that you noticed in her, at every moment, was simply her infinite goodness, her invincible desire to gratify you, to make things easier for you, to do something that would be sure to please you" (4:68).

56. Robert Louis Jackson explores sadistic cruelty in Dostoevskii's characters in "Dostoevsky and the Marquis de Sade: The Final Encounter"; see Jackson, *Dialogues with Dostoevsky*, 144–61. See also F. Kaufman, "Dostojevskij a Markyz de Sade," *Filosofický časopis*, 3 (1968): 384–89; and Sergei Kuznetsov, "Fedor Dostoevskii i Markiz de Sad: Sviazi i pereklichki," in *Dostoevskii v kontse XX veka*, ed. K. A. Stepanian (Moscow: Klassika plius, 1996), 557–74. Beatrice Fink, in her essay on food imagery and symbolism in the works of the marquis de Sade, characterizes the eaters in his fiction as carnivores who seem to share the same *plotoiadnost'* we observe in Dostoevskii's power-hungry human predators. "Sade's libertine does not, in fact, eat," she writes. "He greedily devours; he literally swallows others." See "Food as Object, Activity, and Symbol in Sade," *Romanic Review* 65, no. 2 (1974): 101.

57. Edward Rossmann "The Conflct over Food in the Works of J.-K. Huysmans," *Nineteenth-Century French Studies* 2, nos. 1 and 2 (1973–74): 61. "Appetite for food and the sexual appetite are for Huysmans variations of the general drive to devour or possess everything: food, things, women," Rossmann adds. "For Huysmans man is a devourer, a cannibal on a cosmic scale, whose monstrous appetite would engulf the world, if it could" (63).

58. In his *Diary of a Writer*, Dostoevskii associates this socioeconomic exploitation of the lower classes specifically (and almost exclusively) with the Jews, whom he accuses of being "blood-suckers" (he calls them *krovopiitsy* and *miroedy*). See, for example, the essays "Dreams and Reveries" (21:91–96) and "Apropos of a New Drama" (21:96–105) in *Diary of a Writer* for 1873.

59. See, for example, Straus, *Dostoevsky and the Woman Question*.

60. "What 'stings' Raskolnikov," Joseph Frank writes in his analysis of this scene, "is the bite of these Darwinian reflections, which view the triumph of the stronger as right and just and any help to the weaker as a violation of the laws of nature." See *Dostoevsky: The Miraculous Years*, 107.

61. The emotional "devouring" that occurs between General Ivolgin and Mrs.

Terent'ev seems to be mutual and reciprocal, however; at one point Kolia Ivolgin advises his father not to visit his widow friend, warning him that "she will eat you alive!" (8:110).

62. Straus, *Dostoevsky and the Woman Question*, 89.

63. Nikolai Strakhov reviewed the French translation, *De l'origine des espèces, ou des lois du progrèss chez les êtres organisés par Ch. Darwin*, trans. Clémence-Auguste Royer (Paris, 1862), in *Vremia*, no. 11 (1862).

64. For Darwin's reception in nineteenth-century Russia, see Alexander Vucinich, *Darwin in Russian Thought* (Berkeley and Los Angeles: University of California Press, 1988); Daniel Todes, *Darwin Without Malthus: The Struggle for Existence in Russian Evolutionary Thought* (New York: Oxford University Press, 1989); James Allen Baker, "The Russian Populists' Response to Darwin," *Slavic Review* 22, no. 3 (1963): 456–68, and "Russian Opposition to Darwinism in the Nineteenth Century," *Isis* 65, no. 229 (1974): 487–505; and George L. Kline, "Darwinism and the Russian Orthodox Church," in *Continuity and Change in Russian and Soviet Thought*, ed. Ernest J. Simmons (Cambridge, Mass.: Harvard University Press, 1955), 307–28.

65. Theodosius Dobzhansky, "The Crisis of Soviet Biology," in *Continuity and Change in Russian and Soviet Thought*, 338. James Allen Rogers voices a similar opinion. "The Darwinian controversy in Russia as in Europe," he writes, "went quickly beyond the world of science and became a focal point of philosophical and political disputes." See "Darwinism, Scientism, and Nihilism," *Russian Review* 19, no. 1 (1960): 16.

66. Todes, *Darwin Without Malthus*, 29. As Peter K. Christoff points out, one of the leading Slavophiles maintained that "the best way to constrain man's animal, jungle proclivities was to raise him in a commune." See *K. S. Aksakov: A Study in Ideas*, vol. 3 of Christoff's monumental study, *An Introduction to Nineteenth-Century Russian Slavophilism* (Princeton, N.J.: Princeton University Press, 1981), 368. The peasant commune, according to another Slavophile, "does not comprehend the personal freedom of man alone, which for it is a *wolf's* freedom, not human freedom." See A. Gilferding, *Sobranie sochinenii* (St. Petersburg, 1868), 2:478. Gilferding, in Christoff's words, "saw in the Russian communal principle salvation from jungle-like individualism and social Darwinism" (368 n).

67. A notable exception is the position taken by the radical journal *Russkoe slovo*, to which socialists such as Dmitrii Pisarev and V. A. Zaitsev regularly contributed. Despite their opposition to the current political system in Russia, both Pisarev and Zaitsev favored the industrialization of Russia and supported the doctrine of Social Darwinism. Indeed, they even defended racism and slavery in the United States as a historical necessity, as the struggle for survival was

for them the moving force behind human evolution. See Frank, *Dostoevsky: The Miraculous Years*, 75.

68. Strakhov, "Durnye priznaki," in his *Kriticheskie stat'i (1861–1894)* (Kiev: Izd. I. P. Matchenko, 1902–08), 387, 391.

69. Ibid., 394.

70. Ibid., 396.

71. N. Danilevskii, *Rossiia i Evropa: Vzgliad na kul'turnye i politicheskie otnosheniia slavianskogo mira k Germano-Romanskomu* (St. Petersburg: "Obshchestven-naia pol'za," 1871), 139–41.

72. Danilevskii, *Darvinizm* (St. Petersburg: Izd. M. E. Komarova, 1885–87).

73. "Vzgliad na russkuiu literaturu so smerti Pushkina," *Russkoe slovo*, no. 2, otd. II (1859): 1–63, and no. 3 (1859): 1–39. This essay is reprinted in Apollon Grigor'ev, *Literaturnaia kritika* (Moscow: Khudozhestvennaia literatura, 1967), 157–239.

74. Nikolai Strakhov summarizes Grigor'ev's essay in his preface to *Sochineniia Apollona Grigor'eva* (1876). See Strakhov, *Kriticheskie stat'i (1861–1894)*, 348–57.

75. N. N. Strakhov, *Kriticheskie stat'i ob I. S. Turgeneve i L. N. Tolstom (1862–1885)* (Kiev: Izd. I. P. Matchenko, 1901; repr. The Hague: Mouton, 1968), 246–47.

76. Ibid., 265.

77. Ibid., 284.

78. The issue of "humble" and "predatory" types of personalities is broached quite explicitly in Dostoevskii's *The Eternal Husband*, where Velchinanov exclaims in surprise and exasperation at the vengeful behavior exhibited by Trusotskii, "Why, you really are a 'predatory type!' I thought you were only the 'eternal husband,' and nothing more!" (20:47). The cuckolded husband, for his part, claims to have read about the "predatory type" and the "humble type" in the literary criticism section of a journal, most likely Strakhov's article on Tolstoi's *War and Peace* (20:55). "Much of Dostoevsky's later work," Frank points out, "may well be seen as a dramatization of the conflict between 'predatory' Western (or Western-influenced) types and genuinely Russian 'meek' ones." See Frank, *Dostoevsky: The Stir of Liberation*, 46.

79. Harriet Murav argues that "holy foolishness" serves in Dostoevskii's novels as a site of resistance to the Western-oriented "age of positivism and science" in Russian culture. See *Holy Foolishness: Dostoevsky's Novels and the Poetics of Cultural Critique* (Stanford, Calif.: Stanford University Press, 1992), 8.

80. Witness, for example, the following notebook entry for 1875–76: "The reality and sincerity of the demands of Communism and Socialism and the inevitability of a European upheaval. But here you have science—outside of Christ and with complete faith. The things that must be discovered are: what are the exact scientific relations between people and what is the new moral order

(there is no love, there is only egoism, that is, the struggle for existence)—they firmly believe in science" (24:164).

81. "In his letters and polemical writings Dostoevsky repeatedly juxtaposes Darwin's law with Christ's," writes Liza Knapp. "For Dostoevsky, when Christ turned down the devil's challenge to turn stone into bread he rejected what Darwin would eventually come to represent." See *The Annihilation of Inertia: Dostoevsky and Metaphysics* (Evanston, Ill.: Northwestern University Press, 1996), 114.

82. See B. A. Lewis, "Darwin and Dostoevsky," *Melbourne Slavonic Studies*, no. 11 (1976): 23–32. Lewis argues that the refutation of Social Darwinism constitutes a major theme of *Crime and Punishment*.

83. Ibid., 25.

84. "In literature Darwinism became a topic of direct concern or a target of endless allusions," Alexander Vucinich writes:

> References to the letter or the spirit of Darwinian thought, sometimes of the most subtle nature, became an infallible way of depicting the world outlook and ideological proclivities of the heroes of literary masterpieces. Individual heroes of Dostoevsky's and Tolstoy's literary works provided graphic examples of the myriads of prisms refracting Darwinian science and showing the multiple strands of its impact on current thought and attitudes. More often than not, these heroes were alter egos of their literary creators, giving added scope to Darwinism as an intellectual and social phenomenon. A literary figure took note of Darwinian evolutionism not only by commenting on its scientific principles but also by making use of its metaphors.

See *Darwin in Russian Thought*, 4.

85. Aleksandr Ostrovskii, *Sobranie sochinenii* (Moscow: Khudozhestvennaia literatura, 1960), 7:121–223.

86. Aleksei Pisemskii, *Sobranie sochinenii* (Moscow: Pravda, 1959), 9:285–359.

87. Nikolai Leskov, *Polnoe sobranie sochinenii* (St. Petersburg, 1903), 23:90. Gordanov advises one of his acquaintances, "Living with wolves, act in a wolflike fashion."

88. Gary Cox examines Dostoevskii's novels specifically along the axis of dominance in his *Tyrant and Victim in Dostoevsky* (Columbus, Ohio: Slavica, 1984).

89. "Perhaps Dostoevsky's extensive, and often biting, use of naturalist allegories," Vucinich writes, "owed some debt to Darwin's suggestive ideas"; see *Darwin in Russian Thought*, 110.

90. Everything in such a world, Dostoevskii adds, is reduced to "despotism" over a piece of bread. "Too much spirit," he sadly notes, "is being exchanged for bread" (24:164). For a brief discussion of Dostoevskii's reaction to Darwinism, see G. M. Fridlender, *Realizm Dostoevskogo* (Moscow and Leningrad: Nauka, 1964), 157–63.

91. N. K. Mikhailovsky, *Dostoevsky: A Cruel Talent*, trans. Spencer Cadmus (Ann Arbor, Mich.: Ardis, 1978), 36.

92. Ibid., 12.

93. Ibid. Mikhailovskii maintains that during Dostoevskii's early career the Russian writer's talents were devoted mainly to studying the psychology of the sheep being devoured by the wolf, while in his later career (that is, upon his return from prison and Siberian exile) Dostoevskii turned his attention almost exclusively to the psychology of the wolf devouring the sheep.

94. Ibid., 13.

95. Ivan Turgenev, who read Mikhailovskii's essay, apparently agreed. "He [Mikhailovskii] caught the basic characteristic of his [Dostoevskii's] oeuvre," Turgenev confided to one of his correspondents. See his letter to Mikhail Saltykov-Shchedrin (September 24, 1882) in I. S. Turgenev, *Polnoe sobranie sochinenii i pisem v 28-i tomakh*, ed. M. P. Alekseev (Moscow: Akademiia nauk, 1960–68), vol. 28, bk. 2:49.

96. Maksim Gor'kii, "O 'Karamazovshchine'," *Russkoe slovo* 219 (September 22, 1913), and "Eshche o 'Karamazovshchine'," *Russkoe slovo* 248 (October 27, 1913). Both of these essays are reprinted in Maksim Gor'kii, *O literature* (Moscow: Khudozhestvennaia literatura, 1961), 66–69 and 70–75.

97. Turgenev, *Polnoe sobranie sochinenii i pisem*, vol. 28, bk. 2:51.

98. R. L. Jackson, "Dostoevsky and the Marquis de Sade," 145. Renato Poggioli voices a similar sentiment: "Dostoevsky was never willing to see merely the 'human beast' even in the most degraded human beings." See *The Phoenix and the Spider: A Book of Essays About Some Russian Writers and Their View of the Self* (Cambridge, Mass.: Harvard University Press, 1957), 26.

99. Jacques Catteau discusses *A Raw Youth* as "the novel of the predator" in *Dostoyevsky and the Process of Literary Creation*, trans. Audrey Littlewood (Cambridge: Cambridge University Press, 1989), 265–68.

100. Dostoevskii's portrayal of "predatory" types resembles in a number of important ways that of Dickens. J. R. Kincaid, in *Dickens and the Rhetoric of Laughter* (Oxford: Clarendon Press, 1971), writes that the narrator in *David Copperfield* "speaks of good people as harmless domestic animals and evil people as predatory beasts" (168). In a similar vein, R. D. McMaster examines the extensive use of predatory imagery in another of Dickens's novels. See his essay, "Birds of Prey: A Study of *Our Mutual Friend*," *Dalhousie Review* 40, no. 3 (1960): 372–81. Speaking of the avaricious world of mercantile London that Dickens describes in the novel, McMaster notes that "character after character is a bird, a beast, or a fish of prey in this swamp" (373).

101. Renato Poggioli explores this spider imagery as a symbol for modern man's existential alienation in his essay "Kafka and Dostoyevsky." See *The Kafka Problem*, ed. Angel Flores (New York: Gordian Press, 1975), 107–17. In the

essay "Piccola Bestia," which appeared in *Diary of a Writer* in September 1876 (chap. 1), Dostoevskii relates how a tarantula once crawled about all night in his rented flat in Florence and caused quite an uproar in the building. He then proceeds to use this spider imagery in his ensuing discussion of international politics, where he addresses the so-called Eastern question and especially what he considers the rampant Russophobia that pervades contemporary Europe. "Everyone points at Russia," he notes, "everyone is convinced that the harmful creature each time scurries forth from out of here" (23:107).

102. For recent Russian discussions of the treatment of sexuality in Dostoevskii's fiction (and in particular "Stavrogin's sin"), see Iu. Kariakin, "Khram bez kupola (*Besy* bez glavy 'U Tikhona')," in his *Dostoevskii i kanun XXI veka* (Moscow: Sovetskii pisatel', 1989), 319–24; Tat'iana Kasatkina, "Kak my chitaem russkuiu literaturu: O sladostrastii," *Novyi mir*, no. 7 (1999): 170–82; Irina Rodnianskaia, "Mezhdu Konom i Dostoevskim: Replika Vitaliiu Svintsovu," *Novyi mir*, no. 5 (1999): 213–15; Vitalii Svintsov, "Dostoevskii i otnosheniia mezhdu polami," *Novyi mir*, no. 5 (1999): 195–213; Vitalii Svintsov, "Dostoevskii i stavroginskii grekh," *Voprosy literatury*, no. 2 (1995): 111–42; and M. N. Zolotonosov, "Seks 'Ot Stavrogina': pornograficheskii kommentarii k 'otrechennoi' glave iz romana *Besy*," in Zolotonosov, *Slovo i telo: Seksual'nye aspekty universalii, interpretatsii russkogo kul'turnogo teksta XIX–XX vekov* (Moscow: Ladomir, 1999), 9–78.

103. Susanne Fusso points out that Dostoevskii published this episode from *The Insulted and Injured* (part 3, chap. 10) in the very same issue of *Vremia* that contained his essay, "Otvet *Russkomu vestniku*," in which Cleopatra in Pushkin's *Egyptian Nights* is compared to a man-eating spider, "an image of bestial lust that Dostoevsky was to use again and again"; see *Discovering Sexuality in Dostoevsky*, 4.

104. Ralph Matlaw, "Recurrent Imagery in Dostoevskij," *Harvard Slavic Studies* 3 (1957): 206.

105. See Cox, *Tyrant and Victim in Dostoevsky*. S. K. Somerwil-Ayrton employs Cox's notion of "dominance hierarchy" in Dostoevskii's fictional world as the foundation for a sociological study titled *Poverty and Power in the Early Works of Dostoevskij* (Amsterdam: Rodopi, 1988). "I intend to demonstrate," Somerwil-Ayrton writes

> that all the works analysed in this study reflect Dostoevskij's preoccupation with the psychological effects of the power hierarchy in relation to the possession and to the lack of money in a given stratum of society. Dostoevskij constantly analyses the power wielded by one individual on others, singly and collectively, and shows that the *use* of power by that individual is *misuse* and may easily lead to abuse by the stronger,

exacerbated by weakness or willingness in the victim. Therefore, in each of the analyses in this study I have exposed the underlying elements of the power hierarchy on an axis that I have designated as the *tyrant-victim axis*. (1)

Martin P. Rice, meanwhile, explores the origins of Dostoevskii's concept of a power hierarchy in Hegelian philosophy. See "Dostoevskij's *Notes from Underground* and Hegel's 'Master and Slave,'" *Canadian-American Slavic Studies* 8, no. 3 (1974): 359–69.

106. With regard to the arachnid imagery at work in *The Devils*, Richard Peace notes how "Liza has revealed that Stavrogin is incapable of showing her the spider of evil, and if there is such a spider at all in the novel, it must surely be that weaver of intrigue—Petr Verkhovensky." See *Dostoyevsky: An Examination of the Major Novels* (Cambridge: Cambridge University Press, 1971), 201.

107. In the chapter devoted to *The Idiot* in his book, *The Shape of the Apocalypse in Modern Russian Fiction* (Princeton, N.J.: Princeton University Press, 1989), David Bethea discusses how Dostoevskii came "to associate the railroad with the spread of atheism and the spirit of the Antichrist" (77).

108. In *The Romantic Agony*, trans. Angus Davidson (New York: Oxford University Press, 1970), Mario Praz discusses literary representations of Cleopatra as an algolagnic woman by writers such as Gautier and Pushkin; see 214–16.

109. In her study of consumption in Victorian culture, Houston notes that, as part of the "grotesque realism" of capitalism, aliment is often confused with excrement; see *Consuming Fictions*, 137–38.

110. Dickens's novels, Houston points out, are replete with predatory male characters who are referred to as "boa constrictors"; see *Consuming Fictions*, 108.

111. Alesha's response would seem to parallel Sonia Marmeladova's consternation (and indignation) in *Crime and Punishment* at Raskol'nikov's assertion that in murdering the pawnbroker Alena he had killed not a human being but a foul, noxious "louse" (6:320).

112. Leonid Grossman surmises that Dostoevskii got this image of cannibal flies from Balzac's *Père Goriot*, where Vautrin at one point is heard to remark, "Il faut vous manger les uns les autres, comme des araignées dans un pot." See *Tvorchestvo Dostoevskogo* (Moscow, 1928), 89. It is entirely possible, however, that Dostoevskii took the idea of cannibal insects from a little-known work of Russian literature written by an author with whose oeuvre he seems to have been quite familiar: Prince Vladimir Odoevskii and his beast fable, "Novyi Zhoko," which appeared in 1833 as part of a cycle of stories called *Motley Tales* (*Pestrye skazki*).

113. Michael Holquist, "How Sons Become Fathers," in *Fyodor Dostoevsky's "The Brothers Karamazov*," ed. Harold Bloom (New York: Chelsea House Publishers, 1988), 39–51. Gary Cox likewise examines the Oedipal rivalry between

fathers and sons depicted in *The Brothers Karamazov* in chapter 9 ("Primal Murders") of his book; see *Tyrant and Victim in Dostoevsky*, 86–101. Michael André Bernstein, meanwhile, expropriates Bakhtin's theory of carnival in an innovative way and discusses Ivan Karamazov's murderous intent toward his father as the manifestation of a modern cultural development; see "'These Children that Come at You with Knives': *Ressentiment*, Mass Culture, and the Saturnalia," *Critical Inquiry* 17, no. 2 (1991): 358–85. The classic study on this topic remains, of course, Freud's "Dostoevsky and Parricide," reprinted in *Russian Literature and Psychoanalysis*, ed. Daniel Rancour-Laferriere (Philadelphia: John Benjamins, 1989), 41–57.

114. August Strindberg, *Six Plays*, trans. Elizabeth Sprigge (New York: Doubleday, 1955), 52.

115. Holquist, "How Sons Become Fathers," 40.

116. Mervyn Nicholson, "Eat—or Be Eaten," 198. For a study that provides an overview of the theme of cannibalism in Western literature (from Swift, Flaubert, and the marquis de Sade to Artaud, Genet, and Mailer), see Claude J. Rawson, "Cannibalism and Fiction: Reflections on Narrative Form and 'Extreme Situations,'" *Genre* 10 (1977): 667–711, and 11 (1978): 227–313.

117. According to one of the petitioners who comes to visit the holy fool Semen Iakovlevich in part 2 of *The Devils*, contemporary youth in Russia are already "cannibals" (*liudoedy*) for having issued a writ against this poor old widow (10:258).

118. Tatyana Tolstaya, "In Cannibalistic Times," *New York Review of Books* (April 11, 1991), 3. Roger Dadoun discusses the connection between cannibalism and Stalinism in his essay, "Du cannibalisme comme stade suprême du stalinisme," in *Destins du cannibalisme*, ed. J.-B. Pontalis, special issue of *Nouvelle Revue de Psychanalyse*, no. 6 (Fall 1972): 269–72. For studies on cannibalism, see the following: William Arens, *The Man-Eating Myth: Anthropology and Anthropophagy* (New York: Oxford University Press, 1979); Marvin Harris, *Cannibals and Kings: The Origins of Culture* (New York: Random House, 1977); Eli Sagan, *Cannibalism: Human Aggression and Cultural Form* (New York: Harper, 1974); Reay Tannahill, *Flesh and Blood: A History of the Cannibal Complex* (New York: Stein and Day, 1975); and Peggy Reeve Sanday, *Divine Hunger: Cannibalism as a Cultural System* (Cambridge: Cambridge University Press, 1986).

119. Nikolai Karamzin, *Istoriia gosudarstva rossiiskogo*, 12 vols. (St. Petersburg, 1816–29), 9:152–53. I am quoting here from Harriet Murav, *Holy Foolishness*, 2.

120. Tolstaya, "In Cannibalistic Times," 3.

121. Malcolm Jones, *Dostoyevsky: The Novel of Discord* (New York: Harper and Row, 1976), 22.

122. According to David Bethea, Raskol'nikov's final dream in Siberia demonstrates how Dostoevskii was coming closer to an apocalyptic view of Russian

history. "Raskolnikov," Bethea writes, "is finally made to understand, by the sprung logic of a dream, what his mind has managed to avoid throughout the long and circuitous telling of his story up to this moment: when used to measure morality, reason is a plague . . . presumably emanating from the West, that will bring on the wholesale destruction of humanity"; see *The Shape of the Apocalypse*, 70–71. For a study of dreams in Dostoevskii's fiction, see Michael Katz, *Dreams and the Unconscious in Nineteenth-Century Russian Fiction* (Hanover, N.H.: University Press of New England, 1984), 84–116.

123. Frank, *Dostoevsky: The Miraculous Years*, 146.

124. Kyril FitzLyon, introduction to *Winter Notes on Summer Impressions* by Fyodor Dostoyevsky, trans. Kyril FitzLyon (London: Quartet Books, 1985), vii–viii.

125. Dostoevskii's critique here, as Gary Saul Morson points out, is aimed at the ideal of false Western utopianism: "A cruel parody of Christianity, that ideal is destined to fail, the author proclaims, because it bases love on law and brotherhood on rational self-interest." See *The Boundaries of Genre: Dostoevsky's "Diary of a Writer" and the Traditions of Literary Utopia* (Austin: University of Texas Press, 1981), 25.

126. Bruce Ward discusses the "Geneva ideas" in regard to Versilov's ideology in *A Raw Youth*. See *Dostoyevsky's Critique of the West*, 46.

127. "The binding idea is no more," Lebedev laments, "everything has become soft, everything is flabby and everyone is flabby. We've all, all, all grown flabby" (8:315).

128. Robin Feuer Miller, *Dostoevsky and "The Idiot:" Author, Narrator, and Reader* (Cambridge, Mass.: Harvard University Press, 1981), 202. Malcolm Jones concurs: "Lebedev does not say so explicitly, but *The Idiot* shows how men now consume each other spiritually." See *Dostoyevsky: The Novel of Discord*, 91.

129. In his notebooks for *A Raw Youth*, Dostoevskii writes: "In everything is the idea of decomposition" (16:16) and "Decomposition—this is the principal explicit idea of the novel" (16:17).

130. See, for example, chapter 1 ("Once More on the Subject that Constantinople, Sooner or Later, Must Be Ours") for March 1877 (25:65–67) and chapter 3 ("Peace Rumors. 'Constantinople Must Be Ours'—Is This Possible? Various Opinions") for November 1877 (26:82–87) of Dostoevskii's *Diary of a Writer*.

131. Mochulsky, *Dostoevsky: His Life and Works*, 331.

132. Bakhtin, *Problems of Dostoevsky's Poetics*, 250.

133. Frank, "The World of Raskolnikov," 570. Malcolm Jones, in his study of Dostoevskii's "novel of discord," likewise asserts that the central question facing the author's characters is "whether the fundamental law of human relations is, or should be, cannibalism or active love." See *Dostoyevsky: The Novel of Discord*, 170.

134. Murav, *Holy Foolishness*, 13–14.

135. Bakhtin, *Problems of Dostoevsky's Poetics*, 249.

136. Ibid.

137. As reported by Aleksandr Miliukov in *F. M. Dostoevskii v vospominaniiakh sovremennikov*, ed. A. Dolinin (Moscow: Khudozhestvennaia literatura, 1964), 1:192.

138. Joseph Frank, *Dostoevsky: The Seeds of Revolt, 1821–1849* (Princeton, N.J.: Princeton University Press, 1976), 50.

139. A similar episode occurs in *A Raw Youth*. "One time," Makar Dolgorukii says to Sof'ia Andreevna, recalling an incident that occurred when she was a young girl, "you thought you saw a wolf and ran to me all trembling, but there wasn't any wolf at all." "I remember that," Arkadii's mother replies. "I remember a great deal. My very first memory in life is of seeing your love and kindness for me" (13:330).

140. "If the corruption, which appeared to be foreordained, does not occur and if Alyosha's soul is 'restored,' it is thanks to the 'sisterly' love Grusha shows him," writes Liza Knapp. "This love proves to be a miraculous force, capable of transforming and restoring the human beings it touches." See *The Annihilation of Inertia*, 203.

141. Thompson, *"The Brothers Karamazov" and the Poetics of Memory*, 119.

142. Murav, *Holy Foolishness*, 129.

143. At the beginning of this scene, the petty demon Rakitin is said to be watching Alesha "rapaciously" (*plotoiadno*) from his corner in eager anticipation of the sexual mauling he expects the youngest Karamazov brother will soon receive (14:315). At one point he even exclaims, "What rapaciousness!" (*Ekoe plotoiadie!*) in admiration of what he takes to be Grushen'ka's sexual predatoriness in seducing Alesha (14:324).

144. The episode could easily be seen the other way around, however. Alesha may be said to have pulled Grushen'ka out of hell by "giving her an onion" (by seeing her as a loving spiritual sister rather than as a sexually predatory beast). When Zosima appears to Alesha in his dream during the "Cana of Galilee" chapter, the elder says to him, "You gave a famished woman an onion today" (14:327). This is the way Robin Feuer Miller reads the scene, claiming that "each offers the other an onion" and that "Grushenka gives Alyosha both an onion . . . and a meta-onion." See *The Brothers Karamazov: Worlds of the Novel*, 85, 86.

145. Murav, *Holy Foolishness*, 142.

146. "Dmitry is metaphorically dead," Murav explains, "and his interrogation corresponds to the trials that, according to tradition, await us in the underworld"; ibid., 142.

147. Ibid., 143.

148. Robert L. Jackson writes that "one may perhaps assume that the future rela-

tionship between Dmitry and Grushenka will be characterized by a union of carnal and spiritual elements"; see "In the Darkness," 213.

149. Murav, *Holy Foolishness*, 143.

150. Nearly every social gathering in *The Brothers Karamazov*, Murav points out, is "an occasion for rupture, scandal, 'laceration,' and violence. Only Alyosha's dream of the wedding at Cana of Galilee provides an image of peace. The ending transforms the vision of social harmony into reality. Ilyusha's funeral feast is a feast of brotherly love"; see *Holy Foolishness*, 166. Sven Linnér likewise sees the Cana of Galilee chapter as providing an important model of transcendent harmony in human interrelations, observing that "the scene is transformed from the earthly wedding in Cana into the heavenly banquet, whose host is the Lord resurrected." See *Starets Zosima in "The Brothers Karamazov": A Study in the Mimesis of Virtue* (Stockholm: Almqvist and Wiksell, 1975), 175.

*3. Eating as Pleasure: Tolstoy and Voluptuousness*
(pages 98–157)

1. See, for example, Helena Goscilo, "Tolstoyan Fare: Credo à la Carte," *Slavonic and East European Review* 62, no. 4 (1984): 481–95; Irina Gutkin, "The Dichotomy between Flesh and Spirit: Plato's *Symposium* in *Anna Karenina*," in *In the Shade of the Giant: Essays on Tolstoy*, ed. Hugh McLean (Berkeley and Los Angeles: University of California Press, 1989), 84–99; Karin Horwatt, "Food and the Adulterous Woman: Sexual and Social Morality in *Anna Karenina*," *Language and Literature* 13 (1988): 35–67; Ronald LeBlanc, "Levin Visits Anna: The Iconology of Harlotry," *Tolstoy Studies Journal* 3 (1990): 1–20, Irene Pearson, "The Social and Moral Roles of Food in *Anna Karenina*," *Journal of Russian Studies* 48 (1984): 10–19, and Paul Schmidt, "What Do Oysters Mean?" *Antaeus* 68 (1992): 105–11.

2. Although, as Andrew Wachtel has demonstrated, Tolstoi contributes quite seminally to the myth of a happy gentry childhood in nineteenth-century Russian literature, his quasi-autobiographical account of childhood in *Detstvo* (1852) contains remarkably few, if any, references to food and orality; see *The Battle for Childhood*, 7–57.

3. Bryan S. Turner discusses this Cartesian paradigm in *The Body and Society* (London: Sage Publications, 1996), 9–11, 17–19.

4. R. F. Christian, ed. and trans., *Tolstoy's Diaries* (New York: Scribner, 1985), 2:x. "Ate too much at dinner (gluttony)," Tolstoi reproaches himself, for example, in a diary entry for March 8, 1851. "Ate too many sweets" (46:48).

5. Judith M. Armstrong, *The Unsaid Anna Karenina* (New York: St. Martin's Press, 1988), 18.

6. Ruth Crego Benson, *Women in Tolstoy: The Ideal and the Erotic* (Champaign: University of Illinois Press, 1973), 2.

7. G. W. Spence, *Tolstoy the Ascetic* (New York: Barnes and Noble, 1968), 20.

8. Donald Davie maintains that Merezhkovskii's "brilliantly perceptive but one-sided view of Tolstoy is distorted by his determination to make Tolstoy and Dostoievsky antithetical." See Donald Davie, ed. *Russian Literature and Modern English Fiction* (Chicago: University of Chicago Press, 1965), 7.

9. Dmitrii Merezhkovskii, *Polnoe sobranie sochinenii*, 16 vols. (Hildesheim and New York: Georg Olms, 1973), 7:155.

10. Thomas Mann, "Goethe and Tolstoy," in *Essays by Thomas Mann*, trans. H. T. Lowe-Porter (New York: Vintage Books, 1958), 106.

11. Ibid., 108. In light of the many unflattering things that he had to say about Goethe during his lifetime, Tolstoi himself probably would have resented Mann's analogy. "I don't like Goethe at all. I don't like his self-assured paganism," Tolstoi writes, for instance, in a letter in August 1891 (66:34). Later, in his diary for 1906, Tolstoi writes, "I am reading Goethe and can see all the pernicious influence of this insignificant, bourgeois-egotistical gifted man on the generation I encountered" (55:248). With respect to Goethe's most famous work, Tolstoi once referred to *Faust* as "that trashiest of trash" (63:38).

12. John Bayley, *Tolstoy and the Novel* (New York: Viking Press, 1966), 50.

13. I am quoting here from Boris Sorokin, *Tolstoy in Prerevolutionary Russian Criticism* (Columbus: Ohio State University Press, 1979), 182.

14. "Tolstoy's repudiation of sex is embedded within a complex of polarized feelings about women and sexuality," writes Daniel Rancour-Laferriere, who examines *The Kreutzer Sonata* and its author from a psychoanalytic perspective. "Tolstoy both desired women and punished himself for his desire." See *Tolstoy on the Couch: Misogyny, Masochism and the Absent Mother* (New York: New York University Press, 1998), 3.

15. Gutkin, "The Dichotomy Between Flesh and Spirit: Plato's *Symposium* in *Anna Karenina*," 84.

16. Richard Gustafson, *Leo Tolstoy, Resident and Stranger: A Study in Fiction and Theology* (Princeton, N.J.: Princeton University Press, 1986), 207.

17. Ibid., 207.

18. Armstrong, *The Unsaid Anna Karenina*, 45.

19. A. P. Sergeenko, *Rasskazy o L. N. Tolstom: iz vospominanii* (Moscow: Sovetskii pisatel', 1978), 63.

20. For historical studies that examine the development of the health reform movement in nineteenth-century America (and Sylvester Graham's ideological system in particular), see Stephen Nissenbaum, *Sex, Diet and Debility: Sylvester Graham and Health Reform* (Westport, Conn.: Greenwood Press, 1980) and James C. Whorton, *Crusaders for Fitness: The History of American Health Reformers* (Princeton, N.J.: Princeton University Press, 1982). Ronald M. Deutsch, meanwhile, discusses the food faddism of these health reformers

rather more irreverently and unsympathetically in his popular book *The New Nuts Among the Berries* (Palo Alto, Calif.: Bull Publishing, 1977). I examine Tolstoy's vegetarian views in connection with the health reform movement in nineteenth-century America in "Tolstoy's Way of No Flesh: Abstinence, Vegetarianism, and Christian Physiology," in *Food in Russian History and Culture*, ed. Joyce Toomre and Musya Glants (Bloomington: Indiana University Press, 1997), 81–102.

21. Gustafson, *Tolstoy: Resident and Stranger*, 55.

22. Mikhail Bakhtin, *Problems of Dostoevsky's Poetics*, 122–23.

23. "I can't overcome my sensuality," the twenty-one-year-old Tolstoi complains in a diary entry for June 19, 1850, "the more so since this passion has now become a habit with me" (46:37). "I am tormented by sensuality," he laments less than a year later, on April 17, 1851 (46:59).

24. Gustafson, *Tolstoy: Resident and Stranger*, 56. Judith Deutsch Kornblatt agrees that the drunken and nostalgic Daddy Eroshka emerges as "a highly contradictory character, a former hero now mocked by the younger Cossacks." See *The Cossack Hero in Russian Literature: A Study in Cultural Mythology* (Madison: University of Wisconsin Press, 1992), 94. Appropriately enough, Kornblatt entitles the chapter of her book that deals with *The Cossacks* "The Ambivalent Tolstoi."

25. John Hagan, "Ambivalence in Tolstoy's *The Cossacks*," *Novel: A Forum on Fiction* 3, no. 1 (1969): 36.

26. Hagan explains the author's ambivalence in the following way: "Tolstoy feels the pull of an ethic of love and self-sacrifice as fully as he feels the pull of an amoral freedom from such an ethic; he is Puritan and Primitivist at one and the same time, for he cannot decide whether God resides 'in' Nature and is obeyed by living according to natural impulse, or whether God is 'outside' Nature and is obeyed by resisting natural impulse. This is the crux of the whole matter, and the main point about *The Cossacks* is that it expresses this dilemma without ever resolving it" (ibid., 44).

27. In a letter dated December 28, 1851, for example, Tolstoi writes, "Nothing to excess. That's a principle that I'd be very glad to follow in all things" (59:138).

28. Sergeenko, *Rasskazy o Tolstom*, 62.

29. In *Natasha's Dance: A Cultural History of Russia* (New York: Picador, 2002), Orlando Figes identifies Natasha's dance as one of those scenes from nineteenth-century Russian literature that provides us with "a window on to a nation's inner life" (xxvii). "At its heart," he explains, "is an encounter between two entirely different worlds: the European culture of the upper classes and the Russian culture of the peasantry" (xxvii).

30. Albert Cook, who argues that each book in *War and Peace* has "a prevailing

mood, a phase of the common life to which each character responds in the very act of contributing to create it," characterizes the mood of book 7 as one of "Unearthly Joy." See "The Unity of *War and Peace*," *Western Review* 22 (1958): 250.

31. The meal scene at Uncle's, with its joyful celebration of native foods by members of the extended Rostov family in the Russian countryside, provides a stark contrast to the opening scene of the novel. At Anna Sherer's soirée, set in the artificial atmosphere of aristocratic St. Petersburg, the hostess is said to relish being able serve up two foreign celebrities, le vicomte de Mortemart and l'abbé Morio, as choice morsels of meat to her assembled guests: "the vicomte was served up to the company in the choicest and most advantageous style, like a well-garnished joint of roast beef on a hot dish" (9:14).

32. Benson, *Women in Tolstoy*, 55.

33. Ibid., 65.

34. Ibid., x. "Central to Tolstoy's notion of the family is that it disciplines, justifies, and redeems sexual relations," Benson writes elsewhere in her book. "More than that, it places sex in a natural, biological order which can minimize its erotic and maximize its functional essence" (91).

35. Mary Evans, *Reflecting on Anna Karenina* (London: Routledge, 1989), 12.

36. Amy Mandelker questions the idyll of domesticity that most readers believe Tolstoi is depicting in the epilogue: "Although his masterpiece, *War and Peace* (1863–69), may seem to conclude on a note of connubial bliss, this mood is undercut by the apparent dissolution of the main characters' potential for heroic action and the limitation of their ultimate interests and passions to the everyday world of mundane events and concerns." See *Framing Anna Karenina: Tolstoy, the Woman Question, and the Victorian Novel* (Columbus: Ohio State University Press, 1993), 7.

37. "Both *gourmands* and *gourmets*," insists Benson, "could happily refute any argument based on this particular analogy"; see *Women in Tolstoy*, 68.

38. "But once married," Benson writes of the heroine in *Family Happiness*, "her romantic illusions are destroyed and eventually transformed into a subdued, chastened adaptation to domestic reality"; ibid., 17.

39. Pearson, "The Social and Moral Roles of Food in *Anna Karenina*," 10.

40. Mandelker, *Framing Anna Karenina*, 7.

41. Later, in part 3 of the novel, Tolstoi shows us the moral antipodes in the countryside to this urban scene of decadent gastronomic indulgence at the Moscow restaurant. First of all, there is the scene where Levin shares a simple meal of bread and water with an old peasant during a break from the mowing on his estate, a scene in which, as Goscilo correctly notes (485), food symbolizes a sense of "true communion" between the hero and some simple rural laborers engaged in a common activity (18:268–69). Second, there is the scene where

Levin receives a pleasant impression of spiritual well-being while he watches a peasant family dine together modestly on cabbage soup and kasha (18:344).

42. Goscilo, "Tolstoyan Fare: Credo à la Carte," 482.

43. Roland Barthes, "Lecture de Brillat-Savarin," in Jean-Anthèlme Brillat-Savarin, *Physiologie du goût* (Paris: Hermann, 1975), 8.

44. "Socrates points out that eating is a pleasure because it takes away the pain of hunger," Pearson writes. "But as soon as one is satisfied, the pleasure disappears along with the pain. A false hunger, a type of greed, must be stimulated in order to re-create the possibility of feeling more pleasure. The same is true of sexual pleasure, Tolstoy seems to imply"; see "The Social and Moral Roles of Food in *Anna Karenina*," 13. Tolstoi, in fact, states this belief quite explicitly in a letter of October 27–30, 1895, when he writes, "if life's happiness lies in the satisfaction of one's lusts, then as they are satisfied, one's pleasure decreases and decreases, and one must constantly arouse newer and stronger lusts in order to obtain the same pleasure" (68:240).

45. Pearson, "The Social and Moral Roles of Food in *Anna Karenina*," 11. James W. Brown observes that Balzac is another author who makes a clear distinction in his novels between city appetites and country appetites, contrasting the elegant cuisine and fashionable dining rooms of Parisian bons vivants with the modest fare served by provincial misers. See Brown, *Fictional Meals and their Function in the French Novel*, 30. In the "Glossary of Metafictional Terms" appended to his book, Brown defines "Food-work metonym" as "the peasant ethic whereby the purpose of food is to supply energy for work. Food is a means, not an end in itself: eating to live, not living to eat" (202).

46. In her study of A. N. Engelgardt's correspondence, Cathy A. Frierson explores a number of these same binary oppositions that were utilized by this Russian populist writer (and contemporary of Tolstoi) in his essayistic writings. See *Aleksandr Nikolaevich Engelgardt's Letters From the Country, 1872–1887*, ed. and trans. Cathy A. Frierson (New York: Oxford University Press, 1993).

47. Irina Gutkin, "The Dichotomy Between Flesh and Spirit: Plato's *Symposium* in *Anna Karenina*," 86.

48. Goscilo makes this classical Greek distinction between Levin, who is associated with Plato and the Stoics, and Oblonskii, who is associated with Epicurus and the Hedonists, in "Tolstoyan Fare: Credo à la Carte," 486.

49. Arguing that Stiva "epitomises the pursuit of one alternative that Tolstoy did not allow himself in his own life," Armstrong claims that the author himself actually longed for stolen "rolls" like Oblonskii, but he simply refused to admit it. See *The Unsaid Anna Karenina*, 56, 58–59. In her psychoanalytic reading of *Anna Karenina*, Armstrong thus sees both Levin and Oblonskii as products of the author's self-projection. Tolstoi, she asserts, "allows Stiva, his supposed opposite, to satisfy vicariously all these banned appetites" (65–66).

50. Halmut Kiltz has written an entire book about the erotic dining that transpired in such private dining rooms (*chambres séparées*). See *Das erotische Mahl: Szenen aus dem "chambre séparée" des neunzehnten Jahrhundert* (Frankfurt: Syndikat, 1983).

51. "Levin loves Kitty because she is so apparently distant from sexual desire," explains Mary Evans. "Kitty is the woman innocent of sexuality, Anna the woman inspired and motivated by it." See *Reflecting on "Anna Karenina,"* 69.

52. See, respectively, Benson, *Women in Tolstoy*, 89, and Evans, *Reflecting on "Anna Karenina,"* 1.

53. Pearson, "The Social and Moral Roles of Food in *Anna Karenina*," 12.

54. Goscilo, "Tolstoyan Fare: Credo à la Carte," 488–89.

55. When Vronskii in part 5 is desperately searching for some pastime to occupy him while he is staying with Anna in Italy, Tolstoi compares him to "a hungry animal," one who "seizes every object it meets, in hopes of finding food in it" (19:32).

56. Evans, *Reflecting on Anna Karenina*, 81.

57. "Anna lives by means of her passion," Nikolai Strakhov once observed. "Before this passion, she was spiritually hungry. With suprising subtlety and clarity the author depicts this social life in the capital and at court, a life in which there is no spiritual food of any kind." See "Vzgliad na tekushchuiu literaturu (Ob *Anne Kareninoi*)" in N. Strakhov, *Kriticheskie stat'i ob I. S. Turgeneve i L. N. Tolstom (1862–1885)* (Kiev: Izd. I. P. Matchenko, 1902; repr., The Hague: Mouton, 1968), 358.

58. Goscilo, "Tolstoyan Fare: Credo à la Carte," 488.

59. For a useful distinction between "hunger" (essentially a bodily drive) and "appetite" (a state of mind), see Daniel Cappon, *Eating, Loving and Dying: A Psychology of Appetites* (Toronto: University of Toronto Press, 1973), 21.

60. Gary Saul Morson, "Prosaics and Anna Karenina," *Tolstoy Studies Journal* 1 (1988): 7.

61. Pearson, "The Social and Moral Roles of Food in *Anna Karenina*," 14. "Towards the end," Pearson writes, "Anna thinks more and more on the level of 'dog-eat-dog,' or to use Tolstoy's own reference to Katavasov's scientific research, on the level of 'the cuttlefish's eating habits'" (14).

62. It could be argued that there is a deeper culinary significance to Anna's statement; although "zest" carries the usual meanings of "gusto" and "relish," the word originally denoted the peel of citrus fruit such as lemons and oranges, which was used as a flavoring in recipes.

63. Donna Orwin, *Tolstoy's Art and Thought, 1847–1880* (Princeton, N.J.: Princeton University Press, 1993), 202.

64. Edward Wasiolek, *Tolstoy's Major Fiction* (Chicago: University of Chicago Press, 1978), 130.

65. Even such a staunch opponent of the pro-Anna camp as Gary Saul Morson openly admits that he belongs to the "minority camp" when he holds that the book condemns Tolstoi's heroine. See Morson, "Prosaics and Anna Karenina," 8.

66. See chapter 7, "Intoxicated Consciousness," of *Tolstoy: Resident and Stranger*, especially 349–52, where Gustafson analyzes Natasha's opera episode. As he makes clear in the footnote on 352, Gustafson takes issue with Shklovskii's notion of "defamiliarization" (*ostranenie*), preferring instead to understand the estrangement that Tolstoi's characters sometimes experience as the sense of reality as "alien" (*chuzhoi*).

67. In part 6 we are shown how Levin is angered by the spirit of *prazdnost'* that Oblonskii and Veslovskii bring with them from the city to the countryside. When these two urban bon vivants arrive at Pokrovskoe, we are told that "Levin, who but a minute before had been in the brightest of spirits, was now looking dismally at everyone, dissatisfied with everything. . . . And most repugnant of all was Kitty, for the way she fell in with the merry tone of that gentleman [Veslovskii], who looked upon his arrival in the countryside as a holiday (*prazdnik*) for himself and for everyone else. . . . 'For them it's always a holiday there,' he [Levin] thought, 'while here we have work that is not a holiday affair (*dela ne prazdnichnye*), work which cannot be put off and without which it is not possible to live'" (19:142–43).

68. The restaurant dialogue in part 1, Irina Gutkin observes, "sets the pattern for the Levin-Oblonsky relationship throughout the novel." In all the subsequent meetings between Levin and Oblonskii in the novel, she notes, food and sex are invariably involved; see "The Dichotomy Between Flesh and Spirit: Plato's *Symposium* in *Anna Karenina*," 87. The reader, as a result of this pattern, is in a sense prepared to expect that the two brothers-in-law will somehow become involved with the issue of sexual love after an evening of eating and drinking at the club.

69. Brown, *Fictional Meals and Their Function in the French Novel*, 14. Noting the pervasive tendency within Western cultures to mix the gastronomical with the sexual, Brown observes that "writers have always associated food with sex: but in nineteenth-century France in particular novelists exploit the similarities between sensual and sexual pleasures, perhaps because they were made explicit in the society at large" (50).

70. This pattern of dining, drinking, and whoring is well illustrated in Balzac's *La peau de chagrin* (1831), where Emile and Raphael visit the courtesans Aquiline and Euphrasie after partaking in an orgiastic banquet meal. Indeed, Balzac here indicates not merely a connection between eating and fornicating, but also a hierarchy of carnal desires progressing from oral to sexual gratification. After the sated diners leave the banquet room for the adjoining salon,

Balzac tells us that, compared to the alluring concubines who await them there, "the rich ornaments of the banquet paled to nothing, for what they saw appealed to the most sensual of their senses." See *Oeuvres complètes de Honoré de Balzac* (Paris: Louis Conard, 1925), 27:66.

71. In part 6 of the novel, Vas'ka Veslovskii, one of the more memorable of the Oblonskian playboys in *Anna Karenina*, seems to have brought this pattern of dining, drinking, and whoring with him from the city to the country; during the hunting trip with Levin and Oblonskii at Pokrovskoe we find him one evening eating all of the provisions, drinking vodka, and then making love to the local peasant girls.

72. Sydney Schultze notes that "the same image cluster which attends Anna's arrival in Petersburg is used again when Anna and Levin finally meet"; see *The Structure of Anna Karenina* (Ann Arbor, Mich: Ardis, 1982), 32. She later points out that the frequent mention of heat and the association with the color red (both of which symbolize Anna's inner fire) contribute toward creating a diabolical image of Anna, who is seen as "demonic" (*besovskoe*) by Kitty at the ball in part 1 and who is often referred to as a devil in the original drafts of the novel. Schultze also notes an uncanny parallel: at the same time that Vronskii goes to watch his friend Iashvin play billiards down "in the infernal regions" (*v infernal'nuiu*) of the English Club, Levin is shown riding off to meet Anna. For both these observations, see 130 of Schultze's book.

73. Joan Grossman is one of the first commentators on *Anna Karenina* to entertain seriously the idea that Levin's visit to Anna's suggests a trip to a brothel. "Tolstoy's suggestion is unmistakable," she writes, "that this call parallels a visit to 'those places' of which Kitty thinks with horror, now that she is a married woman and knows such things. Tolstoy is at some pains to underline this hint when the two men actually arrive"; see her essay, "Tolstoy's Portrait of Anna: Keystone in the Arch," *Criticism* 18, no. 1 (1976): 3. See also my "Levin Visits Anna: The Iconology of Harlotry," 1–20.

74. "While following this interesting conversation," the narrator observes, "Levin all the time continued to admire her: her beauty, her cleverness, her good education, together with her simplicity and sincerity. He listened and talked, and all the time thought of her, of her inner life, trying to guess her feelings. And he, who had formerly judged her so severely, now by some strange train of thought was justifying her and at the same time pitying her and fearing that Vronskii did not fully understand her. Toward eleven, when Oblonskii rose to leave (Vorkuev had already gone), Levin felt as if he had only just arrived. He got up regretfully" (19:278).

75. These seductive powers of sexual attraction, according to Tolstoi, are an inherent feature of woman's nature. "A woman is happy and attains all that she can desire," Pozdnyshev asserts in *The Kreutzer Sonata*, "when she bewitches a

man. Therefore, the chief aim of a woman is to be able to bewitch him" (27:38). Pozdnyshev uses the same verb here for "bewitches" (*obvorozhit*) that Kitty had used to describe Anna's effect upon her husband (*obvorozhila*) (19:281). Anna later admits to herself the existence within her of this aggressive desire to seduce: "If I were an immoral woman, I could make her husband fall in love with me—if I wanted to. And I did want to" (19:340).

76. As we shall see later in this chapter, carnal love, according to Pozdnyshev, constitutes a physical addiction just like addiction to morphine, alcohol, or tobacco (27:19). When Tolstoi learned that his daughter Tania was planning to marry, he wrote her a letter (October 14, 1897) in which he not only warned her of the highly addictive nature of sexuality, but even compared sexual passion to a disease—not unlike diphtheria, typhus, or scarlet fever—that should be avoided at all costs. "Right now it seems to you that there is no living without this [feeling of love]," Tolstoi wrote to his daughter. "It seems the same way to drunkards and smokers, but when they are set free [from their addiction], only then do they see what real life is" (70–71:168).

77. Gustafson discusses at some length this notion of "intoxicated consciousness" in chapter 7 of his *Leo Tolstoy: Resident and Stranger*, 338–402.

78. In an English-language film version of *Anna Karenina* (1997), produced by Bernard Rose, the link between the disillusioned views of Tolstoi (as author of *Confession*) and those of Levin (as his alter ego in *Anna Karenina*) is reinforced by having Levin be the one who recounts this Eastern fable (the voice-over is provided by Albert Molina, the actor who plays the role of Levin in the film).

79. Susan Layton argues that Afanasii Fet's lyric poem, "Mine was the madness he wanted . . ." (1888), in which the poet likens lyric creativity to a bee producing honey, should be read as an ironic reply to Tolstoi's Eastern tale about the two drops of honey having lost their sweetness. "I see Tolstoy's *Confession* as Fet's main target," Layton writes; see her "A Hidden Polemic with Leo Tolstoy: Afanasy Fet's Lyric 'Mine was the madness he wanted . . . ,'" *Russian Review* 66, no. 2 (2007): 220–37.

80. Orwin, *Tolstoy's Art and Thought*, 145. It is largely in this sense, no doubt, that Kathryn Feuer is to be understood when she claims that *Confession* should be read as a sequel, or second ending, to *Anna Karenina*. See her essay, "Stiva," in *Russian Literature and American Critics*, ed. Kenneth N. Brostrom (Ann Arbor, Mich.: Ardis, 1984), 347–56.

81. "Don't let us stupefy ourselves, don't let us kill our reason with strong food that is not natural to man, and with stupefying drinks and smoking," Tolstoi writes in a letter of October 27–30, 1895 (68:244).

82. Following his conversion experience, Orwin argues, Tolstoi "rejected the body, and, therefore, nature, as the source of or even a possible participant in higher human goodness." See *Tolstoy's Art and Thought*, 217.

83. Rancour-Laferriere considers the author's asceticism a manifestation of his "moral masochism": that is, his desire to abstain from sex and to suffer physical privations is fueled by his desire to subdue his guilt over matricidal feelings. See *Tolstoy on the Couch*, 144–51.

84. Henrietta Mondry, "Beyond the Boundary: Vasilii Rozanov and the Animal Body," *Slavic and East European Journal* 43, no. 4 (1999): 653.

85. Mikhail O. Menshikov, a literary critic for the journal *Nedelia* who was one of Tolstoi's most zealous followers on issues concerning sexual morality, advocates the same preference of love-as-compassion (*zhalenie*) over love-as-desire (*zhelanie*) in his book *O liubvi* (1899). See Peter Ulf Møller, *Postlude to The Kreutzer Sonata: Tolstoj and the Debate on Sexual Morality in Russian Literature of the 1890s*, trans. John Kendal (New York: E. J. Brill, 1988), 206.

86. "If a man will consciously strive to live not for the stomach, but for the spirit," Tolstoi writes to Chertkov on October 9, 1888, "then his relationship to food will be what it ought to be. But if a man henceforth will arrange tasty dinners for himself, then he will unavoidably fall into illegality and debauchery" (86:177–78).

87. These two selves—the one animal, the other divine—that Tolstoi posited in each human being are delineated quite clearly in the narrator's characterization of the young hero, Dmitrii Nekhliudov, in *Resurrection*. "In Nekhliudov, as in every man, there were two beings," writes the narrator. "One was the spiritual man, seeking only that kind of happiness for himself which would constitute the happiness of all; the other was the animal man, seeking only his own happiness, and ready to sacrifice to it the happiness of the rest of the world. At this period of his insane egoism, which was brought on by his life in St. Petersburg and in the army, this animal man ruled supreme in him and completely crushed the spiritual man" (32:53).

88. For a wide-ranging discussion of the socioeconomic and cultural changes taking place in late imperial Russia, see Catriona Kelly and David Shepherd, eds., *Constructing Russian Culture in the Age of Revolution: 1881–1940* (New York: Oxford University Press, 1998).

89. Laura Engelstein, *The Keys to Happiness: Sex and the Search for Modernity in Fin-de-Siècle Russia* (Ithaca, N.Y.: Cornell University Press, 1992); see esp. chapter 6, "Eros and Revolution: The Problem of Male Desire," 215–53.

90. Paul Birukoff, *The Life of Tolstoy* (London: Cassell, 1911), 97.

91. Aileen Kelly, *Toward Another Shore: Russian Thinkers Between Necessity and Chance* (New Haven, Conn.: Yale University Press, 1998), 82.

92. As Peter Ulf Møller notes in his study of the debate over sexual morality that *The Kreutzer Sonata* helped to launch in Russia during the 1890s, Tolstoi's focus on the sexual instinct and on the sexual aspect of marriage in this novella was truly unprecedented in Russian literature. "With *The Kreutzer Sonata*,"

writes Møller, "Tolstoj introduced the 'sexual question' (*polovoj vopros*) as a theme for debate in Russia." See Møller, *Postlude to The Kreutzer Sonata*, xiii.

93. Robert L. Jackson characterizes *The Kreutzer Sonata* as the most "Dostoevskian" of all Tolstoi's works, seeing Pozdnyshev's behavior just prior to the murder as related to the ethical thinking of the Underground Man. See his essay, "In the Darkness of the Night: Tolstoy's *Kreutzer Sonata* and Dostoevsky's *Notes from Underground*," in R. L. Jackson, *Dialogues with Dostoevsky: The Overwhelming Questions* (Stanford, Calif.: Stanford University Press, 1993), 208–27.

94. Robert Edwards, "Tolstoy and Alice B. Stockham: The Influence of 'Tokology' on *The Kreutzer Sonata*," *Tolstoy Studies Journal* 6 (1993): 94.

95. See Mandelker, *Framing Anna Karenina*, 32. Rancour-Laferriere considers *The Kreutzer Sonata* to be a novella about Tolstoi's misogyny that expresses the "negative pole" of the author's ambivalence toward women, whom he both desired carnally and punished himself for desiring: "Tolstoy's ideal of sexual abstinence derives from guilt over uncontrollable rage at the mother who died on him in early childhood." Tolstoi's matricidal psyche, according to Rancour-Laferriere, is what generated his argument for sexual abstinence; see *Tolstoy on the Couch*, 3, 4, 9.

96. As Nissenbaum points out, Sylvester Graham likewise maintained (albeit for physiological rather than theological reasons) that, with a proper diet, people could subdue their sexual propensity and thus preserve chastity (32). Witness, for example, what Graham writes in his *Lecture to Young Men* about the direct connection between stimulating foods and sexual arousal: "All kinds of stimulating and heating substances; high-seasoned foods; rich dishes; the free use of flesh; and even the excess of aliment; all, more or less, —and some to a very great degree—increase the concupiscent excitability and sensibility of the genital organs, and augment their influence on the functions of organic life, and on the intellectual and moral faculties." See Nissenbaum, *Sex, Diet, and Debility*, 18–19.

97. In *Father Sergius*, for instance, the possibility that the hero will succumb to the sexual temptations of the feeble-minded but voluptuous daughter of a local merchant is foreshadowed in the text by mention of how Sergius no longer threatened his health by fasting, but now indulged his appetite for food and drink, "often eating with special pleasure and not, as before, with revulsion and a consciousness of sin" (31:34). In a narrative as well as a physiological sense, therefore, gastronomical appetite seems to trigger sexual appetite in Tolstoi's story.

98. Tolstoi was not the first person, of course, to link eating meat with sexual arousal. Many of the American health reformers in the nineteenth century likewise preached the sexual dangers of carnivorism. Nissenbaum notes how Sylvester Graham, for example, argued in the 1830s for a meatless diet largely

on the grounds that meat acted as a sexual stimulant, exciting vile tempers and driving men to sexual excesses. See *Sex, Diet, and Debility*, 33–36, 119–20. Indeed, the belief among health reformers that "meat excited libido," Whorton writes, "was a truism"; see *Crusaders for Fitness*, 92. Carol J. Adams examines "Grahamism" (as a dietary method for controlling male sexuality) from a feminist perspective and draws some interesting connections between male power and meat eating. Ethical vegetarianism, according to Adams, represents a feminist way not merely to reject a carnivorous view of the world, but also to rebuke the generally violent and aggressive male discourse that has predominated in our patriarchal culture. See *The Sexual Politics of Meat: A Feminist-Vegetarian Critical Theory* (New York: Continuum, 1990).

99. Colin Spencer, *The Heretic's Feast: A History of Vegetarianism* (London: Fourth Estate, 1993), xiii. "He loved the role of outcast and rebel," William H. Blanchard writes about Tolstoi, "because it made him feel above the crowd." See W. H. Blanchard, *Revolutionary Morality: A Psychosexual Analysis of Twelve Revolutionists* (Santa Barbara, Calif.: ABC-Clio Information Services, 1984), 35. Chapter 3 of Blanchard's book ("Count Leo Tolstoy: Return to God and Nature") examines the moral masochism Tolstoi exhibited as a social rebel and revolutionist (31–43).

100. Tolstoi's conversion to vegetarianism is discussed in my "Vegetarianism in Russia: The Tolstoy(an) Legacy," *Carl Beck Papers in Russian and East European Studies*, no. 1507 (May 2001): 1–39; see esp. 4–7.

101. L. N. Tolstoi, "Pervaia stupen'," *Voprosy filosofii i psikhologii*, kn. 13 (1892): 109–44.

102. Janet Barkas, *The Vegetable Passion: A History of the Vegetarian State of Mind* (London: Routledge and Kegan Paul, 1975), 158.

103. Isaac Skelton, "The Vegetarian Tradition in Russian Literature," unpublished manuscript, 30.

104. "Although mythologized as a vegetarian pacifist, Tolstoy's abstinence [from eating meat] did not initially arise from ethical considerations," Darra Goldstein explains. "Tolstoy struggled against carnal and gustatory temptation alike; the renunciation of sex and meat were equally important for attaining moral purity. Thus his treatise on the first step toward ethical living shows far greater concern with the rigors of asceticism than with compassion for animals. For Tolstoy, the disavowal of meat was simply another step in his quest for moral self-perfection." See "Tolstoy's Table," in *The Vegetarian Hearth: Recipes and Reflections for the Cold Season* (New York: HarperCollins, 1996), 205.

105. This aspect of Foucault's argument is developed most successfully in the second volume of his three-volume *History of Sexuality*; see *The Use of Pleasure*, trans. Robert Hurley (New York: Vintage Books, 1985).

106. "The main concern and the main preoccupation of people is not eating—eating does not require much effort—but rather overeating. People talk about their interests and exalted aims, women about lofty feelings, and they do not talk about food; but their main activity is directed towards food," Tolstoi writes in his diary on May 10, 1891. "All people eat on the average, I think, three times as much as they need" (52:31).

107. Tolstoi was also distressed by the gluttony he saw in his own children. "They eat to excess and amuse themselves by spending money on the labors of other people for their own pleasure," he wrote to Chertkov in 1885 (85:294). "You look for the cause; look for the remedy," he wrote angrily to his wife just a few days later. "The children can stop overeating (vegetarianism)" (83:547).

108. A. P. Chekhov, *Polnoe sobranie sochinenii i pisem*, 20 vols. (Moscow: Khudo-zhestvennaia literatura, 1944–51), 16:133.

109. In a diary entry of June 25, 1890, Tolstoi writes: "I ought to write a book called *Gorging* [*zhran'e*]: Belshazzar's feast, bishops, tsars, and taverns. Meetings, partings, and jubilees. People think that they are occupied with various important matters, but they are occupied only with gluttony" (51:53).

110. "Last night I was still thinking about the Preface to the vegetarian book, that is, about abstinence, and I wrote not badly all morning," Tolstoi records in his diary on June 25 (52:43). On July 13 he writes that he has finished writing the "article about gluttony" (52:44). And again on August 27, he mentions how for the past two days he has been making corrections to the "article about gluttony" (52:50).

111. See the chapter, "O poste," in Solov'ev's *Dukhovnye osnovy zhizni*, in *Sobranie sochinenii Vladimira Sergeevicha Solov'eva* (St. Petersburg: Obshchestvennaia Pol'za, 1901–03), 3:314–19.

112. See Leo Tolstoy, *The Relations of the Sexes*, trans. Vladimir Chertkov (Christ-church, Eng.: Free Age Press, 1901), 37–38.

113. "God sent people food," Tolstoi once quipped, "but it's the devil who sent us cooks." See *Krug chteniia* for 4 March (41:149).

114. "And so there is the meal," Tolstoi writes, "a modest meal. One could augment the pleasure to be derived from this meal even more and more. And people do augment it, and there are no limits to this augmentation: hors d'oeuvres meant to whet the appetite, and entremets, and desserts, and various combinations of tasty treats, and flowers, and decorations, and music played during the meal. And the surprising thing is that the people who gorge themselves every day on such meals—compared to which Belshazzar's feast, which evoked the prophetic warning, is nothing—naïvely believe that for all that they can still lead a moral life" (29:77).

115. In *Die Pfennig-Sonate* (1890), one of the several parodies of *The Kreutzer Sonata* that arose as part of the counterliterature that appeared in the wake of

Tolstoi's controversial novella, Sigmar Mehring pokes fun at this connection Tolstoi makes between sexual and gastronomic abstinence. In Mehring's parodic sequel, the narrator once again meets Pozdnyshev on a train, listening this time to his account of how he killed a second wife. "His account of his second conjugal murder," Møller writes, "is interwoven with a series of nonsensical arguments in favour of total abstinence—from food!" See *Postlude to The Kreutzer Sonata*, 169. "We should never eat," Pozdnyshev asserts in Mehring's sequel. "We should return again to primitive abstinence—that is the ideal condition for all those who are possessed by cultural catarrh. How many wails and how many wants would disappear from the world if only we would free ourselves from the ridiculous habit of eating." I am quoting here from the Russian translation, *Groshevaia sonata* (St. Petersburg, 1890), 9.

116. Vladimir I. Porudominskii, "L. N. Tolstoi i etika pitaniia," *Chelovek* no. 2 (1992): 106.

117. Whorton, *Crusaders for Fitness*; see esp. chapter 2, "Christian Physiology," 38–61. See also Whorton's article, "'Christian Physiology': William Alcott's Prescription for the Millenium," *Bulletin of the History of Medicine* 49 (1975): 466–81.

118. Carroll Smith-Rosenberg, "Sex as Symbol in Victorian Purity: An Ethnohistorical Analysis of Jacksonian America," in *Turning Points: Historical and Sociological Essays on the Family*, ed. John Demos and Sarane Spence Boocock (Chicago: University of Chicago Press, 1978), 213.

119. Tolstoi was acquainted, however, with a number of other nineteenth-century American reformers. Robert Edwards, who explores Tolstoi's relationship with a famous American sexual reformer, notes that the Russian author regularly subscribed to U.S. journals such as *New Christianity* and *World's Advance Thought*; see "Tolstoy and Alice B. Stockham: The Influence of 'Tokology' on *The Kreutzer Sonata*," 90. In the same special issue of that journal ("Tolstoy and Sexuality"), William Nickell discusses Tolstoi's familiarity with two other American sexual reformers; see "The Twain Shall Be of One Mind: Tolstoy in 'Leag' with Eliza Burnz and Henry Parkhurst," *Tolstoy Studies Journal* 6 (1993): 123–51. Jayme A. Sokolow and Priscilla R. Roosevelt, meanwhile, examine the influence of American pacifists such as William Lloyd Garrison and Adin Ballou on Tolstoi's philosophy of nonviolence. See "Leo Tolstoi's Christian Pacifism: The American Contribution," *Carl Beck Papers in Russian and East European Studies*, no. 604 (Pittsburgh, Pa.: University of Pittsburgh Center for Russian and East European Studies, 1987). Finally, Harry Walsh provides an entertaining synopsis of Tolstoi's reception in late-nineteenth-century and early-twentieth-century America in "The Tolstoyan Episode in American Social Thought," *American Studies* 17, no. 1 (1976): 49–68.

120. Nissenbaum, *Sex, Diet, and Debility*, 4.

121. Jayme A. Sokolow, *Eros and Modernization: Sylvester Graham, Health Reform, and the Origins of Victorian Sexuality in America* (Rutherford, N.J.: Fairleigh Dickinson University Press, 1983), 14.

122. Ibid., 163.

123. See, in addition to Møller's *Postlude to "The Kreutzer Sonata,"* Laura Engelstein, *The Keys to Happiness*, esp. chapter 6, "Eros and Revolution: The Problem of Male Desire," 215–53.

124. John M. Kopper discusses a few of these texts in his essay, "Tolstoy and the Narrative of Sex: A Reading of 'Father Sergius,' 'The Devil,' and 'The Kreutzer Sonata'"; see *In the Shade of the Giant*, 158–86.

125. Engelstein, *The Keys to Happiness*, 6.

126. In *War and Peace*, as we recall, Pierre learns a similar lesson: namely, that happiness consists in the satisfaction of simple human needs, while all unhappiness arises not from privation but from superfluity. "A superfluity of the comforts of life destroys all joy in satisfying one's needs," the narrator explains (12:98).

127. The same expression is used in Tolstoi's play, *The Power of Darkness* (1886), in which one of the peasant characters (Mitrich) comments, "A dog goes mad from too much fat. How can a man not get spoiled from too much fat! Look at how I got messed up from too much fat living: I got drunk for three weeks without a break" (26:180).

128. Porudominskii, "Tolstoi i etika pitaniia," 115. Orwin points out that in the Tolstoi family circle, "pie" was a code word for something that made people happy. See *Tolstoy's Art and Thought*, 233 n. 1.

129. S. A. Behrs, *Recollections*. I am quoting here from Aylmer Maude, *The Life of Tolstoy* (London: Oxford University Press, 1930), 2:336. Tolstoi himself once noted that "pie is not eternal, while human reason is" (63:393).

130. Porudominskii, "Tolstoi i etika pitaniia," 115.

131. Maude, *Life of Tolstoy*, 2:336.

132. "Art for pleasure, like the seductive music of the sonata, is analogous to sex for pleasure," Edwards writes in paraphrasing Tolstoi's aesthetic theory. "For Tolstoy, art without a message is like sex without the goal of procreation. His tale [*The Kreutzer Sonata*] serves as a counterbalance to the music of the sonata itself, which is an invitation to carnality. Art without message is equivalent in Tolstoy's view to sex without reproduction, a mutual act of onanism for the pleasure of the artist and the audience, pleasure that has no goal but individual satisfaction." See Edwards, "Tolstoy and Alice B. Stockham," 93.

133. "As regards taste," Tolstoi is quoted once as saying, "an unhealthy taste needs mustard, whereas it produces an unpleasant impression upon a pure taste. So it is in the arts. It is necessary to draw a dividing line and to find where

that artistic mustard begins, and I think it is a problem of enormous importance." See A. B. Goldenweizer, *Talks with Tolstoy*, trans. S. S. Koteliansky
and Virginia Woolf (New York: Horizon Press, 1969), 107–108.

134. Goscilo finds Tolstoi's use of these reductive tropes—through which he compares art to food—both crude and inaccurate. After all, as she reminds us,
"our ingestion of food culminates, literally, in excretion." See "Tolstoyan
Fare: Credo à la Carte," 494.

135. In response to a letter from A. D. Zutphen, a Dutch medical student who had
read in a newspaper about Tolstoi's frugal meals and wrote to inquire about
the writer's diet, Tolstoi wrote, "My diet consists mainly of hot oatmeal porridge, which I eat two times a day with whole wheat bread (graham bread). In
addition to this, at dinner I eat cabbage soup or potato soup, buckwheat porridge or a potato, either boiled or fried in sunflower oil or mustard oil, and
apple and prune compote. Dinner, which I eat together with my family, can
be replaced, as I have tried to do, by simple oatmeal porridge, which serves
as my basic diet. My health not only has not suffered; it has in fact improved
significantly since I have given up milk, butter, and eggs, as well as sugar,
tea and coffee" (67:32). Tolstoi's son Sergei likewise insists that his father's
meatless diet in fact aided his digestion. "My mother considered vegetarianism unhealthy but in Father's case she was wrong," he writes, "because
for his liver complaint it was definitely very appropriate food." See Sergei
Tolstoy, *Tolstoy Remembered by his Son*, trans. Moura Budberg (London: Weidenfeld and Nicolson, 1961), 86.

136. "Lev Nikolaevich is unwell," Sof'ia records in her diary on March 14, 1887.
"He has bad indigestion and his stomach aches, and yet he eats the most
senseless diet: first it's rich food, then vegetarian food, then rum and water,
and so on." See S. A. Tolstaia, *Dnevniki v dvukh tomakh* (Moscow: Khudozhestvennaia literatura, 1978), 1:139.

137. S. A. Tolstaia, *Dnevniki v dvukh tomakh* (Moscow: Khudozhestvennaia literatura, 1978), 1:359. All further citations from Sof'ia Andreevna's diary come
from this two-volume edition and will be cited parenthetically in the text by
volume and page number.

138. Sof'ia was even more upset that two of his daughters were likewise experiencing chronic ill health; this was all due, she insisted, to the vegetarian diet
their father had convinced them to follow. "Yet one more sacrifice to Lev
Nikolaevich's principles!" she noted bitterly (1:360). The stormy relationship that developed between Tolstoi and his wife following his conversion
is chronicled by Louise Smoluchowski, *Lev and Sonya: The Story of the Tolstoy
Marriage* (New York: Paragon House Publishers, 1987) and Lily Feiler, "The
Tolstoi Marriage: Conflict and Illusions," *Canadian Slavonic Papers* 23, no. 3
(1981): 245–60.

139. "It wasn't the vegetarian diet *per se* that hurt Tolstoi's stomach," Porudomin-skii maintains, "but the fact that he ate too much and that he ate poorly combined, heavy simple foods." See "Tolstoi i etika pitaniia," 132.

140. Ibid., 132–33.

141. "I often suffer because his love for me is physical, more than emotional" (2:132), she would write as late as 1897, when Lev Nikolaevich was almost seventy years old.

142. Her husband, on the other hand, considered his occasional sexual lapses as temporary setbacks in his striving for chastity. "I was myself a husband last night," Tolstoi confessed once in 1896, "but that is no reason for abandoning the struggle [for sexual continence]." See Maude, *Life of Tolstoy*, 2:402.

143. Sof'ia seems to have felt that the chances of maintaining gastronomic abstinence were as slim as they were of maintaining sexual celibacy. "Over tea we had a conversation about food, luxury, and the vegetarian diet that Levochka is always preaching," she notes in 1891. "He said that he had seen a vegetarian diet in some German newspaper which recommended a dinner of bread and almonds. I am quite sure that the man who is preaching that keeps to such a *régime* in much the same way as Levochka practices the chastity he preaches in *The Kreutzer Sonata*" (1:160).

144. Those efforts at spiritualization were doomed to be ineffectual, Mann, Merezhkovskii, and Gor'kii would argue, because they were undertaken by such an unregenerate and earthy pagan as Tolstoi.

145. Maude, *Life of Tolstoy*, 2:423.

146. "It's impossible to eat even porridge or peacefully have a roll with tea," Tolstoi observes in a letter written in May 1886, "when you live with the knowledge that right by you there are people you know—children . . . who are going to bed without any bread" (83:568).

147. "I am living abominably," Tolstoi writes in the midst of the famine relief efforts in 1891. "I don't know myself how I got dragged into this abominable affair, this work of feeding the starving, because it isn't for me to feed those by whom I am fed. But I got dragged in, with the result that I now find myself distributing the vomit puked up by the rich" (66:94).

148. Birukoff, *The Life of Tolstoy*, 99.

149. As Porudominskii points out, Tolstoi had a hearty appetite and sometimes forgot about the dietary rules and principles he preached. See "Tolstoi i etika pitaniia," 111. Maude relates one colorful example of the constant battle Tolstoi waged between his head and his stomach: "One day, soon after his conversion to vegetarianism, Tolstoy called on his friend, I. I. Raevsky, at a hotel in Toula. Raevsky was having dinner. Tolstoy began to say that one should not eat meat or gluttonise, and that man's proper food is bread and water. The pudding was brought in, and Tolstoy, still talking, drew the dish

towards himself to take some. 'Eh! No! . . .' protested Raevsky humorously, 'that's also gluttony!' and Tolstoy pushed back the dish and expressed his penitence." See Maude, *The Life of Tolstoy*, 2:218.

150. Anna Seuron, a former housekeeper at the Iasnaia Poliana estate, once claimed that "those who suppose the Count to be an ascetic in the full sense of the word are much mistaken. He has had, and still has, times when he is capable of any amount of self-denial; but with his physique and his senses, the Count can never be a saint." See Maude, *The Life of Tolstoy*, 2:219.

151. Gor'kii, "Lev Tolstoi," in M. Gor'kii, *Sobranie sochinenii* (Moscow: Khudozhestvennaia literatura, 1963), 18:91.

152. Dmitri Merezhkovski, *Tolstoi as Man and Artist, with an Essay on Dostoievski* (Westport, Conn.: Greenwood Press, 1970), 45.

153. Boris Sorokin, *Tolstoy in Prerevolutionary Russian Criticism* (Columbus: Ohio State University Press, 1979), 182.

154. A. P. Sergeenko, describing the modest meal he saw Tolstoi eat in his guest room at the Optina Pustyn monastery just ten days before his death in 1910, writes that Tolstoi's "typical peasant nature was underscored now by the fact that he ate the usual national meal of the Russian peasant—cabbage soup and kasha"; see *Rasskazy o Tolstom*, 79.

*4. Carnality and Morality in Fin de Siècle and Revolutionary Russia (pages 158–226)*

1. For a study of beast imagery in Dostoevskii's works, see V. P. Vladimirtsev, "Poeticheskii bestiarii Dostoevskogo," in *Dostoevskii i mirovaia kul'tura, Al'manakh no. 12*, ed. K. A. Stepanian (Moscow: Raritet, 1999), 120–34. Yokota-Murakami Takayuki, meanwhile, examines Tolstoi's use of animal imagery in "Man Seen as a Beast, Male Seen as an Animal: The Idea of 'Bestiality' Examined through *The Kreutzer Sonata*," in *The Force of Vision: Proceedings of the XIII Congress of the International Comparative Literature Association*, ed. Earl Miner and Toru Haga (Tokyo: International Comparative Literature Association, 1995), 2:611–16. Tolstoi himself strongly objected to the use of predatory imagery to depict human behavior. "If we are going to use metaphors from the animal world, as some people like to do, defending violence and war as necessary aspects of the struggle for existence in the world of animals," he writes in his essay *What Then Must We Do?*, "then we should select social animals, like bees, to compare ourselves to, because, not to mention the love of his neighbor that is innate within him, man is, by his reason and by his very own nature, inclined to serve other people and a common human goal" (25:292–93).

2. As Richard Stites demonstrates in *Revolutionary Dreams: Utopian Visions and Experimental Life in the Russian Revolution* (New York: Oxford University Press, 1989), utopianism during this revolutionary period was not confined

to Marxists and socialists. Indeed, Tolstoyism, Stites notes, provided a highly attractive alternative vision of the coming transformation promised by the October Revolution. "The Tolstoyan movement attracted intellectuals who sought the traditional popular utopia of the past," he writes. "It preached pacifism, withdrawal to the simplicity of rustic life and away from the moral and physical dirt of the cities, a loathing for the state and for public authority in general, an interior mystical religion outside of the bureaucratic state church, opposition to politics in any form and to terroristic violence on the part of state or revolutionary. It was a rejection of passion and anger and even sexual drive" (33–34).

3. This concern is openly expressed by one contemporary, writing under the pen name "The Communist," who fears that Bolsheviks who observe rigorous ascetic practices in their lives would soon be transformed "from militant revolutionaries with rifles and hammers into Gospel-toting Tolstoyans concerned with refraining from sin rather than annihilating the bourgeoisie." See Kommunist, "Asketizm ili Kommunizm?" *Voronezhskaia kommuna*, August 11, 1921, 3. I am quoting from Eric Naiman, *Sex in Public: The Incarnation of Early Soviet Ideology* (Princeton, N.J.: Princeton University Press, 1997), 212.

4. Plato, *The Republic*, 109. All further citations from *The Republic* come from this edition and will be made parenthetically in the text.

5. Peter Ulf Møller, *Postlude to The Kreutzer Sonata: Tolstoj and the Debate over Sexual Morality in Russian Literature of the 1890s*, trans. John Kendal (New York: E. J. Brill, 1988).

6. Engelstein, *The Keys to Happiness: Sex and the Search for Modernity in Fin-de-Siècle Russia* (Ithaca, N.Y.: Cornell University Press, 1992), 218.

7. Igor Kon, *The Sexual Revolution in Russia: From the Age of the Czars to Today*, trans. James Riordan (New York: Free Press, 1995), 31.

8. Dmitrii Merezhkovskii, *L. Tolstoi i Dostoevskii: Vechnye sputniki* (Moscow: Respublika, 1995).

9. See, for example, "Po povodu odnoi trevogi grafa L. N. Tolstogo," *Russkii vestnik*, no. 8 (1895): 154–87.

10. Renato Poggioli, *The Phoenix and the Spider: A Book of Essays About Some Russian Writers and Their View of the Self* (Cambridge, Mass.: Harvard University Press, 1957), 177.

11. Engelstein, *The Keys to Happiness*, 363.

12. Ibid., 379.

13. Rene Fueloep Miller, "Tolstoy the Apostolic Crusader," *Russian Review*, 19, no. 2 (1960): 101–102.

14. "I am an inveterate realist, a disciple of the school of Tolstoi and Dostoevsky," the author writes in his introduction to an English-language translation of *The Millionaire*. "My development was very strongly influenced by Tolstoi," he

adds, "although I never shared his views on 'non-violent resistance to evil.' As an artist he overpowered me, and I have found it difficult not to model my work on his." See Michael Petrovich Artzibashef, *The Millionaire*, trans. Percy Pinkerton (Freeport, N.Y.: Books for Libraries Press, 1915), 8, 9.

15. Otto Boele, introduction to *Sanin: A Novel*, by Mikhail Artsybashev, trans. Michael Katz (Ithaca, N.Y.: Cornell University Press, 2001), 5.

16. The "Christian non-resistance religion of Tolstoy," according to one critic at the time, was one of the great ideas, dominant in contemporary Russian literature and culture, against which a marked revolt was launched in Russia during the post-1905 period, a revolt in which Artsybashev's novel actively takes part. See William Lyon Phelps, *Essays on Russian Novelists* (New York: Macmillan, 1926), 248.

17. See Mikhail Artsybashev, *Sobranie sochinenii v trekh tomakh* (Moscow: Terra, 1994), 1:259, 164. Unless otherwise indicated, all further citations from *Sanin* and Artsybashev's other works will come from this three-volume collection and will be referenced parenthetically by volume and page number directly in the text.

18. Phelps, *Essays on Russian Novelists*, 260.

19. *U Tolstogo 1904–1910: Iasnopolianskie zapiski D. P. Makovitskogo* (Moscow: Nauka, 1979), *Literaturnoe nasledstvo*, tom 90, kniga 3. See the entry for July 10, 1908 (139).

20. Phelps, *Essays on Russian Novelists*, 259.

21. Engelstein, *The Keys to Happiness*, 388.

22. A. S. Prugavin, *O L've Tolstom i o tolstovtsakh: Ocherki, vospominaniia, materialy* (Moscow: I. D. Sytin, 1911), 282.

23. A. Omel'chenko, *Geroi nezdorovogo tvorchestva ("Sanin" roman Artsybasheva)* (St. Petersburg: Sever, 1908), 36.

24. Maude, *Life of Tolstoy*, 2:339.

25. "If Sanin embodies Artsybashev's advocacy of the natural life, free of moral and social constraints," writes Nicholas Luker,

> then the alternative and unnatural way of being is demonstrated by the technology student Iurii Svarozhich, who serves as a foil to the hero Sanin and he thus represents what Artsybashev saw as the positive and negative polarities operative among the Russian intelligentsia around the turn of the century, a neat contrast affirmed by the fact that both characters have their disciples: Sanin is followed by the teacher, Ivanov, and Iurii by the student, Shafrov. Whereas Sanin's behaviour testifies to the joy of being alive in a world brimming with physical promise, Iurii's reflects the profoundly life-denying pessimism that sapped the creative strength of so many members of his generation.

See Nicholas Luker, "Artsybashev's *Sanin*: A Reappraisal," in Luker, *In De-*

*fence of a Reputation: Essays on the Early Prose of Mikhail Artsybashev* (Nottingham, Eng.: Astra Press, 1990), 84.

26. "'Natural' for him never meant 'animal,'" one commentator has observed about Tolstoi, "it meant, as it did for the Stoics, 'naturally human.' And what was 'naturally human' was not to follow animal impulses but to follow uncorrupted reason and conscience." See Henry LeRoy Finch, introduction to *Talks with Tolstoy*, by A. B. Goldenweizer, trans. S. S. Koteliansky and Virginia Woolf (New York: Horizon Press, 1969), 6.

27. For example, when he witnesses Sanin being nestled affectionately by a lovely young peasant woman during the hunting scene depicted in chapter 13, Iurii feels unconscious envy of his comrade (1:140). Soon afterward, following his hunting trip with his future brother-in-law Riazantsev, Iurii is sorely tempted by his hunting partner's suggestion that the two of them return to the place where Sanin had been cavorting with some peasant women: "Iurii blushed deeply in the darkness. A forbidden feeling stirred within him with its animal appetite; unusual and awe-inspiring pictures penetrated his excited brain, but he gained control of himself and replied dryly, 'No. It's time to go home.'" (1:141).

28. Boele, introduction, 6. Laura Engelstein interprets the scene similarly: "In the soothing lull of a warm summer night, with no desire for commitment or sense of remorse, Sanin enjoys a momentary connection with another man's sexually frustrated sweetheart. Indeed, his special role in the narrative is to convince young women who have succumbed to desire that their impulses have improved rather than degraded them"; see *The Keys to Happiness*, 385.

29. Ibid., 385.

30. Ibid., 397. Naiman, who maintains that "sexual desire in the novel frequently surfaces in self-aggrandizing male fantasies" (49) and that "the novel cannot talk about sex without lapsing into a rhetoric of male aggrandizement and female humiliation" (49–50), strongly disagrees with the much more generous assessment that Engelstein (along with Boele and Luker) provides of the author's sexual ethos; Naiman maintains that such scholars fail to recognize the misogynous dimensions of Artsybashev's text. Although the hero claims to respect women and seeks ostensibly to liberate rather than humiliate them, Naiman advises readers not to detach Sanin from *Sanin*, a novel where, in his view, "delight in female humiliation masquerades as a critique of sexual hypocrisy" (51). See *Sex in Public*, 49–51.

31. Luker, "Artsybashev's *Sanin*: A Reappraisal," 94.

32. Phelps, *Essays on Russian Novelists*, 257.

33. Luker, "Artsybashev's *Sanin*: A Reappraisal," 94.

34. Ibid.

35. Naiman, *Sex in Public*, 48.

36. P. V. Nikolaev, "L. N. Tolstoi i M. P. Artsybashev," in *Tolstoi i o Tolstom. Materialy i issledovaniia* (Moscow: Nasledie, 1998), 243.

37. D. S. Mirsky, *A History of Russian Literature*, ed. Francis J. Whitfield (New York: Knopf, 1969), 375.

38. Ibid., 402.

39. Artsybashev, *Vechnyi mirazh* (Berlin: I. A. Gutnov, 1922).

40. A. G. Gornfel'd, *Knigi i liudi. Literaturnye besedy* (St. Petersburg: Zhizn', 1908), 27.

41. Aleksandr Zakrzhevskii, *Karamazovshchina: psikhologicheskie paralleli* (Kiev: Iskusstvo, 1912), 133.

42. In *O brake i bezbrachii. Protiv "Kreitserovoi sonaty" i "Poslesloviia" k nei grafa L. Tolstogo* (Kazan', 1891), A. Gusev writes that in Tolstoi's novella "the sensual, animal interests of people are placed in the forefront." "Tolstoy's work is an example of what we can expect from the depraved times in which we live," Gusev adds, citing a sentiment from Elizabeth Field's "Count Tolstoy in America," which had appeared in *Volzhskii vestnik* earlier that same year: "Tolstoy's psychology is simple physiology." See *O brake i bezbrachii*, 85.

43. W. T. Stead, "Count Tolstoi's New Tale. Introductory," *Review of Reviews*, 1 (1890): 333. I am quoting here from Møller, *Postlude to The Kreutzer Sonata*, 106 n. 39.

44. Zakrzhevskii, *Karamazovshchina*, 133.

45. Naiman, *Sex in Public*, 4.

46. Zudin seems to have a "speaking" name: the Russian word *zud* means "itch" or "urge," while the word *zuda* is a colloquial term that means "bore" (it is related to the verb *zudit'*, "to nag at"). Initially at least, it is not absolutely clear whether Zudin's name is meant to tell us primarily that he is plagued by sexual urges he must strive to overcome (and thus not succumb to his marital "itch" to commit adultery) or that he is a moralistic, Tolstoyan bore for maintaining such a puritanical attitude toward sexual and gastronomical pleasure.

47. Aleksandr Tarasov-Rodionov, *Shokolad*, in *Sobachii pereulok. Detektivnye romany i povest'*, compiled by V. Gellershtein (Moscow: Sovremennyi pisatel', 1993), 274. All subsequent quotations from *Shokolad* will be taken from this edition of Tarasov-Rodionov's novel and will be cited parenthetically in the text.

48. I am quoting from Charles Malamuth's translation of *Shokolad*, which renders the original line ("Eki, podumaesh', strasti!") quite felicitously here. See Alexander Tarasov-Rodionov, *Chocolate: A Novel*, trans. Charles Malamuth (Westport, Conn.: Hyperion Press, 1932), 35.

49. References to Elena's "chocolate-colored" (*shokoladnye* or *shokoladin'ki*) eyes can be found, for example, on 283, 292, 306, 309, 311, and 312. For some reason, Malamuth fails to include "chocolate-colored" in his translation of *shokoladnye* and *shokoladin'ki*, opting to use the more neutral adjective "dark" instead.

50. Not unlike Zudin, Elena Val'ts is given a possibly significant name. As is true in the case of Elena, the old professor's young siren of a wife in Chekhov's *Uncle Vanya*, Val'ts's first name recalls the alluring Helen of Troy, while the dancer's surname is phonetically linked with the Russian word for "waltz" (*val's*), historically considered a rather sinful and seductive dance in Russia. These two onomastic associations reinforce her role in the story as a seductress and femme fatale.

51. The theme of morally reforming a "fallen woman" occupies a cherished position in nineteenth-century Russian literature, informing the works of such writers as Nekrasov, Chernyshevskii, and Dostoevskii. For a discussion of literary attempts in Russia to save an unfortunate prostitute (and thus to bring about her redemption and salvation), see Olga Matich, "A Typology of Fallen Women in Nineteenth-Century Russian Literature," in *American Contributions to the Ninth International Congress of Slavists*, vol. 2: *Literature, Politics, History* (Columbus, Ohio: Slavica, 1983), 325–43; George Siegel, "The Fallen Woman in Nineteenth-Century Literature," *Harvard Slavic Studies*, 5 (1970): 81–107; and Alexander Zholkovskii, "Topos prostitutsii," in A. K. Zholkovskii and M. B. Iampol'skii, *Babel'/Babel* (Moscow: Carte Blanche, 1994), 317–68.

52. Eliot Borenstein, whose book examines the construction of masculinity in early Soviet culture, considers Ostrovskii's *Kak zakalialas' stal'* "the most ascetic of masculine-oriented socialist realist novels." See *Men Without Women: Masculinity and Revolution in Russian Fiction, 1917–1929* (Durham, N.C.: Duke University Press, 2000), 2.

53. Marcia Morris, *Saints and Revolutionaries: The Ascetic Hero in Russian Literature* (Albany: State University of New York Press, 1993), 130.

54. Mikhail Zolotonosov, "Masturbanizatsiia: 'Erogennye zony' sovetskoi kul'tury 1920–1930-kh godov," *Novoe literaturnoe obozrenie*, no. 11 (1991): 94.

55. Louise McReynolds, introduction to *The Wrath of Dionysus*, by Evdokia Nagrodskaia, trans. and ed. Louise McReynolds (Bloomington: Indiana University Press, 1997), xxiv.

56. For discussions of the nineteenth-century Russian radical democrats as ascetic models for the Bolsheviks, see Igor Kon, "Sexuality and Culture," in *Sex and Russian Society*, ed. Igor Kon and James Riordan (Bloomington: Indiana University Press, 1993), 19–20, and Igor Kon, *The Sexual Revolution in Russia*, 29–30.

57. Naiman, *Sex in Public*, 133.

58. Naiman traces the prerevolutionary roots of Bolshevik asceticism in his essay, "Historectomies: On the Metaphysics of Reproduction in a Utopian Age," in *Sexuality and the Body in Russian Culture*, ed. Jane T. Coslow, Stephanie Sandler, and Judith Vowles (Stanford, Calif.: Stanford University Press, 1993), 255–76. See also Borenstein, *Men Without Women*, 26–27, and Jane T. Costlow,

Stephanie Sandler, and Judith Vowles, introduction to *Sexuality and the Body in Russian Culture*, 9–16.

59. Sheila Fitzpatrick, *The Cultural Front: Power and Culture in Revolutionary Russia* (Ithaca, N.Y.: Cornell University Press, 1992), 69.

60. Zalkind was the author of such works as "Sexual Life and Contemporary Youth," *Sexual Fetishism: Toward a Re-Examination of the Sexual Question*, and *The Sexual Question Under the Conditions of the Soviet Public*. See "Polovaia zhizn' i sovremennaia molodezh'," *Molodaia gvardiia*, no. 6 (1923): 245–49, *Polovoi fetishism: K peresmotru polovogo voprosa* (Moscow, 1925), and *Polovoi vopros v usloviiakh sovetskoi obshchestvennosti* (Leningrad, 1926). For a discussion of Zalkind's controversial theory of "revolutionary sublimation," see Kon, *The Sexual Revolution in Russia*, 51–66, and Borenstein, *Men Without Women*, 12–13.

61. That enthusiastic supporter of revolutionary asceticism is none other than the young writer Andrei Platonov, who voices these sentiments in an early essay titled "The Culture of the Proletariat" (1920). See *Chut'e pravdy*, ed. V. A. Chalmaev (Moscow: Sovetskaia Rossiia, 1990), 106. I am quoting here from Borenstein, *Men Without Women*, 201.

62. Naiman, *Sex in Public*, 210.

63. Ibid., 214.

64. Ironically, chocolates were one of the luxury food items that Tolstoi had the most difficulty resisting. After reading *Pervaia stupen'*, in which Tolstoi preaches that we must look upon food as a nutritional necessity rather than a gustatory pleasure, one of his followers confesses that he had trouble reconciling the author's public plea for abstinence with his own private fondness for such culinary treats as aromatic coffee mocha and chocolate bonbons: "After all, these were not essential for maintaining his physical existence. The chocolates especially concerned me. One could get along without them in any case. In the end I explained away my perplexity in the following manner: I told myself that Lev Nikolaevich has always been extraordinarily strict with himself in terms of diet, he eats only boring, monotonous vegetarian cuisine (vegetables, mainly potatoes, and kasha, most often oatmeal porridge). Clearly he has earned the right to indulge himself a little every now and then." See Sergeenko, *Rasskazy o L. N. Tolstom*, 106.

65. "She is not a stupid woman after all," Zudin muses in amazement at the astuteness of Val'ts's observation. "She has hit the nail right on the head" (284).

66. The connection between the revolutionary asceticism practiced by such fictional activists as Chernyshevskii's Rakhmetov and the traditional religious asceticism practiced by Orthodox believers was noted by one of Tolstoi's contemporaries. See L. E. Obolenskii, "Otkrytoe pis'mo L. N. Tolstomu," *Novosti i birzhevaia gazeta* 85 (March 27, 1890): 2. "Obolensky's comparison between Rakhmetov's self-denial and Christian celibacy is a curious revelation of the

fact that the difference between the 1860s and the Christian tradition may not have been so great with regard to sexuality," explains Møller. "Both valued asceticism highly. The *hero*—whether hermit or revolutionary—distinguished himself by sacrificing his sexuality for a greater cause." See, Møller, *Postlude to The Kreutzer Sonata*, 137.

67. See Wendy Goldman, *Women, the State, and Revolution: Soviet Family Policy and Social Life, 1917–1936* (New York: Cambridge University Press, 1993).

68. See, for example, Mervyn Matthews, *Privilege in the Soviet Union: A Study of Elite Life-Styles under Communism* (London: Allen and Unwin, 1978). In a book that describes the system of privilege that flourished in the Soviet Union, David K. Willis devotes an entire chapter ("Food as *Klass*") to the issue of elite restaurants, special food shops, and luxury food deliveries to which high-ranking party officials had access. See *Klass: How Russians Really Live* (New York: St. Martin's Press, 1985), 19–35.

69. V. V. Buznik, "Tema revoliutsii i grazhdanskoi voiny. Rozhdenie novoi prozy: novye temy, konflikty, geroi. Formirovanie sotsial'no-psikhologicheskogo romana novogo mira," in *Istoriia russkogo sovetskogo romana*, ed. V. A. Kovachev (Moscow and Leningrad: Nauka, 1965), 1:101. See also V. N. Chuvakov's biographical entry on Tarasov-Rodionov, "Tarasov-Rodionov, Aleksandr Ignat'evich," in *Kratkaia literaturnaia entsiklopediia*, ed. A. A. Surkov (Moscow: Sovetskaia entsiklopediia, 1972), 7:387–88.

70. See, for example, Eric Naiman, introduction to *Happy Moscow*, by Andrey Platonov, trans. Robert and Elizabeth Chandler (London: Harvill Press, 2001), xvii.

71. Sheila Fitzpatrick, *Everyday Stalinism: Ordinary Life in Extraordinary Times: Soviet Russia in the 1930s* (New York: Oxford University Press, 1999), 89.

72. Ibid., 93.

73. Randi Cox, "'NEP without Nepmen!' Soviet Advertising and the Transition to Socialism," in *Everyday Life in Early Soviet Russia: Taking the Revolution Inside*, ed. Christina Kiaer and Eric Naiman (Bloomington: Indiana University Press, 2006), 126.

74. Ibid., 125.

75. Jukka Gronow, *Caviar with Champagne: Common Luxury and the Ideals of the Good Life in Stalin's Russia* (New York: Berg, 2003), 6.

76. See A. I. Mikoian, *Pishchevaia industriia Sovetskogo Soiuza* (Leningrad: Partizdat, 1936). All subsequent quotations from Mikoian's report will be cited parenthetically in the text.

77. "The Party and the government are all the time following a policy aimed toward lowering prices and widening the supply of food products in the country," Mikoian explains. "As the result of a decrease in state-regulated prices and a decline in market prices, consumption has expanded considerably.

This speaks to the growth of a cultured and prosperous life" (48). In line with the decidedly unascetic tone he takes in his report, Mikoian at one point mocks Hermann Goering, Hitler's minister, for the "monastic" promise he had made recently to go without butter or fat in his own diet so that Nazi Germany might be able to rearm itself (12).

78. Gronow, *Caviar with Champagne*, 9.

79. Cox, "'NEP without Nepmen!'" 144.

80. Gronow, *Caviar with Champagne*, 9.

81. Julie Hessler, "Cultured Trade: The Stalinist Turn Towards Consumerism," in *Stalinism: New Directions*, ed. Sheila Fitzpatrick (London: Routledge, 2000), 183.

82. Ibid., 184.

83. Gronow, *Caviar with Champagne*, 9.

84. Naiman, introduction to *Happy Moscow*, by Platonov, vii, viii.

85. For examinations of Nietzsche's reception and influence in late-nineteenth-century Russia, see Edith W. Clowes, *The Revolution of Moral Consciousness: Nietzsche in Russian Literature, 1890–1914* (DeKalb: Northern Illinois University Press, 1988), and Ann Marie Lane, "Nietzsche Comes to Russia: Popularization and Protest in the 1890s," in *Nietzsche in Russia*, ed. Bernice Glatzer Rosenthal (Princeton, N.J.: Princeton University Press, 1986), 51–68.

86. V. V. Chuiko, "Obshchestvennye idealy Fridrikha Nitsshe," *Nabliudatel'*, no. 2 (1893): 233.

87. Clowes, *The Revolution of Moral Consciousness*, 92–95.

88. N. Ia. Grot, "Nravstvennye idealy nashego vremeni: Fridrikh Nitsshe i Lev Tolstoi," *Voprosy filosofii i psikhologii*, 16 (1893): 129–54.

89. N. K. Mikhailovskii, *Literaturnye vospominaniia i sovremennaia smuta* (St. Petersburg, 1900), 2:464.

90. Clowes, *The Revolution of Moral Consciousness*, 58–60.

91. Ibid., 76.

92. Ibid., 103.

93. Evdokiia Nagrodskaia, *Gnev Dionisa* (St. Petersburg: Severo-Zapad, 1994), 41. All further citations from *Gnev Dionisa* come from this edition and will be made parenthetically in the text.

94. Mania's early mentor, the revolutionary philosopher Ian, could also be considered a Nietzschean, but only in the sense that his philosophy of life strongly advocates the liberation of the flesh and the life of the instincts. Indeed, Ian expresses high praise for Artsybashev's *Sanin*, which he considers "a brilliant protest against petrified moral values." He tells Mania, "There is more said in defense of the individual personality there than in all of West European literature." See Anastasiia Verbitskaia, *Kliuchi schast'ia*, 4 vols. (Moscow: I. M. Kushnerev, 1910), 1:92–93. All further citations from *Kliuchi schastiia*

come from this edition and will be made parenthetically in the text by volume and page number.

95. Zakrzhevskii, *Karamazovshchina*, 120–123.

96. Engelstein, *The Keys to Happiness*, 390. See also Edith Clowes, "Literary Reception as Vulgarization: Nietzsche's Idea of the Superman in Neo-Realist Fiction," in *Nietzsche in Russia*, ed. Bernice Glatzer Rosenthal (Princeton, N.J.: Princeton University Press, 1986), 315–29. Clowes maintains that Sanin "embodies the Nietzschean stereotype of the superman as a moral hedonist" (323).

97. Engelstein, *The Keys to Happiness*, 385.

98. Ibid., 385.

99. Luker, "Afterword," 265.

100. See, for example, 1:60, 1:172, 1:238, 1:249, 1:268.

101. Luker, "Artsybashev's *Sanin*: A Reappraisal," 88.

102. Ibid., 88.

103. Mikhail Agursky, "Nietzschean Roots of Stalinist Culture," in *Nietzsche and Soviet Culture: Ally and Adversary*, ed. Bernice Glatzer Rosenthal (Cambridge: Cambridge University Press, 1994), 268–69.

104. Vera T. Reck and Michael Green, introduction to *Chinese Story and Other Tales*, by Boris Pilnyak, trans. Vera T. Reck and Michael Green (Norman: University of Oklahoma Press, 1988), 3–4.

105. Naiman, *Sex in Public*, 60.

106. Boris Pil'niak, *Golyi god* (Chicago: Russian Language Specialties, 1966), 142, 143–44.

107. Naiman, *Sex in Public*, 60.

108. Gary Browning, *Boris Pilniak: Scythian at a Typewriter* (Ann Arbor, Mich.: Ardis, 1985), 121–22.

109. Boris Pil'niak, *Mashiny i volki* (Munich: Wilhelm Fink, 1971), 27, 138.

110. Ibid., 34.

111. Iurii Dobranov, "Svidetel'stvo o bednosti," *Kniga i proletarskaia revoliutsiia*, no. 1 (1936): 102–103.

112. Agursky, "Nietzschean Roots of Stalinist Culture," 264.

113. Elias Canetti, *Crowds and Power*, trans. Carol Stewart (New York: Viking Press, 1962), 219.

114. Mikhail Bakhtin, *Tvorchestvo Fransua Rable i narodnaia kul'tura srenevekov'ia i renessansa* (Moscow: Khudozhestvennaia literatura, 1990), 310.

115. *Zavist'* in Iurii Olesha, *Izbrannoe* (Moscow: Khudozhestvennaia literatura, 1974), 57. All further citations from Olesha's works come from this edition and will be made parenthetically in the text.

116. This predatory creature also makes its appearance in Olesha's *Tri tolstiaka* (1924), where the muscles of the strongman Lapitup are seen as moving under the skin "like rabbits swallowed by a boa constrictor" (126). Likewise

Tutti, the heir to the Three Fat Men's throne, has been raised with a bestiary so that the future ruler may learn to imitate the predatory behavior of wild animals. "Let him see how the tigers are fed on raw meat and how the boa constrictors swallow up live rabbits. Let him listen to the voices of blood-thirsty beasts and look into their devilishly crimson eyes. Then he will learn to be cruel" (160). Political rule by predatory beasts will later be depicted in Soviet literature by Fazil Iskander in his satiric beast fable, *Kroliki i udavy* (1982). Irina Ratushinskaia, meanwhile, provides a parodic deconstruction of this paradigmatic Soviet predator in her short story, "On the Meaning of Life," where the main character is a vegetarian boa constrictor whose "all-consuming" (*vsepogloshchaiushchaia*) passion is to watch rabbits, not to eat them. See Irina Ratushinskaia, *A Tale of Three Heads*, trans. Diane Nemec-Ignashev (Tenafly, N.J.: Hermitage, 1986), 12–19. I am extremely grateful to Professor Gitta Hammarberg of Macalester College for drawing my attention to this delightful little tale.

117. See chapter 1, "The Creation of the Collective Body," of Naiman's *Sex in Public* for an interesting discussion of Gastev's rolé in formulating the notion of the "collective body" during the 1920s (especially 65–78).

118. "If Kavalerov bears a personal grudge against the Bolshevik regime," Andrew Barratt notes, "Ivan displays an opposition which is more recognizably ideological." See *Yury Olesha's "Envy"* (Birmingham, Eng.: University of Birmingham, 1981), 43. Barratt is paraphrasing here the view expressed by A. Belinkov in *Sdacha i gibel' sovetskogo intelligenta: Iurii Olesha* (Madrid: Ediciones Castilla, 1976).

119. The connection between gastronomical and sexual pleasure is made even more explicit at the lexical level in Russian by the common element (*lakom*) found in such expressions as "tasty morsel" (*lakomyi kusok*), "delicacy" (*lakomstvo*), "gourmand" (*lakomka*), "to treat onself" (*lakomit'sia*), and "to have a sweet tooth" (*byt' lakomkoi*).

120. Robert Payne, introduction to *"Love" and Other Stories*, by Yuri Olyesha, trans. Robert Payne (New York: Washington Square Press, 1967), xv.

121. For a discussion of this Bolshevik debate over sexual morality, see Kon, *The Sexual Revolution in Russia*, 51-66.

122. Naiman discusses "revolutionary asceticism" at some length in *Sex in Public;* see esp. 124–47.

123. For a thorough analysis of the contemporary critical debate that raged over *Sobachii pereulok*, and particularly the issue of how contemporary critics seriously misread Gumilevskii's novel as a celebration of free love, see Gregory Carleton, "Writing-Reading the Sexual Revolution in the Early Soviet Union," *Journal of the History of Sexuality* 8, no. 2 (1997): 229–55. One contemporary critic maintained that Gumilevskii's novel, along with the fic-

tion written by his "brethren writers" Panteleimon Romanov and Sergei Malashkin, leaves the impression that "vulgarity, pornography, depravity, and animal law reign over contemporary youth." See G. Korotkov, "Literatura sobach'ego pereulka," *Rezets* 15 (1927): 15.

124. Gregory Carleton, *Sexual Revolution in Bolshevik Russia* (Pittsburgh, Pa.: University of Pittsburgh Press, 2005), 216.

125. Geoff Woollen makes a somewhat similar distinction in an essay that explores the semantic distinctions—marking the gradations of human animality—between what he calls *bêtomorphisme* and *brutomorphisme* in the treatment of the "beast in man" in Emile Zola's prose fiction. See "Des brutes humaines dans *La Bête humaine*," in *La Bête humaine: texte et explications* (Actes du colloque de Glasgow 1990), ed. Geoff Woollen (Glasgow: University of Glasgow French and German Publications, 1990), 149-72.

126. I. Kyselev, "Pro L'va Gumilevskogo i pro liubov' deshevshu, nizh kvitok u kino," *Student revoliutsii*, no. 4 (1927): 53. I am quoting here from Igal Halfin, *Terror in My Soul: Communist Autobiographies on Trial* (Cambridge, Mass.: Harvard University Press, 2003), 155.

127. Ibid., 164.

128. Ibid., 105.

129. These chapters are, respectively, part 1, chapter 10, and part 2, chapter 4. In Fyodor Gladkov's *Cement* (1925), images of spiders and spider webs are used not only to indicate the neglected state of the abandoned factory (cobwebs dominate the description of Engineer Kleist's quarters there in chapter 5, for instance), but also—as in *Dog Alley*—to warn against the dangers of failing to restrain one's sexual desires. Unlike Gumilevskii's novel, however, *Cement* associates this arachnoid imagery with men rather than women. Thus when the hero Gleb returns home from the war to find that his wife Dasha has been "liberated" and suddenly transformed into an exemplar of the "new" Soviet woman (that is, one who is politically active and socially independent), he attempts to reassert his old-fashioned male dominance in a brutish manner by insisting upon his conjugal right, as a husband, to sleep with his wife. "Frenzied, drunken with the heat of his own blood," the narrator reports, "he carried her to the bed and threw himself down upon her, tearing her shift, hungrily clasping her, as a spider would a fly." See Fedor Gladkov, "Tsement," *Krasnaia nov'*, no. 1 (1925): 90.

130. See Paul Hillyard, *The Book of the Spider: From Arachnophobia to the Love of Spiders* (New York: Random House, 1994), 20.

131. A. V. Gura, *Simvolika zhivotnykh v slavianskoi narodnoi traditsii* (Moscow: Indrik, 1997), 504.

132. Bram Dijkstra, *Evil Sisters: The Threat of Female Sexuality and the Cult of Manhood* (New York: Knopf, 1996).

133. Engelstein, *The Keys to Happiness*, 322.

134. Vasilii Rozanov, *Opavshie list'ia* (Moscow: Sovremennik, 1992), 336–37. Not too many years later, Adolf Hitler—who in his infamous *Mein Kampf* (1925– 26) likewise referred to Jews as bloodsucking spiders that ensnare Christian Aryans in their fatal socioeconomic webs—would indeed attempt to "sweep all the cobwebs" out of Nazi Germany. See Dijkstra, *Evil Sisters*, 425.

135. See Mikhail Zolotonosov, "Akhutokots-Akhum: Opyt rasshifrovki skazki Korneia Chukovskogo o Mukhe," in Zolotonosov, *Slovo i telo: Seksual'nye aspekty, universalii i interpretatsii kul'turnogo teksta XIX–XX vekov* (Moscow: Ladomir, 1999), 79–87. Zolotonosov, who traces the source of the "Jewish semantics" of the spider as an image in modern Russian culture back to Dostoevskii's anti-Semitic characterization of Benjamin Disraeli as a spider in the September 1876 issue of his *Dnevnik pisatelia* (in the chapter "Piccola bestia"), examines Kornei Chukhovskii's "Mukha-Tsokotukha" as a literary text whose imagery shares the values of this subculture of Russian anti-Semitism.

136. Orlando Figes and Boris Kolonitskii, *Interpreting the Russian Revolution: The Languages and Symbols of 1917* (New Haven, Conn.: Yale University Press, 1999); see esp. chapter 6, "Images of the Enemy," 153–86.

137. Leonid Kraev's pamphlet, *Bolshevitskie pauki i khrest'ianskiia mukhi* (Rostovon-Don, 1919), published in the midst of the civil war, constitutes a salient exception to this revolutionary-era pattern of linking the wealthy bourgeoisie with predatory spiders and the impoverished workers with victimized flies. "The Bolsheviks—they are the spiders, and clever, blood-thirsty, loathsome spiders at that," writes the White sympathizer Kraev. "The peasants—they are the flies whose blood is sucked dry, down to the very last drop, by the Bolshevik spiders" (16).

138. This popular pamphlet, Figes and Kolonitskii maintain, probably did more than any other piece of propaganda at the time to raise the class consciousness of the Russian masses. Although *Spiders and Flies* presents this predatory arachnoid imagery primarily in terms of class warfare, Liebknecht does touch upon issues of sexual exploitation as well when he includes, among the ranks of the "spiders" in Russian society, the "young degenerate from a wealthy family who laughs while seducing young women and luring them into debauchery, and who considers it an honor for him to dishonor as many defenseless women as possible!" See V. Libknekht, *Pauki i mukhi* (New York: Novy Mir 1917), 5.

139. Naiman, *Sex in Public*, 128.

140. A. B. Zalkind, *Polovoi vopros v usloviiakh sovetskoi obshchestvennosti*, 23.

141. Halfin, *Terror in My Soul*, 149.

142. T. Ganzhulevich, "Literatura pro molod," *Student revoliutsii*, no. 4 (1927): 51. I am quoting here from Halfin, *Terror in My Soul*, 149.

143. According to the company's Web site (www.tanglefoot.com), the Tanglefoot Company of Grand Rapids, Michigan, developed sticky-coated paper sheets to trap flies in 1887 by combining castor oil, resins, and wax. The Web site claims that this unique product, which was for many years the world's best-selling flypaper, "became as generic a word for flypaper as Kleenex did for facial tissues."

144. Naiman, *Sex in Public*, 166–67.

145. The same seems to hold true for Andrei Platonov, at least early in his career. "In his early essays," Eliot Borenstein observes, "sex is seen primarily as an enslavement to the material, animal world, an impediment in the road to revolutionary awareness; woman, the 'embodiment' of sex, comes to represent everything that must be overcome in order to lead a truly human life." See *Men Without Women*, 194.

146. Carleton, *Sexual Revolution in Bolshevik Russia*, 118.

147. In *Terror in My Soul*, Halfin discusses in some detail the medical signs of neurasthenia noticeable in Gumilevskii's two male characters; see chapter 4, "From a Weak Body to an Omnipotent Mind," 148–208. On several occasions Tolstoi's narrator in "The Devil" strongly suggests that Irtenev is indeed becoming mentally ill: "He [Irtenev] felt that he was losing control over himself, becoming almost insane [*pomeshannym*]" (27:506); "Evgenii found himself in such a semi-insane [*polusumasshedshem*] condition" (27:507); "It seemed to him that he was undergoing some kind of a fit of insanity [*sumasshestviia*]" (27:511). In the story's final paragraph, however, after doctors have explained Irtenev's suicide as the act of a madman [*on byl dushevno-bol'noi*], Tolstoi's narrator insists that if Irtenev is a madman, then all men are madmen: "And truly, if Evgeny Irtenev was mad [*dushevno-bol'noi*], then all such people are mad [*dushevno-bol'nye*], and the maddest of them all [*samye zhe dushevno-bol'nye*], are undoubtedly those who see the signs of insanity [*sumasshestviia*] in other people, which they do not see in themselves" (27:515).

148. "It is no accident," Burov observes, "that for hundreds of years Don Juan was made the hero of poetic works" (62).

149. Tolstoi likewise inveighs against the notion, popular at the time, that sexual activity is necessary for purposes of health. In his "Afterword to *The Kreutzer Sonata*," for example, he explains what his intentions were in writing that controversial novella. "I wished to say, first of all," he writes, "that in our society there has developed the firm conviction—common to all social classes and supported by false science—that sexual union is necessary for one's health and that since marriage is not always a possible option, extramarital sex, which does not obligate the male to anything except the payment of money, is a perfectly natural thing which ought therefore to be encouraged.

This conviction has become so commonly and so firmly held that parents, on the advice of their doctors, are arranging sexual depravity for their children" (27:79). Tolstoi goes on to argue that sexual abstinence is not only quite possible, but also much less harmful and damaging to one's health than is sexual indulgence.

150. The narrator describes Korolev as appearing to thunder forth "almost like the leader, almost like Savonarola" (150) when he delivers his funeral oratory. "Of course, there was nothing ascetic in him," the narrator is quick to add, fearing perhaps that some readers might mistake the young Communist zealot for some kind of sectarian demagogue or Tolstoyan disciple. "On the contrary, his tall, sturdy figure, firmly planted in the fresh soil of the burial mound, spoke of some sort of special *joie de vivre* and life-affirming fortitude" (150). Such denials of asceticism, as Naiman has pointed out, "became a standard trope in discussions of sexuality" in early Soviet Russia; see *Sex in Public*, 129.

151. Halfin, *Terror in My Soul*, 168. "In Gumilevsky's prescription," Halfin explains, "if he is to redeem himself, Khokhorin [sic] must return to manual labor, sublimate his sexual energy, and achieve the transformation from animalistic individualism to proletarian collective consciousness" (207–208).

152. Naiman, *Sex in Public*, 204–206.

153. Borenstein maintains that the ideal of *tovarishchestvo* lies at the very heart of the Bolshevik myth of masculinity. See *Men Without Women*, 23.

154. Naiman, *Sex in Public*, 178.

155. Donna Orwin discusses the "sticky web of love" that Tolstoi thematicizes in his writings in *Tolstoy's Art and Thought, 1847–1880* (Princeton, N.J.: Princeton University Press, 1993), 62, 232 n. 13. Orwin asserts that Tolstoi derived this motif from the "web of kindness" he found in Laurence Sterne's *Sentimental Journey through France and Italy* (1768).

156. Tolstoi's benign web of Christian love does bear some striking affinities, however, to the socialist "web"—the network of intertwined spiritual and emotional ties for people living in the Communist utopia—that Aleksandra Kollontai envisioned during the early years of the Revolution. Naiman discusses Kollontai's web as part of her contribution to the Soviet discourse on "corporeal collectivization" during the early 1920s; see *Sex in Public*, 119.

157. See, for example, Jane T. Coslow, Stephanie Sandler, and Judith Vowles, introduction to *Sexuality and the Body in Russian Literature*, ed. Jane T. Costlow, Stephanie Sandler, and Judith Vowles (Stanford, Calif.: Stanford University Press, 1993), 30. "Dostoevsky foreshadowed much of the 'dark literature' (*chernukha*) in recent Soviet writing," they write, "and his novels explored the psychological complexities of sexual desire and sexual dread a generation before the advent of Freudian psychoanalysis."

158. See, for example, Tat'iana Zabelina, "Sexual Violence Towards Women," in *Gender, Generation and Identity in Contemporary Russia*, ed. Hilary Pilkington (New York: Routledge, 1996), 169–86.

159. Viktor Erofeev, "Markiz de Sad, sadizm i XX vek," in Erofeev, *V labirinte prokliatykh voprosov* (Moscow: Soiuz fotokhudozhnikov Rossii, 1996), 280.

160. See Kon, *The Sexual Revolution in Russia*, esp. chapter 7, "The Beast Has Broken Loose," 107–25.

161. Alexander Genis, "Borders and Metamorphoses: Viktor Pelevin in the Context of Post-Soviet Literature," in *Twentieth-Century Russian Literature: Selected Papers from the Fifth World Congress of Central and East European Studies*, ed. Karen L. Ryan and Barry Scherr (New York: St. Martin's Press, 2000), 301–303.

162. Viktor Pelevin, *Zhizn' nasekomykh: Romany* (Moscow: Vagrius, 1999), 167.

163. Ibid., 328.

164. Ibid., 229.

165. Keith Livers, "Bugs in the Body Politic: The Search for Self in Viktor Pelevin's *The Life of Insects*," *Slavic and East European Journal* 46, no. 1 (2002): 4–5.

166. Ibid., 4, 5.

167. Eliot Borenstein characterizes this infamous "Kremlin buggery scene" between Khrushchev and Stalin in Sorokin's novel as "a Soviet primal scene for post-Soviet times." See his essay, "Stripping the Nation Bare: Russian Pornography and the Insistence of Meaning," in *International Exposure: Perspectives on Modern European Pornography, 1800–2000*, ed. Lisa Z. Sigel (New Brunswick, N.J.: Rutgers University Press, 2005), 232, 233.

168. "Russia Is Slipping Back into an Authoritarian Empire," *Der Spiegel Online*, February 2, 2007.

169. The Russian title of Sorokin's novel, *Pir*, could also be translated into English as *Symposium*. When Sorokin was asked in an interview whether his book had anything in common with Plato's *Symposium*, however, he replied: "No, with Plato there are mainly conversations, while in my novel there is actual feasting. The book consists of thirteen novellas that are all connected in one way or another with food. . . . In *Pir* there are culinary recipes, but in no way is it a cookbook." See "Vladimir Sorokin: Eda—eto eroticheskii akt (material internet izdaniia Arcadia.ru)" in Boris Sokolov, *Moia kniga o Vladimire Sorokine* (Moscow: AIRO, 2005), 112.

170. Vladimir Sorokin, "Nastia," in Sorokin, *Pir* (Moscow: Ad Marginem, 2001), 8. All subsequent citations from "Nastia" come from this edition and will be cited parenthetically in the text.

171. Although the scene of ritual cannibalism in "Nastia" appears highly Dostoevskian (and Nietzschean), what Sorokin has to say about food and eating in an interview conducted at the time when *Pir* was being prepared for pub-

lication sounds very Tolstoyan. "The act of eating has always interested me," Sorokin says during this interview, "both as a physiological act that brings pleasure and as a language of communication that links people together. It is a specific act that consists not only in the social intercourse that takes place around the table, but also in the dishes, in a country's cuisine as a unique semiotic system. One can get to know a people, a country, their history and culture through the language of that country's cuisine. This interests me a lot. The act of eating—this is a kind of erotic act, an act of pleasure. Strictly speaking, eroticism is present in *The Feast* as well, it's just that it is hidden from view by the food." See "Vladimir Sorokin: Eda—eto eroticheskii akt," 112.

172. Tolstoi's name is likewise invoked in the story. Mamut, whose own daughter Arina will be turning sixteen in just two months, expresses some reservations about the morality of taking the life of a living creature—whether it be an animal or a human—in order that its body might be turned into human food. "You're just reasoning like Tolstoi," one of the female guests observes. "I have no divergence of opinion with Count Tolstoi as far as the question of vegetarianism is concerned," Mamut concedes. "But his doctrine of nonresistance to evil . . . well, that's an entirely different matter" (35).

173. Anthropologists have repeatedly noted that torture, mutilation, and cruelty are distinctively human—rather than animal—acts; they seek not the physical destruction or death of the victim, but rather his or her submission to one's will. For discussions of the uniquely human capacity for cruelty (and the myth of the "beast in man"), see J. R. Durant, "The Beast in Man: An Historical Perspective on the Biology of Human Aggression," in *The Biology of Aggression*, ed. Paul F. Brain (Rockville, Md.: Sijthoff and Noordhoff, 1981), 17–46; Erich Fromm, *The Anatomy of Human Destructiveness* (New York: Holt, Rinehart, and Winston, 1973); John Klama, *Aggression: The Myth of the Beast Within* (New York: Wiley, 1988); Anthony Storr, *Human Destructiveness: The Roots of Genocide and Human Cruelty* (New York: Basic Books, 1972); and Johan M. G. van der Dennen, *The "Evil" Mind: Pt. 3. Cruelty and "Beast-in-Man" Imagery* (Groningen, Netherlands: Rijksuniversiteit, 2005).

*5. Conclusion: Dostoevsky, Tolstoy, and the Human Animal*
(pages 227–37)

1. In his essay, "K voprosu o tekstovoj omonimii: *Putešestvie v stranu Guigngnmov* i 'Xolstomer,'" Tomas Ventslova discusses the similarities and differences between Tolstoy's story and part 4 of Swift's novel ("A Voyage to the Country of the Houyhnhnms"). See *Semiosis: Semiotics and the History of Culture*, ed. Morris Halle et al. (Ann Arbor: University of Michigan, 1984), 240–54.

2. See, for example, Ventslova, "K voprosu o tekstovoj omonimii," 240–41.

3. Andrea Rossing McDowell, "Situating the Beast: Animals and Animal Imagery in Nineteenth- and Twentieth-Century Russian Literature" (Ph.D. diss., Indiana University, 2001), 481. In a variant version of Tolstoi's story, Kholstomer reflects upon his fate as a gelding with the following thoughts: "In this, as in many other instances, there is only one salvation for a horse. This salvation is labor: eternal, unceasing labor, with the awareness that this labor will bring no benefit of any kind to oneself and it will hardly bring any kind of benefit to others" (26:480).

4. "There was a time, I can tell you, when I liked to live well and knew how to live well," Serpukhovskoi brags to his host. "Ah, those were the days! Ah, vanished youth! . . . My word, those were good times!" (26:33, 34).

5. "The contrast between Kholstomer's noble old age and the ignoble old age of Serpukhovskoi is displayed more sharply in the 1885 edition of the text than in the original redaction," writes L. D. Opul'skaia in her study of the "creative history" of Tolstoi's story. "The juxtaposition of the horse's entire life and labor to Serpukhovskoi's useless existence, which yields only evil, is underscored even more sharply. And it is only in the final edition of 1885 that a contrast is drawn—tremendous in its denunciatory power—between Kholstomer's death, with its poetic depiction of the she-wolf feeding her cubs the meat of the slaughtered horse, and Serpukhovskoi's death, whose loathsomeness is not diminished but rather is augmented by the magnificence of the funeral ceremony." See Opul'skaia, "Tvorcheskaia istoriia povesti 'Kholstomer,'" in *Literaturnoe nasledstvo* 69, book 1, ed. I. I. Anisimov (Moscow: Akademiia nauk, 1961), 265.

6. See McDowell, "Situating the Beast," 116.

7. Mary Midgely, *Beast and Man: The Roots of Human Nature* (New York: New American Library, 1980), xiii.

8. Margot Norris, *Beasts of the Modern Imagination: Darwin, Nietzsche, Kafka, Ernst, and Lawrence* (Baltimore, Md.: Johns Hopkins University Press, 1985), 3.

9. D. H. Lawrence, *Collected Letters*, ed. Harry T. Moore (New York: Viking Press, 1962), 1:180.

10. Kenneth Inniss, *D. H. Lawrence's Bestiary: A Study of His Use of Animal Trope and Symbol* (The Hague: Mouton, 1962), 20 n. 18.

11. Norris, *Beasts of the Modern Imagination*, 22.

12. See, for example, Aleksandr Zakrzhevskii, *Karamazovshchina. Psikhologicheskie paralleli* (Kiev: Iskusstvo, 1912), 74, and Anna Lisa Crone, "Nietzschean, All Too Nietzschean? Rozanov's Anti-Christian Critique," in *Nietzsche in Russia*, ed. Bernice Glatzer Rosenthal (Princeton, N.J.: Princeton University Press, 1986), 95.

13. Friedrich Nietzsche, *Thus Spoke Zarathustra*, trans. R. J. Hollingdale (Baltimore, Md.: Penguin Books, 1961), 295. It is Norris who characterizes Nietzsche as a "militant carnivore"; see *Beasts of the Modern Imagination*, 92.

14. *U Tolstogo 1904–1910: "Iasnopolianskie zapiski" D. P. Makovitskogo* (Moscow: Nauka, 1979) [*Literaturnoe nasledstvo* 90], bk. 3, 257.

15. *Tainyiporok: Trezvye mysli o polovykh otnosheniiakh*, ed. V. Chertkov (Moscow: Posrednik, 1908), 12.

16. *Literaturnoe nasledstvo* 90, bk. 1, 121, 285, 376; bk. 4, 36.

17. *Literaturnoe nasledstvo* 90, bk. 1, 202.

18. Emil A. Draitser, *Making War, Not Love: Gender and Sexuality in Russian Humor* (New York: St. Martin's Press, 1999), 117–18.

19. Jane T. Costlow, Stephanie Sandler, and Judith Vowles, introduction to *Sexuality and the Body in Russian Culture*, ed. Jane T. Costlow, Stephanie Sandler, and Judith Vowles (Stanford, Calif.: Stanford University Press, 1993), 13.

# Bibliography

Abramson, Paul R., and Steven D. Pinkerton. *With Pleasure: Thoughts on the Nature of Human Sexuality*. New York: Oxford University Press, 1995.

Adams, Carol J. *The Sexual Politics of Meat: A Feminist-Vegetarian Critical Theory*. New York: Continuum, 1990.

Agursky, Mikhail. "Nietzschean Roots of Stalinist Culture." In *Nietzsche and Soviet Culture: Ally and Adversary*, edited by Bernice Glatzer Rosenthal, 256–86. Cambridge: Cambridge University Press, 1994.

Anderson, Benedict. *Imagined Communities: Reflections on the Origin and Spread of Nationalism*. London: Verso, 1991.

Arens, William. *The Man-Eating Myth: Anthropology and Anthropophagy*. New York: Oxford University Press, 1979.

Aristotle. *The Nicomachean Ethics*. Translated by David Ross. Revised by J. L. Ackrill and J. O. Urmson. New York: Oxford University Press, 1998.

Armstrong, Judith M. *The Unsaid Anna Karenina*. New York: St. Martin's Press, 1988.

Artsybashev, Mikhail. *Sanin: A Novel*. Translated by Michael Katz. Ithaca, N.Y.: Cornell University Press, 2001.

———. *Sobranie sochinenii v trekh tomakh*. Moscow: Terra, 1994.

———. *Vechnyi mirazh*. Berlin: I. A. Gutnov, 1922.

Artzibashef, Michael Petrovich. *The Millionaire*. Translated by Percy Pinkerton. Freeport, N.Y.: Books for Libraries Press, 1915.

Bagno, V. E., ed. *Tolstoi ili Dostoevskii? Filosofsko-esteticheskie iskaniia v kul'turakh Vostoka i Zapada*. Saint Petersburg: Nauka, 2003.

Baker, James Allen. "Russian Opposition to Darwinism in the Nineteenth Century." *Isis* 65, no. 229 (1974): 487–505.

———. "The Russian Populists' Response to Darwin." *Slavic Review* 22, no. 3 (1963): 456–68.

Bakhtin, Mikhail. *The Dialogic Imagination: Four Essays*. Edited by Michael Holquist. Translated by Caryl Emerson. Austin: University of Texas Press, 1988.

———. *Problems of Dostoevsky's Poetics*. Translated by Caryl Emerson. Minneapolis: University of Minnesota Press, 1984.

———. *Rabelais and His World*. Translated by Hélène Iswolsky. Cambridge, Mass.: MIT Press, 1968.

———. "Rable i Gogol' (Iskusstvo slova i narodnaia smekhovaia kul'tura)." In Bakhtin, *Voprosy literatury i estetiki*, 484–95. Moscow: Khudozhestvennaia literatura, 1975.

——. *Tvorchestvo Fransua Rable i narodnaia kul'tura srenevekov'ia i renessansa*. Moscow: Khudozhestvennaia literatura, 1990.

——. *Voprosy literatury i estetiki*. Moscow: Khudozhestvennaia literatura, 1975.

Balzac, Honoré de. *Oeuvres complètes de Honoré de Balzac*. Paris: Louis Conard, 1925.

Baratoff, Natalie. *Oblomov: A Jungian Approach (A Literary Image of the Mother Complex)*. New York: Peter Lang, 1990.

Barkas, Janet. *The Vegetable Passion: A History of the Vegetarian State of Mind*. London: Routledge and Kegan Paul, 1975.

Barker, Adele Marie. *The Mother Syndrome in the Russian Folk Imagination*. Columbus, Ohio: Slavica, 1986.

Barratt, Andrew. *Yury Olesha's "Envy."* Birmingham, Eng.: University of Birmingham, 1981.

Barsukov, Nikolai. *Zhizn' i trudy M. P. Pogodina*. Saint Petersburg, 1890.

Barthes, Roland. *Elements of Semiology*. Translated by Annette Lavers and Colin Smith. New York: Hill and Wang, 1967.

——. "Lecture de Brillat-Savarin." In Brillat-Savarin, *Physiologie du Goût*, 7–33. Paris: Hermann, 1975.

——. "Pour une psycho-sociologie de l'alimentation contemporaine." *Annales* 16 (1961): 77–86.

Baudrier, André-Jeanne, ed. *Le roman et la nourriture*. Paris: Presses universitaires de Franche-Comté, 2003.

Bayley, John. "Best and Worst." *New York Review of Books*, 35, nos. 21 and 22 (January 19, 1989), 11–12.

——. *Tolstoy and the Novel*. New York: Viking Press, 1966.

Belinkov, A. *Sdacha i gibel' sovetskogo intelligenta: Iurii Olesha*. Madrid: Ediciones Castilla, 1976.

Belinskii, V. G. *Polnoe sobranie sochinenii*. Moscow and Leningrad: Akademiia nauk, 1953–59.

Benson, Ruth Crego. *Women in Tolstoy: The Ideal and the Erotic*. Champaign: University of Illinois Press, 1973.

Berdyaev, Nicholas. *Dostoievsky*. Translated by Donald Attwater. New York: Meridian Books, 1957.

Bernstein, Michael André. "'These Children that Come at You with Knives': *Ressentiment*, Mass Culture, and the Saturnalia." *Critical Inquiry* 17, no. 2 (1991): 358–85.

Bethea, David. *The Shape of the Apocalypse in Modern Russian Fiction*. Princeton, N.J.: Princeton University Press, 1989.

Bevan, David, ed. *Literary Gastronomy*. Amsterdam: Rodopi, 1988.

Biasin, Gian-Paolo. *The Flavors of Modernity: Food and the Novel*. Princeton, N.J.: Princeton University Press, 1993.

———. *I sapori della modernità: Cibo e romanzo*. Bologna: Il Mulino, 1991.

Billington, James H. *The Icon and the Axe: An Interpretive History of Russian Culture*. New York: Vintage Books, 1970.

Biriukov, Pavel. *Biografiia L'va Nikolaevicha Tolstogo*. 2 vols. Moscow: Gosudarstvennoe izdatel'stvo, 1922.

Birukoff, Paul. *The Life of Tolstoy*. London: Cassell, 1911.

Blanchard, W. H. *Revolutionary Morality: A Psychosexual Analysis of Twelve Revolutionists*. Santa Barbara, Calif.: ABC-Clio Information Services, 1984.

Bloom, Harold, ed. *Fyodor Dostoevsky's "The Brothers Karamazov."* New York: Chelsea House, 1988.

Boele, Otto. Introduction to *Sanin: A Novel*, by Mikhail Artsybashev, translated by Michael Katz, 1–12. Ithaca, N.Y.: Cornell University Press, 2001.

Borenstein, Eliot. *Men Without Women: Masculinity and Revolution in Russian Fiction, 1917–1929*. Durham, N.C.: Duke University Press, 2000.

———. "Slavophilia: The Incitement to Russian Sexual Discourse." *Slavic and East European Journal* 40, no. 1 (1996): 142–47.

———. "Stripping the Nation Bare: Russian Pornography and the Insistence of Meaning." In *International Exposure: Perspectives on Modern European Pornography, 1800–2000*, edited by Lisa Z. Sigel, 232–54. New Brunswick, N.J.: Rutgers University Press, 2005.

Bourdieu, Pierre. *La Distinction*. Paris: Le Minuit, 1979.

Boym, Svetlana. *Common Places: Mythologies of Everyday Life in Russia*. Cambridge, Mass.: Harvard University Press, 1994.

Brautigan, Richard. *The Abortion: An Historical Romance 1966*. New York: Simon and Schuster, 1971.

Breger, Louis. *Dostoevsky: The Author as Psychoanalyst*. New York: New York University Press, 1989.

Brillat-Savarin, Jean-Anthèlme. *Physiologie du goût*. Paris: Hermann, 1975.

Brodsky, Joseph. *Less Than One: Selected Essays*. New York: Farrar, Straus, and Giroux, 1986.

Brostrom, Kenneth N., ed. *Russian Literature and American Critics*. Ann Arbor, Mich.: Ardis, 1984.

Brown, James W. *Fictional Meals and Their Function in the French Novel, 1789–1848*. Toronto: University of Toronto Press, 1984.

Brown, James W., ed. *Littérature et nourriture*. Special issue, *Dalhousie French Studies* 11 (1987).

Brown, Norman. *Love's Body*. New York: Vintage, 1966.

Brown, William E. *A History of Russian Literature of the Romantic Period*. 4 vols. Ann Arbor, Mich.: Ardis, 1986.

Browning, Gary. *Boris Pilniak: Scythian at a Typewriter*. Ann Arbor, Mich.: Ardis, 1985.

Bulgarin, Faddei. Review of Narezhny's *Bursak*. *Literaturnye listki*, part 4, nos. 19–20 (1824): 49.

Buznik, V. V. "Tema revoliutsii i grazhdanskoi voiny. Rozhdenie novoi prozy: novye temy, konflikty, geroi. Formirovanie sotsial'no-psikhologicheskogo romana novogo mira." In *Istoriia russkogo sovetskogo romana*. Edited by V. A. Kovachev, 1:49–183. Moscow and Leningrad: Nauka, 1965.

Canetti, Elias. *Crowds and Power*. Translated by Carol Stewart. New York: Viking Press, 1962.

Cappon, Daniel. *Eating, Loving and Dying: A Psychology of Appetites*. Toronto: University of Toronto Press, 1973.

Carleton, Gregory. *Sexual Revolution in Bolshevik Russia*. Pittsburgh, Pa.: University of Pittsburgh Press, 2005.

———. "Writing-Reading the Sexual Revolution in the Early Soviet Union." *Journal of the History of Sexuality* 8, no. 2 (1997): 229–55.

Catteau, Jacques. *Dostoyevsky and the Process of Literary Creation*. Translated by Audrey Littlewood. Cambridge: Cambridge University Press, 1989.

Charpentier, Françoise. "Le symbolisme de la nourriture dans le *Pantagruel*." In *Pratiques et discours alimentaires à la Renaissance*, edited by Jean-Claude Margolin and Robert Sauzet, 219–31. Paris: Maisonneuve, 1982.

Chekhov, A. P. *Polnoe sobranie sochinenii i pisem*. 20 vols. Moscow: Khudozhestvennaia literatura, 1944–51.

Chertkov, Vladimir, ed. *Tainyi porok: Trezvye mysli o polovykh otnosheniiakh*. Moscow: Posrednik, 1908.

Chopin, Jean. "Oeuvres de Basile Naréjny." *Revue Encyclopédique* 44 (1829): 118–19.

Christian, R. F., ed. *Tolstoy's Diaries*. Translated by R. F. Christian. New York: Scribner, 1985.

Christoff, Peter K. *K. S. Aksakov: A Study in Ideas*. Vol. 3 of *An Introduction to Nineteenth-Century Russian Slavophilism*. Princeton, N.J.: Princeton University Press, 1981.

Chuiko, V. V. "Obshchestvennye idealy Fridrikha Nitsshe." *Nabliudatel'* 2 (1893): 231–47.

Chuvakov, V. N. "Tarasov-Rodionov, Aleksandr Ignat'evich." In *Kratkaia literaturnaia entsiklopediia*, edited by A. A. Surkov, 7:387–88. Moscow: Sovetskaia entsiklopediia, 1972.

Clowes, Edith. "Literary Reception as Vulgarization: Nietzsche's Idea of the Superman in Neo-Realist Fiction." In *Nietzsche in Russia*, edited by Bernice Glatzer Rosenthal, 315–29. Princeton, N.J.: Princeton University Press, 1986.

———. *The Revolution of Moral Consciousness: Nietzsche in Russian Literature, 1890–1914*. DeKalb: Northern Illinois University Press, 1988.

Coe, Richard N. *When the Grass Was Taller: Autobiography and the Experience of Childhood*. New Haven, Conn.: Yale University Press, 1984.

Cook, Albert. "The Unity of *War and Peace*." *Western Review* 22 (1958): 243–55.

Costlow, Jane T., Stephanie Sandler, and Judith Vowles, eds. *Sexuality and the Body in Russian Culture*. Stanford, Calif.: Stanford University Press, 1993.

Cox, Gary. *Tyrant and Victim in Dostoevsky*. Columbus, Ohio: Slavica, 1984.

Cox, Randi. "'NEP without Nepmen!' Soviet Advertising and the Transition to Socialism." In *Everyday Life in Early Soviet Russia: Taking the Revolution Inside*, edited by Christina Kiaer and Eric Naiman, 119–52. Bloomington: Indiana University Press, 2006.

Crone, Anna Lisa. "Nietzschean, All Too Nietzschean? Rozanov's Anti-Christian Critique." In *Nietzsche in Russia*, edited by Bernice Glatzer Rosenthal, 95–112. Princeton, N.J.: Princeton University Press, 1986.

Culler, Jonathan. *Roland Barthes*. N.Y.: Oxford University Press, 1983.

Dadoun, Roger. "Du cannibalisme comme stade suprême du stalinisme." In *Destins du cannibalisme*, edited by J.-B. Pontalis, 269–72. Special issue, *Nouvelle Revue de Psychanalyse*, no. 6 (1972).

Danilevsky, N. *Darvinizm*. Saint Petersburg: M. E. Komarov, 1885–87.

———. *Rossiia i Evropa: Vzgliad na kul'turnye i politicheskie otnosheniia slavianskogo mira k Germano-Romanskomu*. Saint Petersburg: Obshchestvennaia pol'za, 1871.

Danilov, Vladimir. "Ten'er v russkoi literature." *Russkii arkhiv* 53, no. 2 (1915): 164–68.

Davie, Donald, ed. *Russian Literature and Modern English Fiction: A Collection of Critical Essays*. Chicago: University of Chicago Press, 1965.

De Jonge, Alex. *Dostoevsky and the Age of Intensity*. New York: St. Martin's Press, 1975.

Delvig, Anton. *Sochineniia Barona A. A. Delviga*. Saint Petersburg, 1895.

Demos, John, and Sarane Spence Boocock, eds. *Turning Points: Historical and Sociological Essays on the Family*. Chicago: University of Chicago Press, 1978.

Dennen, Johan M. G. van der. *The "Evil" Mind: Pt. 3. Cruelty and "Beast-in-Man" Imagery*. Groningen, Netherlands: Rijksuniversiteit, 2005.

Deutsch, Ronald M. *The New Nuts Among the Berries*. Palo Alto, Calif.: Bull Publishing, 1977.

Dijkstra, Bram. *Evil Sisters: The Threat of Female Sexuality and the Cult of Manhood*. New York: Knopf, 1996.

Diment, Galya, ed. *Goncharov's Oblomov: A Critical Companion*. Evanston, Ill.: Northwestern University Press, 1998.

———. "'Tolstoy or Dostoevsky' and the Modernists: Polemics with Joseph Brodsky." *Tolstoy Studies Journal* 3 (1990): 76–81.

Dobranov, Iurii. "Svidetel'stvo o bednosti." *Kniga i proletarskaia revoliutsiia*, no. 1 (1936): 102–103.

Dobzhansky, Theodosius. "The Crisis of Soviet Biology." In *Continuity and Change in Russian and Soviet Thought*, edited by Ernest J. Simmons, 329–46. Cambridge, Mass.: Harvard University Press, 1955.

Dolinin, A. S., ed. *F. M. Dostoevskii v vospominaniiakh sovremennikov*. Moscow: Khudozhestvennaia literatura, 1964.

Donskov, Andrew, ed. *L. N. Tolstoi–N. N. Strakhov: Polnoe sobranie perepiski / Leo Tolstoy & Nikolaj Strakhov: Complete Correspondence*. 2 vols. Ottawa and Moscow: Slavic Research Group at the University of Ottawa and the State L. N. Tolstoy Museum, 2003.

Dostoevskii, F. M. *Polnoe sobranie sochinenii*. 30 vols. Leningrad: Nauka, 1972–90.

Dostoevsky, Fyodor. *Memoirs from the House of the Dead*. Translated by Jessie Coulson. New York: Oxford University Press, 1983.

Dostoyevsky, Fyodor. *Winter Notes on Summer Impressions*. Translated by Kyril FitzLyon. London: Quartet Books, 1985.

Douglas, Mary. "Deciphering a Meal." *Daedalus* 101, no. 1 (1972): 61–81.

Draitser, Emil A. *Making War, Not Love: Gender and Sexuality in Russian Humor*. New York: St. Martin's Press, 1999.

Durant, J. R. "The Beast in Man: An Historical Perspective on the Biology of Human Aggression." In *The Biology of Aggression*, edited by Paul F. Brain, 17–46. Rockville, Md.: Sijthoff and Noordhoff, 1981.

Durkin, Andrew. *Sergei Asakov and Russian Pastoral*. New Brunswick, N.J.: Rutgers University Press, 1983.

Edwards, Robert. "Tolstoy and Alice B. Stockham: The Influence of 'Tokology' on *The Kreutzer Sonata*." *Tolstoy Studies Journal* 6 (1993): 87–106.

Engelgardt, Aleksandr N. *Letters from the Country, 1872–1887*. Translated and edited by Cathy A. Frierson. Oxford: Oxford University Press, 1993.

Engelstein, Laura. *The Keys to Happiness: Sex and the Search for Modernity in Fin-de-Siècle Russia*. Ithaca, N.Y.: Cornell University Press, 1992.

Enko, T. F. *Dostoevskii—intimnaia zhizn' geniia*. Moscow: MP Teleos, 1997.

Erofeev, Viktor. *V labirinte prokliatykh voprosov*. Moscow: Soiuz fotokhudozhnikov Rossii, 1996.

Evans, Mary. *Reflecting on Anna Karenina*. London: Routledge, 1989.

Fanger, Donald. *Dostoevsky and Romantic Realism: A Study of Dostoevsky in Relation to Balzac, Dickens, and Gogol*. Chicago: University of Chicago Press, 1965.

Farb, Peter, and George Armelagos. *Consuming Passions: The Anthropology of Eating*. Boston: Houghton Mifflin, 1980.

Feiler, Lily. "The Tolstoi Marriage: Conflict and Illusions." *Canadian Slavonic Papers* 23, no. 3 (1981): 245–60.

Feuer, Kathryn. "Stiva." In *Russian Literature and American Critics*, edited by Kenneth N. Brostrom, 347–56. Ann Arbor, Mich: University of Michigan, Department of Slavic Languages and Literatures, 1984.

Figes, Orlando. *Natasha's Dance: A Cultural History of Russia*. New York: Picador, 2002.

——, and Boris Kolonitskii. *Interpreting the Russian Revolution: The Languages and Symbols of 1917*. New Haven, Conn.: Yale University Press, 1999.

Finch, Henry LeRoy. Introduction to *Talks with Tolstoy*, by A. B. Goldenweizer, translated by S. S. Koteliansky and Virginia Woolf, 5–26. New York: Horizon Press, 1969.

Fink, Beatrice. "Food as Object, Activity, and Symbol in Sade." *Romanic Review* 65, no. 2 (1974): 96–102.

Fischler, Claude. *L'Homnivore: Le goût, la cuisine et le corps*. Paris: Odile Jacob, 1990.

FitzLyon, Kyril. Introduction to *Winter Notes on Summer Impressions*, by Fyodor Dostoyevsky, translated by Kyril FitzLyon, v–xiv. London: Quartet Books, 1985.

Fitzpatrick, Sheila. *The Cultural Front: Power and Culture in Revolutionary Russia*. Ithaca, N.Y.: Cornell University Press, 1992.

——. *Everyday Stalinism: Ordinary Life in Extraordinary Times: Soviet Russia in the 1930s*. New York: Oxford University Press, 1999.

Forster, E. M. *Aspects of the Novel*. New York: Harcourt, Brace, and World, 1954.

Foucault, Michel. *The Use of Pleasure*. Translated by Robert Hurley. New York: Vintage Books, 1985.

Frank, Joseph. *Dostoevsky: The Mantel of the Prophet, 1872–1881*. Princeton, N.J.: Princeton University Press, 2002.

——. *Dostoevsky: The Miraculous Years, 1865–1871*. Princeton, N.J.: Princeton University Press, 1995.

——. *Dostoevsky: The Seeds of Revolt, 1821–1849*. Princeton, N.J.: Princeton University Press, 1976.

——. *Dostoevsky: The Stir of Liberation, 1860–1865*. Princeton, N.J.: Princeton University Press, 1986.

——. *Dostoevsky: The Years of Ordeal, 1850–1859*. Princeton, N.J.: Princeton University Press, 1984.

Freud, Sigmund. "Dostoevsky and Parricide." In *Russian Literature and Psychoanalysis*, edited by Daniel Rancour-Laferriere, 41–57. Philadelphia: John Benjamins, 1989.

——. *A General Introduction to Psychoanalysis*. Translated by Joan Rivière. New York: Pocket, 1971.

——. *Three Essays on Sexuality*. Translated by James Strachey. New York: Basic Books, 1962.

Fridlender, G. M. *Realizm Dostoevskogo*. Moscow and Leningrad: Nauka, 1964.

Frierson, Cathy. *Peasant Icons: Representations of Rural People in Late Nineteenth-Century Russia*. Oxford: Oxford University Press, 1993.

Fromm, Erich. *The Anatomy of Human Destructiveness*. New York: Holt, Rinehart, and Winston, 1973.

Fusso, Susanne. *Discovering Sexuality in Dostoevsky*. Evanston, Ill.: Northwestern University Press, 2006.

Genis, Alexander. "Borders and Metamorphoses: Viktor Pelevin in the Context of Post-Soviet Literature." In *Twentieth-Century Russian Literature: Selected Papers from the Fifth World Congress of Central and East European Studies*, edited by Karen L. Ryan and Barry P. Scherr, 294–306. New York: St. Martin's Press, 2000.

Gigante, Denise, ed. *Gusto: Essential Writings in Nineteenth-Century Gastronomy*. New York: Routledge, 2005.

Gilferding, A. *Sobranie sochinenii*. Saint Petersburg, 1868.

Givens, John. "Wombs, Tombs, and Mother Love: A Freudian Reading of Goncharov's *Oblomov*." In *Goncharov's Oblomov: A Critical Companion*, edited by Galya Diment, 90–109. Evanston, Ill.: Northwestern University Press, 1998.

Gladkov, Fedor. "Tsement," *Krasnaia nov'*, no. 1 (1925): 66–110; no. 2 (1925): 73–109; no. 3 (1925): 47–81; no. 4 (1925): 57–87; no. 5 (1925): 75–111; no. 6 (1925): 39–74.

Goldenweizer, A. B. *Talks with Tolstoy*. Translated by S. S. Koteliansky and Virginia Woolf. New York: Horizon Press, 1969.

Goldman, Wendy. *Women, the State, and Revolution: Soviet Family Policy and Social Life, 1917–1936*. New York: Cambridge University Press, 1993.

Goldstein, Darra. "Domestic Porkbarreling in Nineteenth-Century Russia; or, Who Holds the Keys to the Larder?" In *Russia—Women—Culture*, edited by Helena Goscilo and Beth Holmgren, 125–51. Bloomington: Indiana University Press, 1996.

———. "Tolstoy's Table." In *The Vegetarian Hearth: Recipes and Reflections for the Cold Season*, 205–49. New York: HarperCollins, 1996.

Goody, Jack. *Cooking, Cuisine and Class*. Cambridge: Cambridge University Press, 1968.

Gor'kii, Maksim. *O literature*. Moscow: Khudozhestvennaia literatura, 1961.

———. *Sobranie sochinenii*. Moscow: Khudozhestvennaia literatura, 1963.

Gornfel'd, A. G. *Knigi i liudi. Literaturnye besedy*. Saint Petersburg: Zhizn', 1908.

Goscilo, Helena. "Tolstoyan Fare: Credo à la Carte." *Slavonic and East European Review* 62, no. 4 (1984): 481–95.

Graffy, Julian. "Passion Versus Habit in *Old World Landowners*." In *Nikolay Gogol: Text and Context*, edited by Jane Grayson and Faith Wigzell, 34–49. New York: St. Martin's Press, 1989.

Grieco, Allen J. *Themes in Art: The Meal*. London: Scala Books, 1991.

Grigor'ev, Apollon. *Literaturnaia kritika*. Moscow: Khudozhestvennaia literatura, 1967.

———. "Vzgliad na russkuiu literaturu so smerti Pushkina." *Russkoe slovo*, no. 2, otd. II (1859): 1–63 and no. 3 (1859): 1–39.

Gronow, Jukka. *Caviar with Champagne: Common Luxury and the Ideals of the Good Life in Stalin's Russia*. New York: Berg, 2003.

Grossman, Joan. "Tolstoy's Portrait of Anna: Keystone in the Arch." *Criticism* 18, no. 1 (1976): 1–14.

Grossman, Leonid. *Tvorchestvo Dostoevskogo*. Moscow: Sovremennye problemy, 1928.

Grot, N. Ia. "Nravstvennye idealy nashego vremeni: Fridrikh Nitsshe i Lev Tolstoi." *Voprosy filosofii i psikhologii* 16 (1893): 129–54.

Gura, A. V. *Simvolika zhivotnykh v slavianskoi narodnoi traditsii*. Moscow: Indrik, 1997.

Gusev, A. *O brake i bezbrachii. Protiv "Kreitserovoi sonaty" i "Poslesloviia" k nei grafa L. Tolstogo*. Kazan', 1891.

Gustafson, Richard. *Leo Tolstoy, Resident and Stranger: A Study in Fiction and Theology*. Princeton, N.J.: Princeton University Press, 1986.

Gutkin, Irina. "The Dichotomy between Flesh and Spirit: Plato's *Symposium* in *Anna Karenina*." In *In the Shade of the Giant: Essays on Tolstoy*, edited by Hugh McLean, 84–99. Berkeley and Los Angeles: University of California Press, 1989.

Hagan, John. "Ambivalence in Tolstoy's *The Cossacks*." *Novel: A Forum on Fiction* 3, no. 1 (1969): 28–47.

Halfin, Igal. *Terror in My Soul: Communist Autobiographies on Trial*. Cambridge, Mass.: Harvard University Press, 2003.

Harper, Kenneth E. "Under the Influence of Oblomov." In *From Los Angeles to Kiev: Papers on the Occasion of the Ninth International Congress of Slavists*, edited by Vladimir Markov and Dean S. Worth, 105–18. Columbus, Ohio: Slavica, 1983.

Harris, Marvin. *Cannibals and Kings: The Origins of Culture*. New York: Random House, 1977.

Hessler, Julie. "Cultured Trade: The Stalinist Turn towards Consumerism." In *Stalinism: New Directions*, edited by Sheila Fitzpatrick, 182–209. London: Routledge, 2000.

Hillyard, Paul. *The Book of the Spider: From Arachnophobia to the Love of Spiders*. New York: Random House, 1994.

Hingley, Ronald. Introduction to *Memoirs from the House of the Dead*, by Fyodor Dostoevsky, translated by Jessie Coulson, vii–xviii. New York: Oxford University Press, 1983.

Hinz, Evelyn J., ed. *Diet and Discourse: Eating, Drinking and Literature*. Winnipeg: University of Manitoba Press, 1991. Special issue, *Mosaic: A Journal for the Interdisciplinary Study of Literature* 24, nos. 3–4 (1991).

Holquist, Michael. "How Sons Become Fathers." In *Fyodor Dostoevsky's "The Brothers Karamazov,"* edited by Harold Bloom, 39–51. New York: Chelsea House, 1988.

Horwatt, Karin. "Food and the Adulterous Woman: Sexual and Social Morality in *Anna Karenina.*" *Language and Literature* 13 (1988): 35–67.

Houston, Gail Turley. *Consuming Fictions: Gender, Class, and Hunger in Dickens's Novels.* Carbondale, Ill.: Southern Illinois University Press, 1994.

Hubbs, Joanna. *Mother Russia: The Feminine Myth in Russian Culture.* Bloomington: Indiana University Press, 1988.

Inniss, Kenneth. *D. H. Lawrence's Bestiary: A Study of His Use of Animal Trope and Symbol.* The Hague: Mouton, 1962.

Iskander, Fazel. *Rabbits and Boa Constrictors.* Translated by Ronald E. Peterson. Ann Arbor, Mich.: Ardis, 1989.

Jackson, Robert L. *Dialogues with Dostoevsky: The Overwhelming Questions.* Stanford, Calif.: Stanford University Press, 1993.

Jeanneret, Michel. *Des mets et des mots: banquets et propos de table à la Renaissance.* Paris: Librairie José Corti, 1987.

———. *A Feast of Words: Banquets and Table Talk in the Renaissance.* Translated by Jeremy Whiteley and Emma Hughes. Chicago: University of Chicago Press, 1991.

———. "Ma patrie est une citrouille: thèmes alimentaires dans Rabelais et Folengo." In *Littérature et gastronomie: Huit études,* edited by Ronald W. Tobin, 113–48. Paris and Seattle: Papers on French Seventeenth-Century Literature, 1985.

Jones, Malcolm. *Dostoyevsky: The Novel of Discord.* New York: Harper and Row, 1976.

Kaplan, Fred. *Dickens: A Biography.* New York: Morrow, 1988.

Karamzin, Nikolai. *Istoriia gosudarstva rossiiskogo.* 12 vols. Saint Petersburg, 1816–29.

Kariakin, Iu. *Dostoevskii i kanun XXI veka.* Moscow: Sovetskii pisatel', 1989.

Karlinsky, Simon. "Dostoevsky as Rorschach Test." *New York Times Book Review.* June 13, 1971, p. 1, 16, 18, 20, 22–23.

Kasatkina, Tat'iana. "Kak my chitaem russkuiu literaturu: O sladostrastii." *Novyi mir,* no. 7 (1999): 170–82.

Kashina-Evreinova, A. *Podpol'ie geniia (Seksual'nye istochniki tvorchestva Dostoevskogo).* Petrograd: Tret'ia strazha, 1923.

Katz, Michael R. *Dreams and the Unconscious in Nineteenth-Century Russian Fiction.* Hanover, N.H.: University Press of New England, 1984.

Kaufman, F. "Dostojevskij a Markyz de Sade." *Filosofický časopis* 3 (1968): 384–89.

Kelly, Aileen. *Toward Another Shore: Russian Thinkers Between Necessity and Chance.* New Haven, Conn.: Yale University Press, 1998.

Kelly, Catriona, and David Shepherd, eds. *Constructing Russian Culture in the Age of Revolution: 1881–1940*. New York: Oxford University Press, 1998.

Kilgour, Maggie. *From Communion to Cannibalism: An Anatomy of Metaphors of Incorporation*. Princeton, N.J.: Princeton University Press, 1990.

Kiltz, Halmut. *Das erotische Mahl: Szenen aus dem "chambre séparée" des neunzehnten Jahrhundert*. Frankfurt: Syndikat, 1983.

Kincaid, J. R. *Dickens and the Rhetoric of Laughter*. Oxford: Clarendon Press, 1971.

Kinser, Samuel. *Rabelais' Carnival: Text, Context, Metatext*. Oxford: Oxford University Press, 1990.

Kjetsaa, Geir. *Fyodor Dostoyevsky: A Writer's Life*. Translated by Siri Hustvedt and David McDuff. New York: Viking Penguin, 1987.

Klama, John. *Aggression: The Myth of the Beast Within*. New York: Wiley, 1988.

Kline, George L. "Darwinism and the Russian Orthodox Church." In *Continuity and Change in Russian and Soviet Thought*, edited by Ernest J. Simmons, 307–28. Cambridge, Mass.: Harvard University Press, 1955.

Knapp, Liza. *The Annihilation of Inertia: Dostoevsky and Metaphysics*. Evanston, Ill.: Northwestern University Press, 1996.

Kolb, Jocelyne. *The Ambiguity of Taste: Freedom and Food in European Romanticism*. Ann Arbor: University of Michigan Press, 1995.

Kolb-Seletski, Natalia. "Gastronomy, Gogol, and His Fiction." *Slavic Review* 29, no. 1 (1970): 35–57.

Kommunist. "Asketizm ili Kommunizm?" *Voronezhskaia kommuna*, August 11, 1921.

Kon, Igor. *The Sexual Revolution in Russia: From the Age of the Czars to Today*. Translated by James Riordan. New York: Free Press, 1995.

———. "Sexuality and Culture." In *Sex and Russian Society*, edited by Igor Kon and James Riordan, 15–44. Bloomington: Indiana University Press, 1993.

Kopper, John M. "Tolstoy and the Narrative of Sex: A Reading of 'Father Sergius,' 'The Devil,' and 'The Kreutzer Sonata.'" In *In the Shade of the Giant: Essays on Tolstoy*, edited by Hugh McLean, 158–86. Berkeley and Los Angeles: University of California Press, 1989.

Kornblatt, Judith Deutsch. *The Cossack Hero in Russian Literature: A Study in Cultural Mythology*. Madison: University of Wisconsin Press, 1992.

Koropeckyj, Roman. "Desire and Procreation in the Ukrainian Tales of Hryhorii Kvitka-Osnov'ianenko." *Canadian Slavonic Papers* 44, nos. 3–4 (2002): 165–73.

Korotkov, G. "Literatura sobach'ego pereulka." *Rezets* 15 (1927): 14–16.

Kovachev, V. A., ed. *Istoriia russkogo sovetskogo romana*. vol. 1. Moscow and Leningrad: Nauka, 1965.

Kraev, Leonid. *Bolshevitskie pauki i khrest'ianskiia mukhi*. Rostov-on-Don, 1919.

Kuznetsov, Sergei. "Fedor Dostoevskii i Markiz de Sad: Sviazi i pereklichki." In *Dostoevskii v kontse XX veka*, edited by K. A. Stepanian, 557–74. Moscow: Klassika plius, 1996.

Kvitka-Osnov'ianenko, Grigorii. *Pan Khaliavskii*. Kiev: Dnipro, 1984.

———. *Proza*. Moscow: Sovetskaia Rossiia, 1990.

LaBriolle, François de. "Oblomov n'est-il qu'un paresseux?" *Cahiers du monde russe et soviétique* 10, no. 1 (1969): 38–51.

Lane, Ann Marie. "Nietzsche Comes to Russia: Popularization and Protest in the 1890s." In *Nietzsche in Russia*, edited by Bernice Glatzer Rosenthal, 51–68. Princeton, N.J.: Princeton University Press, 1986.

Lary, N. M. *Dostoevsky and Dickens: A Study of Literary Influence*. London: Routledge and Kegan Paul, 1973.

Lavrin, Janko. *Goncharov*. New Haven, Conn.: Yale University Press, 1954.

Lawrence, D. H. *Collected Letters*. Edited by Harry T. Moore. 2 vols. New York: Viking Press, 1962.

Layton, Susan. "A Hidden Polemic with Leo Tolstoy: Afanasy Fet's Lyric 'Mine was the madness he wanted . . . .'" *Russian Review* 62, no. 2 (2007): 220–37.

LeBlanc, Ronald D. "Alimentary Violence: Eating as a Trope in Russian Literature." In *Times of Trouble: Violence in Russian Literature and Culture*, edited by Marcus Levitt and Tatyana Novikov, 154–77. Madison: University of Wisconsin Press, 2007.

———. "An Appetite for Power: Predators, Carnivores, and Cannibals in Dostoevsky's Novels." In *Food in Russian History and Culture*, edited by Joyce Toomre and Musya Glants, 124–45. Bloomington: Indiana University Press, 1997.

———. "Food, Orality, and Nostalgia for Childhood: Gastronomic Slavophilism in Midnineteenth-Century Russian Fiction." *Russian Review* 58, no. 2 (1999): 244–67.

———. "Gluttony and Power in Iurii Olesha's *Envy*." *Russian Review* 60, no. 2 (2001): 220–37.

———. "Levin Visits Anna: The Iconology of Harlotry." *Tolstoy Studies Journal* 3 (1990): 1–20.

———. "The Monarch as Glutton: Vasily Narezhny's *The Black Year*." In *Diet and Discourse: Eating, Drinking, and Literature*, edited by Evelyn J. Hinz, 53–67. Winnipeg: Mosaic, 1991.

———. "Oblomov's Consuming Passion: Food, Eating, and the Search for Communion." In *Goncharov's Oblomov: A Critical Companion*, edited by Galya Diment, 110–135. Evanston, Ill.: Northwestern University Press, 1998).

———. "Saninism Versus Tolstoyism: The Anti-Tolstoyan Subtext in Mikhail Artsybashev's *Sanin*." *Tolstoy Studies Journal* 18 (2006): 16–32.

———. "The Sweet Seduction of Sin: Food, Sexual Desire, and Ideological Purity in Alexander Tarasov-Rodionov's *Shokolad*." *Gastronomica: The Journal of Food and Culture* 3, no. 4 (2003): 31–41.

———. "Teniers, Flemish Art, and the Natural School Debate." *Slavic Review* 50, no. 3 (1991): 576–89.

———. "Teniersism: Seventeenth-Century Flemish Art and Early Nineteenth-Century Russian Prose." *Russian Review* 49, no. 1 (1990): 19–41.

———. "Tolstoy's Body: Diet, Desire, and Denial." In *Cultures of the Abdomen: Diet, Digestion and Fat in the Modern World*, edited by Christopher E. Forth and Ana Carden-Coyne, 147–66. London: Palgrave Macmillan, 2004.

———. "Tolstoy's Way of No Flesh: Abstinence, Vegetarianism, and Christian Physiology." In *Food in Russian History and Culture*, edited by Joyce Toomre and Musya Glants, 81–102. Bloomington: Indiana University Press, 1997.

———. "Trapped in a Spider's Web of Animal Lust: Human Bestiality in Lev Gumilevsky's *Dog Alley*." *Russian Review* 65, no. 2 (2006): 171–93.

———. "Unpalatable Pleasures: Tolstoy, Food, and Sex." *Tolstoy Studies Journal* 6 (1993): 1–32.

———. "Vegetarianism in Russia: The Tolstoy(an) Legacy." *Carl Beck Papers in Russian and East European Studies*, no. 1507. Pittsburgh, Pa.: University of Pittsburgh Center for Russian and East European Studies, 2001.

Lermontov, Mikhail. *Sobranie sochinenii v chetyrekh tomakh*. Moscow and Leningrad: Akademiia nauk, 1958–59.

Leskov, Nikolai. *Polnoe sobranie sochinenii*. Saint Petersburg, 1903.

Levin, Eve. *Sex and Society in the World of the Orthodox Slavs, 900–1700*. Ithaca, N.Y.: Cornell University Press, 1989.

———. "Sexual Vocabulary in Medieval Russia." In *Sexuality and the Body in Russian Culture*, edited by Jane T. Costlow, Stephanie Sandler, and Judith Vowles, 41–52. Stanford, Calif.: Stanford University Press, 1993.

Lévi-Strauss, Claude. *Structural Anthropology*. Garden City, N.Y.: Doubleday, 1967.

Lewis, B. A. "Darwin and Dostoevsky." *Melbourne Slavonic Studies*, no. 11 (1976): 23–32.

Libknekht, V. *Pauki i mukhi*. New York: Novy Mir, 1917.

Linnér, Sven. *Starets Zosima in "The Brothers Karamazov": A Study in the Mimesis of Virtue*. Stockholm: Almqvist and Wiksell, 1975.

Livers, Keith. "Bugs in the Body Politic: The Search for Self in Viktor Pelevin's *The Life of Insects*." *Slavic and East European Journal* 46, no. 1 (2002): 1–28.

Losev, Lev. "Poetika kukhni." In Vail' and Genis, *Russkaia kukhnia v izgnanii*, 3–20. Los Angeles: Almanakh, 1987.

Loshchits, Iurii. *Goncharov*. Moscow: Molodaia gvardiia, 1977.

Luker, Nicholas. *In Defence of a Reputation: Essays on the Early Prose of Mikhail Artsybashev*. Nottingham, Eng.: Astra Press, 1990.

Lyngstad, Alexandra, and Sverre Lyngstad. *Ivan Goncharov*. New York: Twayne, 1971.

Magarshack, David. *Gogol: A Life*. New York: Grove, 1957.

Makovitskii, D. P. *U Tolstogo 1904–1910: "Iasnopolianskie zapiski" D. P. Makovitskogo*. Literaturnoe nasledstvo, vol. 90. Moscow: Nauka, 1979.

Mandelker, Amy. *Framing Anna Karenina: Tolstoy, the Woman Question, and the Victorian Novel*. Columbus: Ohio State University Press, 1993.

Mann, Thomas. "Goethe and Tolstoy." In *Essays by Thomas Mann*, translated by H. T. Lowe-Porter, 76–179. New York: Vintage Books, 1958.

Margolin, Jean-Claude, and Robert Sauzet, eds. *Pratiques et discours alimentaires à la Renaissance*. Paris: Maisonneuve, 1982.

Marin, Louis. *Food for Thought*. Translated by Mette Hjort. Baltimore, Md.: Johns Hopkins University Press, 1989.

———. *La parole mangée et autres essais théologico-politiques*. Paris: Librairie des Méridiens–Klincksieck, 1986.

Marinelli, Peter V. *The Pastoral*. London: Methuen, 1971.

Marlowe, James E. "English Cannibalism: Dickens After 1859." *Studies in English Literature, 1500–1900* 23, no. 4 (1983): 647–66.

Matich, Olga. "A Typology of Fallen Women in Nineteenth-Century Russian Literature." In *American Contributions to the Ninth International Congress of Slavists*. Vol. 2: *Literature, Politics, History*, edited by Paul Debreczeny, 325–43. Columbus, Ohio: Slavica, 1983.

Matlaw, Ralph. "Recurrent Imagery in Dostoevskij." *Harvard Slavic Studies* 3 (1957): 201–25.

Matthews, Mervyn. *Privilege in the Soviet Union: A Study of Elite Life-Styles under Communism*. London: Allen and Unwin, 1978.

Mays, Milton. "Oblomov as Anti-Faust," *Western Humanities Review* 21, no. 2 (1967): 141–52.

McDowell, Andrea Rossing. "Situating the Beast: Animals and Animal Imagery in Nineteenth- and Twentieth-Century Russian Literature." Ph.D. diss., Indiana University, 2001.

McLean, Hugh. "Gogol's Retreat from Love: Toward an Interpretation of *Mirgorod*." In *Russian Literature and Psychoanalysis*, edited by Daniel Rancour-Laferriere, 101–22. Philadelphia: John Benjamins, 1989.

———, ed. *In the Shade of the Giant: Essays on Tolstoy*. Berkeley and Los Angeles: University of California Press, 1989.

McMaster, R. D. "Birds of Prey: A Study of *Our Mutual Friend*." *Dalhousie Review* 40, no. 3 (1960): 372–81.

McReynolds, Louise. Introduction to *The Wrath of Dionysus*, by Evdokiia Nagrodskaia, translated and edited by Louise McReynolds, vii–xxviii. Bloomington: Indiana University Press, 1997.

Mehring, Sigmar. *Groshevaia sonata*. Saint Petersburg, 1890.

Merejkovski, Dmitry. *Tolstoi as Man and Artist; with an essay on Dostoïevski*. Westport, Conn.: Greenwood Press, 1970.

Merezhkovskii, Dmitrii. *L. Tolstoi i Dostoevskii: Vechnye sputniki*. Moscow: Respublika, 1995.

———. *Polnoe sobranie sochinenii.* 16 vols. Hildesheim and New York: Georg Olms, 1973.

Mersereau, John, Jr. *Russian Romantic Fiction.* Ann Arbor, Mich.: Ardis, 1983.

Meshcheriakov, V. P. "Lukavyi letopisets pomestnogo byta." In Kvitka-Osnov'ianenko, *Proza,* 3-20. Moscow: Sovetskaia Rossiia, 1990.

Midgely, Mary. *Beast and Man: The Roots of Human Nature.* New York: New American Library, 1980.

Mikhailovskii, N. K. *Literaturnye vospominaniia i sovremennaia smuta.* Saint Petersburg, 1900.

Mikhailovsky, N. K. *Dostoevsky: A Cruel Talent.* Translated by Spencer Cadmus. Ann Arbor, Mich.: Ardis, 1978.

Mikoian, Anastas I. *Pishchevaia industriia Sovetskogo Soiuza.* Leningrad: Partizdat, 1936.

Miller, Rene Fueloep. "Tolstoy the Apostolic Crusader." *Russian Review* 19, no. 2 (1960): 99–121.

Miller, Robin Feuer. *The Brothers Karamazov: Worlds of the Novel.* New York: Twayne Publishers, 1992.

———. *Dostoevsky and "The Idiot:" Author, Narrator, and Reader.* Cambridge, Mass.: Harvard University Press, 1981.

Mirsky, D. S. *A History of Russian Literature: From Its Beginnings to 1900.* Edited by Francis J. Whitfield. New York: Vintage Books, 1958.

Mochulsky, Konstantin. *Dostoevsky: His Life and Work.* Translated by Michael A. Minihan. Princeton, N.J.: Princeton University Press, 1967.

Møller, Peter Ulf. *Postlude to The Kreutzer Sonata: Tolstoj and the Debate on Sexual Morality in Russian Literature of the 1890s.* Translated by John Kendal. New York: E. J. Brill, 1988.

Mondry, Henrietta. "Beyond the Boundary: Vasilii Rozanov and the Animal Body." *Slavic and East European Journal* 43, no. 4 (1999): 651–73.

Morris, Marcia. *Saints and Revolutionaries: The Ascetic Hero in Russian Literature.* Albany: State University of New York Press, 1993.

Morson, Gary Saul. *The Boundaries of Genre: Dostoevsky's "Diary of a Writer" and the Traditions of Literary Utopia.* Austin: University of Texas Press, 1981.

———. "Prosaics and Anna Karenina." *Tolstoy Studies Journal* 1 (1988): 1–12.

Murav, Harriet. *Holy Foolishness: Dostoevsky's Novels and the Poetics of Cultural Critique.* Stanford, Calif.: Stanford University Press, 1992.

Mykhed, Pavel. "O prirode i kharaktere smekha v romanakh V. T. Narezhnogo." *Voprosy russkoi literatury* 2 (1983): 87–92.

Nagrodskaia, Evdokiia. *Gnev Dionisa.* Saint Petersburg: Severo-Zapad, 1994.

———. *The Wrath of Dionysus.* Translated and edited by Louise McReynolds. Bloomington: Indiana University Press, 1997.

Naiman, Eric. "Historectomies: On the Metaphysics of Reproduction in a Utopian Age." In *Sexuality and the Body in Russian Culture*, edited by Jane T. Costlow, Stephanie Sandler, and Judith Vowles, 255–76. Stanford, Calif.: Stanford University Press, 1993.

———. Introduction to *Happy Moscow*, by Andrei Platonov, translated by Robert and Elizabeth Chandler, xi-xxxvii. London: Harvill Press, 2001.

———. *Sex in Public: The Incarnation of Early Soviet Ideology.* Princeton, N.J.: Princeton University Press, 1997.

Nicholson, Mervyn. "Eat—or Be Eaten: An Interdisciplinary Metaphor." In *Diet and Discourse: Eating, Drinking and Literature*, edited by Evelyn J. Hinz, 191–210. Winnipeg, Canada: Mosaic, 1991.

Nickell, William. "The Twain Shall Be of One Mind: Tolstoy in 'Leag' with Eliza Burnz and Henry Parkhurst." *Tolstoy Studies Journal* 6 (1993): 123–51.

Nikolaev, P. V. "L. N. Tolstoi i M. P. Artsybashev." In *Tolstoi i o Tolstom. Materialy i issledovaniia*, edited by K. K. Lomunov, 221–44. Moscow: Nasledie, 1998.

Nilsson, Nils Åke. "Food Images in Čechov. A Bachtinian Approach." *Scando-Slavica* 32 (1986): 27–40.

Nissenbaum, Stephen. *Sex, Diet and Debility: Sylvester Graham and Health Reform.* Westport, Conn.: Greenwood Press, 1980.

Nietzsche, Friedrich. *Thus Spoke Zarathustra.* Translated by R. J. Hollingdale. Baltimore, Md.: Penguin Books, 1961.

Norris, Margot. *Beasts of the Modern Imagination: Darwin, Nietzsche, Kafka, Ernst, and Lawrence.* Baltimore, Md.: Johns Hopkins University Press, 1985.

Obolenskii, L. E. "Otkrytoe pis'mo L. N. Tolstomu." *Novosti i birzhevaia gazeta* 85 (March 27, 1890).

Odoevskii, Vladimir. *Pestrye skazki.* Durham, Eng.: University of Durham, 1987.

Olesha, Iurii. *Izbrannoe.* Moscow: Khudozhestvennaia literatura, 1974.

Olyesha, Yuri. *"Love" and Other Stories.* Translated by Robert Payne. New York: Washington Square Press, 1967.

Omel'chenko, A. P. *Geroi nezdorovogo tvorchestva ("Sanin" roman Artsybasheva).* Saint Petersburg: Sever, 1908.

Opul'skaia, L. D. "Tvorcheskaia istoriia povesti 'Kholstomer.'" In *Literaturnoe nasledstvo* 69, book 1, edited by I. I. Anisimov, 257–90. Moscow: Akademiia nauk, 1961.

Orwin, Donna. *Tolstoy's Art and Thought, 1847–1880.* Princeton, N.J.: Princeton University Press, 1993.

Ostrovskii, Aleksandr. *Sobranie sochinenii.* Moscow: Khudozhestvennaia literatura, 1960.

Otradin, M. V. "'Son Oblomova' kak khudozhestvennoe tseloe." *Russkaia literatura* no. 1 (1992): 3–17.

Payer, Pierre J. *The Bridling of Desire: Views of Sex in the Later Middle Ages.* Toronto: University of Toronto Press, 1993.

Payne, Robert. Introduction to *"Love" and Other Stories*, by Yuri Olyesha, translated by Robert Payne, ix–xxiii. New York: Washington Square Press, 1967.

Peace, Richard. *Dostoyevsky: An Examination of the Major Novels.* Cambridge: Cambridge University Press, 1971.

———. *Oblomov: A Critical Examination of Goncharov's Novel.* Birmingham, Eng.: University of Birmingham, 1991.

Pearson, Irene. "The Social and Moral Roles of Food in *Anna Karenina*." *Journal of Russian Studies* 48 (1984): 10–19.

Pelevin, Victor. *The Life of Insects.* Translated by Andrew Bromfield. New York: Penguin, 1999.

Pelevin, Viktor. *Zhizn' nasekomykh: Romany.* Moscow: Vagrius, 1999.

Phelps, William Lyon. *Essays on Russian Novelists.* New York: Macmillan, 1926.

Pil'niak, Boris. *Golyi god.* Chicago: Russian Language Specialties, 1966.

———. *Mashiny i volki.* Munich: Wilhelm Fink, 1971.

Pilnyak, Boris. *Chinese Story and Other Tales.* Translated and with an introduction and notes by Vera T. Reck and Michael Green. Norman: University of Oklahoma Press, 1988.

Pisemskii, Aleksei. *Sobranie sochinenii.* Moscow: Pravda, 1959.

Plato. *The Republic.* Translated by Raymond Larson. Arlington Heights, Ill.: Harlan Davidson, 1979.

Platonov, Andrei. *Chut'e pravdy.* Edited by V. A. Chalmaev. Moscow: Sovetskaia Rossiia, 1990.

———. *Happy Moscow.* Translated by Robert and Elizabeth Chandler. London: Harvill Press, 2001.

Poggioli, Renato. "Gogol's 'Old-World Landowners': An Inverted Eclogue." *Indiana Slavic Studies* 3 (1963): 4–72.

———. "Kafka and Dostoyevsky." In *The Kafka Problem*, edited by Angel Flores, 107–17. New York: Gordian Press, 1975.

———. *The Phoenix and the Spider: A Book of Essays About Some Russian Writers and Their View of the Self.* Cambridge, Mass.: Harvard University Press, 1957.

Polevoi, P. N. *Istoriia russkoi slovesnosti s drevneishikh vremen do nashikh dnei.* Saint Petersburg: A. F. Marks, 1900.

Pontalis, J.-B., ed. *Destins du cannibalisme.* Special issue, *Nouvelle Revue de Psychanalyse*, no. 6 (1972).

Praz, Mario. *The Romantic Agony.* Translated by Angus Davidson. New York: Oxford University Press, 1970.

Probyn, Elspeth. *Carnal Appetites: FoodSexIdentities.* London: Routledge, 2000.

Prugavin, A. S. *O L've Tolstom i o tolstovtsakh: Ocherki, vospominaniia, materialy.* Moscow: I. D. Sytin, 1911.

Rancour-Laferriere, Daniel, ed. *Russian Literature and Psychoanalysis*.
Philadelphia: John Benjamins, 1989.

———. *The Slave Soul of Russia: Moral Masochism and the Cult of Suffering*. New
York: New York University Press, 1995.

———. *Tolstoy on the Couch: Misogyny, Masochism and the Absent Mother*. New York:
New York University Press, 1998.

Ratushinskaia, Irina. *A Tale of Three Heads*. Translated by Diane Nemec-Ignashev.
Tenafly, N.J.: Hermitage, 1986.

Rawson, Claude J. "Cannibalism and Fiction: Reflections on Narrative Form and
'Extreme Situations.'" *Genre* 10 (1977): 667–711 and 11 (1978): 227–313.

Reck, Vera T., and Michael Green. Introduction to *Chinese Story and Other Tales*,
by Boris Pilnyak, translated by Vera T. Reck and Michael Green, 3–14.
Norman: University of Oklahoma Press, 1988.

Rice, Martin P. "Dostoevskij's *Notes from Underground* and Hegel's 'Master and
Slave.'" *Canadian-American Slavic Studies* 8, no. 3 (1974): 359–69.

Rodnianskaia, Irina. "Mezhdu Konom i Dostoevskim: Replika Vitaliiu Svintsovu."
*Novyi mir*, no. 5 (1999): 213–15.

Rogers, James Allen. "Darwinism, Scientism, and Nihilism." *Russian Review* 19,
no. 1 (1960): 10–23.

Rosenthal, Bernice Glatzer, ed. *Nietzsche and Soviet Culture: Ally and Adversary*.
Cambridge: Cambridge University Press, 1994.

———, ed. *Nietzsche in Russia*. Princeton, N.J.: Princeton University Press, 1986.

Rossman, Edward. "The Conflict over Food in the Works of J.-K. Huysmans."
*Nineteenth-Century French Studies* 2, nos. 1 and 2 (1973–74): 61–67.

Rozanov, Vasilii. *Opavshie list'ia*. Moscow: Sovremennik, 1992.

———. "Po povodu odnoi trevogi grafa L. N. Tolstogo." *Russkii vestnik* no. 8 (1895):
154–87.

Ryan, Karen L., and Barry P. Scherr, eds. *Twentieth-Century Russian Literature:
Selected Papers from the Fifth World Congress of Central and East European
Studies*. New York: St. Martin's Press, 2000.

Sagan, Eli. *Cannibalism: Human Aggression and Cultural Form*. New York: Harper,
1974.

Sanday, Peggy Reeve. *Divine Hunger: Cannibalism as a Cultural System*.
Cambridge: Cambridge University Press, 1986.

Schmidt, Paul. "What Do Oysters Mean?" *Antaeus* 68 (1992): 105–11.

Schofield, Mary Anne, ed. *Cooking by the Book: Food in Literature and Culture*.
Bowling Green, Ohio: Bowling Green State University Popular Press, 1989.

Sergeenko, A. P. *Rasskazy o L. N. Tolstom: iz vospominanii*. Moscow: Sovetskii
pisatel', 1978.

Schultze, Sydney. *The Structure of Anna Karenina*. Ann Arbor, Mich.: Ardis,
1982.

Siegel, George. "The Fallen Woman in Nineteenth-Century Literature." *Harvard Slavic Studies* 5 (1970): 81–107.

Simmons, Ernest J., ed. *Continuity and Change in Russian and Soviet Thought*. Cambridge, Mass.: Harvard University Press, 1955.

Skelton, Isaac. "The Vegetarian Tradition in Russian Literature." Unpublished manuscript.

Smith, Alison K. *Recipes for Russia: Food and Nationhood Under the Tsars*. DeKalb: Northern Illinois University Press, 2008.

Smith-Rosenberg, Carroll. "Sex as Symbol in Victorian Purity: An Ethnohistorical Analysis of Jacksonian America." In *Turning Points: Historical and Sociological Essays on the Family*, edited by John Demos and Sarane Spence Boocock, 212–47. Chicago: University of Chicago Press, 1978.

Smoluchowski, Louise. *Lev and Sonya: The Story of the Tolstoy Marriage*. New York: Paragon House Publishers, 1987.

Sokolov, Boris. *Moia kniga o Vladimire Sorokine*. Moscow: AIRO, 2005.

Sokolow, Jayme A., and Priscilla R. Roosevelt. "Leo Tolstoi's Christian Pacifism: The American Contribution." *Carl Beck Papers in Russian and East European Studies*, no. 604. Pittsburgh, Pa.: University of Pittsburgh Center for Russian and East European Studies, 1987.

Solov'ev, Vladimir. *Sobranie sochinenii Vladimira Sergeevicha Solov'eva*. Saint Petersburg: Obshchestvennaia Pol'za, 1901–03.

Somerwil-Ayrton, S. K. *Poverty and Power in the Early Works of Dostoevskij*. Amsterdam: Rodopi, 1988.

Sorokin, Boris. *Tolstoy in Prerevolutionary Russian Criticism*. Columbus: Ohio State University Press, 1979.

Sorokin, Vladimir. *Pir*. Moscow: Ad Marginem, 2001.

———. "Russia Is Slipping Back into an Authoritarian Empire." *Der Spiegel Online*, February 2, 2007.

Spence, G. W. *Tolstoy the Ascetic*. New York: Barnes and Noble, 1968.

Spencer, Colin. *The Heretic's Feast: A History of Vegetarianism*. London: Fourth Estate, 1993.

Steiner, George. *Tolstoy or Dostoevsky: An Essay in the Old Criticism*. New York: Dutton, 1971.

Stilman, Leon. "Oblomovka Revisited." *American Slavic and East European Review* 7, no. 1 (1948): 45–77.

Stites, Richard. *Revolutionary Dreams: Utopian Visions and Experimental Life in the Russian Revolution*. New York: Oxford University Press, 1989.

———. *The Women's Liberation Movement in Russia: Feminism, Nihilism, and Bolshevism, 1860–1930*. Princeton, N.J.: Princeton University Press, 1978.

Stone, Harry. *The Night Side of Dickens: Cannibalism, Passion, Necessity*. Columbus: Ohio State University Press, 1994.

Stoppard, Tom. *Arcadia*. London: Faber and Faber, 1993.

Storr, Anthony. *Human Destructiveness: The Roots of Genocide and Human Cruelty*. New York: Basic Books, 1972.

Strakhov, Nikolai. *Kriticheskie stat'i (1861–1894)*. Kiev: Izdatel'stvo I. P. Matchenko, 1902–08.

———. *Kriticheskie stat'i ob I. S. Turgeneve i L. N. Tolstom (1862–1885)*. Kiev: Izdatel'stvo I. P. Matchenko, 1901; repr. The Hague: Mouton, 1968.

Straus, Nina Pelikan. *Dostoevsky and the Woman Question: Rereadings at the End of a Century*. New York: St. Martin's Press, 1994.

Strindberg, August. *Six Plays*. Translated by Elizabeth Sprigge. New York: Doubleday, 1955.

Svintsov, Vitalii. "Dostoevskii i otnosheniia mezhdu polami." *Novyi mir*, no. 5 (1999): 195–213.

———. "Dostoevskii i stavroginskii grekh." *Voprosy literatury*, no. 2 (1995): 111–42.

Szathmary, Louis. "The Culinary Walt Whitman." *Walt Whitman Quarterly* 3, no. 2 (1985): 28–33.

Takayuki, Yokota-Murakami. "Man Seen as a Beast, Male Seen as an Animal: The Idea of 'Bestiality' Examined through *The Kreutzer Sonata*." In *The Force of Vision: Proceedings of the XIII Congress of the International Comparative Literature Association*, edited by Earl Miner and Toru Haga, 2:611–16. Tokyo: International Comparative Literature Association, 1995.

Tannahill, Reay. *Flesh and Blood: A History of the Cannibal Complex*. New York: Stein and Day, 1975.

Tarasov-Rodionov, Aleksandr. *Shokolad: Povest'*. In *Sobachii pereulok. Detektivnye romany i povest'*, compiled by V. Gellershtein, 265–383. Moscow: Sovremennyi pisatel', 1993.

Tarasov-Rodinov, Alexander. *Chocolate: A Novel*. Translated by Charles Malamuth. Westport, Conn.: Hyperion Press, 1932.

Thompson, Diane Oenning. *"The Brothers Karamazov" and the Poetics of Memory*. Cambridge: Cambridge University Press, 1991.

Tobin, Ronald W., ed. *Littérature et gastronomie: Huit études*. Paris and Seattle: Papers on French Seventeenth-Century Literature, 1985.

———. "Les mets et les mots: Gastronomie et sémiotique dans *L'Ecole des femmes*." *Semiotica* 51 (1984): 133–45.

———. "Qu'est-ce que la gastrocritique?" *XVII siècle*, no. 217 (2002): 621–30.

———. *Tarte à la crème: Comedy and Gastronomy in Molière's Theater*. Columbus: Ohio State University Press, 1990.

Todes, Daniel. *Darwin Without Malthus: The Struggle for Existence in Russian Evolutionary Thought*. New York: Oxford University Press, 1989.

Tolstaya, Tatyana. "The Age of Innocence." *New York Review of Books*, October 21, 1993, p. 24.

———. "In Cannibalistic Times," *New York Review of Books*, April 11, 1991, p. 3.

Tolstoi, L. N. "Pervaia stupen'." *Voprosy filosofii i psikhologii* 13 (1892): 109–44.

———. *Polnoe sobranie sochinenii*. 90 volumes. Moscow: Khudozhestvennaia literatura, 1928–58.

Tolstoy, Leo. *The Relations of the Sexes*. Translated by Vladimir Chertkov. Christchurch, Eng.: Free Age Press, 1901.

Tolstoy, Sergei. *Tolstoy Remembered by his Son*. Translated by Moura Budberg. London: Weidenfeld and Nicolson, 1961.

Turner, Bryan S. *The Body and Society*. London: Sage Publications, 1996.

Turner, Alice K., and Anne L. Stainton. "The Golden Age of Hell." *Arts and Antiques*, no. 1 (1991): 46–57.

Turgenev, I. S. *Polnoe sobranie sochinenii i pisem v 28-i tomakh*. Moscow: Akademiia nauk, 1960–68.

Vail', Petr, and Aleksandr Genis. *Russkaia kukhnia v izgnanii*. Los Angeles: Almanakh, 1987.

Ventslova, Tomas. "K voprosu o tekstovoj omonimii: *Putešestvie v stranu Guigngnmov* i 'Xolstomer.'" In *Semiosis: Semiotics and the History of Culture*, edited by Morris Halle et al., 240–54. Ann Arbor: University of Michigan, 1984.

Verbitskaia, Anastasiia. *Kliuchi schast'ia*. Moscow: I. M. Kushnerev, 1910.

Verbitskaya, Anastasya. *Keys to Happiness: A Novel*. Translated and edited by Beth Holmgren and Helena Goscilo. Bloomington: Indiana University Press, 1999.

Vetrinskii, Ch., ed. *F. M. Dostoevskii v vospominaniiakh sovremennikov, pis'makh i zametkakh*. Moscow: Sytin, 1912.

Viazemskii, Petr A. *Zapisnye zapiski (1813–1848)*. Edited by V. S. Nechaev. Moscow: Akademiia nauk, 1963.

Vigel, V. *Zapiski*. Moscow: Krug, 1928.

Visson, Lynn. "Kasha vs. Cachet Blanc: The Gastronomic Dialectics of Russian Literature." In *Russianness: Studies on a Nation's Identity*, edited by Robert L. Belknap, 60–73. Ann Arbor, Mich.: Ardis, 1990.

Vladimirtsev, V. P. "Poeticheskii bestiarii Dostoevskogo." In *Dostoevskii i mirovaia kul'tura, Al'manakh no. 12*, edited by K. A. Stepanian, 120–34. Moscow: Raritet, 1999.

Vucinich, Alexander. *Darwin in Russian Thought*. Berkeley and Los Angeles: University of California Press, 1988.

Wachtel, Andrew. *The Battle for Childhood: Creation of a Russian Myth*. Stanford, Calif.: Stanford University Press, 1990.

Walsh, Harry. "The Tolstoyan Episode in American Social Thought." *American Studies* 17, no. 1 (1976): 49–68.

Ward, Bruce K. *Dostoyevsky's Critique of the West: The Quest for the Earthly Paradise*. Waterloo, Ontario: Wilfred Laurier University Press, 1986.

Wasiolek, Edward. *Dostoevsky: The Major Fiction*. Cambridge, Mass.: MIT Press, 1964.

———. *Tolstoy's Major Fiction*. Chicago: University of Chicago Press, 1978.

Whorton, James C. "'Christian Physiology': William Alcott's Prescription for the Millenium." *Bulletin of the History of Medicine* 49 (1975): 466–81.

———. *Crusaders for Fitness: The History of American Health Reformers*. Princeton, N.J.: Princeton University Press, 1982.

Wigzell, Faith. "Dream and Fantasy in Goncharov's *Oblomov*." In *From Pushkin to Palisandriia: Essays on the Russian Novel in Honor of Richard Freeborn*, edited by Arnold McMillin, 96–111. New York: St. Martin's Press, 1990.

Williams, Raymond. *The Country and the City*. New York: Oxford University Press, 1973.

Willis, David K. *Klass: How Russians Really Live*. New York: St. Martin's Press, 1985.

Wolfe, Linda, ed. *The Literary Gourmet*. New York: Random House, 1962.

Woodward, James. *The Symbolic Art of Gogol: Essays on his Short Fiction*. Columbus, Ohio: Slavica, 1981.

Woollen, Geoff. "Des brutes humaines dans *La Bête humaine*." In *La Bête humaine: texte et explications*, edited by Geoff Woollen, 149–72. Glasgow: University of Glasgow French and German Publications, 1990.

Yermakov, Ivan. "The Nose." In *Gogol from the Twentieth Century: Eleven Essays*, edited and translated by Robert A. Maguire, 155–98. Princeton, N.J.: Princeton University Press, 1974.

Zabelina, Tat'iana. "Sexual Violence Towards Women." In *Gender, Generation and Identity in Contemporary Russia*, edited by Hilary Pilkington, 169–86. New York: Routledge, 1996.

Zakrzhevskii, Aleksandr. *Karamazovshchina: Psikhologicheskie paralleli*. Kiev: Iskusstvo, 1912.

Zalkind, Aron. "Polovaia zhizn' i sovremennaia molodezh'." *Molodaia gvardiia* no. 6 (1923): 245–49.

———. *Polovoi fetishism: K peresmotru polovogo voprosa*. Moscow, 1925.

———. *Polovoi vopros v usloviiakh sovetskoi obshchestvennosti*. Leningrad, 1926.

Zholkovskii, Aleksandr. "Topos prostitutsii." In Zholkovskii and M. B. Iampol'skii, *Babel'/Babel*, 317–68. Moscow: Carte Blanche, 1994.

Zolotonosov, Mikhail N. "Akhutokots-Akhum: Opyt rasshifrovki skazki Korneia Chukovskogo o Mukhe." *Novoe literaturnoe obozrenie*, no. 2 (1993): 262–82.

———. "Masturbanizatsiia: 'Erogennye zony' sovetskoi kul'tury 1920–1930-kh godov." *Novoe literaturnoe obozrenie*, no. 11 (1991): 93–99.

———. *Slovo i telo: Seksual'nye aspekty, universalii i interpretatsii kul'turnogo teksta XIX–XX vekov*. Moscow: Ladomir, 1999.